CAMBRIDGE STUDIES IN RUSSIAN LITERATURE

The poetic imagination of Vyacheslav Ivanov

Vyacheslav Ivanov, poet, philosopher and critic, played a key role in the formation of early twentieth-century Russian literature as leader of the religious branch of the Symbolist movement, and his influence spread to Europe after his emigration to Italy in 1924. Pamela Davidson explores Ivanov's poetic method, relating his art to his central beliefs (in particular his interpretation of the ancient Greek religion of Dionysus and of the teachings of Vladimir Solovyov), and considering the ways in which he attempted to embody these ideas in his own life.

She focuses on Ivanov's interpretation of Dante, and in so doing opens up new perspectives on the wider question of Russia's relation to the Western cultural tradition and Catholicism. Detailed analyses of Ivanov's pre-revolutionary poetry and of his translations from Dante form the basis of the second part of the study, and extensive use is made of unpublished archival materials from the Soviet Union and Italy.

CAMBRIDGE STUDIES IN RUSSIAN LITERATURE

General editor MALCOLM JONES

Vyacheslav Ivanov: portrait by A. S. Glagoleva-Ulyanova, 1915–16

The poetic imagination of Vyacheslav Ivanov

A Russian Symbolist's perception of Dante

PAMELA DAVIDSON

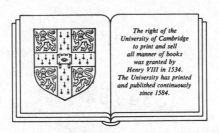
CAMBRIDGE UNIVERSITY PRESS

CAMBRIDGE

NEW YORK   NEW ROCHELLE

MELBOURNE   SYDNEY

Published by the Press Syndicate of the University of Cambridge
The Pitt Building, Trumpington Street, Cambridge CB2 1RP
32 East 57th Street, New York, NY 10022, USA
10 Stamford Road, Oakleigh, Melbourne 3166, Australia

First published 1989

Printed in Great Britain at the University Press, Cambridge

British Library cataloguing in publication data
Davidson, Pamela, 1954–
The poetic imagination of Vyacheslav
Ivanov: a Russian symbolist's perception
of Dante. – (Cambridge studies in Russian literature).
1. Poetry in Russian. Ivanov, Vyacheslav
I. Title
891.71′42

Library of Congress cataloguing in publication data
Davidson, Pamela.
The poetic imagination of Vyacheslav Ivanov: a Russian
symbolist's perception of Dante / Pamela Davidson.
p.   cm. – (Cambridge studies in Russian literature)
Bibliography: p.
Includes index.
ISBN 0–521–36285–7
1. Ivanov, V. I. (Viacheslav Ivanovich), 1866–1949 – Criticism and
interpretation.   2. Dante Alighieri, 1265–1321 – Influence – Ivanov.
I. Title.   II. Series.
PG3467.I8Z64   1989
891.71′3–dc19   88–20319

ISBN 0 521 362857

334793

For E.V.K.

Contents

Illustrations

x

Preface

Vyacheslav Ivanov and Dante Alighieri, although six centuries apart in time and representatives of completely different cultures, are linked by a surprising inner affinity of spirit. Both were poets of an intellectual and philosophical cast of mind who sought to interpret their experience and art in the light of a religious world-view. Both tried to relate the events and cultural trends of their time to a wider spiritual perspective; Dante's world was medieval Florence, Ivanov's world was early twentieth-century Russia. Ivanov was aware of this affinity and felt strongly drawn to Dante throughout his life-time. This study uses a comparative approach to explore Ivanov's perception of Dante as a way of reaching a deeper understanding of the creative method of a leading Russian Symbolist.

The research for this study could not have been undertaken without the support of several institutions. While studying at St Antony's College, Oxford (1976–9), I received a series of scholarships from the British Council which made it possible for me to spend over a year working in the state literary archives of Moscow and Leningrad. My subsequent tenure of a travelling research fellowship at The Queen's College, Oxford (1979–81), enabled me to make further research trips to the Soviet Union, to America to participate in the first international symposium on Ivanov at Yale University, and to Rome to work in the poet's archive. Further grants from the University of Birmingham (1981–4) and the University of Surrey (1984–7) made it possible for me to take part in the second and third symposia, held at the Universities of Rome and Pavia in 1983 and 1986.

I have also benefited greatly from the encouragement and help of many individuals. My original enthusiasm for Dante was kindled by the excellent teaching of Patrick Boyde while I was a student at Cambridge. My interest in Ivanov owes a great deal to the stimulating company of many friends in Moscow and Leningrad, particularly to the generous guidance of two Ivanov scholars, Nikolai

Kotrelyov and Sergei Averintsev. I am most grateful to Dimitry Ivanov and the late Lidiya Ivanova for their warm support and invaluable practical assistance in Rome. Many helpful suggestions were made at different stages by Henry Gifford, Sergei Hackel and Mark Everitt. I would also like to thank my typist, Linda Guess. Closer to home, I owe a special debt of gratitude to my sister, Caroline Davidson and husband, Edward Kissin, for their helpful criticism.

June 1987   PAMELA DAVIDSON
London

Notes on the text

TRANSLATIONS

All the translations from Russian in the text are my own. Verse passages are first quoted in the original, and then followed by a literal prose version, designed to reproduce the meaning of the original as closely as possible.

The translations from the *Divina Commedia* are taken from Charles S. Singleton's version. All other translations from Italian are my own.

TRANSLITERATION

The British system of Cyrillic transliteration has been adopted, omitting diacritics. In proper names, *y* has been used for final ий and ый, *yo* has replaced ё, and the apostrophe for ь has been omitted.

Abbreviations

The following abbreviations have been used in the text and notes.

ANSSR	Arkhiv Akademii Nauk SSSR, Leningrad
'AP'	'Avtobiograficheskoe pis'mo'
CA	Cor Ardens
Con.	Convivio
ed.	edited by
ed.khr.	edinitsa khraneniya
'ER'	'Ellinskaya religiya stradayushchego boga'
GBL	Gosudarstvennaya biblioteka im. Lenina, Otdel rukopisei, Moscow
GLM	Gosudarstvennyi literaturnyi muzei, Moscow
GPB	Gosudarstvennaya publichnaya biblioteka im. Saltykova-Shchedrina, Otdel rukopisei, Leningrad
IMLI	Institut mirovoi literatury im. Gorkogo, Moscow
Inf.	Inferno
k.	karton
KZ	Kormchie zvezdy
LN	Literaturnoe nasledstvo
Mon.	Monarchia
NP	Novyi put'
NS	New Style
NT	Nezhnaya taina
op.	opis'
Par.	Paradiso
Purg.	Purgatorio
'RD'	'Religiya Dionisa'
SS	Sobranie sochinenii
tr.	translated by
TsGALI	Tsentral'nyi gosudarstvennyi arkhiv literatury i iskusstva, Moscow

VFP	*Voprosy filosofii i psikhologii*
VN	*Vita Nuova*
VZh	*Voprosy zhizni*
ZOR	*Zapiski Otdela rukopisei*

Introduction

ciascuna cosa riceva . . . secondo
lo modo de la sua vertù e de lo suo essere   Dante (1304)

. . . And so, Dante is a Symbolist!   Ivanov (1912)

Some writers are chiefly remembered for their active contribution
to the literary life of their day. Others seem to stand outside this
process, and only assume their true importance after death. Vyacheslav Ivanov (1866–1949) was both. As a major poet and the
leading theoretician of the Russian Symbolist movement, he
played a key role in shaping the literature of his time, and received
wide recognition from his contemporaries. His deeper significance,
however, goes far beyond this. In the long term, he is most likely to
be remembered for the unique voice which he developed in his
poetry and prose to convey a mystical and teleological vision of
human life, history and culture. He believed that 'in every place . . .
there is a Bethel and a Jacob's ladder – in the centre of every
horizon', and devoted his life's work to the creation of just such a
ladder.[1] The present study concentrates more on the nature of this
'ladder' than on the surrounding plane; it is not a work of literary
biography, but an attempt to explore the way in which the poet's
vision took form and expressed itself through his art.

A bird's eye view of Ivanov's life and works reveals a design of
remarkable symmetry. Four main phases can be distinguished,
each of which lasted for approximately twenty years. The first
phase (1866–86) took place in Moscow, and covers the poet's
childhood, his early enthusiasm for religion and poetry, his education at a classical gymnasium and his first two years at university,
devoted to ancient languages and history. The period ends with
Ivanov's marriage to Darya Mikhailovna Dmitrievskaya, the sister
of a close childhood friend.

The second phase (1886–1905) opens with the departure of the
young scholar, aged twenty, for Berlin in order to pursue his

academic studies. For the next nineteen years he lived abroad.
Until the completion of his dissertation on Roman antiquity in
1895, he and his wife were based in Berlin, Paris and Rome. Their
marriage ended in divorce in 1895, two years after Ivanov's first
meeting with Lidiya Dimitrievna Zinoveva-Annibal, his second
wife and the major love and inspiration of his life. For the next ten
years, Ivanov and Lidiya Dimitrievna travelled all over Europe
together, spending periods of time in Greece, England, Italy,
France and Switzerland, and only occasionally visiting Russia.
Their daughter Lidiya was born in 1896, and they were formally
wedded in 1899, after Lidiya Dimitrievna finally succeeded in
obtaining a divorce from her first husband.

The fruits of Ivanov's scholarly and literary work began to
appear in print towards the end of this period. His lectures on the
ancient Greek religion of Dionysus, first delivered in Paris in 1903,
were serialized in the Russian periodical press between 1904 and
1905. His first two collections of poetry, *Pilot Stars* (*Kormchie
zvezdy*, 1903) and *Transparency* (*Prozrachnost'*, 1904) were followed by a tragedy in verse, *Tantalus* (*Tantal*, 1905). During a
spring visit to Russia in 1904 he and his wife made their entrée into
the leading circles of Moscow and St Petersburg literary life.

The third phase (1905–24) took place almost entirely in Russia
(St Petersburg, Moscow, Baku) and marks the most intense stage
of Ivanov's involvement in the literary life of his country. In 1905
he and his wife returned to Russia and settled in St Petersburg.
Their home rapidly became one of the focal points of the capital's
literary and cultural life. Ivanov established himself as the leader of
religious Symbolism – a literary movement initiated by a younger
group of poets, Aleksandr Blok, Andrei Bely and Sergei Solovyov.
The heady atmosphere of these days reached a peak with his
collection of verse, *Eros*, published in 1907, but was abruptly
curtailed by the sudden death of Lidiya Dimitrievna in the same
year. Ivanov dedicated two works to her memory – his first collection of literary and philosophical essays, *By the Stars* (*Po zvezdam*,
1909), and a two-volume collection of verse, *Cor' Ardens* (1911),
consisting of poems written since 1904, both before and after his
wife's death.

A few years after the death of Lidiya Dimitrievna, Ivanov
married her daughter from her previous marriage, Vera Konstan-
tevna Shvarsalon. From 1912 to 1913 the couple lived abroad, in

Switzerland, France and Italy. The birth of their son Dimitry in 1912 was commemorated in the poet's fourth collection of verse, *Tender Mystery* (*Nezhnaya Taina*, 1912). When the family returned to Russia in the autumn of 1913, they settled in Moscow. Ivanov continued to write poetry (later collected in the posthumous edition of his works, *Evening Light*, *Vechernii svet*, 1962), including two longer works, an autobiographical poem begun in 1913, *Infancy* (*Mladenchestvo*, 1918), and a lyric-philosophical melopoeia, *Man* (*Chelovek*, 1939), composed between 1915 and 1919. He also published translations of Alcaeus and Sappho (1914) and Petrarch (1915), and worked on versions of Aeschylus, Dante and Novalis. Two further collections of essays, *Furrows and Boundaries* (*Borozdy i mezhi*, 1916) and *Matters Native and Universal* (*Rodnoe i vselenskoe*, 1917), containing reflections on the war and the spirit of the Slavic peoples, were followed by a second tragedy, *Prometheus* (*Prometei*, 1919). In 1920 he composed two outstanding cycles of sonnets, 'The Winter Sonnets' ('*Zimnie sonety*') and 'De Profundis Amavi', and wrote part of the celebrated *Correspondence from Two Corners* (*Perepiska iz dvukh uglov*, 1921), a series of letters on the role of culture and memory exchanged with his friend, the literary historian Mikhail Gershenzon.

This exceptionally fruitful period came to a sudden halt after the tragic death of Vera at the age of thirty in August 1920. Ivanov left Moscow and travelled to Baku where he spent three and a half years at the University as professor of Classical Philology and Poetics. During this period he returned to academic work, publishing his doctoral dissertation *Dionysus and Predionysianism* (*Dionis i pradionisiistvo*, 1923) and lecturing on a wide variety of topics, ranging from Greek antiquity to medieval and Renaissance literature and Russian culture. In May 1924 he visited Moscow, renewed contact with many old literary friends, and received permission – first requested in 1919 – to travel abroad.

The last phase of Ivanov's life (1924–49), like the second, took place outside Russia. In August 1924 he travelled to Italy with his two children and settled in Rome. He joined the Catholic church in 1926, and then moved to Pavia where he spent the next eight years living at the Collegio Borromeo and teaching modern and ancient languages at the University. In 1934 he returned to Rome for the rest of his life. During his final period he taught Slavonic languages and Russian literature at the Russian Catholic Seminary 'Russicum' and at the Eastern Institute of the Vatican.

During his years in Italy Ivanov made an important contribution to European culture, while remaining deeply rooted in the Russian tradition. He met and exchanged ideas with many prominent European intellectuals such as Charles Du Bos, Gabriel Marcel, Jacques Maritain, Alessandro Pellegrini, Benedetto Croce and Martin Buber. His literary work was characterized by a general move from poetry to prose. Between the remarkable 'Roman Sonnets' ('*Rimskie sonety*') of 1924 and the 'Roman Diary' ('*Rimskii dnevnik*') of 1944, he wrote very little verse (only about a dozen poems), and did not begin to assemble his last collection of poetry, *Evening Light*, until 1946. His major project of the period was a prose work, 'The Tale of Prince Svetomir' ('*Povest' o tsareviche Svetomire*'), which he began in 1928 but never completed. It deals with historical and personal themes in a highly complex, allegorical manner. He also contributed numerous articles on literary and religious topics to leading Italian, Swiss, French and Russian émigré journals, and produced a book on Dostoevsky, loosely based on earlier essays and published in Germany in 1932. Towards the end of his life he prepared new editions of various Scriptural texts for the Vatican; these included the Acts of the Apostles, The Revelation of St John and the Book of Psalms.

The picture which emerges from this brief outline is one of remarkable discontinuity of both time and place. Almost as many years were spent outside Russia as in it (some forty-six years in Europe compared to forty-seven in Russia), and for long stretches of time the poet had no fixed address and was constantly on the move. He was married three times, and each marriage ended in tragic circumstances. He lived through an epoch of historical upheavals, witnessing three Russian revolutions, two world wars, and the rise of totalitarianism in both Europe and Russia.

And yet the most striking feature of this life is its inner coherence and unity. Ivanov was not divided by the changes and contradictions which surrounded him, but encompassed and transcended them. Although his life was split between Russia and the West, he felt equally at home in both worlds and never saw himself as an outsider. When he returned to Russia in 1905 after living abroad for almost two decades, he managed to overcome the substantial differences of age and background which set him apart from the younger religious Symbolists and became the leader of a movement which they had established in his absence. Later, after his move to Italy in 1924, he never cultivated the image of the writer in exile, as was the case with many other notable writers of his generation who emigrated after the revolution (Vladimir Nabokov or Ivan Bunin, for example). He was a Russian in Europe and a European in Russia, and even succeeded in bridging the gap between the religions of both cultures by adopting the Catholic faith in 1926. During a traumatic period of history which saw the gradual erosion and decay of culture and civilization in both East and West, he devoted himself to building up an essentially spiritual vision of the world through a wide range of writings, including poetry, prose, tragedy, autobiography, translations, essays on religion, philosophy, aesthetics and literature. As his friend and contemporary Fyodor Stepun put it, he was a true 'European Russian', and the 'most versatile, but at the same time the most integral figure of the Russian Symbolist school'.[2]

In this respect Ivanov stands in marked contrast to many of his contemporaries. Marina Tsvetaeva (1891–1945), for example, also spent many years in Europe after the revolution, but her reaction to similar circumstances was quite different. She regarded time and space as the great dividers of human life, and her distinctive poetic voice consistently records her painful awareness of fragmentation and separation, rendered all the more acute by the intensity of her longing for unity and wholeness. By contrast, the paradoxically far more varied voice of Ivanov constantly testifies to the inner unity of his vision. For him, space and time were relative concepts, categories of the inner world rather than of the outer. In the middle of the Second World War he wrote the following lines:

И ныне теснотой укромной,
Заточник вольный, дорожу;
В себе простор, как мир огромный,
Взор обводя, не огляжу;
И светит памяти бездомной
Голубизна за Летой темной, –
И я себе принадлежу.   (*SS* III, 626)

And now, a voluntary captive,
I cherish my cramped seclusion;
Turning my gaze, I cannot encompass

The expanse within me, like a vast world;
And to homeless memory shines out
The blueness beyond dark Lethe –
And I belong to myself.

The ideal which gave rise to this inner unity was based on a profound awareness of the spiritual essence underlying the material phenomena of this world. Following Aristotle, Ivanov regarded this essence as a final cause, being both the source and the ultimate goal of human existence. Spirit and matter are not static aspects of reality, but form part of a dynamic chain of being. The material constantly seeks to transform itself into the spiritual. This goal cannot be reached by negating or denying the material side of reality, but only by transforming it. The energy informing this drive towards spiritualization is Eros, and the process of transformation involves a constantly self-renewing cycle of sacrifice, death and new life. The path of Eros is therefore likened to the way of the cross, and the reward for those who follow it is compared to the rose which blooms from the cross, a symbolic revelation of the world's inner spirit.

These ideas owed a great deal to the poet's study of Dionysiac mysticism, and to Vladimir Solovyov's teaching on Sophia, the spiritual essence inherent in the material world. They are at the root of his understanding of the meaning of every life, including his own. The opening lines of his autobiographical poem, *Infancy*, written in 1913, allude to this directly:

Вот жизни длинная минея,
Воспоминаний палимпсест,
Ее единая идея –
Аминь всех жизней – в розах крест.   (*SS* 1, 230)

Here is the long chronicle of a life,
A palimpsest of memories,
Its single idea –
The amen of all lives – is a cross in roses.

Eros, understood in this way, is present in every area of human endeavour. It informs the purpose of man's life, the meaning of earthly love, the course of history, viewed as a teleological process, and the mission of art, defined in theurgic terms. According to the doctrine of realist symbolism which Ivanov developed, words can be raised to the level of mythic symbols, just as matter can be spiritualized, through the transforming, creative power of Eros.

Few of Ivanov's contemporaries held such a carefully worked out and coherent world-view which embraced life as well as art. Those who aspired to such an ideal were often unable to command true faith in the visions which they constructed for themselves. Blok, for example, after his early intuition of the Beautiful Lady, spent the rest of his life measuring his distance from this ideal, often in tones of ironic bitterness and disillusionment. Such feelings were entirely foreign to Ivanov whose ideal was not a projection of his artistic fancy, but the substance of his life's faith. Although it was articulated through a complex system of intellectual arguments, its fundamental appeal was essentially poetic and emotional. As such it exerted a profound and magnetic influence on his contemporaries and successors. One could agree or disagree with it, but one could not fail to be affected by it in some way.

Osip Mandelshtam (1891–1938) was one of the many poets who succumbed on an emotional level to the attraction of Ivanov's system, without, however, entirely accepting it on an intellectual level. When Ivanov's first book of essays, *By the Stars*, came out in 1909, he wrote him an admiring letter of congratulations:

Allow me first a few reflections on your book. It seems to me that one cannot argue with it – it is captivating – and destined to win many hearts.

Does a person who steps under the vaults of Notre Dame really reflect on the truth of Catholicism, and not just become a Catholic by virtue of his being under those vaults?

The splendour of your book is like the beauty of great architectural creations and astronomic systems. Every true poet, *if* [my italics. P.D.] he were able to write books on the basis of the exact and immutable laws of his own art – would write like you.[3]

The 'if' is a major one and deserves underlining. Although this letter was written at the very beginning of Mandelshtam's poetic career, before the emergence of the Acmeist movement as a separate school, it already reveals both the force of his attraction to religious Symbolism, and the source of his divergence. Further on in the letter he comments on the excessive 'roundness' (*kruglost'*) of Ivanov's book – its lack of angles renders it impenetrable, the system is too coherent for his taste. He singles out one image in particular from the book as most suggestive: that of the dissenter who does not agree to join the circular dance and leaves the magic circle, covering his face with his hands.[4] Here he seems to be

unconsciously anticipating the dynamics of the Acmeists' relation
to the Symbolists – Ivanov's 'circle' or closed system provided them
with a common point of departure from which, however, they
chose to diverge, preferring the role of dissident disciples.
Later, in an essay of 1923, Mandelshtam acknowledged the full
extent of the Acmeists' debt to Ivanov; although their tastes
differed, they had taken many of their ideas directly from the
Symbolists, and Ivanov in particular had contributed a great deal
to the development of Acmeist theory.[5]

Ivanov's influence extended beyond his contemporaries and
immediate successors to subsequent generations. His vision of art
as a system of symbolic signs and his work on Dostoevsky were
taken up and developed by the critic Mikhail Bakhtin and, through
this channel, reached a modern audience.[6] To this day his work
provides the most important model in the Russian tradition of an
artist who sought to integrate religion and culture, both in theory
and in practice, rather than regarding them as distinct or conflicting
forces. In this sense his example serves as a powerful antidote both
to the civic and aesthetic schools of art, and to the trend set by
Tolstoy whose advocacy of religion led him to reject secular culture
as a corrupting influence. In the West the significance of Ivanov's
thought and scholarship has also been widely acknowledged. The
German historian of culture, Ernst Robert Curtius, for example,
described the *Correspondence from Two Corners* as the 'most
important statement about humanism since Nietzsche'.[7]

It therefore comes as something of a surprise to find that scholarship on Ivanov is still in its infancy, both in the Soviet Union and in
the West. Most of the literature which appeared on the poet before
his emigration either revolved around current polemics or was
memoir-like in emphasis, concentrating more on the legendary
Ivanov of the tower than on the close study of his work. From the
end of the 1920s until the mid 1960s, virtually no material was
published on Ivanov in the Soviet Union. This silence was part of a
general pattern affecting the fates of many writers throughout the
period when the official canon of socialist realism in art was
imposed with extreme rigour. Ivanov's case was further complicated by two additional factors: his religious convictions and his
emigration after the revolution. In more recent years Soviet
research has therefore tended to skirt these areas by concentrating
on less sensitive topics, such as Ivanov's participation in the institu-

tions of Soviet cultural life in Baku, his work as a translator, or the history of his relations with more established figures such as Valery Bryusov or Aleksandr Blok.[8] The approach has generally been descriptive and documentary rather than analytical.

A significant milestone in the Soviet rediscovery of Ivanov was reached in 1976 with the publication of a small volume of the poet's verse and translations, introduced by Sergei Averintsev.[9] The most important contribution to the renaissance of Ivanov studies has however been the major edition of the poet's works undertaken in the West by Olga Deschartes (1894–1978), a close friend of the family, and Dimitry Ivanov, the poet's son. The first volume appeared in 1971, and includes an extensive introduction by Deschartes which remains the most comprehensive treatment of the poet's life, works and thought available to date. Four of the six projected volumes have so far been published.

Since the end of the 1960s, a slow but steady stream of books and monographs on Ivanov has appeared, including studies of the poet's verse and poetic theory by Carin Tschöpl (1968), of his aesthetics and philosophy by James West (1970) and Fausto Malcovati (1983), and of his contribution as a Symbolist poet and philosopher of culture by Johannes Holthusen (1982).[10] Growing interest in the poet has led to the establishment of a society for the study of his works, Convivium, and to a series of international symposia held at the Universities of Yale, Rome and Pavia.

However, most of the critical attention devoted to Ivanov has been directed at his thought and ideas, rather than at the study of his actual poetry. For this reason, as recently as 1981 Vladimir Markov was still able to claim that Ivanov is 'the last great Russian poet of his century who remains to be established as such'.[11] Many readers and students may well have been put off Ivanov's poetry by its reputation for difficulty and erudite obscurity. And yet, it is precisely because of these qualities that the poetry merits special attention and can benefit so greatly from detailed textual analysis. Its difficulty derives from the complexity of the ideas on which it is based and of the images chosen for their expression. However, as Averintsev has underlined, in Ivanov's poetry there is always an exact and deep correlation between ideas and imagery which, in the case of other Symbolists, is often either entirely lacking or confusingly approximate.[12] Furthermore, as Ilya Serman has shown, following the theory developed by Tynyanov in *Archaists and Innovators*, the obscure and archaic aspects of Ivanov's verse have often been fruitful sources of inspiration and innovation.[13] Therefore, although Ivanov's poetry undoubtedly does require an intellectual effort on the part of its reader, if this challenge is met, the rewards are rich. Indeed, much of the pleasure of reading Ivanov's poetry derives precisely from the dual nature of the demands which it makes; it appeals both to the intellectual faculties, and to the lyrical, intuitive side of the reader's aesthetic sensibility.

The present study aims to illuminate the poetry by considering it in relation to two major areas – the poet's central ideas and beliefs, and the personal experience of his life-time. The particular approach which has been adopted – that of Ivanov's interpretation of Dante – leads straight to the heart of the poet's creative method. It reveals the inner structure of his world-view and enables one to see how this determined his perception of other cultures and his creation of poetic images within this context.

Generally speaking, the study of the refraction of one culture through another, or of one writer's works through those of another, can afford many insights into the psychology of the receiver of the influence. A writer's interpretation of another author's works often highlights the features which are most characteristic of that writer's spiritual outlook and creative process. This is perhaps particularly striking in the case of Russia's approach to the literature of Western Europe. Russia's geographical and historical isolation from the mainstream of Western European culture has led to a remarkable intensity of interest in the West, coupled with a peculiar 'Russianness' of perception. Foreign influences are desired and sought after, but they are understood subjectively, in Russian terms, and assimilated into the national tradition. This combination of attitudes – both out-going and inward-looking – constitutes one of the central tensions in Russian history, leading to constant oscillations between spells of Slavophile fervour and waves of Westernizing enthusiasm in the search for a balance between these two extremes.

In 1876 the death of George Sand prompted Dostoevsky to enter some reflections on the peculiar nature of Russia's approach to Western literature into his writer's diary:

We Russians have two motherlands: our Rus and Europe . . . a great deal, a very great deal of what we have taken from Europe and transplanted to our country has not just been copied by us . . . but has been grafted into our organism, into our flesh and blood; . . . I maintain and repeat that every European poet, thinker and philanthropist is always most fully and intimately understood and accepted in Russia, out of all the countries of the world apart from his own . . . This Russian attitude to world literature is a phenomenon which is almost unparalleled to the same degree among other nations throughout world history . . . every poet-innovator of Europe, everyone who appears there with a new idea and a new source of strength, cannot fail to immediately become a Russian poet as well, cannot bypass Russian thought, cannot fail to become an almost Russian force.[14]

Dostoevsky reconciled the inherent tension between the Westernizing and Slavophile elements implicit in his view by claiming that it was only by fully accepting foreign influences that Russia could fulfil its mission of universal service to humanity. Furthermore, as he stresses, these foreign influences would be entirely Russianized. In this way the Russian tradition would safeguard the truly universal elements in Western culture. The true Slavophile must therefore recognize that he has two motherlands, Russia and Europe.

Within Europe, Russians have turned to different countries, taking from each that which was most appropriate to its needs and aspirations at any given time. In particular, France, Germany, England and Italy have played significant roles in the development of Russian culture. Language was not necessarily a barrier. Before the revolution, French was the established language of the aristocracy and it was common to find a resident English tutor or governess in the homes of the nobility. At the beginning of the nineteenth century the Russian Romantics took a great deal from their English and German counterparts, most notably from Byron, Walter Scott, Goethe and Schiller. Pushkin tried his hand at translating Byron and imitated him in his early verse, while Zhukovsky met Goethe and addressed poems to him. The Russian novel also owed much to the English and French traditions; Turgenev spent many years living in France and corresponded extensively with Flaubert, and Dostoevsky borrowed elements of his narrative technique from the novels of Balzac, George Sand and Dickens. Towards the end of the century, as prose began to give way to poetry, the emerging school of Russian Symbolists followed the lead set by Baudelaire and the French Symbolists. In all these

cases however, the end product remained peculiarly and distinct-
ively Russian. One wonders, for example, what Shakespeare
would have made of Turgenev's view of Hamlet as the prototype of
a uniquely Russian phenomenon – that of the 'superfluous man'
(*lishnii chelovek*) who cannot find a place for himself in society?[15]
Individual writers in the West have often been able to generate
whole movements or substantial followings in Russia. This is not
only true of major authors of the past; it also applies to lesser and
more recent figures, such as Archibald Cronin or Jack London,
whose popularity in Russia vastly exceeds their reputation at
home.

The case of Italy is somewhat different. One cannot name a
comparable range of authors whose impact on Russian culture as
individuals equals that of their French, German or English
counterparts. The influence of Italy has generally been more
diffuse and pervasive, depending less on the legacy of specific
writers. In part it has derived from the special magnetic attraction
which Italy has always exercised on Russians. This feeling is an
emotional, intuitive response to the country, based on a mysterious
sense of inner affinity which defies rational analysis. More than any
other country, Russians have traditionally regarded Italy as their
second homeland. This idea has expressed itself in many striking
ways, ranging from the belief in Moscow as the third Rome to the
parallel between imperial Rome and Stalinist Russia developed by
Mikhail Bulgakov in *Master and Margarita*. Its most tangible
manifestation can be found at the heart of Russia in the churches of
the Moscow Kremlin, some of which were built by Italian archi-
tects, specially invited to Russia for the purpose. The Cathedral of
the Dormition was designed by Fioravanti, a Florentine architect
nicknamed 'Aristotle' for his prowess, and the Cathedral of the
Archangel was the work of a Venetian, Alevisio Novi. In a very
beautiful and evocative poem of 1916, Osip Mandelshtam refers to
the twin Italian and Russian souls of these churches, and takes
their Italianate features as the basis for a poetic reverie on the
miraculous resurrection of 'Florence in Moscow'.[16]

There are several facets to the question of Italy's significance for
the Russian artistic imagination. The country often served as a
bridge which enabled Russians to reestablish their links with the
classical world of ancient Rome and Greece by retracing a path
back through the Italian Renaissance and Middle Ages. In this

sense, Italy played a role not unlike that of the Crimea which had also once formed part of the Byzantine Empire and served in a similar way as a stepping-stone for Russians between their culture and ancient Greece.[17]

Another aspect of Italy's fascination lay in its role as the seat of the Roman Catholic church. The breach between Greek and Latin Christendom, usually assigned to the great schism of 1054, resulted in the formation of two different churches, the Orthodox in the East and the Roman Catholic in the West. Russians thus found themselves on the other side of a great rift, isolated from the mainstream of European culture by their religion as well as by geographical and historical factors. Ecumenically-minded Christians from either side sought to bridge the gap, and for many Russian intellectuals, disenchanted with their own church for political reasons, Roman Catholicism offered an exotic alternative structure of religious experience.

Pavel Muratov has written with great perceptiveness about the Russian feeling for Italy in his inspiring study of the country, first published in 1911. As he points out in the preface, for Russians a trip to Italy was never just a casual affair; it was always something of a spiritual pilgrimage which invariably had profound repercussions on the visitor's soul. He distinguishes two peak periods in the history of Russian Italomania. The first occurred in the 1840s when many Russians travelled to Italy, sometimes settling there for years and converting to Catholicism. Through paintings and works of literature they secured a firm place for Italy in the Russian artistic imagination and laid the foundation for the Russian sense of Italy as a second or spiritual motherland. Gogol, for example, spent many years living in Rome where he wrote the first part of *Dead Souls*. When he returned to Rome after a period of absence, his reactions overwhelmed him:

When at last I saw Rome for the second time, oh, how much better it seemed to me than the first time! It seemed to me that it was as if I had seen my motherland which I had been absent from for a few years and which only my thoughts had inhabited. But no, that was not it: it was not my motherland but the motherland of my soul which I had seen, where my soul lived even before me, before I was born into this world . . . [18]

The second period of Russian Italomania began in the 1890s and carried on through the 1900s into the early 1910s. Numerous artists, poets and writers went on pilgrimages to Italy and committed their impressions to paper in the form of travelogues, diaries, letters and poems. The works of Annensky, Merezhkovsky, Gippius, Volynsky, Balmont, Baltrushaitis, Kuzmin, Voloshin, Bryusov, Blok, Bely, Sergei Solovyov, Ellis and Vyacheslav Ivanov abound in such reminiscences and reflect the deep feelings which these writers developed for the country and sometimes for Catholicism as well.

For Russians, the supreme embodiment of both Italy and Catholicism was the medieval poet Dante Alighieri (1265–1321), the founder and leading figure of the Italian literary tradition. Their interest in Dante was a natural extension of their more general attraction to Italy, and developed within the framework outlined by Dostoevsky in his comments on the Russian attitude to Western literatures. There was on the one hand an avid reaching out towards Dante and determination to come to terms with him as the major poet of Italy and of Catholicism; on the other hand there was also a constant attempt to present Dante in Russian terms, to adapt him to meet the particular needs of the age. There have consequently been as many Russian Dantes as there have been major periods in Russian thought and individual writers within these periods.[19]

Not surprisingly, this interest in Dante has been at its strongest during the peak periods of Russian Italomania. In particular, the second period outlined by Muratov was most propitious. It coincided with the general revival of interest in spiritual matters which swept Europe at the end of the nineteenth century. In Russia this renaissance of religious feeling led to the formation of a new poetic movement, designed to counteract the predominantly positivist trend of late-nineteenth-century prose. In its early stages Russian Symbolism was a largely aesthetic movement with some decadent overtones, modelled on the French movement, and led by figures such as Merezhkovsky, Balmont and later Bryusov. Towards the end of the century a new group emerged which, under the influence of the religious philosopher Vladimir Solovyov, sought to develop an alternative form of Symbolism based on mystical rather than aesthetic principles. Although the previous generation of Symbolists had turned to Dante and, in the case of Balmont and Merezhkovsky, even translated him, it was for the second wave of Symbolists – for writers such as Blok, Bely, Ellis, Sergei Solovyov and Vyacheslav Ivanov – that Dante became a figure of such central importance.

There were several reasons for this. Some relate to Dante's role as a representative of Catholicism and the Middle Ages, others are specific to Dante himself. In general, nostalgia for the Middle Ages was a fairly widespread phenomenon in late-nineteenth-century Europe as a result of the resurgence of interest in religion. The Middle Ages were extolled as a golden age exemplifying the ideal unity of culture and religion. One of the most influential expressions of this trend was the Pre-Raphaelite movement in England which, with its deliberate cult of the Middle Ages and of Dante, spread to Europe and Russia. For the Russian religious Symbolists, searching for a new form of mystical art, the European Middle Ages were the obvious model to turn to, particularly as Russia had not had such a period in her own history. During the Russian Middle Ages, Byzantine chronicles and religious texts were widely translated but there was not as yet any secular culture. Russian literature did not establish itself until the eighteenth century when, under the influence of the Enlightenment and of Peter the Great's policy of Europeanization, it followed a mainly secular line of development. Some nineteenth-century thinkers, such as Khomyakov, Vladimir Solovyov, Tolstoy or Dostoevsky tried in different ways to mend this rift between culture and religion, but it was not until the religious Symbolists established their own movement that this became a trend of more than individual significance. For the religious Symbolists Dante – as the supreme representative of medieval culture – was the prototype of the ideal artist who succeeded in integrating religion and art on the deepest level.

As a direct consequence of the fusion of religion and culture which prevailed in the European Middle Ages, there was a far greater wealth of religious symbolism, liturgical, iconographic and literary, available in the Catholic tradition than in Russian Orthodoxy. Dante's works reflect this richness and provided an important source of religious imagery for the Russian Symbolists' attempts to develop a new poetic lexicon for the expression of spiritual ideas. Many works of the Symbolist period attempted to import Catholic liturgical motifs into the Russian tradition. The *Little Flowers* of St Francis were first translated in 1904,[20] and the tendency reached a peak in 1911 with the publication of three heavily 'Catholic' collections of verse, Ellis's *Stigmata*, Baltrushaitis's *Earthly Rungs* (*Zemnye stupeni*) and Vyacheslav Ivanov's *Cor Ardens*.

Various other features of the Catholic tradition were also particularly attractive to Russian intellectuals and artists. It was important, for example, that the intellectual aspect of religion was much more highly developed in Catholicism than in Russian Orthodoxy. The Eastern church placed its main emphasis on the mystical and sensual aspects of worship, attaching greater importance to the values of humility and simple piety than to scholarly learning. The Latin tradition, by contrast, offered a blend of philosophy and theology which was unknown in the East. Scholastic philosophers of the Middle Ages such as Thomas Aquinas had constructed entire systems designed to reconcile Christian dogma with the teachings of Aristotle and Plato. This intellectual element is very prominent in Dante's works which constantly seek to provide philosophical explanations of problems of faith. This was particularly appealing to a generation of poets whose approach to religion often stemmed more from the mind than from the heart.

Another important difference between the two traditions concerns their view of the relations between the flesh and the spirit. Russian Orthodoxy regards matter as potentially spirit-bearing, and constantly works towards the reconciliation of the spirit with the flesh through the sanctification of the material world (the cult of icons is a direct expression of this belief). The Catholic tradition tends towards greater asceticism, regarding the flesh as an obstacle to be overcome in the pursuit of higher goals. This difference is reflected in the contrast between the characteristic architectural styles of the two religions. The soaring spires, towers, buttresses and vaults of Gothic architecture convey a sense of restless upward striving, while the rounded domes and cupolas of Russian churches evoke greater tranquillity, suggesting the descent of holiness onto earth.[21]

The same difference finds expression in certain doctrinal areas of divergence. The Russian Orthodox never accepted the systematic definition of Purgatory, and a comparison of the topography of the after-life in the two traditions is very revealing. The Russian vision of the after-life is fairly vague and undefined; the term *khozhdenie po mukam* suggests a series of aimless wanderings over a vast area of unspecified torments. The Catholic vision is far more structured and hierarchical, with a strong emphasis on the vertical. Dante's journey in the *Commedia* either takes him downwards, descending through the circles of Hell into the pit of the abyss, or upwards, climbing the terraces of Mount Purgatory and ascending through the spheres of Paradise. The degrees of damnedness or blessedness are graded down to the minutest detail; the circles of Hell are fenced round with outlying and preliminary zones, further divided into subsidiary ditches. Such a detailed artistic vision had no counterpart in the Eastern tradition and provided the religious Symbolists with ready-made forms for the expression of their own sense of life as a mystical journey and of this world as a spiritual entity masked to a greater or lesser extent by its material form. Dante's vision was a particularly fruitful source of inspiration for those who felt drawn to a more intellectual, structured and hierarchical view of the spiritual life than the Russian tradition could offer.

Besides these factors – which were all common to the Catholic medieval tradition – there was a further characteristic which was specific to Dante and of special appeal to the religious Symbolists. This was the fact that Dante was both pilgrim and poet; his works combine the example of a life, viewed as a spiritual journey, with the art which arose from this experience. Dante himself was acutely aware of the close relationship between biographical experience and art, and constantly draws attention to it in his works, monitoring his spiritual development and discussing its reflections in his art.

This alliance of life and art was a particularly potent combination for the religious Symbolists who were seeking to implement their ideals in life as well as in art. As Bely pointed out in his memoirs of the period, Dante's influence was enormous not just because the problems he addressed were central to the preoccupations of the religious Symbolists, but also because he provided them with the example of a life which embodied these ideals and could serve as a model.[22] It was of great significance in this respect that love had played such an important role in Dante's spiritual development. The figure of Beatrice bridged the gap between personal and universal experience, between physical and spiritual love. In the *Vita Nuova* the religious Symbolists were able to find an account of the experience of love as the origin of a spiritual journey, and in the *Commedia* they could follow the record of a mystical journey of the soul, guided by Beatrice, towards its final union with the divine essence. In both these works, the author's spiritual experience is paralleled by an account of his literary experience as a poet, seeking to find adequate forms for the expression of his vision. Dante's works were thus a rich source of inspiration for the relig-

1 Vyacheslav Ivanov with a portrait of Lidiya Zinoveva, Pavia, late 1932

ious Symbolists on many different levels, providing them not only with a possible model for their understanding of love and spiritual experience, but also for its literary expression, and ultimately even for an aesthetics of Symbolism.

Inevitably, the interest in Dante which was generated by all these factors, while being widespread, was also often superficial. Not all the Symbolists could read Dante in the original, fewer still studied him in any depth. Dante was more often invoked as a source of poetic images or set ideas, than as one of complex philosophical or religious concepts. The repertoire of images was fairly standard:

the gates of Hell, the martyred lovers, Francesca and Paolo, or the guiding figures of Virgil and Beatrice. Certain ideas were taken over from Dante's works, but again these tended to be limited to a few set notions: the view of the individual's life as a spiritual path, the role of love as a guiding force in this journey (linked to the figure of Beatrice), the need to pass through Hell and acquire a knowledge of sin as a stage of the mystic way (an idea often exploited for decadent ends), and the sense of a strong hierarchical structure of damnation and beatitude pervading the universe.

Ivanov's approach to Dante, while arising out of the same general context as that of his contemporaries, differed in two major respects. It was not only based on a much closer knowledge of Dante's works and deeper understanding of his ideas, but, more importantly, it was also intimately related to his own spiritual outlook, thereby causing him to turn to Dante on a much more profound level than the other Symbolists. In terms of first-hand knowledge of Dante, Ivanov had several advantages. The three years which he spent in Italy at the beginning of his poetic career (1892–5) enabled him to attain a level of fluency in Italian which was not matched by any of the other Symbolists. Furthermore, his academic training and grounding in classical antiquity gave him a profound insight into the roots of European culture, and a conscientious thoroughness and depth of approach in his study of other writers. It is plain from materials in his archive that he spent considerable amounts of time working on a close textual study of the *Vita Nuova* and *Commedia*, as well as researching the historical background to the period in some detail.[23] None of the other religious Symbolists ever undertook a similar academic study of Dante's works.

However, the fact of Ivanov's greater familiarity with Dante's works is not in itself sufficient to explain the entirely different quality of his approach. It is only a manifestation of the fundamentally intellectual character of his attitude to Dante on a deeper level. It is important to remember that Ivanov began his career as an academic, and retained the interests and methods of a scholar throughout his later literary work. His approach to religion and art was never purely intuitive; it was always accompanied by a strong philosophical orientation. This intellectual tendency was also typical of the literature of medieval Catholicism. Dante saw no clash between faith and reason or between the aesthetically beautiful and the intellectually satisfying. Many of his works are devoted to an elucidation of the relation between these different aspects of revealed truth; in the *Commedia* questions of faith are illuminated through rational and philosophical exposition, and in the *Vita Nuova* and the *Convivio* he subjects his own poetry to detailed prose analysis and commentary.

There was therefore a certain inner affinity between Ivanov's and Dante's modes of thinking and creative methods. This caused Ivanov to feel a particular closeness to Dante, and enabled him to gain a deeper insight into his works. The similarity between the two poets was noted by a number of Ivanov's contemporaries. The religious philosopher, Sergei Bulgakov, for example, dwelt at some length on the strong intellectual element in Ivanov's poetry, and compared him to Dante in this respect, using the term 'poet-thinker' of both writers.[24] Later, the same comparison was developed in a suggestive manner by the literary critic and medieval scholar Evgeny Anichkov. In the section of his work on modern Russian poetry devoted to Ivanov, he wrote that it is impossible to reach an understanding of Ivanov just through his poetry. This is because Ivanov's poems are often related to some external cause (*povod*), and derive their innermost meaning from his extremely complex world-view (*miroponimanie*). In this respect he compared Ivanov to Petrarch and Dante whose verse also derived from a world-view which it did not express directly. For this reason Dante had felt a need to write commentaries to clarify his own poetry – hence the prose section of the *Vita Nuova*. In order to understand Ivanov through his poetry, one would require extensive scholia elucidating the inner meaning of his more difficult verse.[25]

However, Ivanov was not simply a poet of an intellectual nature, he was also an intellectual of a poetic nature. The point was well put by Bryusov in a review of recent Russian literature which he wrote for the English journal *The Athenaeum* in 1903. On the basis of Ivanov's first collection of verse, *Pilot Stars*, Bryusov made a perceptive comment which remains valid for the whole of Ivanov's work:

The volume of poems of Viacheslav Ivanov, entitled 'Pilot Stars', deserves our attention. Of Ivanov I have previously spoken. Certainly his opinions are clearly expounded in his verses. He expresses many philosophic perplexities, which are frequently embodied in the form of classical antiquity. He deals with such questions in his verses as ordinarily are treated in close-reasoned prose, but even while deciding them he remains a poet.[26]

This combination of highly intellectual, academic elements with an intuitive, poetic approach requires a particular method of analysis. As Anichkov correctly points out, one cannot hope to understand Ivanov's poetry without understanding the ideas from which it derives. On the other hand, one cannot attempt to analyse the ideas as purely academic, objective concepts. Although Ivanov was an intellectual type of poet, his intellectual academic side was never without its poetic, personal dimension.

The need to cater for these two aspects – the intellectual and the poetic – calls for a two-pronged approach which is reflected in the structure of this study. The first part is primarily devoted to the ideas and beliefs which caused Ivanov to turn to Dante and determined the way in which he interpreted him. This involves a discussion of Ivanov's ideal of Dionysiac Eros (unique to him), and of his interpretation of Solovyov's teaching on Sophia (shared with the other religious Symbolists). It also includes an examination of the way in which the ideal of mystical love which arose from these combined influences crystallized around the events of the poet's own life, thereby creating a unique and unrepeatable fount of experience which formed the basis of much of his poetry. The investigation of these three areas – constituting what Anichkov described as the 'world-view' and 'external cause' underlying Ivanov's verse – prepares the ground for the discussion of Ivanov's works which follows.

In the second part the approach is more text-orientated. A selection of poems drawn from Ivanov's first three major collections, *Pilot Stars*, *Transparency* and *Cor Ardens*, are analysed in detail, and the treatment of Dantesque images in these poems is related to the themes explored in Part I. Finally, the texts of Ivanov's translations from Dante's three major works, the *Vita Nuova*, *Convivio* and *Divina Commedia*, are published, together with a commentary on the background to these projects and on the poet's method of translation.

The texts chosen for detailed study are taken from the key period from the early 1900s through to the First World War. These years saw the emergence, flowering and decline of religious Symbolism, and were also central to Ivanov's development as a poet.

Close analysis of the texts reveals certain tendencies which were
not only typical of Ivanov's own creative process, but also endemic
to the movement which he led. More than any other movement in
Russian literature, the Symbolists turned obsessively to other cultures and world history in search of support for their own ideas. In
Ivanov's case this phenomenon was intensified by his belief in the
cult of memory as the prerequisite of prophecy and poetry. And
yet, for all their ostensibly outward orientation, the Symbolists
remained fundamentally inward-looking, and their approach to
other cultures and figures from the past was essentially ahistorical.
They were more interested in history and other literatures as a
source of mythological types or universal ideas which could be used
to illustrate their own beliefs. The way in which Ivanov interpreted
the figure of Dante provides a valuable insight into this process.
Images from Dante were taken up and adapted in such a way as to
facilitate their assimilation into the tradition which Ivanov was
trying to build. The arts of poetry and translation thus became a
means for the substantiation of the poet's own spiritual ideal.

PART I

APPROACHES AND THEMES

1

Ivanov's Dionysiac ideal and Dante

Formation: a Christian upbringing and classical education

The three traits which are usually considered characteristic of
Ivanov – the fervent profession of the Christian faith, a high level
of academic scholarship and a sense of poetic vocation – were all
bequeathed to him at the outset of his life by his mother. In a brief
autobiographical note written in 1917, Ivanov paid tribute to the
decisive influence which his mother exerted on his life; she brought
her son up in an atmosphere of mystical Russian Orthodox belief
and piety, wished him to be highly educated and to become a
poet.[1] But Ivanov did not achieve a stable synthesis of these three
elements without first going through a period of reaction during
which he rebelled against his Christian upbringing, pursued a line
of academic research unsuited to his nature, and regarded himself
as a scholar rather than as a poet.

The start of this period of reaction occurred in February 1881
when Ivanov, as he subsequently recorded, made the sudden and
painless discovery around the date of his fifteenth birthday that he
was no longer a believing Christian but an atheist and revolutionary (*SS* II, 13). This phase of adolescent atheism lasted for five
years; it covered the final three years of Ivanov's education at the
First Moscow Gymnasium as well as his first two years at university, and was largely responsible for determining the course of his
academic studies for some years to come.

In atheist circles philological studies were considered frivolous,
whereas the study of history, while lacking the prestige of the social
sciences, could nevertheless be considered to serve the cause of
revolutionary ideals. When the director of Ivanov's gymnasium,
who recognized the natural philological bent of his pupil's talents,
advised Ivanov to take advantage of a state grant to go to Leipzig

and study philology, the suggestion was turned down; Ivanov preferred to support himself rather than to receive money from the Tsarist regime.

In 1884 Ivanov joined the University of Moscow as a student of the Faculty of History and Philology; he devoted himself almost entirely to the study of history despite his greater aptitude for classical philology. This was recognized by the university authorities who awarded him a prize for his work on classical languages.[2] Ivanov concentrated on history however, determined to find the answer to social problems through this field of study; he invested his studies with an almost religious fervour, regarding university life as a form of 'sacred banquet' (SS II, 14). When he set off for Berlin after two years at the University of Moscow to study history under the supervision of the famous historian of Ancient Rome, Theodore Mommsen (1817–1903), he was still fired by his faith in the social value of the study of history. He described his sense of mission in the following lines, written upon his departure from Russia:

> Я верою пошел руководимый,
> Дабы найти в пыли священных книг
> Волшебный щит и меч неодолимый.   (SS II, 16)

> I set off led by faith
> In order to find among the dust of sacred books
> A magic shield and invincible sword.

When Ivanov arrived in Germany, his world-view underwent an abrupt and substantial change; he experienced a resurgence of interest in mystical, spiritual matters, and shed his adolescent atheism. However, for some years he continued to pursue the purely historical line of research which he had adopted under the influence of his atheist views. During the nine semesters which he spent at the University of Berlin from the autumn of 1886 until the spring of 1891, he worked on the history of Ancient Rome and of the Byzantine Empire, specializing in questions such as the system of state taxation in Egypt under the Roman Empire, Latin and Greek palaeography, Roman law, the exarchate of Ravenna, and Byzantine institutions in Southern Italy. While in Berlin, he also started work on his dissertation on the Roman system of taxation. During the spring of 1891, he moved to Paris at the instigation of his Berlin supervisor, Otto Hirschfeld, in order to continue work on his dissertation in the Bibliothèque Nationale and write it out in Latin. After a year in Paris, he moved to Rome for a further three years during which he did some additional work on archaeology and continued to improve his dissertation. At the end of 1895, he finally submitted his dissertation to the Berlin University authorities and received their official approval on 1 January 1896.[3]

In later years, Ivanov came to regard the historical research which he embarked on in Berlin as marking the beginning of a series of wanderings which took him further and further astray from the true object of his affections and natural destiny – the study of classical philology and in particular of the Hellenic soul (SS II, 17). His religious interests eventually led him to abandon the study of Ancient Rome in favour of the spiritually more rewarding subjects of Hellenism and classical philology. However, this transition was a gradual, not a precipitate one. After submitting his dissertation he continued for a while to work on Roman antiquity, but invested his studies with his new interest in Christianity. During the late 1890s he worked in the reading-room of the British Museum in London for almost a year, collecting material on the historical and religious roots of the Christian faith in the universal mission of Rome.

It was not until the early 1900s, during a year spent in Athens, that Ivanov finally settled down to the full-time study of a subject which was more deeply in tune with the nature of his religious interests, and with which he had gradually become increasingly preoccupied over the previous ten years. When Ivanov renewed his interest in religion after moving to Germany in 1886, he found that his previously unquestioning approach to Christianity had given way to a new period of intensive mystical searching. He felt dissatisfied with the state of religious feeling current in contemporary society and was critical of modern Christianity which, in his view, had been steadily deteriorating since the Reformation and had lost touch with its vital roots in Earth and in Nature. This loss could only be repaired by a return to mysticism, the primitive essence of all religions which enables the individual to reaffirm his unity with the Spirit of the universe. He therefore called for a revitalization of the Christian faith through a rediscovery of its mystical roots.[4]

In his search for a new mystical form of religion, Ivanov turned to the two traditions with which he was already familiar through his

childhood upbringing and education – Christianity and classical
antiquity – and sought to develop a new approach to them.
Throughout the 1890s and more intensively during the early 1900s,
his main concern was to establish a synthesis of the mystical
elements in these two traditions which would provide him with a
solid historical and scholarly basis for his new religious intuitions.

Influences: Christian thinkers and Nietzsche

Two sets of influences played a particularly important role in this
search. During the early part of his residence in Berlin, Ivanov was
strongly influenced by the mystical and philosophical teachings of
Vladimir Solovyov, Khomyakov, Dostoevsky and Schopenhauer.
These writers enabled him to invest the Christian faith of his
childhood with new mystical content. Solovyov's ideas in particular
were instrumental in forming his perception of Dante, as will be
discussed in chapters 2 and 3 below.

Towards the end of the Berlin period, these influences were
supplemented by a second major source. Friedrich Nietzsche's
ideas on Dionysus and Apollo entirely changed Ivanov's approach
to classical antiquity and paved the way towards his understanding
of the mystical essence of Hellenic culture.[5]

Ivanov was one of the first Russian writers to become interested
in Nietzsche's ideas. These were being widely discussed in
Germany at the beginning of the 1890s, and the first article on
Nietzsche in the Russian press appeared in 1892.[6] By this time
Ivanov's interest in Nietzsche was already established. When he
travelled from Berlin to Paris in the spring of 1891, there were, as
he records, 'little volumes of Nietzsche' among his luggage (*SS* II,
19).

It was as a result of reading these works that Ivanov first began to
develop his ideas about the Dionysiac principle in Greek culture.
In particular, Nietzsche's first major work, *The Birth of Tragedy
out of the Spirit of Music*, published in 1872, had an enormous and
lasting influence on him.[7] This work popularized one of the most
influential of modern polarities, that between Apollo and Dionysus, the two art-deities of the Greeks. Apollo was associated by
Nietzsche with the drive to individuation, the principle of artistic
order, the art of sculpture and the state of dream. Dionysus on the
other hand was identified with the drive to unity and oneness, the

spirit of elemental chaos, the art of music and the state of ecstatic intoxication. Nietzsche denied the existence of any absolute moral or religious truths, and treated the Apollo–Dionysus polarity on a purely aesthetic level. He condemned Christianity as the weak man's response to the world, and demanded the extinction of all values derived from Christian teaching such as humility or charity in order to give full rein to the individual's will to power. He identified this force with the Dionysiac and anti-Christian principle of elemental chaos which he posited as his ideal; he wished to replace the worship of Christ with the cult of Dionysus.

Nietzsche's anti-Christian position evoked reactions of shock and indignation in Russian intellectual circles.[8] Ivanov's encounter with his ideas took place at a time when he was searching for a new form of mystical Christianity, and he naturally found the philosopher's anti-religious position untenable; for Ivanov any system of aesthetics was necessarily the expression of a religious point of view.[9] The main impulse behind Ivanov's work when he finally settled down to write up his ideas on Dionysus in Athens was therefore the desire to demonstrate the superiority of a religious interpretation of the cult of Dionysus over Nietzsche's aesthetic treatment of the subject. In later years, looking back on his work in Athens on Dionysus, he wrote: 'This study was prompted by an insistent inner requirement: only by this method was I able to overcome Nietzsche in the sphere of questions of religious consciousness' (SS II, 21).[10]

Ideal: a synthesis of Christianity and Dionysiac mysticism

The product of Ivanov's reflections on the cult of Dionysus took the form of a series of lectures which he delivered in the spring of 1903 in Paris at the Higher School of Social Sciences for Russians. Valery Bryusov was in Paris at the time, and made Ivanov's acquaintance at one of the lectures. He was most impressed, and later wrote to Ivanov from Moscow to inform him that Merezhkovsky wished to publish his lectures in his journal Novyi put'.[11] Ivanov agreed to this proposal, and his lectures were subsequently published in the form of a series of articles, at first under the title 'The Hellenic Religion of the Suffering God' in Novyi put' in 1904 and then in Voprosy zhizni, the journal which took over from

Novyi put', under the title 'The Religion of Dionysus'.[12] In this way, through the agency of Bryusov and Merezhkovsky, Ivanov's ideas on Dionysus entered the mainstream of Russian Symbolist culture.

At the very beginning of his series of articles, Ivanov makes it clear that he has undertaken his study of the cult of Dionysus in order to clarify contemporary religious and philosophical searchings and the problems which these present; in other words, the presentation of the cult of Dionysus is a matter of relevance to contemporary Christianity.[13] This is borne out by the structure of the articles; the argument culminates in the two final sections of the last article, entitled 'Dionysus and Hellenism – Dionysus and Christianity' and 'Conclusion: general historical and philosophical deductions. Dionysus and the religious problem'.[14] Ivanov's point of departure in approaching the study of Dionysus was his Christian mystical ideal; he wished first to establish the nature of the cult of Dionysus as an essentially religious phenomenon, and secondly to demonstrate that it should be regarded as the spiritual antecedent and historical basis of the new Christian mystical ideal which he proposed for his age.[15]

Ivanov's first task was therefore to define the mystical essence of the cult of Dionysus. In the course of his articles he describes and analyses the various external forms, myths and rituals which surround the cult of Dionysus, and peels these off as outer masks to reveal the central mystical idea from which they derive their existence and meaning. He concludes that 'this god is always only a mask and is always a single orgiastic essence'.[16]

How is this 'orgiastic essence' to be defined? It is important to realize that the features which are commonly associated with the cult of Dionysus – a state of drunken intoxication and oblivion, an overflowing abundance and fertility – are but the outward manifestations of a state of ecstasy which is itself intimately connected with the experiences of sacrifice and suffering.[17] Ivanov sees this general Dionysiac principle at work in the very character of the winemaking process: wine, which creates a state of intoxication or ecstasy, is made by a process which involves an act of sacrifice, the crushing and pressing of whole grapes.[18]

The 'orgiastic essence' which is at the heart of the cult of Dionysus can therefore be seen to consist of two essential elements – ecstasy and sacrifice. These are inextricably bound to each other in an eternally self-renewing cycle which leads through sacrifice and suffering to the experience of ecstasy which in turn leads to further sacrifice. This cycle embodies the mystical principle which is at the heart of the universe, that of a 'force searching for deliverance from its own excess through suffering and death, and of an ecstatic delight in life which turns into the joy of destruction'.[19]

In Ancient Greece this cycle was celebrated through the cult of Dionysus. Dionysus, as the god of vegetation, was seen as a figure of both suffering and ecstasy, for his myth embodied the yearly cycle of death and resurrection by which nature is governed. His death was mourned in winter, and his resurrection from the dead was celebrated every spring. Through this cycle man is in touch with the mystical forces which inform the universe. He longs to overcome the limitations of his individual self and to merge with these forces in order to become part of the greater whole.[20] The longing which he experiences is mystical in character, it is the feeling of Eros which is the driving impulse behind his spiritual searchings.

To penetrate the mystical essence of the universe, a person must bring the Dionysiac cycle of sacrifice and ecstasy within the framework of his own experience. This means transcending the limitations of his individual self and requires an act of sacrifice; the individual must first lose himself if he is to find himself again within the divine whole. As Ivanov writes: 'the passionate longing for God breaks down the limited individuality of man: where love awakens, the self dies'.[21]

The experiences of suffering and death lead to the ecstasy of rebirth; this is the essence of the individual's Dionysiac mystical experience, summed up by Ivanov in the following terms: 'Dionysiac intoxication is the state of emerging from the boundaries of the self; the destruction and the merging of individuation; the terror of this liberation and of the submersion into the unity and first principle of reality.'[22]

Ivanov regarded the experience of sexual love both as the original source and as the intimate analogue of the Dionysiac mystical experience. The Platonic tradition holds that the feeling of Eros, the aspiration towards the highest form of beauty and good, originates in man's love of physical beauty. Ivanov followed this view, and believed that the experience of sexual ecstasy, requiring man

to transcend the limitations of his individual self to achieve union
with another being, was the primitive essence of Dionysiac mystical ecstasy and therefore of all mystical and religious experience in
general. In his view the religion of Dionysus actually originated in
the cult of sexual ecstasy.[23]

Ivanov felt that contemporary Christianity would only regain its
natural vitality by returning to the mystical ideal embodied in the
cult of Dionysus, and consequently urged his contemporaries to
recover their full spiritual stature by imitating the ancients: 'we
must reject ourselves and become ancient in spirit in order to
restore the presently diminished image of man'.[24]

This return to pagan antiquity is not motivated by a romantic,
escapist nostalgia for the past, but by the desire for a synthesis of
the present with the past.[25] Ivanov is therefore concerned to prove
the compatibility of the two traditions, to demonstrate that the
Christian faith can accommodate elements of pagan antiquity. In
his view, the synthesis which he advocates is not simply a matter of
wishful thinking, it was once a matter of historical fact, and should
become so once more. In the final section of the work, he places
great emphasis on the historical continuity between the religion of
Dionysus and Christianity. He argues that Christianity in its early
phase was close to the ecstatic spirit of Dionysiac mysticism. The
cult of Dionysus prepared the pagan world for the reception of
Christianity, and many aspects of the cult of Dionysus are the
direct antecedents of elements of the Christian tradition. To illustrate this point he relates the images and symbols which occur in
the parables of the Gospels to Dionysiac mythology; he links, for
example, the Christian celebration of Christ's resurrection from
the dead at Easter to the main Dionysiac spring festival, the Great
or City Dionysia, which celebrated the spring-time resurrection of
Dionysus, the god of vegetation, from his winter sleep.[26]

These parallels are the outer manifestations of a deeper internal
affinity. The sacrificial–ecstatic nature of Dionysiac mysticism
passed on into the heart of Christianity. Dionysus, both man and
god, is the prototype of Christ, and the passion of Dionysus is the
central and distinguishing characteristic of the Dionysiac religion in
the same way as the Passion of Christ, which it prefigures, is the
heart of Christianity.[27] In both religions the experience of suffering
and sacrifice is the necessary prelude to the experience of mystical
ecstasy, and death precedes resurrection. In this sense, the life of

Christ and the lesson which it teaches reflect the mystical core of the Dionysiac religion.

It should be emphasized that Ivanov's exploration of these affinities was related to his interest in the inner *psychology* of religion; he regarded Dionysiac mysticism as a certain *method* which could profitably be reaffirmed within a Christian context. This approach did not detract from his view of Christ and the church as part of a radically new revelation (a subject elaborated in his later writings), nor did it reduce the two religions to identical manifestations of equal spiritual value.

Historical models: Dante and the Renaissance

This new brand of Christianity based on Dionysiac mysticism was the spiritual ideal which Ivanov proposed for his age. Naturally, he wished to identify periods in the history of culture which could be seen to exhibit this ideal and therefore be presented as models for the present age to emulate.

Ivanov formulated the general principle which determined his view of history in the following terms:

Hellenism in Europe is an eternally living force ... It can be established as a matter of historical fact that European thought constantly and regularly returns to the genius of Ancient Greece for new stimuli and fertilization. And then the genius of Ancient Greece once more celebrates its resurrection ... It is particularly appropriate for us to speak of 'resurrection' because we are speaking of Dionysus. 'This is the god of resurrection', taught the Neoplatonists. For the European spirit Ancient Greece has always been a source of life and of renewed youth.[28]

When applied to history, this theory produced the following results. Since the early phase of mystical Christianity which retained its close link with the ecstatic character of Dionysiac mysticism, there had been three periods in history embodying this beneficial return to the sources of Hellenism. The first of these was the Renaissance. The second was the German Romantic movement, stimulated by Lessing's and Winckelmann's rediscovery of classical antiquity which entered the mainstream of European culture through the works of Goethe and Schiller. Finally, the period which Ivanov termed 'our most recent Renaissance', and which owed its vitality to the spirit of music. This period was initiated by Beethoven who first resuscitated the Dionysiac spirit.

He was followed by Wagner, and the ideas implicit in their music were further developed by Nietzsche.

Although Ivanov was critical of the Renaissance for being dominated by Rome rather than Greece, of German romanticism for being insufficiently Dionysiac in spirit, and of Nietzsche for not having developed a religious approach to Dionysus, nevertheless, these three periods in their broad outlines were closely associated by him with the life-giving spirit of Hellenism.[29] The period which he invokes most frequently as an example of his spiritual ideal is the Renaissance; this is of particular significance since Ivanov's concept of the Renaissance shaped his approach to Dante.

The Renaissance is conventionally described as a period falling between the fourteenth and sixteenth centuries during which art and letters underwent a considerable revival under the influence of classical models. Ivanov's definition of the Renaissance was a rather broader one, however; it encompassed a period normally described as the late Middle Ages or pre-Renaissance, covering the thirteenth and fourteenth centuries. Ivanov was particularly interested in this early phase because of its strongly religious character; this was more suited to the mystical synthesis of traditions which he was advocating than the later humanist phase of the Renaissance.

Ivanov's definition of the Renaissance therefore began with the medieval sculptor Nicolò Pisano who imported ancient architectural motifs from the south of Italy to Pisa; Pisano's celebrated work of 1260, the Pulpit which stands in the Baptistery at Pisa, exhibits clear signs of classical influence, and can thus be viewed as an early example of Christian art incorporating elements from the heritage of classical antiquity.

It is because of this rather eccentric use of the term Renaissance that Ivanov was able to regard Dante – who was born five years after Pisano's Pulpit was built – as the main representative of a period which he advanced as the embodiment of his spiritual ideal. Ivanov wished to see in Dante a Christian mystic who incorporated the legacy of classical antiquity into his spiritual outlook. It is clear that Dante could meet the first requirement of Ivanov's spiritual ideal – that of Christian mystical content. A question which, however, deserves more detailed attention is the extent to which Dante's Christian mysticism can rightly be considered, as Ivanov would have it, to be closely related to the spirit of classical antiquity.

DANTE'S ATTITUDE TO PAGAN ANTIQUITY

Literary debt

It is undoubtedly true that the legacy of classical antiquity was widely reflected in Dante's works, as indeed it was in the culture of the late Middle Ages in general. Although at one time it was the practice to refer to the Middle Ages as the 'Dark Ages', it has long since been accepted by historians that a renaissance of sorts, a revival of culture and classical learning, was already launched in Western Europe by the middle of the eleventh century. Indeed, from a purely literary point of view, the medieval debt to classical antiquity was extensive.

To establish a foothold in the Graeco-Roman world, Christianity was obliged from an early date to take on many of the outer characteristics of the pagan culture which it was trying to penetrate. By presenting itself in terms familiar to men of a classical upbringing, it was able to make rapid progress in converting pagans to the new religion. This assimilation of pagan elements was a matter of necessity as well as expediency; the classical literary tradition was the only one which was available to the new Christian writers as a model for their own writings. Although the early Christians condemned the representatives of classical antiquity as pagans, they admired and imitated them as writers; they took over the secular art forms of the classical world and filled these with Christian content.

This dual attitude was inherited by the Christian writers of the Middle Ages. Although many medieval writers regarded secular subjects with suspicion, the study of classical literature, and in particular of Virgil, nevertheless formed the basis of their education in the arts of Grammar and Rhetoric.

A further important factor which determined the medieval attitude to the literature of classical antiquity was the disappearance of the study of Greek. Although Greek was the original language of the Gospels, it was superseded by Latin, the language of the church after Rome established itself as the centre of Christianity. As a result, the Greek element which had originally been so closely entwined with Roman civilization receded into the background. During the Middle Ages, knowledge of Greek was a rarity. Homer, for example, was only known as a famous name, and the

chief representative of classical antiquity was a poet not of Greece
but of Ancient Rome – Virgil.[30]

These attitudes are reflected in Dante's works. Dante regarded
the great poets of classical antiquity as his literary mentors, and
pays open tribute to their influence many times. In the fourth canto
of the *Inferno*, for example, he meets Homer, Horace, Ovid and
Lucan, all of whom are confined to Limbo on the borderline of
Hell; Virgil, who is accompanying Dante on his journey, is normally the fifth member of their company. In describing the poets,
Dante uses various forms of the word 'onore' ('honour') seven
times, stressing the veneration which is due to them. The poets
invite Dante to join them and he becomes the sixth person in their
group – a clear indication of Dante's sense of debt and affiliation to
the great writers of classical antiquity.

Dante, like most of his contemporaries, did not know Greek,
and his inclusion of Homer in this group is based on received
opinion. The other four members of the group are all Roman
writers whose influence on Dante has been well documented.[31] In
keeping with the spirit of the age, the most important of these
poets and the major poet of classical antiquity for Dante was
Virgil; it is significant that in the passage cited above, Homer gives
Virgil a special greeting, calling upon the other members of the
group to honour 'l'altissimo poeta' ('the great Poet' – *Inf.* IV, 80).[32]

Dante wrote in both Latin and Italian at a time when the
vernacular literatures were only just emerging from under the
shadow of Latin. He looked towards Latin as the mother tongue of
Italian, and regarded Virgil, the supreme Latin poet and, in the
medieval mind, master of the Latin language, as his literary
mentor. He makes the special character of this relationship quite
clear in a speech which he addresses to Virgil at their first meeting:

> 'O de li altri poeti onore e lume,
>   vagliami 'l lungo studio e 'l grande amore
>   che m'ha fatto cercar lo tuo volume.
> Tu se' lo mio maestro e 'l mio autore,
>   tu se' solo colui da cu'io tolsi
>   lo bello stilo che m'ha fatto onore . . .'   (*Inf.* I, 82–7)

> 'O glory and light of other poets,
>   may the long study and the great love
>   that have made me search your volume avail me!
> You are my master and my author.

You alone are he from whom I took
the fair style that has done me honour . . .'

This is a clear tribute to Virgil as the master poet and Dante's
teacher in literature, with particular reference to the *Aeneid*, the
volume which Dante has lovingly studied. When discussing different parts of this work, Dante always refers to Virgil in terms of
highest praise; 'nostra maggior musa' ('our greatest Muse' – *Par.*
xv, 26), 'lo maggiore nostro poeta' ('our major poet' – *Con.* iv, xxvi,
8) and even 'divinus poeta noster Virgilius' ('our divine poet Virgil'
– *Mon.* ii, iii, 6).[33]

The claim that Dante's works are related to classical antiquity
would thus seem to be justified on a literary level. Ivanov,
however, intends by his spiritual ideal a more substantial relationship than one of purely literary influence. He is making a claim for
an affinity between the mystical traditions of classical antiquity and
the Middle Ages. The question of Dante's approach to pagan
antiquity must therefore be considered from the spiritual, religious
point of view – when Dante refers to Virgil as 'divinus poeta noster
Virgilius', how exactly is this divine quality attributed to Virgil to
be understood?

Philosophy and ethics

The medieval debt to the literature of classical antiquity was
paralleled by a similar revival of interest in the thought and philosophy of classical antiquity. Pagan philosophy was however a
more delicate area to deal with from the theological point of view.
The eleventh-century revival of interest in classical learning
gathered momentum throughout the twelfth century during which
ancient Greek thought, particularly that of Aristotle, became more
and more widely available through translations into Latin from the
original Greek or from Arabic versions. The main challenge faced
by the thirteenth century was the assimilation of this new array of
classical texts into the Christian tradition. By the time Dante began
writing in the 1280s, this task had largely been achieved. St Alber-
tus Magnus (died 1280) and St Thomas Aquinas (died 1274) succeeded in incorporating Aristotle's empirical logic and many of his
teachings into Christian theology. Aquinas also made extensive use
of the metaphysics of Platonism. Platonic doctrines had become
interwoven with Christian teaching from an early stage, following

the interpretation of platonic forms as the creative thoughts of God. Through the works of Plotinus, St Augustine, Dionysius the Pseudo-Areopagite and Boethius, Platonic doctrine passed into the teachings of the twelfth-century mystic, St Bernard of Clairvaux, into Aquinas's system and into the mainstream of medieval thought.[34]

Apart from Plotinus who was not a Christian, all of the theologians and philosophers mentioned above in connection with the Christian absorption of pagan philosophy are to be found in Dante's *Paradiso*, either in the Sphere of the Sun, associated with Wisdom, or in the Empyrean. Through the works of these thinkers, Dante therefore had access to a body of Christianized Aristotelian and Platonic thought on which he was able to draw freely. The influence of Aristotle was particularly strong; his works are quoted by Dante more frequently than any other body of writings apart from the Bible.[35] In the Middle Ages Aristotle was referred to simply as 'the Philosopher'; for Dante, he is ''l maestro di color che sanno' ('the Master of those who know' – *Inf.* IV, 131), and Virgil, addressing Dante, refers to Aristotle as 'l maestro vostro' ('your master' – *Par.* VIII, 120).

Finally, as well as incorporating elements of pagan philosophical systems into his works, Dante also draws extensively on the history and mythology of classical antiquity for illustrations in support of his arguments. Throughout the *Commedia* moral lessons are derived with equal ease from classical and Scriptural sources. This general tendency is well illustrated by the standard pattern of moral instruction followed on the terraces of Mount Purgatory. Here the repentant sinner is presented with images of virtue and sin drawn in turn from Christian, Jewish and classical sources. No differentiation is made between these varied examples.[36]

Religious reservations

There is clearly ample evidence that Dante drew extensively on the writings of classical antiquity not only for literary inspiration but also for philosophical concepts and examples of moral instruction. One might therefore be tempted to agree with Ivanov's portrayal of Dante as a Christian writer whose world-view was grounded in the wisdom of classical antiquity. However, to accept this view would entail ignoring the clear limitations which Dante places upon the role which classical antiquity can play within his spiritual outlook. The precise boundaries of these limitations can be sensed with greatest clarity in relation to two particular examples: the fate which Dante assigns to the virtuous heathen of pagan antiquity, and the role which Virgil, the main representative of this category, plays within the framework of Dante's mystical journey in the *Commedia*.

The problem of the fate allotted to the virtuous heathen of pagan antiquity in the Christian scheme of salvation was an acute one for Dante. Although the church had at an early stage recognized the need for a special zone on the border of Hell to accommodate those who, according to the Christian doctrine of salvation, were excluded from the full blessedness of the beatific vision, but did not nevertheless deserve active punishment, only two categories of humans were admitted into this area: the Jewish patriarchs of the Old Covenant who were regarded as Christians by anticipation, and Christians who had died unregenerate such as unbaptized infants. The Jewish patriarchs were accommodated in the *Limbus patrum*, while the infants were assigned to the *Limbus puerorum*. There was no place for the virtuous heathen of pagan antiquity in either of these two limbos. This view was the canonical one in Dante's time; it was upheld, for example, by Thomas Aquinas, Dante's immediate predecessor and usual authority in matters of theology. It is a tribute to the extent of Dante's respect for the virtuous heathen of pagan antiquity that he went beyond traditional church ruling and extended the concept of the *limbus puerorum* in order to include the virtuous heathen.[37]

Although Dante's Limbo constitutes the first circle of Hell, it lies outside of Hell proper, on its border, as the name Limbo implies. The souls of Limbo move among pleasant surroundings and do not undergo any active torment. Among them Dante distinguishes a specially honoured group who are in a blaze of light which overcomes the surrounding darkness. These are the great poets of antiquity; they move forward to greet Dante and Virgil and lead them to a fresh green meadow where Dante observes two further groups of virtuous heathen: warriors of the ancient world, mainly connected with the founding of the Roman Empire, and the philosophers and scholars of pagan antiquity, grouped around their leader Aristotle (*Inf*. IV, 67–151).

The relatively pleasant conditions in which the virtuous heathen of Limbo find themselves, and the special attention which Dante devotes to their description only serve however to underline their fundamentally tragic plight. Although Dante has paid a substantial tribute to them by allowing them a place in Limbo, he has in no way departed from the very firm distinction drawn by Aquinas and fundamental to the Christian faith between the spheres of reason and revelation. The world of the virtuous heathen is in the final analysis a 'cieco mondo' ('blind world' – *Inf.* IV, 13); its light remains encircled by darkness, for it is no more than the light of natural reason, limited, and not extended by the illumination of divine grace. Whereas Limbo is the eternal station of the virtuous heathen in the after-life and marks the end of their journey, for Dante it is only a beginning, a point of departure.

Through the personage of Virgil, Dante is able to incorporate a dynamic treatment of this predicament into the very structure of the *Commedia*. Limbo is a static area in the topography of the after-life, but Virgil, who belongs to this world, is allowed by special dispensation to emerge from it in order to accompany and guide Dante on his journey; this provides a clear illustration of the exact limits to which the wisdom of pagan antiquity can reach within the framework of a Christian mystical journey.

Virgil's journey teaches us two main points about this matter; firstly, that pagan wisdom may be considered as a preparation for Christian revelation; but secondly, that it cannot operate in the sphere of Christian truth from which it remains firmly excluded. Virgil represents the operation of human reason directed towards the revelation of grace but deprived of it. This two-fold principle is demonstrated on a personal level, in the context of Dante's mystical journey, and on a general level, in terms of the historical relations between pagan antiquity and the Christian era.

The personal level is illustrated by Virgil's role as a guide to Dante in the *Commedia*. Dante's journey through Hell, Purgatory and Paradise is a journey of the soul towards the final Beatific Vision and knowledge of God. According to Aquinas, the path followed by man in his mystical journey falls into three stages, described in the following terms:

Man's knowledge of divine things is threefold. The first is when man, by the natural light of reason, rises through creatures to the knowledge of God. The second is when the divine truth which surpasses the human intelligence comes down to us by revelation, yet not as shown to him that he may see it, but as expressed in words so that he may hear it. The third is when the human mind is raised to the perfect intuition of things revealed.[38]

Dante's journey in the *Commedia* follows this pattern, and for each separate stage a different guide is provided. Virgil takes Dante as far as the 'natural light of reason' can guide him, Beatrice guides him through the truths which are revealed to man through grace, and St Bernard of Clairvaux is his guide in matters of purely intuitive contemplation. Although the natural wisdom of pagan antiquity which Virgil embodies is thus allowed to play a certain role within the scheme of a Christian mystical journey, this role is firmly circumscribed. When Virgil parts with Dante he tells him that he has now reached a stage of the journey where he can see no further – without the operation of divine grace, the necessary factor for the next stage of the journey. His words are: 'se' venuto in parte/dov'io per me più oltre non discerno' ('[you] are come to a part where I of myself discern no further onward' – *Purg.* XXVII, 128–9). As in Limbo, there is no confusion between reason and revelation, and although Virgil can serve as a guide for the first preparatory stage, he is firmly excluded from the latter stages of the journey. At their very first meeting in the opening canto of the *Inferno*, Virgil informs Dante that he will be his guide through Hell and Purgatory, but that if Dante should then wish to ascend to the spirits of the blest, he shall be guided by a spirit fitter for that purpose than Virgil (*Inf.* I, 122). Virgil explains that he is not allowed admittance into the city of God because he was a rebel to His law. Dante therefore, taking the point, entreats Virgil to lead him onwards out of the dark wood 'per quello Dio che tu non conoscesti' ('by that God whom you did not know' – *Inf.* I, 131).

Virgil frequently acknowledges the limitations of his powers. He is often obliged to admit his inadequacy, his inability to cope with a situation or deal with a given question; on many occasions he must refer Dante to Beatrice or Statius who have the Christian understanding through grace which he lacks. He relates the limitation of human reason which is unable to comprehend certain religious mysteries such as the Trinity to the condition of the pagans; if the natural reason of pagan antiquity had been all-powerful, there would have been no need for the Christian revelation and the longing of the virtuous heathen to know God would not be doomed to remain forever as it was in their life-time: essentially incomplete and unsatisfied (*Purg.* III, 34–45).

As a representative of pagan antiquity, Virgil is also able to illustrate the relation of natural reason to Christian revelation within a general historical context. Through his example pagan antiquity is shown to have been a historical period which prepared the way for Christianity but was itself excluded from the light of divine revelation. The encounter between Virgil and Statius which takes place in Purgatory clearly illustrates the gulf which separates the two worlds. Virgil lived, to quote his own words, 'nel tempo de li dèi falsi e bugiardi' ('in the time of the false and lying gods' – *Inf.* I, 72); he died in 19 BC before the Advent of Christ, and, because of this historical timing, could not be a Christian and find salvation (*Inf.* IV, 37–42). Statius, who was born *c.* AD 45, was able to convert to Christianity. Accordingly, Virgil is doomed to a life of desire without hope in Limbo for all eternity, whereas we encounter Statius making his way up Mount Purgatory, destined eventually for Paradise.

On the other hand, Virgil is presented as a prophet of Christianity whose works were directly instrumental in the conversion of the pagan world to Christianity. This attitude was common in the Middle Ages, and was based on the Christological interpretation of Virgil's fourth *Eclogue* first advanced by the emperor Constantine. Virgil's poem was composed in the dawn of the Roman Empire, forty years before the birth of Christ. It speaks of a glorious time which is about to begin and of a child just born under whom the iron age shall cease and a golden era spring up throughout the world which he shall rule in peace. Many Christians followed Constantine and regarded this poem as an inspired prophecy – whether conscious or unwitting – of the coming of Christ. The *Eclogue* became known as the Messianic one, and was the chief factor in the medieval glorification of Virgil. Many popular legends arose telling of the conversion of pagans to Christianity under the influence of Virgil's words.[39]

Dante believed in Virgil's special role as a witness to the providential destiny of the Roman Empire, under which Christianity was brought to birth in the time of Augustus. He shared the common medieval view of Virgil's fourth *Eclogue* as a prophecy of Christianity, and appears to have deliberately staged the scene of Virgil's encounter with Statius to demonstrate the importance of

Virgil's role as a prophet of Christianity. Although there is no historical evidence for Statius's conversion to Christianity, he presents Statius as a poet who converted from paganism to Christianity under the influence of Virgil. When Virgil and Statius first meet, Virgil asks what caused Statius to convert to Christianity. Statius replies that Virgil was his first guide in literary matters and also – after God – in spiritual matters. He compares Virgil to one who goes by night and carries the light behind him – who is himself unenlightened, but who illuminates the path of those who follow him. This role of Virgil's is explicitly related by Statius to the fourth *Eclogue* from which he quotes a line in free translation (*Purg.* XXII, 55–72). Statius's dual debt to Virgil, both literary and religious, is summed up in his statement to Virgil: 'Per te poeta fui, per te cristiano' ('Through you I was a poet, through you a Christian' – *Purg.* XXII, 73).

Clearly therefore, although pagan antiquity may be a rich source of literary inspiration and of moral and philosophical teachings for Dante, and although it may even be viewed as a preparatory stage leading up to Christianity, it is nevertheless placed on an entirely different plane and excluded from the light of religious revelation or truth.[40]

IVANOV'S IMAGE OF DANTE

Intellectual inconsistencies

Although Dante may justifiably be regarded as a religious thinker who incorporated elements of pagan antiquity into the Christian mystical tradition, Ivanov's spiritual ideal amounted to far more than a simple revival of interest in classical antiquity, Greek or Roman. He was advocating a return to the Greek tradition and, more specifically, to the Dionysiac religion, regarded as the true spirit of Hellenism and as a prefiguration of the ideal, primitive essence of Christianity. Since he regarded the pre-Renaissance as one of the main periods to have experienced the beneficial return to the sources of Hellenism, he was bound to view Dante, the chief representative of the period, as a writer whose spiritual outlook exhibited Dionysiac traits.

In order to lend substance to this view, Ivanov attempted to build a chain linking Dante to Dionysus with Virgil as intermediary. On the basis of the great importance attached by medieval Christian mystics to Virgil's Messianic *Eclogue*, he established the first link in this chain, that between Dante and Virgil. In a late essay on Virgil, he discusses the Middle Ages' particular appreciation of Virgil and intimate grasp of his unique historical greatness as an intermediary figure linking the pagan world of classical antiquity to Christianity. In this context he makes frequent reference to Dante, and in particular to the latter's presentation of Statius. He cites Statius's conversion to Christianity under the influence of Virgil's Messianic *Eclogue*, quoting Dante's words spoken by Statius 'Per te poeta fui, per te cristiano' ('Through you I was a poet, through you a Christian'). He also discusses the medieval view of Virgil as a theurgic poet, and special feeling for the *Aeneid* because of its eschatological elements. Here again he quotes Dante's words spoken by Statius who refers to the *Aeneid* as his 'mamma/ ... e ... nutrice' ('mother and nurse' – *Purg.* xxi, 97–8).[41]

This link, as noted above, was indeed reflected in Dante's *Commedia*. However, Ivanov attempts to trace it back one step further, reaching from Dante through Virgil to Dionysus. In his early work on the religion of Dionysus, he claimed that it was through Dionysiac mysticism that the pagan world had been prepared for the Messianic message of Virgil's *Eclogue* and for the acceptance of the Christian faith. Indeed, it was precisely because of the hidden presence in Christianity of original Dionysiac truths that the pagan world had been able to accept the new religion.[42]

It is possible that Statius was a particularly important example for Ivanov because he could be seen as a link in this chain. Statius was the author of the *Thebaid*, an epic poem about the city of Thebes, the birthplace of Bacchus and centre of his cult. 'Cantai di Tebe' ('I sang of Thebes') are his words in *Purgatorio* (xxi, 92) and we know that Dante described Thebes as 'la città di Baco' ('the city of Bacchus' – *Inf*, xx, 59). Dante in fact represents Statius as having secretly converted to Christianity while still completing the *Thebaid* (*Purg.* xxii, 88–91). He can therefore in some sense be seen as a figure linking the cult of Dionysus to Christianity through the intermediary of Virgil's influence.

There are, however, two major drawbacks inherent in Ivanov's attempt to relate Dante to Dionysiac mysticism through a chain of this type. Firstly, as far as the general idea of a return to the Greek

tradition is concerned, Dante knew no Greek and therefore had no
direct access to the Hellenic world; his vision of classical antiquity
was entirely dominated by the Latin writers of Ancient Rome.
Ivanov did in fact recognize that the early Renaissance as a period
was inadequate to his spiritual ideal in this respect, for its understanding of the true spirit of the Hellenic world was incomplete,
limited by the Roman forms through which it perceived classical
antiquity.[43]

The second point concerns Ivanov's understanding of pagan
mysticism as anticipating the primitive essence of Christianity.
Ivanov claimed that his view of the cult of Dionysus as an essentially mystical phenomenon was closer to the medieval understanding of pagan antiquity than the generally accepted contemporary
view.[44] By this he wished to imply that medieval artists shared his
awareness of Dionysiac mysticism. And yet, although representations of Dionysus did survive in the art of the Christian Middle
Ages, they were by no means conceived in the same spirit as that in
which Ivanov viewed them.[45] The references which Dante makes
to Bacchus in the *Commedia*, for example, number only three, and
do not betray any significant interest in the god's cult. Aspects of
the cult of Bacchus are evoked by Dante in order to be contrasted
unfavourably with Christian practice and condemned. Several of
the diviners and soothsayers who are punished in hell are associated with Thebes, 'the city of Bacchus'; the slothful who run along
the terrace of Purgatory to cleanse themselves of their sin are
compared to the Thebans running and worshipping Bacchus; the
hymn of praise to the Trinity sung by the spirits in the sphere of
wisdom in Paradise is contrasted with the hymns sung to Bacchus
and Apollo in antiquity.[46]

Ivanov's desire to view Dante as a Christian mystic continuing
the tradition of Dionysiac mysticism was clearly incompatible with
Dante's condemnation of Bacchic rites and firm exclusion of pagan
antiquity from the truth of Christianity. For Dante there was no
spark of religious truth or mystical essence in pagan antiquity
which could serve as a basis for Christianity. The only elements of
pagan antiquity which could be absorbed into the Christian scheme
were non-religious and rational, either literary, philosophical or
ethical. In terms of religious spirit there was no area of overlap
between the two realms. As Etienne Gilson wrote in *The Spirit of
Medieval Philosophy*: 'The Christians never considered themselves

as merely completing Greek religion, but always thought that they were merely completing Greek philosophy.'[47]

For Dante, Christianity was not a continuation or further development of some strand inherent in pagan antiquity; it was a radical new departure, breaking with the old. It was a revelation, and the relation of pagan antiquity to this revelation could only be one of blindness preceding the light, or, at best, as in the case of Virgil, of prophecy, but never one of identity or inner affinity.

Poetic coherence

Ivanov never attempted to provide any theoretical justification for the discrepancy between the image of Dante which he presented and the historical reality of Dante's own attitude to pagan antiquity. Although he was aware on an intellectual level that Dante's attitude fell within the traditional confines of Latin-dominated Christian thinking, he was not concerned with Dante as a historical figure; he was interested in him as a vehicle which he could invest with his projected spiritual ideal of a synthesis of Greek and Christian mysticism. It is as if, having found Nietzsche's views on Dionysus lacking in the religious dimension, he turned to the figure of Dante as a religious thinker who could be made to reflect the Dionysiac aspects of Nietzsche's teaching, extended into the sphere of Christian mysticism.[48] Although his approach to spiritual questions was often couched in scholarly, historical language, it was essentially an artistic and intuitive one. Ivanov was a poet, not a theologian, and he was quite prepared to reconcile doctrines which were incompatible on a theoretical or theological level on an altogether different plane of generalized poetic truth.

Ivanov did not approach pagan and Christian mysticism as abstract theoretical systems; he approached them through their embodiment in the myths and poetry of their age. Dionysiac mysticism was to be found in the myths surrounding the cult of Dionysus and in the dithyrambic verse of Greek tragedy, just as Dante's mysticism was to be found in his poetry. It was primarily on this level of poetry that Ivanov attempted to establish a relationship of continuity between Dionysiac mysticism and Dante. For Ivanov poetry was the sacred vessel through which universal mystical truths could be expressed. Greek tragedy was one of the earliest art forms to fulfil this function – the function of 'great art' (*bol'shoe iskusstvo*) as Ivanov termed it. In his view, Dante was the last representative of true 'great art' in the history of culture, for his art expressed the universally acknowledged mystical truths of his time.[49]

Through poetry, defined in this way as the voice of divine truth, Ivanov was able to trace a line from classical antiquity to Dante. This poetic rather than theological basis for the link between Dante and pagan antiquity comes across clearly in a late essay of 1938 entitled 'Thoughts on Poetry'. Here, Ivanov defines the essence of a poetry as a form of mystical utterance or 'incantation' (*zaklinanie*), safeguarded by the Muses, the daughters of Zeus and Memory. Christianity, in its struggle with the heritage of pagan antiquity, struck a blow at the classical idea of the poet's sacred mission. Apart from the utterances of the sibyls and Virgil's fourth *Eclogue*, the church would not accept the spiritual value of the literary heritage of classical antiquity. But the poets were not prepared to relinquish their trust in beauty as something sacred. Ivanov quotes two examples: Dante, who could not write his Christian works without appealing to the Muses of classical antiquity, and Raphael's depiction of Poetry, sitting up in the clouds, surrounded by an inscription from Virgil testifying to the divine quality of poetic inspiration.[50] Both Dante and Raphael, artists of the Renaissance, are viewed as continuing the classical tradition of belief in poetry as a divinely inspired vehicle for the expression of sacred truths. For Ivanov both examples reflect the synthesis of Greek wisdom and Christian revelation which was his spiritual ideal.

Ivanov tried, therefore, to establish the link between Dante and classical antiquity on the basis of both cultures' common faith in the sacred character of poetry. His main method for substantiating this link was however necessarily one of poetic creation rather than of intellectual demonstration. He could not prove that Dante was inherently Dionysiac; he could however create an image of Dante invested with Dionysiac traits, and by this means lend substance to intuitions or ideals which intellectually he could not defend.

One example may serve to illustrate this general tendency to develop an idea which can only be hinted at in prose more fully through its embodiment in poetry. In the fifth chapter of 'The Hellenic Religion of the Suffering God' Ivanov explores the link between the Dionysiac religion and the cult of dead souls inhabiting trees. Since the cult of Dionysus is rooted in the cult of the dead, and trees wère in antiquity the refuge place of dead souls, he sees in the legends of dead souls inhabiting trees manifestations of the Dionysiac religion. As examples he quotes the legends of Daphne, Cyparissus, Atys, Philemon and Baucis.

Having established the image of dead souls inhabiting trees as a Dionysiac one, Ivanov calls the reader's attention to the memorable episode of the souls of the suicides imprisoned in trees, described by Dante in *Inferno* XIII.[51] In this canto, we learn that the souls of suicides fall after death into a savage and trackless wood where they sprout into trees; the Harpies, by feeding on their leaves, cause them to wail in pain. Dante plucks a twig from one of these trees which drips blood and cries out in protest.

Dante's image is of pagan origin; as he points out in line 48 of the same canto, it is borrowed from Virgil's *Aeneid*.[52] He has absorbed it into the framework of his Christian teaching, regarding it as a fitting symbol of the punishment deserved by the suicide who in his life deprived his own body of its natural movement. Ivanov's deliberate reference to this passage from Dante in the context of his treatment of the same type of image as a manifestation of the cult of Dionysus seems to imply that Dante's image also has its roots in the Dionysiac religion; once more Ivanov is trying to establish a line of spiritual kinship reaching back from Dante through Virgil to Dionysiac mysticism.

In prose, Ivanov cannot present this idea logically; he can only hint at it by juxtaposing the elements which he would like the reader to connect. Poetry, however, is a medium which is much better suited to the conveying of intuitively grasped affinities. Phenomena of entirely different origins can be presented side by side; within the framework of a unified poetic text they appear as coherent parts of a single whole. This is well illustrated by a poem in which Ivanov returned to the idea which he had originally advanced in prose and presented it, more fully developed, as a poetic truth.

In August 1909, Ivanov wrote a sonnet at the request of S. Makovsky, the editor of *Apollon*, for the first issue of the journal. The poem first appeared under the title 'Apollini' in the opening issue of *Apollon*. Later it was included in 'To the Poet' ('*Poetu*'), a cycle of three poems which formed the closing epilogue to the second book of *Cor Ardens*. The text of the poem is as follows:

Когда вспоит ваш корень гробовой
Ключами слез Любовь, и мрак суровый,
Как Смерти сень, волшебною дубровой,
Где Дант блужал, обстанет ствол живой, –

Возноситесь вы гордой головой,
О гимны, в свет, сквозя над мглой багровой
Синеющих долин, как лес лавровый,
Изваянный на тверди огневой!

Под хмелем волн, в пурпуровой темнице,
В жемчужнице - слезнице горьких лон,
Как перлы бездн, родитесь вы - в гробнице.

Кто вещих Дафн в эфирный взял полон,
И в лавр одел, и отразил в кринице
Прозрачности бессмертной? - Апполон.   (*SS* II, 358–9)

When Love waters your buried root
With springs of tears, and bleak gloom,
Like Death's canopy, by a magic grove
Where Dante wandered surrounds the living trunk –

You rise up with your proud heads,
O hymns, into the light, shining translucent over the crimson
    darkness
Of blue valleys, like a laurel wood
Carved out against the fiery firmament!

Under the intoxicating waves, in a purple dungeon,
In the pearl-oyster lachrymatory of the bitter expanses,
Like pearls of the abyss, you are born in the tomb.

Who took soothsaying Daphnes into ethereal captivity
And clad them in laurel, and reflected them in the well
Of immortal transparency? – Apollo.

In this poem, Ivanov develops the association which he had made earlier in prose between Dante's image of the souls of the suicides, trapped in trees, and the myth of Daphne, changed into a laurel. As before, these two images are seen as manifestations of the fundamental principle of Dionysiac mysticism – that death itself contains the seeds of life; this belief is however now extended from the sphere of life into the sphere of poetry, viewed as one of the most intense expressions of life which comes from death and is then immortalized through art.

The poem begins with an address to 'hymns' – songs of praise in honour of a deity or hero, and the original form of poetry. Hymns have their root in death, but when this root is watered with the tears of suffering love, then the death-like gloom of Dante's magic wood will be found to surround a living trunk, and the hymns will grow up above the gloom into the light, like a wood of laurels.

This complicated image has its origin in Dante's description of the magic wood in *Inferno* xiii. The dead souls which inhabit the trees of this wood will reveal the life which is inherent in them when prompted by suffering love. This life manifests itself through dripping blood and speech. The speech is here understood by Ivanov as an image for poetry. This interpretation accords well with Dante's own text. The soul who speaks forth after Dante plucks a twig from his branch is Pier della Vigna, a famous poet as well as the chief adviser of the Emperor Frederick II. His speech is highly embellished and full of literary conceits reminiscent of his own poetic style. He speaks at the prompting of Dante's pitying heart (ll. 82–4), just as the 'hymns' or trees of Ivanov's poem grow after their roots are watered by tears of love.

The first two verses of Ivanov's poem can therefore on one level be read as a reference to the poetic speech of Pier della Vigna whose words, solicited by pitying love, rise out of apparent death, above the dark wood and into the light of eternal fame. The third verse of the poem restates the same idea – that poetry is born out of death – through a different image. In the last verse this idea is related to the deity after whom Makovsky's new journal was named and for whom the poem was intended. The culmination of the poet's task is to show that Apollo, who presides over the arts and over poetry in particular, and who is traditionally identified with the forces of order and light, has his roots in the Dionysiac cult of death. Ivanov wishes to provide a poetic demonstration of Nietzsche's thesis that 'the highest goal of tragedy and of all art is attained' when 'Dionysus speaks the language of Apollo; and Apollo, finally, the language of Dionysus'.[53]

To do so, Ivanov makes use of Apollo's role in the myth of Daphne. For him, Daphne's transformation into a laurel was a perfect Dionysiac image of the life which can be contained within a dead form. Indeed, on the very day he completed the writing of this sonnet, he was still pursuing his work on Dionysus and writing about Daphne in this context, as he records in his diary (*SS* II, 796). The following extract from Ovid's account of the myth of Daphne brings out the features which Ivanov took up in his poem in a Dionysiac context quite clearly; after describing Apollo's pursuit of Daphne, Daphne's appeal to her father, the river god Peneus, and consequent transformation into a laurel, Ovid continues with the following description of Apollo:

Even as a tree, Phoebus loved her. He placed his hand against the trunk, and felt her heart still beating under the new bark. Embracing the branches as if they were limbs he kissed the wood: but, even as a tree, she shrank from his kisses. Then the god said: 'Since you cannot be my bride, surely you will at least be my tree. My hair, my lyre, my quivers will always display the laurel . . . Further, as my head is ever young, my tresses never shorn, so do you also, at all times, wear the crowning glory of never-fading foliage'.[54]

Ivanov sees in this myth a clear manifestation of the Dionysiac idea of death being transmuted into life through suffering love. Apollo is himself responsible for the creation of this image of life in death; it was he who caused Daphne to be imprisoned in mid-flight in the form of a laurel. Having brought about this death, however, Apollo then seeks to release the living principle from the dead form. The object of his passion eluded him through death, but he was able to transcend this loss through his suffering love by making the symbol of Daphne's dead form, the laurel, sacred to his divinity, and turning it into an emblem of unfading foliage and poetic immortality.

The poem provides an example of the way in which Ivanov uses poetic methods to assimilate Dante into a Dionysiac context and present him as a figure endowed with the features of his spiritual ideal. It is constructed around a series of metamorphoses which starts with the image of the tree's root, develops into Dante's magic wood, then into the laurel wood and finally into Daphne transformed into a laurel. Through this sequence of poetic images Ivanov is able to establish a link between an episode from Dante's *Commedia* and the myth of Apollo and Daphne, and to present both of these as manifestations of the same Dionysiac principle. The fact that Dante's views were in many ways incompatible or at variance with the Dionysiac elements of Ivanov's ideal did not act as a deterrent; on the contrary, as the example reveals, the need to overcome these inherent tensions by weaving webs of syncretic imagery was one of the fundamental stimuli inspiring Ivanov's Muse.

2

Vladimir Solovyov and Dante

The spiritual ideal which Ivanov evolved during his student years in Europe was composed of two main elements, the Dionysiac and the Christian. The first of these was strongly coloured by Nietzsche's ideas, while the second owed much to the influence of various Christian thinkers among whom the Russian philosopher and poet Vladimir Solovyov (1853–1900) played a role of special importance. Although his influence was for a time partially eclipsed by Ivanov's fascination with Nietzsche and Dionysus, it later reasserted itself and was a substantial factor in the composition of Ivanov's spiritual idea. It is of particular interest for our subject as certain aspects of Solovyov's teaching contributed directly to the formation of the Symbolists' and Ivanov's perception of Dante. To see how this came about, it is necessary to first consider the nature of Solovyov's beliefs and the impact which these had on his own interest in Dante.

SOLOVYOV'S TEACHING ON SOPHIA

The idea of Sophia

One of the principal drives behind Solovyov's teaching was a sense of dissatisfaction with the historical development and contemporary state of Christianity. In October 1891 he gave a lecture entitled 'On the Decline of the Medieval World-View' in which he analysed the source of the spiritual decline of Christianity and urged his audience to return to a truer form of Christian faith. In his view Christianity was in its essence a religion of God-manhood, and its mission was to transform humanity and the world into the Kingdom of God, to turn the Flesh into Spirit. As he wrote: 'The meaning of Christianity lies in transforming human life in accordance with the truths of faith ... Christianity is *the religion of divine incarnation and of the resurrection of the flesh.*'[1]

53

Christianity had however betrayed its original mission. After a few centuries, the true spirit of Christianity had given way to a false version of the faith; this new version was no longer a religion of martyrdom and conviction, but a state religion of convenience. The pagans who accepted the new religion once it became established were happy to pay lip-service to an idea, but did not want their ordinary lives to be affected. This attitude led to a fatal split between the earthly life of the Flesh – which could remain untouched – and the life of the Spirit – which was reduced to the profession of a few articles of faith. By swearing allegiance to a few dogmas, a pagan could become a Christian while ignoring the fundamental imperative of Christianity to make religion a part of everyday life, the 'norm of reality' or the 'law of life',[2] to transform the life of the Flesh into Spirit.

In Solovyov's view medieval Christianity was the direct result of this original distortion, and the product of a false compromise between paganism and Christianity. One of the main thrusts of his teaching was therefore to attack all forms of dualism which tended to dissociate the material world from the spiritual. The teaching on Sophia which he evolved was a response to his desire to affirm the unity of the Creator and His creation, of the Spirit and the Flesh; it was a way of emphasizing the spiritual divine element which is inherent in the material world and not distinct from it.

Sophia is first defined in one of Solovyov's earliest works, the 'Lectures on God-Manhood', a series of twelve lectures dating from the late 1870s. In the seventh lecture Solovyov formulated a distinction between two types of unity in the world – the unity of the active principle, and the unity of the multiplicity which this active principle creates. The first is termed 'producing unity' (*edinstvo proizvodyashchee*) or 'unity in itself as a principle' (*edinstvo kak nachalo (v sebe)*), and the second is termed 'resultant unity' (*edinstvo proizvedennoe*) or 'unity in manifestation' (*edinstvo v yavlenii*). The mystic name of the second type of unity is Sophia, defined as 'God's body, the matter of the Deity permeated by the principle of divine unity'.[3] In other words Sophia is the divine basis or essence of that which, as created, is distinct from God; it is the living soul of the created world. The concept of *khokhma* or wisdom occurs in the Old Testament as both a human and divine quality; translated into Greek as σοφια (*sophia*), it passed into the vocabulary of Christian theology, and was applied by St Paul to the person of Christ, in whom wisdom was regarded as incarnate; it was also connected with the third person of the Trinity as one of the gifts of the Holy Ghost.[4]

Solovyov further developed the idea of Sophia in *La Russie et l'Eglise Universelle*, first published in Paris in 1889. Here he described Sophia as the protecting guardian-angel of the world, the substance of the Holy Spirit which hovered over the world at its creation:

La Khocma, la Σοφια, la Sagesse divine n'est pas l'âme, mais l'ange gardien du monde couvrant de ses ailes toutes les créatures pour les élever peu à peu à l'être véritable comme un oiseau qui couve ses petits. Elle est la substance de l'Esprit-Saint qui s'est porté sur les eaux ténébreuses du monde naissant.[5]

Solovyov continued to describe the three distinct and successive but essentially indivisible manifestations of Sophia: the Virgin Mary (the feminine principle of Sophia), Christ (the masculine principle), and the church or ideal humanity, the social or universal realization of Sophia in the future, the bride of the Word of God who will be known by the name of Sophia. This final universal incarnation of Sophia has particularly attracted the Russian religious soul; the Russian churches dedicated to Saint Sophia and the representations of Sophia in Russian iconography as a distinct divine being refer to this third future manifestation of Sophia as redeemed humanity, and are in this sense distinct from Greek usage which identified Sophia with the Logos.[6]

Sophia and love

Had the concept of Sophia remained the object of purely abstract theological speculation, it would no doubt not have exerted the powerful influence which it did on the poetic imagination of the religious Symbolists. However, because Solovyov incorporated the idea of Sophia into the heart of a carefully worked out theory on the meaning of love, both physical and spiritual, and provided a specific illustration of his theory by the example of his life, the Symbolists were able to link the idea to their own experience of love and view Sophia as part of a personal reality.

Solovyov expounded his ideas on love in 'The Meaning of Love', a series of articles which first appeared between 1892 and 1894.[7]

This work had an enormous influence on all the religious Symbolists including Ivanov. It provided them with a common point of
departure in their search for an understanding of the nature of love
and of its role in life and in art.

In 'The Meaning of Love' the unity of the created world or
Sophia is identified as a female principle and termed the 'eternal
Feminine' (*vechnaya Zhenstvennost'*).[8] This principle is inherent in
every created being; indeed, the individual is merely a particular
manifestation of this created unity. Therefore when we love the
ideal image of a person we are in fact loving the essence of created
unity or the 'eternal Feminine'.[9]

The object of true love is therefore twofold, consisting both of
this ideal created unity or 'eternal Feminine' and of a real, individual person. In the following passage Solovyov explores the
implications of this view:

> The object of true love is not simple but twofold: we love, first, the ideal
> being (ideal not in an abstract sense, but in the sense of belonging to
> another higher realm of being) which we must bring into our ideal world,
> and secondly, we love the natural human being which provides the living
> personal material for this realization, and which is idealized through this
> process not in our subjective imagination, but in the sense of being actually
> and objectively transformed or regenerated. Thus, true love is indivisibly
> both *ascending* and *descending* (*amor ascendens* and *amor descendens*
> ...).[10]

The task of true love is therefore one of transformation – to
bring Sophia down to earth and to incorporate the ideal of the
'eternal Feminine' into one's life by loving one of her individual
manifestations. According to Solovyov, the 'eternal Feminine' is
herself longing to be given fulfilment and realized in this way, for
this is the natural end towards which world history is moving.[11]

The act of love becomes therefore one of the primary ways for
man to link himself to God:

> The complete realization, the transformation of an individual feminine
> being into a ray of the divine eternal Feminine, inseparable from its
> radiant source, will be the real, not only subjective but also objective
> reunion of the individual human being with God, the reinstatement of the
> living and immortal image of God in man.[12]

Sexual love in particular is one of the most effective means for
implanting the divine at the very centre of one's existence:

In sexual love, rightly understood and truly realized, this divine essence finds a means for its complete and final embodiment in the individual life of man, for the deepest and at the same time most outwardly sensible and real union with him.[13]

Solovyov elevates sexual love to such a high status because he regards it as the 'finest flowering of individual life'.[14] A person's worst enemy is false individualism; when the self is cut off from the unity of the created world through egoism, it is spiritually dead. At the other extreme, the truly fulfilled individual is the person who has overcome his personal egoism, renounced his individuality and transcended it in order to be in touch with divine unity: 'True individuality is a certain definite form of universal unity, a certain definite way of apprehending and assimilating the whole.'[15]

Sexual love enables a person to transcend his individual limitations in exactly this way:

Through love we come to know the truth of another not in abstraction but in reality, and actually transfer the centre of our life beyond the confines of our empirical separateness; and in doing so we manifest and realize our own truth, our own absolute significance, which consists precisely in the power of transcending our actual phenomenal existence and of living not only in ourselves but also in another.[16]

For this reason, Solovyov can make the following statement: 'the meaning of human love in general is the *justification and salvation of individuality through the sacrifice of egoism*'.[17] Precisely because sexual love is grounded in the physical nature of man, it is the only force capable of truly transforming that nature into something spiritual.[18] Accordingly, Solovyov regards sexual love as the type and ideal of all loves, and refers to the *Song of Songs* to support his point.[19]

The connection between mystical love of Sophia and the love of a real woman which Solovyov advanced in his theoretical writings could also be related to certain episodes from his own life. The most well-known source of information on Solovyov's personal experience of Sophia is 'Three Meetings' ('*Tri svidaniya*'), a long autobiographical poem written in 1898 to describe the three visions of Sophia which the poet had during his lifetime.[20] The first of these took place in Moscow in 1862 when Solovyov was a young boy; the second occurred in 1875 in the reading-room of the British Museum, and the third in 1876, in the Egyptian desert near Cairo.

In each of these visions, Sophia, although incorporeal, is described as a beautiful woman. In the first and third visions, she appears in full stature, while in the second vision only her face is revealed. She is bathed in azure, and referred to as the 'eternal friend' (*podruga vechnaya*), the 'radiance of the divine being' (*siyan'e bozhestva*), and the 'image of feminine beauty' (*obraz zhenskoi krasoty*).[21]

Solovyov's 'Sophiological' cycle also contains poems which were written at the time of the last two visions. For example, 'All in azure today appeared ...' ('*Vsya v lazuri segodnya yavilas'* ...') and 'My queen has a high palace ...' ('*U tsaritsy moei est' vysokii dvorets* ...') were composed in Cairo in 1875 and 1876 respectively. In both poems Solovyov refers to Sophia as his 'queen' (*tsaritsa*).[22]

There is no mention of any real woman in connection with the last two apparitions of Sophia related in 'Three Meetings'. However, the first vision which occurred when Solovyov was nine years old arose directly as a result of his love for an entirely real little girl of the same age. This provided an example of the connection between the love of a real woman and the revelation of Sophia which Solovyov upheld in his theoretical works.

Furthermore, there is evidence from other sources that certain women did play an important part in Solovyov's life and in the formation of his views. Solovyov has left an account of a significant encounter with a young lady named Julie which took place in a train in May 1872, exactly ten years after the first youthful vision described in 'Three Meetings'.[23] K. Mochulsky, Solovyov's biographer, relates this particular episode to Solovyov's change of worldview and conversion to Christianity in 1872.[24]

Mochulsky also discusses Solovyov's friendship with Sofya Petrovna Khitrovo (1837–96). She attended the 'Lectures on God-Manhood', and Solovyov addressed a number of poems to her; in the first of these, written in 1878, he addresses her as 'Madonna'.[25] Significantly, she was also connected with Solovyov's later translations from the *Vita Nuova*, discussed below.

Mochulsky further points out that 'The Meaning of Love' was written immediately after (and, he suggests, as a result of) Solovyov's last love for a married woman, Sofya Mikhailovna Martynova.[26] This is supported by letters from Solovyov to Sofya Martynova, written in 1892 in an ironic tone, lamenting the fact that

Sofya has ceased to be his Sophia or Madonna and has turned into an ordinary woman. Solovyov addresses Sofya as 'hitherto Sophia and Madonna', regrets that his Madonna has flown away, and refers to the change as the 'loss of the rainbow radiance or attributes of the divine Sophia'. He even encloses a poem, 'You were once a Madonna for me ...' ('*Madonnoi byla dlya menya ty kogda-to ...*'), an acrostic upon Sofya's new name *Matryona*.[27]

Finally, towards the very end of Solovyov's life, a spinster living in Nizhnii-Novgorod named Anna Schmidt wrote to him and announced that she was an incarnation of Sophia and his mystical bride. Solovyov agreed to meet her and they entered into an extensive correspondence. She made a particular impact on the Symbolist poets because she introduced herself to them after Solovyov's death and polemized with them on the nature of Sophia.[28]

These odd biographical incidents and references to real women as Sophia or Madonna were seen by the religious Symbolists as indications that Solovyov had embodied his ideal in real life. Combined with the philosopher's theoretical writings and poetry, they helped to establish the idea that the love of a real woman in life would lead to the mystical love of Sophia and ultimately of God. This idea was subsequently a major factor in determining the religious Symbolists' understanding of the theme of love in Dante's works.

Sophia and poetry

Solovyov's belief in the objective reality of Sophia naturally determined his view of the function of art in general and of poetry in particular. Indeed, at the end of his seventh 'Lecture on God-Manhood', after defining the idea of Sophia, he wrote that the innate desire to penetrate the kingdom of the divine or of 'eternal beauty' was particularly characteristic of the poet whose connection with Sophia is an extremely close one; he depends on it both for his vision of the truth, and for the artistic inspiration to express this truth. Just as man's task is to bring Sophia down to earth through love, so the poet's task is to bring Sophia or Beauty down to earth by intuiting her nature and finding artistic forms in which to capture her essence.[29]

Solovyov developed his ideas on the connection between Sophia and poetry in a series of writings on aesthetics and poetry, largely

completed during the last decade of his life. In 1889 he wrote
'Beauty in Nature', choosing as an epigraph Dostoevsky's formula
'Beauty will save the world'. Solovyov believed that the task of the
aesthetically beautiful was to transform reality. If present stan-
dards of artistic beauty did not reflect this truth, it was because this
process of transformation was only in its infancy: 'in our hands are
only the fragmentary rudiments of true art'.[30]

The fulfilment of this task – the final realization of Sophia –
would coincide with the end of world history. Art was consequently a matter of the utmost importance, a form of inspired
prophecy.[31] As a consequence of this view, the two main subjects
of true lyric poetry were defined by Solovyov as the eternal beauty
of nature and the infinite power of love. Both of these themes are
closely connected with the cult of Sophia. Love is one of the main
channels through which man can link himself to Sophia, and to
praise the beauty of nature, the living body of Sophia, is to worship
the divine spirit of Sophia inherent in the material world.[32]

In searching for a theoretical basis for his aesthetics, Solovyov
turned back to an unexpected source – Chernyshevsky's dissertation 'The Aesthetic Relations of Art to Reality', first published in
1854. In an essay of 1894 he advanced this work as the first step
towards establishing a valid new system of aesthetics. He was
reacting against the currently fashionable doctrine of art for art's
sake and against Nietzsche's attack on morality as a form of
weakness. The two fundamental theses of Chernyshevsky's dissertation upon which Solovyov believed that any future system of
aesthetics must be based were the belief in the objective reality of
beauty (which in Solovyov's terms meant the true existence of
Sophia), and the recognition of the inadequacy of art (which had so
far failed to reflect the ideal transforming power of beauty). Solovyov upheld Chernyshevsky's insistence that art must serve the
goals of humanity, and defined the task of aesthetics as the need to
'link artistic creation with the supreme goals of human life' – by
ultimate goals we know that he means the realization of Sophia.[33]

Although Solovyov did not in fact go on to construct a detailed
theory of aesthetics along these lines, he did write a series of essays
on the work of various poets from the standpoint of his central
premise. These essays illuminate in different ways the poet's relation to Sophia. In 1895, for example, he wrote an article on the
publications of a new group of poets who called themselves the

Russian Symbolists (almost all of the poems published in these booklets were in fact by Bryusov, masking under different pseudonyms). He described the work of these poets as a travesty of the true task of poetry; its consistent misuse of language and imagery revealed its decadent, dilettante character, and total lack of an underlying philosophy.[34]

Solovyov preferred to write about poets whose work reflected some aspect of the transcendent faith in Sophia. True poetry of this type, being based on a proper philosophical outlook, necessarily contains a marked intellectual element. For this reason he makes frequent use of the term 'poet-thinker' (*poet-myslitel'*), applying it to each of the poets about whom he chooses to write in connection with their perception of Sophia: Tyutchev, Aleksei Tolstoy and Polonsky.[35]

By extending his teaching on Sophia into the sphere of art and by putting these ideas into practice in his own poetry, Solovyov laid the foundations for a system of aesthetics based on a theurgic view of art. Furthermore, by choosing to write about the work of various poets from this point of view, he established the beginning of a sense of a tradition of poets of Sophia. It was by taking up and developing this approach that the religious Symbolists came to view Dante in the light of Solovyov's teaching on Sophia in relation to love and poetic creation. They saw themselves as poets of Sophia, continuing a tradition which they had received from Solovyov but which could be traced back through earlier poets to Dante.

In this respect the Symbolists were to a large extent following the lead of Solovyov's own references to Dante. Although these are not presented in the form of a separate essay, as in the case of the other poets mentioned above, they nevertheless created a certain framework for interpreting Dante in terms of the philosopher's ideas. A useful example is provided by a passage from an essay on Polonsky in which Solovyov compares the Russian poet's world-view to Dante's. He finds that for Polonsky this world is not a Dantesque Hell, bereft of hope, but a Purgatory, a place where the material can be transformed into the spiritual. For this reason, he writes, the various extremes of Dante's three realms can be contained within the single world of Polonksy's poetry.[36]

The argument seems to be that Polonsky, as a poet of Sophia, was committed to a belief in the transforming power of the spiritual

element inherent in the material world, and did not therefore need
to project his vision into the Dantesque extremes of darkness
without hope or of spirituality without flesh. Later, the religious
Symbolists developed the implications of this comparison; they
tended to use Dantesque images to introduce a sense of hierarchy
and extremes into their Sophiological poetry. Frequently, this
involved encompassing Dante's three realms within the single
realm of the Sophiological outlook. This led to the tendency
(prominent in Ivanov's poetry) of presenting Dante's *Inferno* in a
purgatorial light, as a realm of darkness which contains within itself
the seeds of its own transformation into a spiritual entity.

This is just one example of the way in which the Symbolists were
able to build on Solovyov's references to Dante. The next section
considers in greater detail the foundation on which they were
building – the image of Dante presented in Solovyov's works.

SOLOVYOV'S APPROACH TO DANTE

Sophia and the union of the churches

Solovyov's interest in Dante was closely related to his desire for a
union between the Russian Orthodox and Roman Catholic
churches. Although his religious views were initially of a Slavophile nature which tended to be hostile to the Catholic church,
from the early 1880s onwards they underwent a marked change; he
became increasingly interested in the relations between the two
churches and in ways of promoting their union while retaining the
individual characteristics of each.[37]

Solovyov regarded Sophia as a universal ideal for all mankind.
In his view, the process of world history would culminate in the
realization of Sophia under whose protection ideal humanity would
be united in one church. If the spirit of Sophia was not to be
conceived in narrowly parochial terms but was to be a truly universal goal, it had to be inherent in the Catholic as well as the Russian
Orthodox tradition; the Latin church was also moving towards the
realization of Sophia, whether through the cult of love, poetry, or
the implementation of certain socio-historical forms of
government.

Here Dante was able to play an important role in Solovyov's
thought. Traditionally regarded as the major poet of the Catholic

tradition, for Solovyov he was 'le plus grand des écrivains catholiques'[38] and a symbolic representative of the 'other' tradition with which the Russian church should unite. Not surprisingly, in Solovyov's comments on Dante there is a marked tendency to dwell on those elements in the Italian poet's writings which could be seen to reflect the presence of the idea of Sophia in the Catholic tradition. These elements centred on two of the three forms which Solovyov attributed to Sophia – ideal humanity, the future universal realization of Sophia, and the Virgin Mary, an individual historical incarnation. Solovyov found a reflection of the first of these forms of Sophia in Dante's ideas on theocracy, and of the second in the Catholic cult of the Virgin Mary and its connection with Dante's love of Beatrice.

Sophia and theocracy

In his critique of the medieval world-view as a compromise between paganism and Christianity, Solovyov singled out as a particular shortcoming the Middle Ages' exclusive preoccupation with the individual's salvation and lack of concern for the moral welfare of society as a whole. In his view, this problem was more acute in the Byzantine tradition than in the West where some attempts had been made to deal with it.[39]

Amidst the representatives of the Western tradition, Dante would seem to fall outside the scope of Solovyov's criticism. He took an active part in the political and social life of his day, and directed his entire vision at the correction of the faults of the society which he lived in. Even when he reached the pinnacle of his mystic journey in the highest realms of Paradise, his thoughts still turned to Florence.[40] His Latin treatise, the *Monarchia*, was entirely devoted to arguing the need for a universal monarchy.

Solovyov clearly recognized this fact. Indeed, he first turned to Dante as a writer on socio-political problems. In 1883 he wrote a series of articles which were published in the same year under the title 'The Great Dispute and Christian Politics' in I. S. Aksakov's Slavophile periodical *Rus'*.[41] The articles dealt with the historical reasons for the split between Byzantium and Rome and with the need for a union between the two churches. In this context Solovyov raised the question of universal monarchy as the ideal form of government, and turned to Dante as one of his main sources of inspiration. In June 1883 he wrote to Aksakov that he had been reading Uniate polemics of the sixteenth century in Polish and Dante in Italian in the course of his work on 'The Great Dispute'. A letter written to Aksakov a few months later in November reveals more about the precise nature of this interest in Dante. As a Slavophile Aksakov clearly did not welcome the references in Solovyov's articles to the idea of a universal Emperor. Solovyov had in fact already withdrawn a passage on this subject from his previous article, but he insists on his loyalty to the concept of universal monarchy in his letter, commenting that it is not his own idea, but the 'eternal aspiration of all nations' (*vekovechnoe chayanie narodov*) – a phrase which recalls the terms in which he refers to Sophia elsewhere. He singles out two thinkers who have been inspired by this idea – Dante and Tyutchev – and announces his intention of providing a complete exposition of the idea of universal monarchy, largely in the words of Dante and Tyutchev, in a full edition of 'The Great Dispute', unhampered by the restrictions of Aksakov's editorial policy.[42]

Dante's *Monarchia* was evidently one of the main sources for Solovyov's ideas on universal monarchy.[43] The Western emphasis in 'The Great Dispute' gave the Catholics much satisfaction but led to a rupture with the Slavophiles who labelled Solovyov as a papist who had betrayed the Russian national ideal.[44] However, it is clear that Solovyov's choice of two writers, representative of the Catholic and Russian Orthodox traditions, reflected his desire to unify the two traditions through adherence to a composite ideal of universal monarchy under which the realization of ideal humanity or Sophia could be achieved. Dante's ideas were thus indirectly brought within the framework of the philosopher's Sophiological teaching.

Solovyov planned an ambitious sequel to this work, *The History and Future of Theocracy* (*Istoriya i budushchnost' teokratii*). However, out of the three projected volumes, only the first, covering the philosophy of Biblical theocracy, was published in 1887. Had the work been completed, it would clearly have included an examination of Dante's views on theocracy.[45] The theme of the need for a strong form of state government to ensure the salvation of society continued to preoccupy Solovyov; he returned to it in one of his latest works, 'The Justification of the Good' (1894–7), once more presenting Dante as an example of a great poet who was fully aware of this need, and referring to the views which Dante expressed on the subject in the *Divina Commedia* and *Monar-chia.*[46]

Sophia and the Virgin Mary

The association between Dante and Sophia which Solovyov developed on the basis of his ideas on theocracy was important, but did not have as strong an influence in determining the Symbolist perception of Dante as a poet of Sophia as the second area of association did – that of the link between the Virgin Mary and Sophia. This link provided a most important stepping-stone from the Russian Orthodox to the Catholic tradition; it bridged the gap between the Solovyovian tradition of mystical love of Sophia through the love of a particular woman and the Catholic tradition of an association between the cult of the Virgin Mary and the love of an earthly woman.

Solovyov regarded the Virgin Mary as one of the individual historical incarnations of Sophia and emphasized the close association between the two figures in his theoretical works. In his view the long-standing tradition established in both Latin and Greek liturgy of applying Biblical references to Wisdom or Sophia to the figure of the Virgin Mary had received doctrinal sanction in the dogma of the Immaculate Conception of Mary, defined by Pius IX in 1854.[47] This dogma had not been accepted by the Russian Orthodox church, and in underlining his allegiance to it and presenting it as a confirmation of the mystical faith in Sophia, Solovyov was trying to close the gap between the two churches. For similar reasons he speculated on the link between the medieval Catholic cult of the Madonna and the 'Grand Etre' created by the French philosopher Auguste Comte (1798–1857) to serve as the basis of his new 'religion of humanity'. Comte's 'Grand Etre' was a feminine image of ideal, unified humanity. Solovyov interpreted it as a figure of Sophia, and was struck by the fact that the French philosopher was elaborating his theory of a Sophiological incarnation of perfect humanity at precisely the same moment in history as the medieval cult of the Virgin Mary culminated in the formulation of the dogma of the Immaculate Conception.[48]

Although in his prose writings Solovyov always made it clear that Sophia and the Virgin Mary were quite separate figures, however closely they might be associated, this distinction was subsequently blurred by the religious Symbolists who tended to present a composite, syncretic figure in their poetry, combining elements from both traditions. In doing so they were taking their lead not only from the parallels which Solovyov drew between the two figures in his theoretical works, but also from the closer weaving together of the two traditions which took place in his poetic works and translations. These presented a less clearly defined, more fluid feminine image which could be seen with greater ease in a syncretic light.

This point was made by a number of the Symbolists' contemporaries. Georgy Chulkov (1879-1939), for example, the mystical anarchist and close associate of the religious Symbolists, insisted that the heart of Solovyov's views on Sophia and the main source of his influence were to be found in his poetry, not in his philosophical writings. Although he emphasized that Solovyov had not identified Sophia with the Virgin Mary, he realized that he had prepared the ground for this association; in the following passage he first quoted a statement by Bryusov on the subject, and then added his own comment: '"The Worship of the Eternal Feminine leads to the worship of the one who is her purest image", i.e. of the Virgin Mary. Here there is as yet no affirmation of the identity of Sophia and Mary.'[49]

Chulkov's views were echoed by the essayist and critic Vasily Rozanov (1856-1919); he wrote that Solovyov's monastic cast of mind and visions of the Eternal Feminine had led to the spread of the Catholic cult of the Virgin Mary in Russia, and to a bridging of the gap between Russian Orthodoxy and Catholicism. Like Chulkov, Rozanov attributed this to the influence of Solovyov's poetry rather than to that of his theological writings.[50]

The religious Symbolist Sergei Solovyov took the point even further; he argued that the distinction between the Virgin Mary and Sophia was a matter for theologians only: 'The distinction between these two principles is a matter of theology. In terms of religious feeling, Sophia merges with the Virgin Mary as a single *feminine hypostasis of the Divine Being*.'[51]

Two particular works of Vladimir Solovyov contributed to the formation of these views by providing a poetic presentation of the Catholic themes of the cult of the Virgin Mary and of the love of a woman in a Sophiological light: these were his translations from the verse of two major poets of the Catholic tradition, Petrarch and Dante.

Solovyov's translation of Petrarch

Solovyov's translation of part of a *canzone* by Petrarch dates from the summer of 1883 and was clearly part of the same general move towards the Catholic tradition which inspired him to read Dante in Italian and write 'The Great Dispute' at the time. It was published under the title 'From Petrarch. Hymns and Prayers to the Blessed Virgin Mary', and consists of seven sections of which the first six are a translation of the first six sections of the final *canzone* (CCCLXVI) of Petrarch's 'Sonetti e canzoni in morte di Madonna Laura'. The seventh section of Solovyov's work is an original composition in the Petrarchan manner, although it is not presented as such.[52]

Petrarch's *canzone*, as Solovyov's title indicates, is a hymn of praise and series of prayers addressed to the Blessed Virgin Mary. Placed at the conclusion of his book of poems lamenting the death of his earthly beloved Laura, it serves to present the Virgin Mary as a spiritual figure in whom the love of a mortal woman, transcended through death, can culminate. The story of Petrarch's love for Laura could be interpreted in Sophiological terms according to which the earthly woman is a physical manifestation of Sophia. The transition from Laura to the Virgin Mary (one of Sophia's incarnations) can thus be viewed in terms of the more general graduation from the love of a real woman to the mystic love of Sophia which Solovyov had taught was the true meaning of love.

This interpretation is implicit in the style of Solovyov's translation. One can take as an example the opening lines of the *canzone*. In the original they read as follows:

> Vergine bella, che di sol vestita,
>   Coronata di stelle, al sommo Sole
>   Piacesti si che 'n te sua luce ascose ...[53]

> Beautiful Virgin, clothed with the sun,
>   Crowned with the stars, you so pleased
>   The supreme Sun that he hid his light in you ...

The image of a woman clothed with the sun and crowned with stars is drawn from the Book of Revelation 12.1: 'And there appeared a great wonder in heaven; a woman clothed with the sun, and the moon under her feet, and upon her head a crown of twelve stars.' This passage has traditionally been interpreted by Christians as referring either to the Virgin Mary or to the church. Petrarch is making use of the first of these interpretations and incorporating the line into his address to the Virgin Mary; she so pleased God the Father, the supreme Sun, that he hid his light, the Person of Christ, in her.

Solovyov was familiar with this Christian tradition of interpretation, and indeed cited it in *La Russie et l'Eglise Universelle*. However, he did so to prove his point that the Virgin Mary or the church are different manifestations of a single underlying substantial basis – Sophia, or the Divine Wisdom inherent in the material world.[54] For him the woman clothed with the sun was ultimately an image of Sophia. This becomes quite clear in the preface which he wrote to the third edition of his poems in 1900; here he cites the Biblical reference to the 'woman clothed with the sun' who is already in labour and about to give birth to the truth as an image for Sophia or Eternal beauty through which the world will be saved.[55]

In Solovyov's translation of Petrarch's lines, the Virgin Mary is addressed in terms which are no longer so clearly associated with Christ and carry a strong Sophiological connotation, given the context established earlier on in the book by the preface and the other Sophiological poems:

> В солнце одетая, звездо-венчанная,
> Солнцем превышним любимая Дева!
> Свет Его вечный в себе ты сокрыла.[56]

> Clothed with the sun, crowned with the stars,
> Virgin beloved by the supreme Sun!
> You hid His eternal light in yourself.

Later in his translation Solovyov introduces a line which is absent from the original, referring to the future labour (*gryadushchie rody*) of the Virgin;[57] this addition, when read in conjunction with the reference in the preface to Sophia as a woman who is 'already suffering the pains of labour' (*uzhe muchaetsya rodami*) further reinforces the link between Petrarch's Virgin Mary and Solovyov's ideal of Sophia.

There are numerous other phrases throughout the translation

which have the same effect. Some of these, such as 'heavenly queen' (*tsaritsa nebesnaya*) for 'del ciel regina' or 'Wisest Virgin among the wise' (*Mezhdu premudrymi Deva Mudreishaya*) for 'Vergine saggia' correspond fairly closely to the original but still have a strong Sophiological ring about them.[58] Solovyov introduces the word 'imperishable' (*netlennyi*) twice, in the second and third sections of his translation, although it is not used by Petrarch.[59] It is one of his favourite epithets for Sophia who was indeed bodiless, unlike the Virgin Mary.

The style of Solovyov's translation from Petrarch established a basis for presenting the Catholic cult of the Virgin Mary in a Sophiological light; the translations from the *Vita Nuova* then extended this tradition into the realm of Dante's writings.

Solovyov's translations of Dante

Solovyov translated two sonnets from Dante's *Vita Nuova*. The first of these, 'Everything in my thoughts immediately dies ...' (*'Vse v myslyakh u menya mgnovenno zamiraet ...'*), is a translation of the sonnet from chapter xv beginning 'Ciò che m'incontra, ne la mente more ...' ('That which rises up against me dies away in my mind ...'). It was completed in St Petersburg in 1886, three years after the translation from Petrarch, and published in the same year in *Vestnik Evropy*. It was subsequently included in the first collection of Solovyov's verse, published in 1891, and in each of the following editions.[60]

The sonnet describes the piteous state into which Dante is thrown by the sight of Beatrice. The passers-by who see Dante in this state and do not show him any compassion are guilty of committing a sin; Beatrice's mockery has destroyed their capacity for feeling pity.

The second translation, 'My thoughts are full of love alone ...' (*'Polny moi mysli lyubov'yu odnoyu ...'*) is a version of the sonnet from chapter xiii, 'Tutti li miei penser parlan d'Amore ...' ('All my thoughts speak of Love ...'). It also deals with Dante's confused state of mind, and describes the conflicting thoughts which argue within him about the nature of his love, causing him either to weep or to hope. Dante can only bring these thoughts into harmony by calling on his enemy, Lady Pity.

This translation was first discovered among the papers of Sofya

Petrovna Khitrovo, in an undated letter addressed to her by Vladimir Solovyov. Since this letter also includes the text of the first
translation described above and dated 1886, the second translation
is likely to date from the same year. It is interesting to note that
Sofya Khitrovo, one of the main figures closely connected with
Solovyov's cult of Sophia, was in this way also directly associated
with Solovyov's translations from the *Vita Nuova* dealing with
Dante's love for Beatrice. The second translation did not appear
until 1909 in the second volume of Solovyov's collected letters.[61]
After this date it was included in the subsequent editions of Solovyov's verse, next to the first translation.[62]

From 1891 onwards, therefore, the first of the two translations
from the *Vita Nuova* was published alongside Solovyov's Sophiological poetry; by the third edition of 1900 this had grown to include
'Three Meetings', and by the sixth edition of 1915, the second
translation from the *Vita Nuova* was also incorporated into the
collection. Although there was nothing overtly Sophiological
about Solovyov's translations from Dante, the fact that they were
presented alongside a translation from Petrarch and original poetry
in which Sophia did play an important role served to create a sense
of a single Sophiological tradition which could absorb Beatrice and
Dante as well as Laura and Petrarch into its framework. This laid
the foundation for the Symbolist understanding of Dante as a
predecessor of Solovyov and poet of Sophia.

Dantesque motifs in Solovyov's poetry

The sense of a single unified tradition linking Dante to Solovyov
was further reinforced by the fact that Solovyov, after first infusing
Catholic themes with Sophiological content, then borrowed the
imagery of Catholic poetry and used it in his own Sophiological
verse. This process is clearly reflected in his major poem 'Three
Meetings' (1898). The very concept of this work – to write a
retrospective autobiographical account of the development of an
experience of mystical love from the childhood love of a real girl to
later purely abstract visions – is remarkably close to the idea of the
Vita Nuova. This parallel is underlined in the note which Solovyov
appends to his poem about the history of its composition. He writes
that his desire was to reproduce in verse 'the most significant part
of that which has so far happened to me in my life', and that after

two days of memories his little autobiography was ready on the third day, and pleased certain poets and certain ladies.[63] The tone of this note is very Dantesque; the desire to reproduce that which is most significant, the insistence on the role of memory, the deliberate reference to the number three and the singling out of poets and ladies as his audience are all features which occur in the *Vita Nuova*.[64]

The number three and its multiple nine were one of the specific motifs which Solovyov took up from Dante's work and echoed in his poem. In chapter XXIX Dante dwells at some length on the symbolism of these numbers which play an important role in his relationship with Beatrice; he explains their significance in relation to the Trinity. The architectural composition of the *Vita Nuova* is determined entirely according to the numbers three and nine, and Dante also attaches great importance to the fact that he and Beatrice were both in their ninth year when they first met.[65]

Three and nine are also important numbers in 'Three Meetings', both in its structure and in relation to the question of age. Solovyov's poem consists of an introduction of three verses, followed by three parts dealing with the three visions of which the last and longest comprises thirty verses. The importance of the number three is emphasized in the introduction: 'Was it not three times that you revealed yourself to a living gaze' (*Ne trizhdy l' ty dalas' zhivomu vzglyadu*).[66] In the first main section of the poem describing the poet's initiation into love, the fact that he and the little girl were both nine years old at the time is underlined: 'I'm nine years old, *She* . . . she too is nine' (*Mne devyat' let*, Ona . . . *ei – devyat' tozhe*).[67]

Although the spirit of Solovyov's poem is entirely different from that of the *Vita Nuova*, these outward similarities are clearly not accidental and played an important part in allowing the Symbolists to link the figure of Beatrice to Sophia.

3

The Symbolist view of Dante as a poet of Sophia

Vladimir Solovyov's teaching on Sophia was one of the most important influences on the world-view of the religious Symbolists and on their understanding of love and poetry. In a way which is often characteristic of emergent movements, the new poets sought to consolidate their position by establishing a tradition of predecessors with roots reaching far back into the past. Solovyov had already set a precedent for the sense of a tradition of poets of Sophia in his essays on various Russian poets of the nineteenth century. The Symbolists carried this tendency a step further; they developed it to include not only the poets whom Solovyov had written about, but also two of the poets whom he had translated: Dante and Petrarch. Both these poets had loved earthly women, Beatrice and Laura, and through them had risen to the mystical love of the Virgin Mary and ultimately of God. It was easy for the Symbolists to see in this a manifestation of Solovyov's ideal of love of Sophia through the love of an earthly woman, celebrated in poetry, particularly since Solovyov had associated Sophia with the Virgin Mary and had introduced both Petrarch and Dante into a Sophiological context by translating their poetry.

Through Solovyov, the Symbolists therefore reached back to Petrarch and Dante as their spiritual and poetic precursors. Since, however, the immediate source of their ideas was in Solovyov, not in Dante, this in effect meant that they were either applying Solovyovian concepts to their understanding of Dante, or simply borrowing images from the Catholic or Dantesque traditions and using these to express essentially Solovyovian ideas.

The main poets who contributed to the formation of this tradition of interpretation of Dante were Blok, Bely, Sergei Solovyov and Ivanov. In 1915 the religious philosopher Sergei Bulgakov singled out these names in a discussion of the remarkable impact of Vladimir Solovyov's verse on contemporary poets. His comments were prompted by the appearance of a new edition of Vladimir

Solovyov's poetry, prepared by Sergei Solovyov. He described Blok, Bely and Ivanov as a single group of poets who had all 'come out' of Vladimir Solovyov and combined this dominant influence with that of other poets, including Dante and Petrarch.[1]

Although the ways in which these poets contributed to the Sophiological tradition of interpretation of Dante varied considerably, they derived from a common source and exercised a considerable influence on each other's development. A major role was played by Blok who became a legend in his own life-time and was widely regarded by his contemporaries as a disciple of both Solovyov and Dante. Bely made an important contribution to the theoretical analysis of the tradition, basing much of his argument on the example of Blok's life and works. Ivanov, who lived outside Russia for many years before 1905, came into contact with Solovyov's ideas earlier, and combined them in an idiosyncratic way with his Dionysiac ideal of Eros. However, his approach was nevertheless part of the common tradition evolved by the religious Symbolists as a group, and should be considered within this context not as an isolated phenomenon but as a particular manifestation of a general current.

BLOK

Early interest in Solovyov

In his autobiography of 1915, Blok notes that the first two most influential events of his life were seeing Vladimir Solovyov from a distance (in February 1900, a few months before the philosopher's death) and his friendship with Mikhail and Olga Solovyov.[2] The juxtaposition of these two events is significant, for it was to a large extent through the intermediary of the philosopher's younger brother, Mikhail Solovyov (1862–1903), a historian, teacher and translator, and his wife, Olga Mikhailovna (1852–1903), also a translator, that the legacy of Vladimir Solovyov was passed on to the younger generation of religious Symbolists.

Blok began to visit Mikhail Solovyov and his wife regularly from 1898.[3] The two families were related (Olga Mikhailovna and Blok's mother were cousins), and the proximity of their country estates near Moscow, Shakhmatovo and Dedovo, made contact easy. Blok particularly valued his friendship with them because they were the first people outside his immediate circle to pay attention to his poetry.[4] Their son, Sergei Solovyov, was also a poet, and he and Blok formed a close friendship on the basis of their shared interests.

Blok's serious interest in Vladimir Solovyov appears to date from the spring of 1901 when his mother gave him a volume of Solovyov's verse as an Easter present. This work, as Blok later noted, confirmed and strengthened all the feelings of mystical intuition which he had previously held.[5] He wrote of this period: 'At that time, in connection with acute mystical and romantic experiences, my entire being was taken over by the poetry of Vladimir Solovyov.'[6] Sergei Solovyov recalls that Blok settled down to the serious study of Vladimir Solovyov and began to read the latter's 'Lectures on God-Manhood' in the autumn of 1901, after he had transferred from the faculty of law to the philological faculty at the University of St Petersburg.[7]

During this period the Solovyov family played an important role in fostering Blok's interest in Vladimir Solovyov. Mikhail Solovyov was responsible for the major eight-volume edition of Vladimir Solovyov's collected works which appeared between 1901 and 1903. His interest in his brother's legacy and absorption in the task of editing his works made his home in Moscow one of the major centres for the young 'Solovyovites', as Bely termed them.[8] As each new volume came out, Mikhail Solovyov would post it to Blok in St Petersburg.[9]

When Blok wrote in November 1902 to thank him for the fourth volume in the series, he brought up a subject which had apparently first been raised during the previous year in August – the suggestion that he should edit a collection of Vladimir Solovyov's humorous verse. Blok was very keen to undertake the project, possibly with the cooperation of Sergei Solovyov and Bely in Moscow; he felt that his love for Vladimir Solovyov was even greater than before, and that he could now approach the task in a proper spirit of religious seriousness. Mikhail Solovyov was not however able to take up Blok's suggestion immediately, and after his death a few weeks later in January 1903 the matter was dropped.[10]

Blok's interest in Vladimir Solovyov continued, now further stimulated by Sergei Solovyov, who sent him the eighth volume in the series when it appeared.[11] After Blok's marriage in the summer

of 1903, Sergei Solovyov thought it appropriate to suggest that
Blok should read Solovyov's work on theocracy, *The History and
Future of Theocracy*; Blok replied in November that he had in fact
already read this work during the previous winter but planned to
reread it now in greater depth; in the meantime, during the
autumn, he had been reading another work by Solovyov, 'The
Spiritual Foundations of Life'.[12]

Lyubov Dmitrievna Mendeleeva and the cult of Sophia

This period of Blok's immersion in Solovyov's poetry and philosophical works was closely connected with the culminating phase
of his relationship with Lyubov Dmitrievna Mendeleeva before
their marriage in August 1903. Blok had first met Lyubov Dmitrievna during his childhood, and then again as a young man in
1895. He began to fall in love with her in 1898, and the most
intense phase of their courtship commenced in the 'mystic
summer' of 1901. In her memoirs Lyubov Dmitrievna describes
her meetings with Blok after October 1901 when they began to
visit the churches of St Petersburg together; Blok spoke to her
about Vladimir Solovyov, the World Soul (Sophia), Sofya Petrovna
Khitrovo and the poem 'Three Meetings'. Lyubov Dmitrievna felt
that she was being placed on a pedestal which she could not
comprehend.[13]

Blok was evidently trying to put into practice the theory of love
of Sophia through the love of an earthly woman which Solovyov
had advanced in 'The Meaning of Love' and illustrated in his own
poetry. He was supported in his view of Lyubov Dmitrievna as an
earthly manifestation of Sophia by both Sergei Solovyov and Bely,
and this was the central theme of his poetry of the time.[14] It can be
sensed in some of the 1900 verses of 'Ante Lucem' and is developed with particular intensity in the collection *Verses about the
Beautiful Lady* (*Stikhi o Prekrasnoi Dame*), written between 1901
and 1902 and first published at the end of 1904. Poems such as 'I
have forebodings of Thee. The years pass by – . . . ' ('*Predchuvst-
vuyu Tebya. Goda prokhodyat mimo* – . . . ', 4 June 1901) with its
epigraph from Vladimir Solovyov's poetry describe quite explicitly
the painful feeling of love and anticipation of Sophia, mixed with
the fear of future deception.[15]

Blok as a Dantesque poet: *Verses about the Beautiful Lady*

Blok's relationship with Lyubov Dmitrievna and the *Verses about the Beautiful Lady* served as the basis on which the traditional view of Blok as a Dantesque poet developed. This view largely derived from an association of Blok's experience of love and early poetry with Dante's love of Beatrice and record of it in the *Vita Nuova*. It was advanced by Blok's contemporaries during the 1900s, and became so firmly established during the 1910s that it was regularly repeated in a number of works written on Blok during the early 1920s and thereafter. In 1921, for example, the critic V. Zhirmunsky wrote that a shared mystical awareness of the divine element in love linked Blok to Dante's *Vita Nuova*, both directly and through the intermediary of Vladimir Solovyov. In similar fashion K. Chukovsky commented in the following year that Blok's transformation of a neighbouring girl, Lyubov Dmitrievna, into the abstract ideal of the *Verses about the Beautiful Lady* followed exactly the same pattern as Dante's transformation of his neighbour's daughter, Beatrice Portinari, into an ideal image. The sense of a tradition linking Blok to Dante even formed the subject of an entire book by N. Minsky entitled *From Dante to Blok*, published in 1922.[16]

However, in most of these works, the accepted view of Blok as a Dantesque poet is presented as an established fact with little analysis of the evidence or of the nature of the connection. In considering the evidence in Blok's own work to support the association, it is worth emphasizing from the outset that Blok followed Vladimir Solovyov in closely linking the figure of Sophia to the Virgin Mary; this provided both him and his readers with a framework for the incorporation of Catholic poets such as Dante and Petrarch into the Sophiological tradition.

There are numerous examples of Blok's association of Sophia with the Virgin Mary in his letters and poems of the early 1900s. In a letter to Sergei Solovyov in November 1903, for instance, immediately after discussing his plans to reread Vladimir Solovyov's work on theocracy, Blok announces his intention of writing a dissertation on iconographic representations of the Virgin Mary. This shows a tendency towards association which is more explicitly revealed in a later letter of 1905 to G. Chulkov; here Blok refers to Sophia and the Virgin Mary as manifestations of a single essence which, following Vladimir Solovyov, he terms the 'Eternal Feminine'.[17]

It is not surprising therefore that in some of the *Verses about the Beautiful Lady* Sophia and the Virgin Mary seem to merge into a single composite figure. For example, in 'I enter dark churches . . .' (*'Vkhozhu ya v temnye khramy* . . .', 25 October 1902) Blok describes waiting for the apparition of a feminine Being in a church while looking at an icon depicting her features by candlelight. Lyubov Dmitrievna's memoirs reveal that the incident described in this poem was based on her regular visits with Blok to an icon of the Virgin Mary which they regarded as 'theirs' in the Kazan cathedral.[18] And yet Blok deliberately chooses to describe this figure in terms such as 'Beautiful Lady' (*Prekrasnaya Dama*) or 'Eternal Wife' (*Vechnaya Zhena*) which evoke both the Western Catholic and the Russian Sophiological traditions.

This association is reflected in the discussion of the title of a group of poems which Blok sent to Bryusov in February 1903 for publication in the almanach *The Northern Flowers* (*Severnye tsvety*). In his accompanying letter Blok referred to the poems as 'verses about the Beautiful Lady', but requested that they should be published under the title 'About the eternal feminine' (*O vechno-zhenstvennom*) as this was the essential theme of the collection.[19] Blok's choice of title accurately reflected his primary allegiance to the Solovyovian cult of Sophia. Bryusov, however, preferred to publish the poems under the title 'Verses about the Beautiful Lady'; this evoked the Western medieval Catholic tradition of knightly love of the 'gentil donna' which Dante and his contemporaries had received from the Provençal troubadours. The fact that this title was finally adopted illustrates the tendency prevalent at the time to use imagery with Dantesque associations to describe concepts or themes of an essentially Solovyovian character.

If one examines the *Verses about the Beautiful Lady* for internal evidence to substantiate their association with Dante, one finds that although one poem carries an epigraph from a sonnet by Petrarch,[20] the collection does not in fact contain any direct references to Dante. The association of the *Verses* with Dante was latent rather than explicit, and it was not until many years later in 1918 that Blok decided to make it plain by adding a prose commentary to the *Verses*, modelled on the *Vita Nuova*.

However, there is evidence from other sources that Blok was
developing an interest in Dante around the time of the composition
of the *Verses*, and that he associated the figure of the Beautiful
Lady with Dante's Beatrice. By the early 1900s he already knew
Dante's two major works, the *Commedia* and the *Vita Nuova*. The
Commedia figures in a list of recently purchased books which he
drew up in 1902, and the copy of the *Inferno* which he kept in his
library at Shakhmatovo was apparently liberally annotated by
him.[21] By 1903 he was also familiar with the Italian original of the
Vita Nuova – an interest which he shared with his cousin Sergei
Solovyov. Following the tradition established by Vladimir Solovyov of incorporating the *Vita Nuova* into the Sophiological tradition by translating sonnets from it, Sergei Solovyov translated the
first sonnet of the *Vita Nuova* ('A ciascun'alma presa e gentil core
...' – 'To every captive soul and gentle heart ...') and entered his
version into Blok's exercise book of poetry. Blok wrote to him
about the translation on 8 October 1903; although he was critical of
Sergei's poetry, he expressed great admiration for his translation:
'Your translations, on the other hand, including the *Vita Nuova*,
amaze me and arouse my gratitude.' His criticism of one particular
word in the translation reveals his close knowledge of the original.[22]

In fact, Blok most probably already knew the *Vita Nuova* in
1901. He must have seen the translation of a sonnet from this work
which was included in the collection of Vladimir Solovyov's verse
given to him by his mother that year at Easter. Furthermore, the
work's influence on his perception of his relationship with Lyubov
Dmitrievna can be sensed from an entry at the beginning of his first
notebook, dated 26 September 1901. Here he records a dream in
which he meets a woman who stretches out her hand to him and
utters something obscure to him about his love for her. In response
Blok hands her a book of Vladimir Solovyov's poems. Just as he is
about to have a prophetic vision, he wakes up and the dream comes
to an end.[23]

The content of the dream as well as the vivid and direct style in
which it is recorded are strongly reminiscent of the dreams or
mystical visions which form such an important part of Dante's *Vita
Nuova*. In these dreams the figure of Love or Beatrice often
appears to Dante who cannot always understand the obscure words
which he hears being uttered; his vision or dream is broken by his

awakening, and then recorded by him in prose.[24] This typically Dantesque sequence is reflected in Blok's notebook entry which shows clearly how the Solovyovian and Dantesque traditions were associated in his mind at the time when he was writing the *Verses about the Beautiful Lady*.

The loss of the ideal and Beatrice

Although the Beautiful Lady disappeared from Blok's verse in 1905, Blok insisted that he never lost his faith in her objective existence. Throughout his poetic career and numerous changes of outlook, she remained a fixed point of reference.[25] Strangely, it was only after her disappearance, during this later post-1905 period, that Blok openly established the link between the Beautiful Lady and Beatrice. In writings of this period, he frequently looked back to the Beautiful Lady as an example of the ideal which he and his age had lost, and used the name Beatrice in this context to refer to the Beautiful Lady in her pure original form.

For example, in 1908 he wrote an essay on irony in which he decried one of the chief diseases of his age: the loss of faith in a pure, absolute ideal, and the consequent inability to distinguish between Beatrice and lesser images of a vulgar nature: 'In the face of cursed irony – everything is the same to them: good and evil, a bright sky and a stinking pit, Dante's Beatrice and Sologub's *Nedotykomka*. Everything is mixed up, as if in a tavern and in gloom.[26]

In the following year, he wrote 'The Song of Hell' (*'Pesn' ada'*), a long poem in terzinas in which he turned to Dante's *Inferno* as a source of images for his sense of the 'infernalism' of the world around him. But even here he still did not lose sight of the original pure ideal, and his sense of tragedy derived precisely from his awareness of the gap which separated him from that which he had lost:

Где спутник мой? – О, где ты, Беатриче? –
Иду один, утратив правый путь,
В кругах подземных, как велит обычай,

Средь ужасов и мраков потонуть.[27]

Where is my companion? – O where are you, Beatrice? –
I walk alone, having lost the right way,
In the circles of the underworld, as custom rules,

To drown among the horror and the gloom.

Blok commented on these lines in a note: 'The present not only lacks a heavenly companion (*sputnitsa*), divine Wisdom, but also lacks the earthly wisdom of Virgil, the pagan, who accompanied Dante in Hell and handed him over to Beatrice at the entrance to heaven.'[28]

This note shows that Blok associated Beatrice with Sophia; significantly, he uses a capital letter for the divine Wisdom of Beatrice, as opposed to Virgil's earthly wisdom. Blok clearly regarded his journey from the intuition of Beatrice to the *Inferno* as representative of more than his own individual experience; in his view it was symptomatic of the spirit of the age, and illustrated the path followed by his generation of religious Symbolists. In an essay of 1910, 'On the Present State of Russian Symbolism', he once more defined the present stage of religious Symbolism in relation to Dante; without the intuition of Beatrice, art becomes an *Inferno*, as he had shown in 'The Song of Hell':

Art is *Hell*. It was not without reason that V. Bryusov bade the artist: 'Like Dante, your cheeks must be scorched by the flame of the underworld'. The countless circles of Hell can only be crossed without dying by a person who has a companion, a teacher and a guiding dream about She who will lead him to a place which even the teacher dares not enter.[29]

Blok's projection of his individual feelings onto the experience of his generation was extremely important; it was adopted by the other Symbolists and enabled them to take up Blok's Dantesque symbolism and regard it as emblematic of their own development.

1918 *Vita Nuova* project

Towards the end of his life, in 1918, Blok made a final attempt to return once more to the lost ideal of his youth, the Beautiful Lady. Typically, this took the form of trying to establish the link between the Beautiful Lady of his early verse and Beatrice, the image of this ideal in its pure, original form. For this purpose he planned to write a prose commentary which would link together the *Verses* and explain their relation to the events of his past in the manner of Dante's *Vita Nuova*. On 28 August 1918, the date of the feast of the Assumption of the Virgin Mary, he made the following entry in his notebook: 'I have conceived the idea, like Dante once did, of filling in the gaps between the lines of *Verses about the Beautiful*

Lady with a simple explanation of events. But towards night I was
already tired. Surely this task is not already beyond the strength of
my exhausted mind?'[30]

The idea behind this project was further clarified in a preface to a
projected edition of the *Verses* which Blok drafted on the same
day. After hinting at the concealed meaning between the lines of
his early book, accessible only to a small circle of readers, he
lamented the subsequent misinterpretations of his development as
a poet and relationship to the ideal of the Beautiful Lady. His
attempts to elucidate the meaning of his early poetry in later
editions had been unsuccessful and had led him to the following
thoughts:

... I felt lost in the wood of my own past until it occurred to me to make
use of the device which Dante chose when he was writing the *Vita Nuova*.
Requesting the help and quiet advice of Her who is the subject of this
book, I wish to succeed in writing the rest of it in simple words which
would help others to understand its only necessary content.[31]

The desire to write a retrospective account in simple prose of the
events of the past which led to the composition of a series of early
poems in order to set these poems in their proper context and
thereby make plain their innate significance – this was the very
impulse which inspired Dante to present the poems of his youth in
a small book, linked by connecting passages of clear prose
designed to make their origin and meaning transparent to the
reader. Like Dante, Blok's concern is not so much to describe a
youthful experience of love as to provide a prose clarification of the
poetry which arose from this experience.

Blok began work on this project two days later on 30 August, the
fifteenth anniversary of his marriage to Lyubov Dmitrievna.[32] The
first section of his account, completed on this date, covers the
period from 1897 until the end of 1901. The second section, written
a few weeks later on 11 September, provides a more detailed
month-by-month account of the events of 1901 from January to
May.[33] Blok's decision to begin his account on the anniversary of
his marriage is evocative of the symbolic importance attached by
Dante to all dates connected with his relationship with Beatrice in
the *Vita Nuova*. Furthermore, his detailed descriptions of the times
and places of his meetings with Lyubov Dmitrievna, his relation of
these events to the poetry he was writing at the time, and his
interpretation of his relationship in the light of Solovyov's teaching

on Sophia directly echo the approaches which inform the structure of the *Vita Nuova*. Dante also devotes much space to the precise account of his meetings with Beatrice, explains how these found their way into his early poetry, and analyses both in terms of his growing understanding of their spiritual meaning.

Blok's fear that he would lack the strength to carry out this task proved justified. He wrote virtually no original poetry after 1918, and did not complete the project. However, his wish to undertake it is nevertheless evidence of the underlying affinity which he perceived between the Sophiological tradition of love poetry, inherited from Solovyov, and the Catholic tradition of mystical love established by Dante in the *Vita Nuova*.

If, however, one returns to Blok in the early 1900s, it is clear that although he contributed through his poetry and personal interests to the development of the link between Dante and Sophia which was already latent in Solovyov's works, he did not himself make this association explicit at the time. He provided the example in his life and poetry, but it was Bely who supplied its theoretical interpretation, and succeeded in creating the sense of an established tradition running from Dante through Vladimir Solovyov to the religious Symbolists.

BELY

The link between Solovyov and Dante

Bely began to develop an interest in Vladimir Solovyov in 1900, about a year earlier than Blok. The fact that he lived in Moscow rather than in St Petersburg meant that he could regularly visit his friend Sergei Solovyov and discuss matters of religious and literary interest with him and his parents, Olga and Mikhail Solovyov. It was in their flat that Bely met Vladimir Solovyov in the spring of 1900; they held a long conversation which he later described as a decisive influence on his life.[34] When the philosopher died a few months later, Bely recorded his sense of trauma: 'I was knocked out for the whole week, it seemed to me that with the death of Solovyov, my own path in life [*put'*] had also suddenly come to an end: for he had become my teacher in the path of life.'[35]

That autumn Bely spent much time involved in intense discussions of Sophia and the 'Three Meetings' with Mikhail and Sergei

Solovyov. As well as avidly reading Solovyov's poetry, he also studied his philosophical works, attaching particular importance to 'The Meaning of Love'.[36] This work provided him and his generation of religious Symbolists with a model on which to base their experience of love. In his autobiographical notes, he gave some examples of its remarkable impact. In 1901, which he regarded as the year of the 'dawn' (*zarya*) when the feeling of mystical tension and anticipation engendered by Solovyov's works reached a peak, he and Blok and Sergei Solovyov were *all* pursuing romantic attachments inspired by the idea of Sophia. He described his own beloved of the time as an icon-like symbol of Sophia whom he had served with all the devotion of a medieval knight.[37]

Later, looking back on January of that year, he discussed the way in which Dante's and Petrarch's love poetry was taken up in this context; after dwelling on his own love for a woman referred to alternately as his 'Lady' (*Dama*) or as his 'Beatrice', he continued:

I emphasize: in January 1901 a dangerous 'mystical' explosive was implanted in us which gave rise to many false rumours about the 'Beautiful Lady'; the root of this lay in the fact that in January 1901 Borya Bugaev [Bely] and Seryozha Solovyov, who were in love with a society lioness and a schoolgirl from Arsenev's grammar school, plus Sasha Blok, who was in love with Mendeleev's daughter, jotted down 'mystical' verse and became interested in the love poetry of Goethe, Lermontov, Petrarch, Dante.[38]

The question of exactly how these two traditions – Solovyovian and medieval Catholic – could be combined was of considerable interest to the religious Symbolists and particularly to Bely. This is reflected in Bely's account of the main subjects which he and Blok discussed in their correspondence of 1903. His list, compiled after Blok's death in 1921, includes the following points: the nature of the Beautiful Lady and her relation to Solovyov's teaching on the future of theocracy; the connection between Solovyov's concept of Sophia and the philosopher's own experience of love (based on 'Three Meetings' and his friendship with Sofya Khitrovo); the relation between Sophia and Plato's Eros, Dante's Beatrice, the medieval cult of courtly love and Goethe's 'Ewig-Weibliche'. Bely added that for him and Blok the main challenge at that time had consisted in trying to combine the philosophical ideas of Vladimir Solovyov, Hegel and Auguste Comte with the particular reflections of these systems of thought in the lives of individuals like Dante and Goethe.[39]

Bely's comments provide a typical illustration of the way in which the religious Symbolists blended different traditions syncretically – the central core of their preoccupations clearly revolved around Solovyov's ideal of Sophia, and Dante and Petrarch were brought in as examples illustrating the importance of embodying the ideal of mystical love in one's life and expressing it through poetry. It is significant that both Bely and Blok were interested in these questions at the same time, although it was a year before their first meeting; as Bely put it: 'the problem of the age raised all these questions'.[40]

The association of the Virgin Mary with Sophia provided the stepping-stone between Dante and Solovyov for Bely, just as it had for Vladimir Solovyov and Blok. In his article 'On Theurgy' (1903), Bely quoted Vladimir Solovyov's definition of Sophia and several poems which he described as addressed to Sophia; these included verses by Vladimir Solovyov, the medieval hymn 'Mater Dei sine spina – peccatorum medicina' and a few lines identified as Petrarch's but in fact taken from the seventh, original section of Vladimir Solovyov's 'Hymns and Prayers to the Blessed Virgin Mary'.[41] The last two examples are actually addressed to the Virgin Mary but Bely is identifying her with Sophia. In the case of Petrarch he was evidently following the lead provided by Vladimir Solovyov's Sophiological rendering of Petrarch's *canzone* to the Virgin Mary.

Anna Schmidt, Solovyov's disciple, otherwise known as the Sophia of Nizhnii Novgorod, noted the implication of Bely's words, and wrote a long letter of protest to Bryusov, the editor of *Vesy*, in which she tried to correct what she regarded as a fundamental and widespread distortion of the philosopher's teaching. Taking up Bely's mixture of examples she listed a series of points from the works of Solovyov to prove that although he associated the Virgin Mary with Sophia, he would never have accepted their confusion or identity.[42]

The disagreement illustrates the difference between the approaches of theology and of the poetic imagination. The religious Symbolists were concerned with the fashioning of a new poetic tradition through syncretic images and had little concern for the strictures of more academic approaches. Thus, when Bely reviewed a new Russian translation of Scartazzini's book on Dante in 1905, he adopted a somewhat patronizing attitude; he describes the work as extremely limited, for, in his opinion, the respected Dante scholar did not understand the Italian poet with the same lively spirit as the Russian Symbolists and was unaware of his particular relevance to the present age.[43]

Most of Bely's review is in fact devoted to an analysis of the current revival of interest in Dante. He attributes this to the link which exists between all forms of religious symbolism throughout the ages, and which causes the Russian Symbolists to turn towards Dante as an artist who developed a complete system of religious symbols. In his view, one particular element of Dante's mysticism has led contemporary thinkers to feel a strong sense of affinity with him; this is the poet's transformation of Beatrice into Divine Wisdom.

Beatrice as Sophia

Bely's view that Beatrice was transformed into Divine Wisdom or Sophia deserves consideration as a typical manifestation of the religious Symbolists' understanding of Dante in terms of Solovyov's teaching. Beatrice was indeed transformed from an earthly woman into an abstract figure; she first appears in the *Vita Nuova* as a real person with whom Dante falls in love; initially his love depends on her physical existence, but after her death he learns to love her spiritual essence, preserved in his memory and imagination; this raises his love from a narrow physical level to a higher spiritual one.

It is possible to understand this development, as the Symbolists did, in terms of Solovyov's theory of love. Through the love of an earthly woman, Beatrice, a manifestation of Sophia or of the divine essence inherent in humanity, Dante learns to love this divine essence in a purer form. The parallel can be carried through into the area of poetry, since Dante, as a poet who writes of his love for Beatrice, can be considered in Solovyovian terms as a poet of Sophia.

While it is possible to maintain this analogy on a very general level, the question of Beatrice's actual transformation into Sophia is rather more problematic. In the *Commedia*, Beatrice is already among the blessed in heaven; she is no longer alive, and the nature of her role as an abstract figure can be understood more clearly. Following the request of the Virgin Mary, passed on through an intermediary intercessor, Beatrice descends to the underworld where she asks Virgil to guide Dante through Hell and Purgatory in order to save him from the wicked ways into which he has fallen. In the Earthly Paradise, at the top of Mount Purgatory, she meets Dante and takes over Virgil's role. She guides Dante up through the spheres of Paradise and hands him over to St Bernard who prays to the Virgin Mary to grant Dante his final vision of the Holy Trinity.

Throughout the *Commedia* is is clearly emphasized that Virgil's role is limited to explaining the visible things which can be understood through reason, while Beatrice's function is to guide Dante through questions of faith which require the light of revelation. Accordingly Beatrice has traditionally been viewed by commentators as a figuration of revelation or theology.

Bely's view that Beatrice was transformed into Sophia is incompatible with the traditional interpretation of Dante's text in two major ways. Firstly, although Beatrice in her role as instructress in theology is clearly wise, this is not the same as regarding her as Wisdom incarnate. She is an incarnation of divine revelation, not of wisdom, and Bely has evidently introduced his difference of emphasis to bring Dante more firmly in line with the Solovyovian tradition of Sophia.

Secondly, Bely's complete allegorization of Beatrice is at odds with the figural interpretation of her dual significance as a real person who at the same time embodied certain spiritual values. Erich Auerbach has provided a useful analysis of Beatrice's role in terms of the concept of *figura* developed by the early Christian tradition of figural interpretation of the Old Testament scriptures. This allows both for the historical reality of Beatrice's physical existence and for the fulfilment of this reality in the spiritual role which she plays in Dante's life. Dante begins to understand the significance of this spiritual role more fully after Beatrice's death; she remains for him, however, at all times a real person, not an abstraction.

Auerbach comments that while nineteenth-century romantic realism tended to overemphasize the human Beatrice, the fashion in the twentieth century had been to regard her as a purely symbolic, allegorical figure, 'to do away with her entirely, to dissolve her in an assortment of increasingly subtle theological concepts'.[44] Bely's interpretation of Beatrice's role clearly reflects this trend towards complete allegorization, and detracts from the greater complexity of Beatrice's dual figural significance. Sergei Bulgakov made this distinction clear in his essay on V. Solovyov and A. Schmidt. Although he also followed the general tradition of viewing Dante's love for Beatrice in terms of Solovyov's teaching, he would not accept the equation of Beatrice with Sophia: 'For Dante Beatrice is the incarnation or image [*lik*] of Sophia, and yet she is nevertheless not Sophia. She has a fixed biography in this world which is continued in the heavens.'[45]

The poetic tradition: from Dante through Solovyov to the Symbolists

It is clear from these examples that Bely was more interested than Blok in trying to establish a theoretical basis for the synthesis of Dante and Solovyov which the religious Symbolists were advancing. It was he, for example, who explicitly formulated the sense of a tradition linking the religious Symbolists through Vladimir Solovyov to Dante. Significantly, he took Blok's poetry as his point of departure in elaborating this theory. In a review of Blok's second collection of poetry, *Joy beyond Hope* (*Nechayannaya radost'*, 1907), he divided the sources of the world-view expressed in the *Verses about the Beautiful Lady* into two categories – intellectual and poetic. The intellectual roots of Blok's poetry were in the Greek philosophers and Gnostic mystics who first elaborated the idea of a world-soul or eternal feminine principle (Plato, Philo, Plotinus and Schelling are included in this list). Its poetic roots were in the hymns of Dante, Petrarch and Goethe who linked the abstract intellectual concept to their personal experience and created symbolic images of the eternal feminine in their poetry. Fet and Lermontov dealt with the same issues unconsciously. Finally, Vladimir Solovyov synthesized the intellectual theories with the poetic hymns, and presented a new vision of the imminent descent of Sophia on to earth. This was the point at which Blok's poetry began.

After thus establishing *Verses about the Beautiful Lady* as the culmination of a tradition which reached back through Solovyov to Dante, Bely turned to the subject of his review, the collection *Joy beyond Hope*. He regarded the parodic Satanic elements which had entered Blok's work by this stage as a betrayal of the purity of the original tradition: the theme of the Beautiful Lady had been forsaken for a new·world of marshes and devils.[46]

In this way, Blok's works played a vital role in laying the foundation for the Symbolists' sense of a tradition linking them to Dante through Solovyov. The *Verses about the Beautiful Lady* provided a personal and lyrical expression of Solovyov's ideas on Sophia which the Symbolists were able to relate to the *Vita Nuova*. They were helped in this interpretation by Blok's understanding of his own development – and by extension of the Symbolists' path – in terms of Dantesque categories. Blok's view of Beatrice as a figure of Sophia in her pure, incorruptible essence, and of the post-Beautiful-Lady stages of Symbolism as a Dantesque *Inferno*, lacking the guidance of Beatrice, were readily adopted by the other religious Symbolists. Bely, for example, quoted Blok's comments on the disease of irony and vulgarization of Beatrice in a passage from his memoirs describing the development of Symbolism; he also cited lines from 'The Song of Hell' about the loss of Beatrice to illustrate Blok's change of orientation.[47] In a similar way, Sergei Solovyov linked Blok's use of the image of Beatrice to Vladimir Solovyov's vision of Sophia in 'Three Meetings'; he regarded the figure of Beatrice as Blok's 'guardian-angel', who had later been overshadowed by darker figures of the Astarte type. His memoirs of Blok end with the hope that the deceased poet would agree with this distinction and allow himself to be ranged on the side of purity with Dante: 'And now, all the more, he will not complain about my attempt to separate the pure gold of his poetry from the clouded, dark-lilac alloys – that gold which is destined to shine in its immortal wreath next to the gold of Dante – the poet of the *Vita Nuova*.'[48]

The association of Beatrice with Sophia thus not only provided the religious Symbolists with a model of the individual's experience of mystical love of Sophia in life and of its expression in poetry; it also gave them a means of introducing into Solovyov's teaching on Sophia the Catholic sense of hierarchy and progression which is so strongly reflected in the various stages of Dante's journey in the *Commedia*. The imagery of Dante's works and the figure of Beatrice in particular became for them a way of measuring their distance from their final goal – to bring Sophia down to earth by embodying her in their lives through love, and in art through poetry.

IVANOV

Influence of Solovyov

Ivanov saw himself as forming part of a common tradition, originating in the teachings of Vladimir Solovyov and upheld by the fraternity of religious Symbolists. This sense of spiritual kinship is clearly reflected in the following verses from a poem which he addressed to Blok in 1912:

> Пусть вновь – не друг, о мой любимый!
> Но братом буду я тебе
> На веки вечные в родимой
> Народной мысли и судьбе.
>
> Затем, что оба Соловьевым
> Таинственно мы крещены;
> Затем, что обрученьем новым
> С Единою обручены.
>
> Убрус положен на икону:
> Незримо тайное лицо.
> Скользит корабль по синю лону:
> На темном дне горит кольцо.   (*SS* III, 10)[49]

> So be it once again – not a friend, o my beloved!
> But a brother I will be to you
> Forever in our dear
> Nation's thought and fate.
>
> Because we both by Solovyov
> Were mysteriously christened,
> Because by a new betrothal
> We are betrothed to Her, the Only One.
>
> The cloth has been put over the icon:
> The mysterious face is invisible.
> The ship glides across the blue expanse:
> On the dark sea-bed burns a ring.

Ivanov wrote these lines in response to a poem which Blok had addressed to him earlier that year. In his poem Blok had described the initial phase of his relationship with Ivanov in terms of a meeting in a Dantesque infernal circle which had later been succeeded by a period of estrangement. Ivanov responded to the

image of the Dantesque circle (*krug*) which had linked them both
in the past with the image of the ring (*kol'tso*) which binds them
together in eternity through their shared allegiance to Solovyov
and Sophia; this indissoluble bond transcends friendship and is
described as a mystical rite of initiation. Ivanov may no longer be
Blok's friend, but he will forever remain his spiritual brother.

It is important, however, to realize that this sense of a common
tradition established itself retrospectively, with hindsight, and was
composed of individual approaches which varied considerably in
their origins. Blok and Bely each began to evolve an approach to
Solovyov in the early 1900s, but did not actually meet until 1904.
Until the same year, Ivanov's interest in Solovyov had also been
developing along quite independent lines. It was only after his visit
to Russia in the spring of 1904 and final return the following year
that the various threads began to weave themselves into a single
fabric.

The question of Ivanov's place within the tradition can therefore
be considered in terms of two main phases – the first covering his
years abroad and leading up to his return to Russia in 1905, and the
second beginning after he took up residence in St Petersburg and
joined the mainstream of the Russian Symbolist movement. While
elements of Dante and Solovyov are present and even to some
extent blended in the initial phase, they only acquired the characteristic features of the Symbolist interpretation of Dante in the
light of Solovyov's ideas after 1905. This becomes clear if one
compares Ivanov's first two collections of verse, written before his
return to Russia, with his later poetry. Although *Pilot Stars* and
Transparency contain many elements which anticipate the later
fuller merging of Solovyovian and Dantesque traditions, this tendency becomes much more pronounced in *Cor Ardens*.

Ivanov was fourteen years older than Blok and Bely, and, not
surprisingly, as many years in advance of them in his first contact
with Solovyov's ideas. He began to study the works of Solovyov in
1886 after his move from Moscow to Berlin, at a time when Blok
and Bely were still in their infancy. He was able to meet Solovyov
over a number of years before the philosopher's death in 1900, and
the first stage of his literary formation took place directly under the
latter's supervision and encouragement.[50]

Ivanov's poetry was first brought to the attention of Solovyov in
1895 by his first wife, Darya Mikhailovna, who acted without her

husband's knowledge. Although 1895 was the year in which Solovyov launched his biting attack on the Russian Symbolists in his
reviews of Bryusov's booklets, he took a different view of Ivanov's
verse, recognizing its indisputable originality. He sent an encour-
aging telegram to Ivanov, expressing his desire to arrange for the
poems to be published. At his instigation, a number of Ivanov's
poems were printed in various journals a few years later, in 1898
and 1899.

This initial contact was followed by a meeting later the same
year.[51] Solovyov correctly predicted to Ivanov that he would
outgrow his obsession with Nietzsche. For the next five years
Ivanov visited Solovyov whenever he returned to Russia from
abroad. Although the meetings were infrequent, Ivanov attached
the greatest importance to them. 'Every time, a meeting with him
was an education for the soul', he wrote in his unpublished autobiography of 1904. Later, he summed up his debt to Solovyov in
the following words: 'He was both the patron of my muse and the
confessor of my heart.'[52]

In the summer of 1900, Ivanov and his second wife Lidiya
Dimitrievna visited Solovyov in St Petersburg, a few months
before his death. Solovyov was the first judge of *Pilot Stars* and
gave his blessing to the title of this work. He reassured Ivanov that
although he was making his literary début alone, he would be
welcomed into the fraternity of other poets soon after the publication of his book.[53]

When Solovyov died on 31 July 1900, the loss was felt as keenly
by Lidiya Dimitrievna as by Ivanov. On 1 August she wrote to her
husband:

I have just read that Vladimir Sergeevich has left us in this life. Where is
he? Where is that person whose eyes I was just recently looking into with
joy and love? My soul is even quieter, even humbler. There is no need for
sharp misery before this new mystery, although I cry and cannot do
otherwise. I see him before me, alive and full of kindness.[54]

At the end of 1900 Ivanov wrote a poem entitled 'Verses on the
Holy Mountain' ('*Stikh o svyatoi gore*'), clearly intended as a
tribute to Solovyov's memory. The words which the philosopher
spoke on his death-bed, 'The work of the Lord is hard' (*Trudna
rabota Gospodnya*), are appended to the poem as an epigraph.[55]
The poet describes the building of a church on a holy mountain in
Russia. The builders cannot see what they are building, and pray to

the 'Heavenly Queen' or 'Most Pure Mother' to make the invisible church visible. This figure, who in a characteristically Solovyovian manner combines features of both the Virgin Mary and of Sophia, promises that she will descend to earth at an appointed time to redeem Russia and the world.

Pilot Stars: disparate influences

'Verses on the Holy Mountain' was published in *Pilot Stars*, a work which reflects a great variety of disparate and unharmonized influences – including those of Dionysus, Dante and Solovyov. Ivanov commented on the syncretic character of his work in a preface which he wrote for *Pilot Stars* in Carmel in May 1901; the style of this preface is remarkably heavy and clumsy, which perhaps explains why it was not included in the final version of the book:

> The poetic harvest of a long and drawn-out series of 'years of study and wanderings' inevitably betrays contradictions of form and interest [*uvlecheniya*], and the strictest selection will not transform the collection into a unified whole; but the constant contemplation of transcendent guiding principles is also a form of unity, and this is what has given the collection its overall title which received the blessing of he to whose great memory this book would have been dedicated with reverence, if another more sacred duty had not turned it into an *ex-voto* offering to the deceased mother of the poet.[56]

Ivanov's mother died in 1896 and *Pilot Stars* is dedicated to her memory rather than to that of Vladimir Solovyov. There is, however, much evidence of the philosopher's influence throughout the book, starting with the direct tribute paid to him in the opening verses of the first section, 'Beauty' ('*Krasota*' – *SS* 1, 517). This poem is dedicated to Solovyov and describes a female figure, Beauty, who links the higher world to the lower world and is served by an earthly pilgrim whose vision she has transformed. Beauty serves Adrastia (a surname of the Greek goddess Nemesis, identified with fate), and Ivanov explains in a note to the poem that those who serve Adrastia are wise (*SS* 1, 859). This makes it quite clear that Ivanov's figure of Beauty is an image of Solovyov's Sophia. In other words Ivanov is emphasizing from the start that he belongs to the tradition of poets serving Sophia established by Solovyov.

In his preface Ivanov insisted that the disparate influences on his first work were unified through the common preoccupation with transcendent truths from which they all derived. It is true that the Solovyovian and Dantesque images in the book are related to this central preoccupation, but they nevertheless remain distinct rather than being merged into a single whole. For example, as the title of his work, Ivanov has chosen the Dantesque image of the guiding stars; this image recurs throughout the *Commedia* as a symbol of the transcendent truths which guide man in his spiritual life and the poet in his art.[57] To make the Dantesque character of his title explicit, Ivanov has appended to it an epigraph from the *Purgatorio* which takes up the image of the guiding stars within the context of Dante's spiritual journey:

> Poco potea parer li del di fuori
> Ma per quel poco vedev'io le stelle
> Di lor solere e piu chiare e maggiori   (*SS* I, 513)[58]

> Little of the outside could be seen there,
> but through that little I saw the stars
> brighter and larger than their wont.

Within the first few opening pages of *Pilot Stars* we move from these Dantesque images to the Solovyovian evocation of Sophia described in 'Beauty'; Dante and Solovyov are presented side by side, but there is as yet little attempt to synthesize them into a common tradition.

In his essay on Ivanov, written in April 1905, Blok took up these Dantesque and Solovyovian images and worked them into a single tradition.[59] He quoted the epigraph from the *Purgatorio*, and interpreted the description of Dante looking out from within a narrow passage-way at the top of Mount Purgatory to the light of the stars above as symbolic of the contemporary artist's attempt to grope his way out of the dark cave of present art to the pure Symbolist art of the future. Blok regarded *Pilot Stars* as a preparatory work leading up to *Transparency*, and described the transition from one work to the other in terms of images drawn from Ivanov's poetry – the poet had been led by the light of the guiding stars to a vision of Sophia, partially revealed in 'Beauty' and then more fully in 'Transparency', one of the opening poems of *Transparency*. This interpretation of Ivanov's development in terms of Solovyovian and Dantesque images is typical; it reflects the common Symbolist tendency to use Dantesque images to introduce a sense of ordered progression by stages into the poet's journey towards Sophia.

Transparency: the beginning of the synthesis

Transparency is indeed a more unified work than *Pilot Stars*, and
anticipates the later fuller fusion of Solovyovian and Dantesque
traditions, introduced as separate strands in the first collection.
The following poem, '"Transcende te ipsum"', can be considered as an example of the beginning of the process of welding
together the different traditions, Dionysiac, Solovyovian and
Dantesque.

> Два жала есть у царственного змия;
> У ангела Порывов – два крыла.
> К распутию душа твоя пришла:
> Вождь сей тропы – Рахиль; и оной – Лия.
>
> Как двум вожжам послушны удила,
> Так ей – дела, а той – мечты благие.
> Ей Отреченье имя, – чьи дела;
> Той – Отрешенье. Вечная София –
>
> Обеим свет. Одна зовет: 'Прейди
> Себя, – себя объемля в беспредельном'.
> Рахиль: 'Себя прейди – в себя сойди'.
>
> И любит отчужденного в Одном,
> А Лия – отчужденного в Раздельном.
> И обе склонены над темным дном.   (*SS* I, 782–3)

The regal serpent has a two-pointed tongue;
The angel of Impulses has two wings.
To a parting of the ways your soul has come:
The ruler of this path is Rachel; and of the other – Leah.

Just as a horse's bit obeys two reins,
So to one belong actions, and to the other – blessed dreams.
Repudiation is the name of the one whose sphere is actions;
The name of the other is Renunciation. Eternal Sophia

Is light to them both. One calls: 'Transcend
Yourself – by embracing yourself in the infinite.'
Rachel says: 'Transcend yourself – descend into yourself.'

And she loves the other in the One,
While Leah loves the other in the Divided.
And both are bowed over the dark deep.

The title of the poem, ' "Transcende te ipsum" ', alludes to the Augustinian precept of 'transcensus sui' which Ivanov interpreted as a Christian formulation of the principle of Dionysiac self-transcendence through Eros.[60] The poem is in fact primarily grounded in Ivanov's Dionysiac ideal. It begins with an evocation of Eros, described as the 'angel of Impulses' (*angel Poryvov*); 'impulse' (*poryv*) refers to the fundamental mystic urge or impulse to self-transcendence, and should be understood as Ivanov defined it in the context of Dionysiac mysticism. Eros is traditionally represented as a winged infant, and here the two wings are used as images of the two paths which man can follow in mystical love.

The Dionysiac ideal of Eros is then clothed in Christian imagery derived from two different traditions, the Dantesque and the Solovyovian. To define the two types of mystical love, Ivanov turns to the images of the sisters from the Old Testament whom Jacob married, Leah and Rachel. There was a well-established medieval Christian tradition of interpreting these two sisters as allegorical figures of the active and contemplative lives. Leah, who bore many children, represented the active way of God; Rachel who bore only one son was regarded as a figure of the contemplative life. This interpretation was made famous by Dante who dreamt of Leah and Rachel at the top of Mount Purgatory before entering Earthly Paradise (immediately after gazing out at the stars from the narrow passageway, the lines chosen by Ivanov as an epigraph to *Pilot Stars*). In Dante's dream Leah is gathering flowers and singing about her sister Rachel who sits all day in front of her mirror contemplating her eyes. Rachel is satisfied with seeing, and Leah with doing (*Purg.* xxvii, 91–108).

Ivanov had already used the images of Leah and Rachel as types of the active and contemplative life in 'The Sphinx' ('*Sfinks*'), a long Dantesque poem written in terzinas and included in *Pilot Stars* (*SS* 1, 643–60). Here he described Leah, picking flowers, and Rachel's eyes just as in Dante's *Purgatorio*; in a note he explained that Leah and Rachel were symbols of the active and contemplative life in Dante's work, following St Thomas Aquinas (*SS* 1, 652, 861).

In ' "Transcende te ipsum" ' Ivanov uses the image again in exactly the same sense. But now the Dantesque tradition is also blended with Solovyov's teaching on Sophia. Both Rachel and Leah are illuminated or guided by Sophia, and seek to transcend the boundaries of their individual selves to achieve mystical union with the divine spirit. Leah achieves self-transcendence through loving the 'other' as embodied in the infinite multiplicity of the world's phenomena; Rachel achieves the same goal by loving the 'other' in the depths of her own being. In Solovyovian terms, they both transcend themselves through love of Sophia, either embodied in the material being of the universe or in her abstract divine essence.

Ivanov's use in this poem of Sophiological terms to describe Dionysian Eros testifies to the remarkable close affinity which he perceived between his Dionysian ideal and Solovyov's teaching on the meaning of love. In both systems the ultimate goal of mystical union with the divine essence of the universe was to be achieved through an experience of sacrifice which would enable the individual to transcend the narrow boundaries of the limited self. In both cases physical love is advocated as the heart of the mystical experience because it embodies in its core the cycle of sacrifice leading to ecstasy, of death leading to life.[61]

Like Ivanov, Solovyov made frequent reference to the importance of the connection between death and life in his writings on love and in his poetry. In 'The Meaning of Love' he refers specifically in this context to the identity of Dionysus, god of fertility, and Hades, god of death, to illustrate the idea that true spiritual life must arise out of the death of the individual's limited self. Some of the phrases which he uses, such as 'whoever supports the root of death will inevitably also taste of its fruits' (*kto podderzhivaet koren' smerti, tot neizbezhno vkusit i ploda ee*),[62] have a strong Dionysiac ring about them and are later echoed by Ivanov in his writings.

Ivanov attached particular importance to 'The Meaning of Love' precisely because he was able to interpret it in terms of the Dionysiac cult of life from death. In an essay of 1910 about Solovyov he wrote:

The question of the meaning of love is intimately connected, like the other side of a single mystery, with the question of man's triumph over death. Perhaps no one since Plato has said anything so deep and so true to life about love and sex as V. Solovyov. He glorified love and restored the human dignity and divine-human purpose of sex, celebrating the 'roses which rise above the black mass' and blessing their 'roots which sink into the dark soil'. And for love – oh, for this above all else! – the last task and the third, secret and supreme feat is the overcoming of death . . .

(*SS* III, 305)

Here Ivanov is paraphrasing an image from Solovyov's poem of 1892, 'We came together not in vain . . .' ('*My soshlis' s toboi ne darom* . . .'), and interpreting it in the light of his own Dionysiac beliefs.[63] The roses, deeply rooted in the dark earth, are presented as a symbol of the Dionysiac as well as Solovyovian belief in the parallel connection between sexual and mystical love, between death or darkness and life or light.

Ivanov's perception of the similarities between Dionysiac mysticism and Solovyov's teaching on love provided him with a framework for incorporating his pagan ideal into the Christian tradition. In Solovyov's emphasis on the need for a new union of the flesh and spirit Ivanov found an echo of his own desire to create a mystical form of Christianity based on its Dionysiac roots. Although Solovyov had not advocated a return to pagan mysticism, like Ivanov he was aware of the potentially Christian elements inherent in classical antiquity. During the summer of 1887 he worked on translations of Virgil's *Aeneid* and of the fourth *Eclogue*, and it is clear from his note to the last translation that he shared the medieval view of Virgil as a prophet of Christianity. He had in fact begun work on his translation of the *Eclogue* in 1883, the same year as he translated verse from the *Vita Nuova* and Petrarch.[64] In subsequent editions of his poetry, translations from all three authors were published alongside each other. This juxtaposition of Solovyov's original verse with works by Dante, Petrarch and Virgil fitted in well with Ivanov's attempt to create a single syncretic tradition in which Dante would appear as the representative of both Dionysiac (mediated through Virgil) and Solovyovian ideals.

' "Transcende te ipsum" ' provides an early example of Ivanov's tendency to interpret and present Dantesque images in terms of both the Dionysiac and Solovyovian elements of his spiritual ideal. After his return to Russia in 1905, this tendency became much more pronounced, as can be seen from the examples drawn from his later poetry discussed in chapter 5. This was no doubt partly because he had now joined the mainstream of the Russian Symbolist movement and had many more opportunities to share his ideas with other like-minded intellectuals and poets through direct discussion. In 1908, for example, he wrote a lengthy letter to Blok in which he discussed the younger poet's latest collection of verse entirely in terms of its relation to the idea of the Beautiful Lady and Sophia.[65] This type of exchange of ideas as well as the simple passage of time were important factors which enabled him to assimilate the various strands of his spiritual ideal into a single more coherent fabric.

Dante and Solovyov as poets of Sophia

By 1910 the religious Symbolists' sense of a tradition linking them through Solovyov to the Catholic Middle Ages and Dante was fully established. This emerges clearly from the lectures which Ivanov and Blok composed at the end of the year in December to be read at meetings convened in honour of the tenth anniversary of Solovyov's death. Both articles appeared together in the following year in an anthology devoted to Solovyov,[66] and both stress the parallel between the Russian philosopher and Dante in different ways.

Blok made a point of building up an association between the Russian mystic of Sophia and the Italian medieval Catholic tradition. He used the term 'knight-monk' (*rytsar'-monakh*) as the title of his talk to describe Solovyov and compared the key poem 'Three Meetings' to a religious medieval Latin inscription which he had once seen in Ravenna. In his description of this poem he underlined its connection with the idea of a new life, thereby hinting at its affinity with the *Vita Nuova*. His sentence 'the poem written at the end of a life-time points to where life begins' deliberately echoes the opening of the *Vita Nuova* in which Dante announces his intention to copy out the words which he finds under the heading '*Incipit vita nova*' in the book of his memory.[67]

Ivanov presented the same view of a common tradition, but placed more direct emphasis on the parallel with Dante. After dwelling on the importance of Solovyov's contribution towards the understanding of love, he turned to his role as the founder of a new school of realist religious Symbolism or theurgic art. Here, he compared Solovyov to Dante and Goethe; all three had inaugurated a new era in poetry, based on the worship of the Eternal Feminine:

The significance of Solovyov, the poet of the heavenly Sophia, . . . can also be defined in relation to the fruits of his poetic activity: in his poetry he initiated a whole movement, perhaps an epoch, in Russian poetry. When the Eternal Feminine is invoked, a certain god begins to stir in the heart of the World Soul – like a child in the womb – and then the poets begin to sing. It was like this after Dante, it was like this – in the figure of Novalis – after the one who said 'Das Ewig-Weibliche zieht uns hinan'. Moreover, as a teacher, V. Solovyov found words which opened the eyes of the poet and of the artist to his true and supreme mission: Solovyov defined true art as a form of theurgic service.   (*SS* III, 306)[68]

Here Ivanov establishes the link between Dante and Solovyov – as between Dante and the classical world – primarily on the basis of their shared faith in poetry as a sacred, theurgic form of art. Many years later, in an essay on Pushkin written in 1937, he once more coupled the names of Dante and Solovyov as artists who aspired to a theurgic form of art which would guide and transform the human race.[69]

In these different ways Ivanov, Bely and Blok all came to regard themselves as the inheritors of a tradition which linked them through Solovyov to Dante. This determined a specific approach to Dante in the light of Solovyov's teaching on Sophia in the realms of love and poetry. In the case of Blok and Bely, this approach was primarily based on the link between the concept of Sophia and Beatrice as an image for the poet's personal ideal. Ivanov extended the parallel into a wider area incorporating the aesthetics of art as a form of divine theurgic service.

4

Ivanov's ideal of mystical love

So far we have considered two of the most important influences which affected Ivanov's spiritual ideal and approach to Dante: Dionysiac mysticism and Solovyov's teaching on Sophia. Both these systems stressed the importance of sexual love as the main means of transcending the limitations of the individual self and achieving mystical union with the divine spirit of the universe. Both Dionysiac Eros and love, in Solovyov's understanding of the term, were seen as cyclical experiences leading through sacrifice to ecstasy, through death to new life, through the physical to the mystical. This made it possible for Ivanov to merge the two systems into a single syncretic ideal, composed of both pagan and Christian elements.

The core of Ivanov's spiritual ideal was therefore the experience of love, and this was the main area in which he turned to Dante as a source of images for its poetic expression. Ivanov's understanding of the Hellenic periods in history had already led him to regard Dante as a major representative of his Dionysiac–Christian ideal, and Solovyov had also laid the foundations for the incorporation of Dante into the Sophiological tradition of mystical love. The fact that the theme of love was central to Dante's works was a further factor in making these a particularly rich source of inspiration for Ivanov; the *Vita Nuova* is the record of Dante's transition from the physical love of Beatrice during her life-time to the spiritual love of God after her death, and the *Commedia* describes a mystic journey inspired by the love of Beatrice and guided by the moving power of divine love.

However, before any discussion of Ivanov's use of Dantesque images in his poetry can take place, it is necessary first to establish the immediate context in which these images arose: Ivanov's experience of love. This was the primary focus of his spiritual ideal and the major inspiration behind his poetry. In general, the Symbolists did not look upon spiritual ideals as intellectual abstractions but as living truths to be experienced in practice as well as preached in theory. The dividing line between art and life was dispensed with in so far as possible. Like art, life was regarded as an ideal area for the creative realization of abstract ideals. The poet Khodasevich provides an excellent analysis of this phenomenon at the beginning of his memoirs. He singles out the desire to 'merge life and creative work together' as the most characteristic manifestation of the spirit of the Symbolist era, and writes: 'The Symbolists did not want to separate the writer from the man, the literary biography from the personal one. Symbolism did not want to be just an artistic school, a literary trend. It constantly strove to become a method for life as well as creative work ...'[1] Love, which allows one to experience a maximum concentration of emotions, was, as Khodasevich remarks, considered a most effective means for this purpose, and was consequently deliberately cultivated by the Symbolists.[2]

Ivanov was no exception to this general tendency. Both Dionysiac mysticism and the teaching of Solovyov on Sophia advanced an ideal of mystical love which was not a matter for merely intellectual contemplation but a method to be adopted and incorporated into life through physical means. Ivanov associated his spiritual ideal with a particular experience which he regarded as the instrument of its revelation and confirmation to him in his life. This was his relationship with Lidiya Dimitrievna Zinoveva-Annibal. Together with lesser and more transitory involvements with Sergei Gorodetsky and Margarita Sabashnikova, this formed the core around which his theories on mystical love crystallized and the basis from which his poetry grew up. His changing perception of these experiences contributed to the formation of his spiritual ideal and to his understanding of Dante within this context.

From adultery to wedlock: L. D. Zinoveva-Annibal
(Italy, 1893–9)

When Ivanov first met Lidiya Dimitrievna in the summer of 1893, he was married and living in Rome with his first wife, Darya Mikhailovna Dmitrievskaya (the sister of his close friend Aleksei Dmitrievsky) whom he had married seven years previously, just before leaving Russia for Germany. After spending some years in

Berlin and in Paris, the couple had moved to Rome in 1892 for
Ivanov to continue work on his dissertation. It was during this
period of residence in Italy, which lasted until 1895, that Ivanov
first met Lidiya Dimitrievna, fell in love with her, and decided to
divorce his first wife.[3]

Lidiya Dimitrievna was separated from her first husband and
had come to Italy with her three children, Aleksandr, Sergei and
Vera, to study music and singing in Florence. In the summer of
1893, her Petersburg acquaintance, the historian, Ivan Mikhailo-
vich Grevs, came to Florence on a visit from Paris, and persuaded
her to accompany him to Rome to meet his friend Ivanov. Grevs
was on his way to visit Ivanov for academic purposes. The two
scholars had first met in 1891 while working in the Bibliothèque
Nationale in Paris, and had developed a friendship on the basis of
their shared interest in Ancient Roman history and Dante.[4]

Ivanov's first meeting with Lidiya Dimitrievna took place in July
and was a great success. The three friends went for walks around
Rome, shared meals and enjoyed each other's conversation. Lidiya
Dimitrievna then returned to Russia for a year. During this period
Ivanov and his family moved from Rome to Florence.

When Lidiya Dimitrievna returned to Italy in 1894, she settled in
Pesaro where she took tuition in music and singing. The development of her relationship with Ivanov can be reconstructed from
this point in some detail from her letters to the poet. On 12
September she wrote to him in Florence, recalling his and his wife's
kindness at their previous meetings, and inviting them to visit her.
Five days later, she wrote again, this time announcing her plan to
accompany her music teacher to Florence for two or three weeks,
and asking Ivanov to help her find accommodation.[5]

On 30 September Lidiya Dimitrievna arrived in Florence.[6] She
began to meet Ivanov regularly, and it is clear from subsequent
letters that their relationship underwent a substantial change of
character during the next few months. The situation began to get
out of control, and around the end of 1894 or beginning of 1895,
Ivanov moved to Rome, leaving his family and Lidiya Dimitrievna
behind in Florence.[7] He was certainly installed in Rome by 18
January 1895 because on this date Lidiya Dimitrievna posted him a
small token of her love from Florence – a lock of golden hair and
two green leaves.[8]

From this point Lidiya Dimitrievna's letters to Ivanov are full of open confessions of love and of yearning to be reunited with him, interspersed with expressions of guilt towards his wife whom she saw periodically in Florence.[9] This rising tide of emotion culminated in a lightning visit which she paid to him in Rome; on 11 March she arrived at midnight and stayed with him for three days in a hotel room before returning to Florence.[10] The climax of the visit was an evening which the two lovers spent together at the Coliseum, described by Ivanov in his poem 'At the Coliseum' ('V Kolizee' – SS 1, 521).[11] The poem 'Golden Happiness' ('Zolotoe schastie') and the cycle 'Songs of Daphnis' ('Pesni Dafnisa' – SS 1, 763–9) were written by Ivanov in March 1895 and reflect his feelings of joy after the visit.

The meeting was tempestuous and, despite its brevity, decisive. In April Ivanov returned to Florence and informed his wife of the situation. Darya Mikhailovna insisted on a divorce, and soon after Ivanov left Florence to accompany her back to Russia.[12]

The first phase of Ivanov's and Lidiya Dimitrievna's relationship was thus brought to a conclusion. It had consisted of three main stages: Rome in July 1893, Florence from September to December 1894, and Rome again in March 1895. Lidiya Dimitrievna summed this up in a letter to Ivanov of June 1895: 'Florence kindled the barely smouldering spark of love which you had ignited at our first meeting, Rome set a hot flame burning.'[13] They both had a strong sense of the importance of the connection between the birth of their love and Italy; in a letter to Ivanov written after his departure from Italy, Lidiya Dimitrievna imagined his nostalgia and passionate longing to return to 'our wonderful Italy', to the 'homeland of our happiness'.[14] This feeling for Italy as the homeland of love had a vital influence on Ivanov's poetic treatment of love and of Dante within this context.

After Ivanov's separation from his first wife in 1895, he and Lidiya Dimitrievna lived together in several countries – including Switzerland, Germany, France, England and Greece – until their eventual return to Russia in 1905. They visited Russia regularly, seeing Vladimir Solovyov on each occasion until his death in 1900. Lidiya Dimitrievna had difficulty in securing a divorce from her previous husband, and for some years she and Ivanov were obliged to disguise the nature of their relationship. In April 1896 their daughter Lidiya was born in Paris. Three years later, in 1899, when the divorce finally came through, the couple were married in a

Greek Orthodox church in Livorno; according to the Greek rite,
vine wreathes entwined with white lamb's wool were placed on
their heads during the ceremony.

Ivanov's perception of his relationship with Lidiya Dimitrievna
was intimately connected with the development of his spiritual
ideal over these years. From their first meeting, he identified
Lidiya Dimitrievna's nature with the Dionysiac principle; through
her, he felt in touch with the Dionysiac forces of the universe of
which his knowledge had previously been purely academic. Nikolai
Berdyaev makes this point clearly in his reminiscences of Ivanov:

L. D. Zinoveva-Annibal was of a quite different nature from V. Ivanov,
more Dionysiac, stormy, impulsive, revolutionary in temperament,
elemental, constantly pushing forward and upward. Such an elemental
female nature, combined with the refined academic manner of V. Ivanov
... created a talented, poetically transformed social atmosphere.[15]

When Ivanov first met Lidiya Dimitrievna, he was still strongly
under the influence of Nietzsche's analysis of the Dionysiac principle as an order-defying, anti-Christian force. Since in its early
phase his relationship with Lidiya Dimitrievna was a passionate
adulterous affair which defied the laws of conventional Christian
morality, it is hardly surprising that he should first have regarded it
as a sinful passion and manifestation of the chaotic and destructive
aspects of the Dionysiac principle in Nietzsche's definition of the
term. In later years, he commented on the extent to which Nietzsche influenced his initial perception of the affair:

Nietzsche was becoming the master of my thoughts to an increasingly full
and powerful extent. This Nietzscheanism helped me to resolve – cruelly
and deliberately but, according to my conscience, correctly – the problem
which I was faced with in 1895 of choosing between the deep and tender
affection which my feeling of love towards my wife had turned into, and
the new love which had totally engulfed me; this love was destined from
then on only to grow and deepen spiritually in the course of my whole life,
but in those early days it seemed to me as well as to the one I loved that it
was just a criminal, dark, demonic passion.   ('*AP*', *SS* II, 19–20)

The Nietzschean character of Ivanov's Dionysiac ideal and the
way in which it was entirely bound up for him at this stage with the
image of Lidiya Dimitrievna can be seen very clearly in a poem
which he wrote on 20 and 21 January 1895, shortly after parting
with Lidiya Dimitrievna and moving from Florence to Rome.[16]

The poem is entitled 'The Funeral Rites in Memory of Dionysus' (*'Trizna Dionisa'*) and reads as follows:

Зимой, порою тризн вакхальных,
Когда Мэнад безумный хор
Смятеньем воплей погребальных
Тревожит сон пустынных гор, –

На высотах, где Мельпомены
Давно умолкнул страшный глас
И меж развалин древней сцены
Алтарь вакхический угас, –

В благоговеньи и печали
Воззвав к тому, чей был сей дом,
Мэнаду новую венчали
Мы Дионисовым венцом:

Сплетались пламенные розы
С плющем, отрадой дерзких нег,
И на листах, как чьи-то слезы,
Дрожа, сверкал алмазный снег . . .

Тогда пленительно-мятежной
Ты песнью огласила вдруг
Покрытый пеленою снежной
Священный Вакхов полукркг.

Ты пела, вдохновеньем оргий
И опьяняясь, и пьяня,
И беспощадные восторги,
И темный гроб земного дня:

«Увейте гроздьем тирсы, чаши!
Властней богов, сильней Судьбы,
Несите упоенья ваши!
Восстаньте – боги, не рабы!

«Земных обетов и законов
Дерзните преступить порог, –
И в муке нег, и в пире стонов
Воскреснет исступленный бог! . . . »

Дул ветер, осыпались розы;
Склонялся скорбный кипарис . . .
Обнажены, роптали лозы:
«Почил великий Дионис!»

И с тризны мертвенно-вакхальной
Мы шли, туманны и грустны;
· И был далек земле печальной
Возврат языческой весны.   (*SS* I, 571–2)

In winter, at the time of the Bacchanalian rites,
When the mad chorus of Maenads
With a commotion of funeral cries
Disturbs the sleep of the deserted mountains –

On the heights where Melpomene's
Fearful voice has long since fallen silent
And where among the ruins of an ancient stage
The Bacchic altar is extinguished –

After calling out in awe and sorrow
To the one whose home this was,
We crowned a new Maenad
With a Dionysiac crown:

Fiery roses intertwined
With ivy, the delight of daring pleasures,
And on the leaves, like someone's tears,
Trembling, shone the diamond snow . . .

Then with a captivatingly stormy
Song you suddenly filled
Bacchus's sacred semi-circle,
Covered with a shroud of snow.

You sang, by the inspiration of the orgies
Both intoxicated and intoxicating,
You sang of unrelenting delights,
And of the dark grave of the earthly day:

'Wreathe your thyrsi and cups with clusters!
More powerfully than the gods, more forcefully than Fate,
Uphold your ecstatic delights!
Rise up – like gods, not slaves!

Dare to cross the threshold
Of earthly vows and laws –
And in the torment of pleasures, and in a feast of laments
The frenzied god will rise again!. . .'

The wind blew; roses scattered;
The mournful cypress bowed . . .
The bare vines murmured:
'The great Dionysus has passed away!'

And from the funereal Bacchanalian rites
We went, clouded and sad;
And far from the sorrowful earth
Was the return of a pagan spring.

The poem is set at the time of the winter Dionysiac festival (it was originally entitled 'The Winter Dionysia' – '*Zimnie Dionisii*');[17] this event took place every year in December and marked the beginning of the annual cycle of festivities celebrating the myth of the death and resurrection of Dionysus, the god of wine, nature and vegetation. The winter Dionysia lamented the god's death but contained a hint of his future resurrection in the simultaneous tasting of the new year's wine.[18] This tension between the lamentation of the death of Dionysus and yet the hope or anticipation of his resurrection is the fundamental theme of Ivanov's poem.

The scene is a ruined theatre which was once dedicated to the cult of Dionysus. Previously, the god was worshipped by Maenads who brought sacrifices to him on a central altar to the accompaniment of ecstatic songs and dance. Now, however, the theatre is abandoned, its altar is out of use, and the Muse of Tragedy has long since fallen silent.

Against this background of death and lamentation, an attempt is made to revive the spirit of Dionysus. A new Maenad (addressed as 'you') is crowned (by the 'we' of the poem) with a wreath of roses and ivy. She begins to sing an intoxicating song calling upon the spirits buried under the snow to rise and join in the worship of Dionysus in an attempt to raise him from his winter sleep.

However, the winter landscape remains unmoved, and the vines murmur that the great Dionysus is dead. The friends leave the funereal scene in despondent moods, and the poem closes with the pessimistic statement that the return of the pagan spring is still far away.

Ivanov's lamentation that the cult of Dionysus is no longer a live force in contemporary culture, his call for its revival and yet recognition that this will not take place for some time is all presented through the prism of his relationship with Lidiya Dimitrievna. This becomes clear if one recalls the incident on which the poem is based. During the winter before Ivanov's departure from Florence, the poet, Lidiya Dimitrievna and Grevs visited the ancient Roman theatre of Dionysus in the hills near Florence at Fiesole. Lidiya Dimitrievna frequently alluded to this visit in her subsequent letters to Ivanov. They both regarded it and the later meeting at the Coliseum in March 1895 as symbolic turning points in their relationship. Lidiya Dimitrievna often coupled the two events together, referring to them simply as 'Fiesole' and 'the Coliseum', and emphasizing their importance.[19]

In the light of this background information, it would appear that the woman in the poem who is crowned a Maenad and who sings a song calling for the resurrection of Dionysus represents Lidiya Dimitrievna who was, indeed, a trained singer. She is the medium through whom Ivanov can communicate with the spirit of Dionysus. At the time of the visit to the theatre at Fiesole, their relationship was still secret, and Ivanov was about to move to Rome. Ivanov, writing this poem in Rome after the parting had taken place, identifies the current stage of his affair with the winter sleep or death of Dionysus, and laments it accordingly. He looks forward, however, to its resurrection, and the last two lines of the poem acquire a prophetic ring in the light of subsequent events; the relationship was 'revived' from its winter sleep by Lidiya Dimitrievna's visit to Rome in March 1895, timed, whether by chance or deliberately, to fall exactly on the eve of the yearly springtime celebration of Dionysus's resurrection from the dead.[20]

Significantly, the Dionysiac forces invoked in the poem are Nietzschean in character; the Maenad's song calls for men to be like gods and dare everything. There is as yet no hint at the Christian dimension of Dionysus; the poem is a prayer for the return of a purely pagan spring.

This poem was one of the verses which Ivanov's wife gave to Vladimir Solovyov for his consideration in 1895, and which were subsequently published at his initiative.[21] As was noted in the previous chapter, when the two men first met later that year, Solovyov predicted that Ivanov would outgrow Nietzsche, and this indeed proved to be the case. Naturally, Ivanov's new perception of the religious significance of Dionysus altered his understanding of his relationship with Lidiya Dimitrievna. In his autobiographical letter, he described the mystical dimension which the Dionysiac character of his affair subsequently acquired:

Through each other, we each found ourselves and more than just ourselves: I would say, we discovered God. Meeting her was like a powerful Dionysiac spring storm after which everything in me was renewed, blossomed and turned green. And it was not only in myself that for the first time the poet revealed and recognized himself, freely and confidently, but also in her: the whole of our shared life, full of deep inner events, can without exaggeration be described for both of us as a period of almost uninterrupted inspiration and intense spiritual burning.

(*SS* II, 20)

This sense of spiritual rebirth was fully shared by Lidiya Dimitrievna. In July 1895, she dwelt on it in a letter to Ivanov, looking back to the time which they had spent together in Florence in 1894:

Do you remember, my dear, last autumn in Florence, my sleepless nights full of the ecstasy of a new life, of new dreams about a previously unimagined happiness? I told you: 'You are witnessing the birth of a person.' I was being born then, freeing myself from the dead weight of the past. The horizon was widening and it seemed to me that the 'word' was descending on me. The word of life, its solution . . .[22]

Ivanov and Lidiya Dimitrievna both came to view their relationship in the light of Ivanov's spiritual ideal in its later form – the Dionysiac essence, not Nietzschean but mystical, and incorporated into a religious framework. The original sense of sin developed a sacrificial, suffering dimension which made it compatible with Christianity. Ivanov was undoubtedly influenced in his progression towards this new understanding by Solovyov's ideas on mystical love which took up the notions of sacrifice and self-transcendence in sexual love within a Christian context.

The ceremony with which the lovers celebrated their marriage in 1899 served as a perfect image of Ivanov's spiritual ideal: the incorporation of Dionysiac motifs (the Greek vine and lamb's wool wreaths) into the Christian ritual. In later years, in a *canzone* included in the fourth book of *Cor Ardens*, Ivanov expressed his sense of the transformation of his early Dionysiac sinful passion (epitomized by the episode in the Coliseum) into a Christian mystery (symbolized by the wedding ceremony):

Наш первый хмель, преступный хмель свободы
    Могильный Колизей
Благословил: там хищной и мятежной

Рекой смесились бешеные воды
  Двух рухнувших страстей.
Но, в ревности о подвиге прилежной,
  Волною агнца снежной
Мы юную лозу от вертограда,
  Где ты была мэнада,
Обвив, надели новые венцы,
Как огненосцы Духа и жрецы.   (*SS* II, 398)

Our first drunkenness, the criminal drunkenness of freedom,
      Was blessed
By the tomb-like Coliseum: there in a wild and stormy
River flowed together the mad waters
      Of two headlong passions.
But, in our fervent zeal for the feat,
      After twining a snowy wave of lamb's wool
Around a young vine from the garden
      Where you were a Maenad,
We donned new crowns
Like firebearers of the Spirit and priests.

Life in the tower: S. Gorodetsky and M. Sabashnikova
(St Petersburg, 1905–6)

Between 1895 and 1903 Ivanov and Lidiya Dimitrievna lived in
almost complete isolation from Russian literary circles; their main
contact in Russia was Vladimir Solovyov, until his death in 1900. In
October 1902 Ivanov's first collection of verse, *Pilot Stars*, was
published.[23] It was favourably reviewed by Bryusov in the March
1903 issue of *Novyi put'*.[24] Ivanov's first personal contact with the
Russian Symbolists followed soon after in April when he met
Bryusov in Paris. This acquaintance led to the publication of his
second collection of verse, *Transparency*, by Bryusov's publishing
house Skorpion. The book's appearance in the spring of 1904
followed a visit which Ivanov and Lidiya Dimitrievna paid to
Russia, marking their official entrée into Moscow and St Petersburg literary circles. In Moscow they met the poets grouped
around Bryusov's publishing house and journal *Vesy* – Balmont,
Baltrushaitis and Bely. In St Petersburg they made the acquaintance of Merezhkovsky, his wife, the poetess, Zinaida Gippius, and
others associated with the journal *Novyi put'*. Both circles
accepted Ivanov into their midst ('*AP*', *SS*, II, 21).

In the spring of 1905, Ivanov and Lidiya Dimitrievna left their home near Geneva permanently and returned to Russia. A new phase began in their lives. They took up residence in St Petersburg in a flat on Tavricheskaya Street which, because of the shape of the building, became known as the tower (*bashnya*). Their home rapidly became one of the principal meeting-places for the intelligentsia of the capital. The regular meetings known as 'Ivanov's Wednesdays' (*Ivanovskie sredy*) started in September 1905 and were attended by a wide variety of intellectuals and artists; they began late in the evening, continued throughout the night, and broke up in the early hours of the morning.[25] Ivanov's continuing preoccupation with Eros was reflected in the style of these gatherings. Nadezhda Chulkova, the wife of Georgy Chulkov who collaborated with Ivanov in spreading the concept of mystical anarchism, recalls in her memoirs that Ivanov called each meeting a symposium, in imitation of Plato.[26] In Ancient Greece a symposium was an after-dinner drinking-party for conversation and intellectual entertainment. The word was used by Plato as the title of his famous work which describes in the form of a dramatic dialogue the discussion of the nature of Eros which takes place at one such all-night drinking-party. Ivanov's use of the term reflects his desire to continue the ancient Greek tradition of late-night discussions of love.

At these meetings, Chulkova further recalls, Lidiya Dimitrievna was known by the name of Diotima, Socrates's instructress in the art of love whose teachings are reported by Socrates in the *Symposium*. To look the part, she wore a Greek tunic and sandals. Ivanov clearly wished to present his wife to St Petersburg society cast in the role of high priestess of love.

According to Chulkova, Lidiya Dimitrievna also held her own meetings on Tuesdays for women only. She called each meeting a *fias*, a word derived from the Greek *thiasos*, meaning a company of persons dancing and singing in honour of a god, especially of Dionysus.[27] At these gatherings she retained her name of Diotima, and gave others the names of various women from past history, mythology and literature. Lyubov Dmitrievna, Blok's wife, was called Beatrice, and Margarita Sabashnikova, the wife of the poet Voloshin, was known as Primavera, a reference to Botticelli's famous painting.[28] This detail is typical of the way in which Ivanov and Lidiya Dimitrievna merged pagan antiquity with Christianity and Dionysus with Dante in the service of Eros.

Soon, however, Ivanov began to feel a need to introduce a new element into his cult of Eros. He and Lidiya Dimitrievna were no longer roaming Europe in semi-clandestine secrecy, but legally married and running an established household in Russia. Ivanov became concerned lest their marriage should become introverted and lose the element of self-transcendence and suffering essential to Dionysiac mysticism. He therefore decided to introduce a third person into their relationship so as to open it up and bring it closer to his ideal of 'collective spirituality' (sobornost'). This decision, taken jointly with Lidiya Dimitrievna, led to two consecutive relationships in the course of 1906, first with the young poet and future Acmeist, Sergei Gorodetsky, and then with the artist Margarita Sabashnikova.

Ivanov's involvement with Gorodetsky should be considered against the background of his entourage and the atmosphere in which he was living at the time. By the beginning of the twentieth century the works of Oscar Wilde and André Gide had become known in Russia and had generated a wave of interest in the figure of the homosexual artist in Bohemian circles.[29] Many of the artists grouped around the *fin de siècle* journal *Mir iskusstva* were homosexual.[30] Ivanov first came into contact with their ideas through a few individuals who had met over their work for the journal and had subsequently formed a small, intimate association of their own. The association was named 'Hafiz's Tavern' (*Kabachok Gafiza*) in honour of Hafiz, the fourteenth-century Persian poet and mystic celebrated for his learning in mystical theology and indulgence in wine and love, themes which predominated in his poetry. The secret of his appeal lay in his combination of the flesh and the spirit as equally valid means for attaining mystical intoxication.

The key members of this association were the poet Mikhail Kuzmin (1872–1936), the musical critic and amateur composer Valter Nuvel (1871–1949) and the artist Konstantin Somov (1869–1939). Kuzmin's biographer, John Malmstad, has speculated on whether or not 'Hafiz's Tavern' was a homosexual club. Although he concludes that this is unlikely, given the danger of such an open association, it was nevertheless a group in which homosexuals were prominent.[31]

Ivanov's association with the group dates from 18 January 1906 when Nuvel brought Kuzmin to one of the gatherings at the tower.[32] An important friendship developed out of this meeting; Ivanov and Kuzmin shared many academic and cultural interests, particularly in Ancient Rome and early Christianity and in medieval and Renaissance Italy. Kuzmin was one of the few people in Ivanov's entourage who could match the older poet's erudition and scholarship.[33]

Ivanov took part in the evenings organized by the disciples of Hafiz or 'Hafizites' (*gafizity*) as he termed them. For him these were essentially a continuation of his own Platonic tradition of symposia with an additional touch of Oriental colour. Not surprisingly, he interpreted Hafiz in the light of his own Dionysiac and Solovyovian beliefs. This syncretic approach had an important precedent; in 1885 Vladimir Solovyov translated eleven love poems by Hafiz, and included these alongside his original verse in each subsequent edition of his poetry. In this way Hafiz came to form part of the Sophiological tradition. Ivanov was aware of this link and drew attention to it many years later: 'I very much regret that I do not know Persian. All Persian poets, members of the Sufi sect, strive to join heaven to earth. It was not without reason that Vladimir Solovyov so loved Hafiz and translated him.'[34]

In honour of the second meeting of the circle, Ivanov and Kuzmin both composed special poems, headed 'To the friends of Hafiz. The second evening supper [*vecherya*], 8 May 1906 in Petro-baghdad'.[35] In one of these poems, 'The Meeting of the Guests' ('*Vstrecha gostei*') Ivanov addresses his companions in Hafiz by a series of code-names current among the initiate of the group. These are worth mentioning because they reflect the esoteric image which the group was trying to project. Ivanov had two names: Hyperion and Rumi. The first is taken from Hölderlin's novel *Hyperion* and refers to its hero, an idealist Greek youth who falls in love with a Greek girl, Diotima, the epitome of beauty. Lidiya Dimitrievna's code-name of Diotima, also used in the poem, thus acquires a dual resonance, deriving both from Plato's *Symposium* and from Hölderlin's *Hyperion*.[36] The second of Ivanov's names, Rumi, refers to Jalal al-Din, a Persian dervish and mystic poet of the thirteenth century who came from Rumi.

Kuzmin was also known by two names, often hyphenated and combined into one, as in this poem: Antinous-Charicles. Antinous was a youth of extraordinary beauty and a favourite of the Emperor Hadrian.[37] Charicles is the name of the hero of a long poem dedicated to Nuvel which Kuzmin composed in 1904. Set in Ancient Rome, the poem introduces the themes of homosexuality and sorcery. Its partly autobiographical characteristics led Kuzmin to be associated with its hero.[38]

Nuvel is referred to as Petronius, one of Nero's favourites, the director of the imperial pleasures and reputed author of the *Satyricon*, a work which combines licentious descriptions of sexual orgies and banquets with learned discourses on literature. In his diary Ivanov refers to Nuvel as Renouveau, alluding to his role as a 'renewed', 'nouvel' Petronius.[39] Nuvel is also addressed in the poem as the Corsair, the hero of Byron's poem of the same name.

Finally, Somov the artist is called Apelles, a Greek court artist of Alexander the Great, and Aladin, presumably an allusion to the magical sorcery of his work.[40]

This eclectic atmosphere was the prelude and background to Ivanov's relationship with Sergei Gorodetsky (1884–1967). Gorodetsky first visited the tower at the end of 1905. In his memoirs he recalled that Blok wished to protect him from Ivanov's Wednesdays which he did not attend until he was taken by the poet Vladimir Pyast. He evoked the atmosphere vividly: candles, Lidiya Dimitrievna in her Greek tunic, long discussions of mystical love and of the cult of Dionysus. He read out some of his poetry and was reminded of the behaviour of the Khlysts, a Russian mystical sect given to the practice of ecstatic rites.[41]

Ivanov welcomed Gorodetsky into his circle and took him under his wing as a young protégé (Gorodetsky was eighteen years his junior). Ivanov clearly wished to model his relationship with the younger poet on the Platonic ideal of Eros, casting himself in the role of spiritual teacher and Gorodetsky in that of disciple. He taught Gorodetsky Greek, initiated him into the mysteries of Dionysiac mysticism, and instructed him in the craft of poetry.[42] However, although Gorodetsky's ideas were strongly influenced by Ivanov at this stage, he nevertheless retained a certain distance and independence of spirit; this mixture of involvement and ironic detachment comes across clearly in a description of an all-night discussion of sex held at the tower and chaired by Berdyaev which he sent to Blok in June 1906.[43]

The development of Ivanov's relationship with Gorodetsky from this point can be traced from the diary and letters which he wrote from 1 June to 18th August 1906.[44] Ivanov described his diary as the record of one of the major turning-points of his life, or, ironically, as the 'bulletin' of his 'ravings'. It was a very intense period in his life, one of 'unprecedented suffering and happiness of an unprecedented completeness' (*SS* II, 752). It is, however, extremely difficult to form an objective assessment of exactly what happened, since no other sources are available. Further speculation is futile, and the following account is therefore limited to reproducing Ivanov's version of events.

For Ivanov the affair with Gorodetsky clearly represented a conscious attempt to implement certain theoretical ideas and to overcome his increasing sense of loneliness and isolation from his entourage. These feelings are frequently noted by him in his diary; possibly, after his return from Russia, he was having to face up to the fact that he was considerably older than most of the members of his circle and came from a completely different background.

In the first entry, dated 1 June, Ivanov records that his decision to start a diary may well have been prompted by the examples of Charicles and Renouveau (Kuzmin and Nuvel). He comments on the gap which divides him from the other 'Hafizites' who attack him for being a 'moralist' full of internal contradictions. He also expresses a constant preoccupation with the question of whether people are truly alive or 'dead'; by this he appears to mean a person's ability to truly *live* by his ideas. He worries that Kuzmin is 'dead', regrets that his step-son Seryozha is 'dead', given his own feeling of Eros towards youths, and finally raises the question as to whether he himself is not 'dead'. His conclusion that 'faith without deeds is dead' seems to anticipate his later decision to take action to allay his fears that he is 'dead' (*SS* II, 744–5).

On 3 June he refers to his and his wife's deep sense of loneliness amidst people (*SS* II, 746). Over a week later he relates a lengthy night-time conversation with Nuvel about homosexual love which included an account of the latter's amorous adventures. In this context Nuvel attacked him for being a dead carrier of an ideology which he failed to practise. Ivanov responded by referring to his latent struggle with the 'demonic influence' of Kuzmin, and spoke of the 'parallelism of sexuality and genius in collective life' and of art as a 'sphere saturated with sexual feeling'. At the end of this entry he recalls an earlier meeting and night-time walk with Gorodetsky along the Neva embankment, and Gorodetsky's 'sweet kiss of farewell' (*SS* II, 747–8).

The poet's interest in homosexual love was further stimulated the following day on 13 June when Kuzmin read out part of his diary to the assembled company at the tower.[45] Ivanov was extremely impressed, and regarded the diary as a work of art. He saw Kuzmin as the 'pioneer of a coming age' when homosexual love would become widespread and accepted, and the function of sex would no longer be viewed as purely reproductive. In his opinion homosexuality was 'inextricably linked with humanism', but should remain associated with heterosexual love so as not to become narrowly exclusive and sterile. He concludes that Kuzmin's diary was a 'lecture édifiante' which enabled him to understand his own feelings more clearly. The reading was predictably followed by a long discussion on the subject of sex (*SS* II, 749–50).

A few days later, Ivanov's painful sense of loneliness reached a new climax; he entered in his diary:

The fifth evening supper of Hafiz (without Gorodetsky). –
I turn to you, o Hafizites. My heart and lips, eyes and ears have turned to you. And here I stand alone among you. So it is, my loneliness is alone with me among you.
So much on the Hafizites. And now not about them. The result of an entire phase of my life going by under the sign of 'collective spirituality' [*sobornost'*] stands out clearly: I am alone, perhaps as never before.

(*SS* II, 751–2)

After one more entry on 17 June, there is a break in the diary which lasts for two months. In the middle of June Lidiya Dimitrievna went abroad to join her children in Switzerland. During her two-month absence, Ivanov wrote sixteen letters to her, and these became his diary for that period, recording the progression of his relationship with Gorodetsky throughout the summer.

From the start Ivanov viewed his relationship with Gorodetsky as a continuation of a pattern set by his relationship with Lidiya Dimitrievna. In a letter of 9 July he compared his feelings of amorous excitement towards Gorodetsky with the beginning of his affair with Lidiya in Florence; later he wrote that he saw Gorodetsky as a mask of Dionysus, but complained that Gorodetsky had told him that he could not love him because he was a man (*SS* II, 758–9).

The climax of the affair occurred on 16 August, immediately before Lidiya Dimitrievna's return from Switzerland. On the previous evening Ivanov took up his diary once more and noted his desire to enter the room in which Gorodetsky was spending the night. He lacked the courage to do so however. The next morning Gorodetsky told him that he would have left immediately if Ivanov had opened his door. He is however tender and affectionate, and assures Ivanov that he loves him more than any other man, but cannot truly love him because of his preference for women. On their way to lunch they read a letter from Lidiya Dimitrievna expressing feelings of envy and the fear that Ivanov is estranged and no longer needs her.

The entry ends with a description of a moment of physical closeness which took place later that evening:

I meet Seryozha at the door ... He is light-hearted and affectionate. He allows himself to be undressed and watches himself in the mirror while I give him a brief lecture on the aesthetics of his body. I persuade him to lie down with me and in the darkness feel at first that I am dying as I embrace him. Then he occasionally responds fleetingly to my kisses, allows me moments of ecstasy. Then he either sleeps or dozes; while I am dying. There is nothing sweeter ... If only he loved me. And yet he *does* love me, whatever he says and however he behaves.

Pathetic notes in which I fail to record a thousandth part of what I am living through. (SS II, 753)

The diary ends two days later on a note of eager impatience awaiting Lidiya Dimitrievna's return. On 21 August she arrived back in St Petersburg and was met at the station by both Ivanov and Gorodetsky. She noted in her diary that she found Gorodetsky's presence unpleasant, but was nevertheless attracted by the new 'richness' which it brought (SS II, 755)

This 'richness' took the form of a series of poems which Ivanov wrote after his wife's return to commemorate the affair. They were first published at the beginning of 1907 in Ivanov's third collection of verse, appropriately entitled *Eros*.[46] The book opens with a poetic address which describes the affair as a new spring which 'darkened' the poet's life – a reference perhaps to a resurrection of the Dionysiac spirit, carrying within it seeds of death as well as ecstasy:

ТЫ, ЧЬЕ ИМЯ ПЕЧАЛИТ СОЗВУЧНОЮ СЕРДЦУ СВИРЕЛЬЮ,

    ЗНАЕШЬ, КОМУ Я СВИВАЛ, ИВОЙ УВЕНЧАН, ТВОЙ МИРТ

ОТ КОЛЫБЕЛИ ОСЕННЕЙ ЛУНЫ ДО ВТОРОГО УЩЕРБА,

    В ГОД, КОГДА НОВОЙ ВЕСНОЙ ЖИЗНЬ ОМРАЧИЛАСЬ МОЯ.

MCMVI (SS II, 362)

YOU WHOSE NAME AROUSES SORROW LIKE THE SOUND OF A REED-PIPE
   CONSONANT TO THE HEART,
      KNOW FOR WHOM I WREATHED, CROWNED WITH WILLOW, YOUR MYRTLE
FROM THE CRADLE OF THE AUTUMN MOON UNTIL THE SECOND WANING,
   IN THE YEAR WHEN MY LIFE WAS DARKENED BY A NEW SPRING.

   MCMVI

The first poem in this collection, 'Snake' ('*Zmeya*' – *SS* II, 363), is
an erotic address dedicated to Diotima, and serves to emphasize the
continuing primacy of Lidiya Dimitrievna's role in Ivanov's cult of
Eros. Many of the other poems are connected with Gorodetsky.
Some, such as 'The Invocation of Bacchus' ('*Vyzyvanie Vakkha*' –
SS II, 368–9) portray him as a mask of Dionysus:

> Чаровал я, волхвовал я,
> Бога-Вакха зазывал я   (*SS* II, 368)

> I enchanted, I made magic,
> I called for Bacchus the god to come

Others such as 'Symposium' ('*Simposion*' – *SS* II, 375–6) relate the
theme of the collection to the Platonic tradition. In some poems,
such as 'The Architect' ('*Zodchii*') and 'The Crater' ('*Krater*' – *SS*
II, 380–1), Ivanov refers quite explicitly to his attempt to create a
sacred union of three for the worship of Eros; in 'The Architect',
for example, he writes:

> Я башню безумную зижду
> Высоко над мороком жизни,
> Где трем нам представится вновь,
> Что в древней светилось отчизне,
> Где нами прославится трижды
> В единственных гимнах любовь.

> I am building a mad tower
> High up above the gloom of life,
> Where that which shone forth in the ancient homeland
> Will appear to the three of us once again,
> Where love shall be thrice glorified
> By us in unique hymns.

Addressing the god Eros he concludes with the following wish:

> И сплавь огнежалым перуном
> Три жертвы в алтарь триедин!   (*SS* II, 380)

> And fuse with a fire-tipped thunderbolt
> Three sacrifices into a triune alter!

This last poem illustrates the poet's attempt to integrate the Dionysiac cult of a sacrificial–ecstatic erotic experience into a Christian framework by describing the triple sacrifice in terms evocative of the Trinity.

By the end of October 1906, the Gorodetsky episode was clearly over.[47] Ivanov and Lidiya Dimitrievna were not, however, ready to renounce their theoretical ideal; they decided to make a second attempt at enriching their relationship by introducing a third person, and this time turned their attention to a woman.

Margarita Sabashnikova (1882–1974) was the sister of the publisher Mikhail V. Sabashnikov and the first wife of the poet Maksimilian Voloshin. She and her husband were both admirers of Ivanov's poetry. By late October 1906 they were living in the tower on the floor below Ivanov and his wife.[48] As in the case of Gorodetsky, Ivanov began to teach his new protégée Greek and instructed her in the art of poetry.[49] Deschartes argues on the basis of an entry in Ivanov's diary dated 29 June 1909 ('my love was in the rhythm of 3, not 2 – fortunately the marriage union [brak] did not take place' – SS II, 778) that the relationship never developed beyond the realm of dreams and poetic fantasy.[50] However, it seems clear from other entries in the diary that it contained a strong erotic element. On 26 August 1909, for example, Ivanov records a long, intimate conversation with Gorodetsky: 'I was intimate with him about myself as, perhaps, never before. I spoke openly about Margarita, omitting only the sensual aspect' (SS II, 795–6).

The affair received its poetic expression in a cycle of seventeen sonnets entitled 'Golden Veils' ('Zolotye zavesy'), first published in 1907 in an anthology produced by Ivanov's publishing house 'Oræa'.[51] This volume contained contributions from a number of writers and poets, including members of Ivanov's immediate circle – L. Zinoveva-Annibal, M. Sabashnikova, M. Voloshin, S. Gorodetsky and M. Kuzmin. It opened and closed with poems by Ivanov, and the cycle 'Golden Veils' was significantly printed immediately after Sabashnikova's contribution.

As with the Gorodetsky poems in Eros, the continuing importance of Lidiya Dimitrievna was emphasized by the inclusion in the cycle of a sonnet on Lidiya's name, bearing the dedication 'Ad Lydiam' (*SS* II, 388–9). Apart from one other poem,[52] all the remaining sonnets in the cycle are connected with Sabashnikova. Although they do not carry an explicit dedication, the association is clear from internal textual evidence, and Margarita's name is actually mentioned at the end of the ninth sonnet in the cycle.[53] In a number of the poems, discussed in chapter 5, Ivanov makes use of Dantesque motifs for the description of Eros.

Death of L. D. Zinoveva-Annibal and marriage to V. Shvarsalon (1907–13)

Throughout the winter of 1906–7 Lidiya Dimitrievna suffered from poor health. For a time she went into hospital, and during her absence the Wednesday gatherings were suspended. By early January 1907 she was home again, and for a short period the meetings resumed.[54] In the summer she left St Petersburg with Ivanov and went to live at Zagore, a village near Lyubavichi in the province of Mogilyov. An epidemic of scarlet fever broke out in the neighbouring settlement. Lidiya Dimitrievna caught the infection while helping to nurse sick children, and died within seven days, on 17 October 1907. At the end of the month Ivanov and his step-daughter Vera brought her body back to St Petersburg to be buried.[55]

Lidiya Dimitrievna's death marked a major turning-point in Ivanov's life. Sabashnikova, as the third person in the triangle, no longer had a role to play, a fact which she was apparently slower to appreciate than Ivanov. Their relationship was finally ended by Ivanov with some difficulty in the summer of 1909.[56] By this date Ivanov was already obsessed with the idea that he should marry his step-daughter Vera as a means of continuing his relationship with Lidiya. Vera was the daughter of Lidiya's first marriage to Konstantin Shvarsalon, and was seventeen at the time of her mother's death. There are already clear hints at the nature of Ivanov's feelings for her in his diary of 1908. In the first entry, for example, dated 13 June, he wrote that he longed for Vera with 'all the passion' of his 'avid affection', and two days later he recorded a dream in which Lidiya appeared to be offering Vera to him (*SS* II, 771–2). By the summer of 1909 these feelings had become more explicit. On numerous occasions Ivanov heard Lidiya's voice

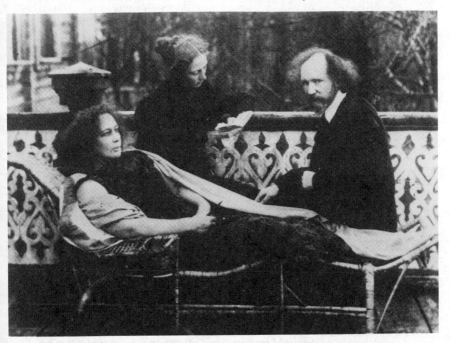

2 Vyacheslav Ivanov, Lidiya Zinoveva-Annibal and Vera, Zagore,
October 1907

speaking to him, urging him to take her daughter as her gift to him
to further their relationship. Often he transcribed her words in a
trance. In some of these entries Vera is referred to by the code-
name of Dorothea (from the Greek δωρα Θεων, 'gifts from the
gods'). On 28 June, for example, Ivanov noted in his diary:

L. said to me: 'Your one duty is Dorothea. She must form a rose in the
cross of our love.'
    I am hurrying to come to you to be together with you. Dorothea is my
gift her living body is for you. Lidiya. Ora Sempre.   (*SS* II, 777)[57]

The following summer, in 1910, Ivanov travelled to Rome to
pursue his research on the religion of Dionysus. He was joined by
Vera who had been studying in Athens under the supervision of
Professor Zelinsky, the Russian classicist. In Rome, the city where
the poet's relationship with Lidiya Dimitrievna had taken a decisive turn fifteen years earlier, Ivanov and Vera decided to follow

the injunctions of Lidiya's voice and link their lives together as man and wife.[58]

Nadezhda Chulkova has left an interesting account in her memoirs of a visit which she and her husband paid to Ivanov and Vera in Rome at this time. In October Chulkov sent Ivanov a postcard of Giotto's portrait of Dante from Florence, announcing his intention of coming to Rome. Ivanov replied warmly, and the visit took place soon after.[59] It is clear from Chulkova's account that she disapproved of the new situation:

He [Ivanov] invited us to dine at his favourite trattoria. Over dinner he drank a fair amount of wine and became tipsy. Vera looked at him reproachfully when he became too animated in conversation. It was 17 October (Old Style) – the third anniversary of the death of his wife and Vera's mother – Lidiya Dimitrievna. But none of us mentioned her name during the meal. It seemed to me that Vera was behaving more like a friend with Vyacheslav Ivanovich than like a daughter with her step-father. And Vyacheslav Ivanovich sometimes let slip ironic little comments aimed at Vera. I felt grieved and pained. We had already heard in Russia that Vyacheslav Ivanovich was marrying Vera.[60]

In November 1910, Ivanov and Vera returned to St Petersburg. They left again in 1912 for Switzerland and France. Vera was expecting a child, and in July she gave birth to a son, Dimitry.[61] Ivanov's fifth collection of poems, *Tender Mystery* (*Nezhnaya taina*), written during the summer of 1912 in Savoie, commemorates the mystery of this new life, born from death. It was the sequel to *Cor Ardens*, a substantial work published in two parts in 1911, reflecting the development of events in the poet's life between 1904 and 1910.

Towards the end of 1912, Ivanov and Vera moved to Rome for almost a year.[62] In the spring of 1913 they travelled to Livorno where they were married in the same Greek Orthodox church by the priest who had married Ivanov and Lidiya Dimitrievna in 1899. Apparently the Russian synodal church would not have agreed to sanctify their marriage. On this occasion, however, the Maenad's wreath of wool and vine leaves was replaced by a simple gilt wreath.[63]

In the autumn of 1913 Ivanov and Vera returned to Russia. They settled in Moscow rather than in St Petersburg. Seven years later, on 8 August 1920, Vera died from ill-health and hunger in Moscow. Ivanov spent the next four years at the University of Baku and then emigrated to Italy in 1924.[64] He never remarried.

From this outline it becomes clear just how closely Ivanov's experience mirrored the theoretical ideal of mystical love which he espoused. He applied the general principles of both the Dionysiac and the Solovyovian systems to his own life, regarding the experience of Eros as the heart of mysticism, and human relationships as the primary means of embodying this spiritual ideal in reality. This approach informed his relationship with Lidiya Dimitrievna; it was also the inspiration behind his decision to embark on affairs with Gorodetsky and Sabashnikova, and eventually to marry Vera.

Furthermore, each of these individual experiences of Eros was understood by Ivanov in terms of the Dionysiac and Solovyovian categories of ecstasy and sacrifice. The pattern was set by his relationship with Lidiya Dimitrievna. This developed from an initial experience of ecstasy, at first Nietzschean and chaotic in character, but subsequently absorbed into a Christian context through a sense of sacrificial suffering, and eventually sanctified in marriage. The excess of life contained in the original experience of ecstasy resolved itself in death; but this in turn led to a renewal of life through Lidiya Dimitrievna's daughter, Vera, who became Ivanov's third wife.

Ivanov's relationship with Vera moved through the same cycle of ecstasy, death and new life (the son born from their marriage). His affairs with Gorodetsky and Sabashnikova also reenacted the pattern of ecstasy leading to sacrificial death, although here the death was a metaphorical one – the death of the relationship – rather than the actual death of the beloved person. All four relationships fell outside the framework of conventional Christian morality; like Ivanov's Dionysiac ideal, they were a purely mystical method, not bound by ordinary moral strictures.

EROS AND AMOR

It is not difficult to see how Ivanov was able to relate the understanding of the cyclical nature of love which he formed on the basis of his experience to the account which Dante gives of his relationship with Beatrice in the *Vita Nuova*; this also follows a cycle of initial ecstasy leading through suffering and death to new spiritual love.

However, the fact that Ivanov was approaching Dante from the standpoint of an ideal formed of Dionysiac and Solovyovian elements meant that a certain amount of distortion of Dante's text inevitably took place. He tended to take up Dantesque images and infuse them with Dionysiac and Solovyovian content; sometimes this meant divesting them of features which were incompatible with the teachings of Dionysus or Solovyov, or adapting them in order to integrate them into a new context.

Specific examples of this process of adaptation, drawn from Ivanov's poetry and translations of Dante, will be considered below in the second part of this study. At this stage, however, it will be useful first to define the main areas of difference between Ivanov's and Dante's concepts of mystical love, and to consider in general terms how Ivanov's attempt to reconcile these differences affected his presentation of Dante. This will establish an overall framework determining the basic patterns of distortion which the individual examples will later be seen to reflect.

The difference between the Dionysiac concept of Eros which Ivanov adopted and Dante's concept of Amor or mystical love is a matter of crucial importance, for the precise way in which mystical love is defined determines the character of its natural outcome, the mystic journey. The Dionysiac concept of Eros was deeply rooted in sexual love. Accordingly, it is a cyclical, recurrent experience or method, leading from ecstasy through sacrifice to death and then to new life and renewed ecstasy; it describes a series of concentric deepening circles rather than a linear journey with a clearly defined beginning and end.

Dante's Amor differs from these intrinsic characteristics of Eros in two fundamental ways, both in its relation to sexual love and in the resulting character of the mystic journey which it inspires.

Mystical love and sexual love

The first of these points of difference should be considered within the wider context of the traditional Christian attitudes which Dante shared. The association between sexual and mystical love can be traced back to the Christian tradition of allegorical interpretations of the Song of Songs. This anthology of love poems, attributed to Solomon and his beloved, the Shulamite, describes the sexual love of the Shulamite for her lover; it has been understood by Christian commentators since Origen as an allegory of the mystical love of the individual soul or of the church for God.

This reading passed on to the Latin-speaking world where it received its most classic exposition in the writings of the twelfth-century monk and mystic, St Bernard of Clairvaux, on the Song of Songs. Through St Bernard the image of sexual union between the bride and her lover to describe the spiritual marriage of the soul with God became widespread and passed into the medieval and later tradition of mystical writings. For example, in the sixteenth century, St Teresa of Avila and St John of the Cross both made much use of sexual imagery in their accounts of their mystical experiences. St John of the Cross's major work, the *Spiritual Canticle*, is a poem based on the idea of the Song of Songs; it is constructed as a dialogue between lover and beloved, and the stages of seeking, courtship and consummation are taken as images for the stages of purgation, illumination and union of the mystic way.

However, although Christian writers made use of the language and images of sexual love to describe the soul's mystical love of God, they did not establish a relationship of identity or a causal link between these two phenomena such as Ivanov would have. On the contrary, they regarded the two forms of love as of quite disparate orders.

Dante followed the tradition established by St Bernard. His admiration for the saint is clear from his portrayal of him in the last cantos of *Paradiso*. St Bernard is his guide during the final stages of his journey in the Empyrean, and prays directly to the Virgin Mary for Dante to be granted his culminating vision of the Holy Trinity (*Par.* xxxi-xxxiii). Like St Bernard Dante is careful to maintain the distinction between sexual and mystical love.[65] Although his love for Beatrice is the initial impulse which causes him to embark on his mystic journey, it is no more than a stepping-stone leading to the pure love of God;[66] it is never presented as an analogous type of experience and Dante clearly did not perceive any innate affinity between the nature of sexual and mystical love. Beatrice's death makes the purely spiritual nature of his love for her quite explicit; he loves the divine spark which is inherent in her, not her physical person.

Dante presents a clear exposition of the relationship between physical love and the mystic love of God in the central cantos of *Purgatorio* (xvi-xvii). Here love is defined as the cause or motive of *all* actions, whether good or bad (*Purg.* xvii, 103–5 and xviii,

14–15). This provides a very general basis for the association of physical and spiritual love. However, Dante qualifies his statement with an important distinction between two types of love. First, there is man's love of the primal good, or of his Creator, God. At the moment of his creation, the human soul is endowed with a natural love of its Creator to whom it desires to return. This desire is the feeling of mystical love or Amor, the love of the primal good, the only true source of lasting satisfaction, peace and rest for the soul (*Purg.* xvi, 85–90 and xvii, 127–9).

The second type of love is the love of secondary goods, of people or of material things. This love is of an entirely different order. It is a potential source of sin if it in any way distracts the soul from the love of the primal good. It must therefore be strictly controlled and measured (*Purg.* xvii, 91–102 and 133–5).

For this purpose man has been endowed with 'the faculty that counsels' (*Purg.* xviii, 62) or 'free will' (*Purg.* xvi, 71). He possesses both an inherent knowledge of the primal good (and hence the ability to distinguish between good and evil), and the faculty of free choice to determine the course which his love shall follow.

There is clearly therefore a fundamental difference between Dante's attitude and Ivanov's view of sexual love as the essence of mystical love. Dante drew a sharp dividing line between the two types of love. In his view, sexual love, coming within the category of love of secondary goods, is not only quite distinct from the mystical love of the primal good, but may even impede it; it is therefore only admissible if subject to a strict system of moral discipline.

This principle is well illustrated by the example of Francesca and Paolo, the adulterous lovers who are punished for the sin of excessive sexual love in the second circle of the *Inferno*, together with the other 'carnal sinners, who subject reason to desire' (*Inf.* v, 38–9). Because they failed to control their lust they are condemned to eternal torment and forever cut off from the knowledge and love of God.

This firm demarcation between sexual and mystical love is so fundamental to Dante's thought that it is embodied in the very structure of his journey in the *Commedia*. Dante cannot begin his ascent through the heavenly spheres of Paradise until he has purged himself of the sin of sexual love by passing through a wall of fire on the final terrace of Mount Purgatory. In other words, his mystical love of God can only be perfected *after* he has cleansed himself of sexual love.

Mystical love and moral discipline

The second, closely related area of difference concerns Ivanov's and Dante's views of the mystic journey determined by love. It follows from Dante's understanding of the correct relationship between love of the primal good and love of secondary goods that all love must be governed by moral choice. Since man is endowed with the ability to conform his love of lesser goods to his love of the primal good, his natural desire for mystic union with God, the source of the primal good, must carry with it a moral dimension. This was the foundation of the moral system of the Middle Ages which Dante inherited from Aquinas.

The mystic journey is therefore always at the same time a moral journey. This is reflected in the traditional Christian division of the mystic journey of the soul into three successive stages, the Purgative, the Illuminative and Unitive. The first stage of the spiritual life requires the purgation or purification of the soul in order to prepare it for illumination and union. This involves the eradication of bad habits and the cleansing through repentance from past sins.

In the *Commedia* the mystic and moral journeys are inextricably bound together. Moral discipline is an intrinsic part of Dante's mysticism because love is defined as a moral as well as a mystic category, the root of sin as well as of mystic aspirations. In *Inferno* Dante is obliged to acquire a full understanding of the various deformations of the soul's capacity to love which constitute sin. Then, in *Purgatorio*, he must purge himself completely of all evil tendencies. On each of the seven terraces of Mount Purgatory, one of the seven P's (from the Latin *peccatum*, 'sin') representing the seven deadly sins is removed from his brow. Only then may he begin his ascent through the different degrees of blessedness represented by each of the spheres of Paradise.

The existence of this moral factor is undoubtedly the single most important element which distinguishes Dante's Amor from Ivanov's understanding of Eros. In an article on mysticism written in 1896 for the Brockhaus and Efron encyclopaedia, Vladimir Solovyov underlined the importance of this factor as the main feature which set orthodox medieval mysticism apart from other varieties of mysticism. He began by tracing mysticism back to the mysteries and secret rituals connected with the cult of Dionysus in Ancient Greece. Pursuing his subject through the ages, when he came to the period of medieval mysticism, he drew a sharp distinction between what he termed orthodox and heretical branches of mysticism. Orthodox mysticism insisted on the indispensability of certain moral conditions for the fulfilment of the soul's mystic journey towards union with God. This journey could only proceed by stages (Solovyov named the purgative, illuminative and unitive stages discussed above), and even the highest degree of mystic communion with God could not absolve the soul from the observance of the lower commandments of a moral order.

Solovyov further pointed out that the heretical tendency, unlike orthodox mysticism, had absorbed pagan and pantheistic elements into its teaching and had taken over from the Gnostics the principle that all forms of experience are equally valid for the attainment of mystic perfection; everything is allowed, and no moral strictures are placed upon man's aspirations.[67]

Solovyov has pinpointed the area which is at the heart of the difference between Ivanov's Dionysiac Eros and Dante's Amor. Dante was a representative of the orthodox branch of medieval mysticism (he followed the teachings of St Bonaventura, cited by Solovyov as one of the major representatives of the orthodox tradition).[68] Ivanov on the other hand, as a follower of Dionysus, did not regard the moral dimension as an essential element of mystical experience. This attitude emerges clearly from the concluding section of his articles on the religion of Dionysus. Here he writes that all true forms of mysticism and religion originate in the essence of Dionysiac mysticism – in the individual's rejection of self in order to find union with the divine spirit of the universe. The experience of ecstasy constitutes the essence of all religious experience, and any form of fixed dogmatic teaching is intrinsically alien to this essence. The Greeks generally resisted all kinds of religious dogmatism, and, as Ivanov continues to argue, there is even less ground for trying to ascribe a fixed system of morals to their religion. Although ethical systems have always, if only in potential, existed alongside religion, they do not form part of its essence. The link between morals and religion is an extrinsic and consequently weak one. According to Ivanov, the later tendency to introduce morals into religion coincided with the first symptoms of religious decline. For similar reasons, the Orphic mystics' attempts to work out a doctrine of retribution for the after-life did not meet with much success. The only form of purgation which the Greeks would accept was a purely mystical ritualistic type of purification, achieved through cathartic mysteries, but quite independent of any dogmatic structure of moral values.

Ivanov's attitude to the link between morals and religion can best be summed up in his own words: 'And so, therefore, morals also do not belong to the essence of religion; for the Greeks were highly religious.'[69]

Distortions of Dante

Given these views, one might expect Ivanov to condemn Dante for upholding a religious system which was closely linked to a fixed moral structure. However, Ivanov's tendency was to redefine rather than to reject elements which were incompatible with his spiritual ideal. He wished to see in Dante and in the Renaissance a continuation or reaffirmation of the original Dionysiac spirit. He therefore simply ignored or adapted those elements of Dante's thought which – as Solovyov pointed out – clearly distinguished Dante's branch of orthodox medieval mysticism from its pagan or gnostic predecessors.

This tendency is clearly illustrated by the various examples of Ivanov's use of Dantesque images analysed in the next chapter. In general, these reflect two major types of distortion, resulting directly from the two fundamental areas of difference between Ivanov's and Dante's concepts of mystical love. The first of these concerns the relationship between mystical love and physical love. Here Ivanov tends to ignore Dante's clear differentiation between the two types of love and condemnation of excessive sexual love. He may, for example, take up images connected with the carnal sin of Francesca and Paolo and lend these a mystic dimension. Or he may make use of Dantesque images associated with Amor, but divest them of their moral dimension, thereby presenting Amor in a Dionysiac light as a cyclical or chaotic force undifferentiated from Eros.

The second type of distortion affects Dantesque images connected with the mystic journey. Here again Ivanov suppresses the moral element in Dante's works. He either ignores the moral structure which underpins Dante's universe – the fixed hierarchy of sins, retribution, purgation and reward – or treats it as a purely mystic category. This is particularly evident in his presentation of Dante's images of sin. In the *Commedia* sin is an area of darkness and spiritual blindness, entirely shut off from the light of grace and leading nowhere. Dante may pass through the *Inferno* as a spectator in order to observe and be warned, but the sinners themselves cannot move; they are doomed to an eternity of uncomprehending torment without issue.

In Ivanov's understanding however, sin is not necessarily just a moral category; it may become a method for transcending the boundaries of the individual self, and a possible first stage of initiation in the mystic journey. Because of its connection with suffering, it may acquire a sacrificial dimension which allows it to be absorbed into the Dionysiac mystic cycle. Its dark demonic qualities then become images of the death which precedes resurrection in the Dionysiac cycle. Dante's images of sin accordingly become more purgatorial than infernal in character. Frequently this is achieved through a deliberate confusion of Dante, the spectator of sin, with Dante, the sinner.

Rings and 'New Masks'

In 1904 Ivanov wrote an essay entitled 'New Masks' as an introduction to a play by his wife, *Rings (Kol'tsa)*.[70] These two works complement each other and provide a most valuable source for understanding the concept of mystical love which Ivanov and his wife developed on the basis of their shared experience; they also illustrate the way in which this concept – when applied to Dante – led to a considerable distortion of the latter's ideas.

Lidiya Dimitrievna began her play in Paris in 1903 during the period when Ivanov was delivering his lectures on the religion of Dionysus.[71] Not surprisingly, it is closely based on the ideas on Dionysiac Eros which her husband was developing at the time in his scholarly work and poetry. Indeed, in many ways it can be read as a dramatization of the spiritual path to be travelled by a person who embraces the principles of Dionysiac Eros.

The action of the play revolves around three principal characters: Aglaya, Aleksei, her husband, and Anna, the wife of Aglaya's dead brother and the mistress of Aleksei. Aglaya is the central character of this triangle, and each of the three acts of the drama records a specific stage in her spiritual development. She is named after one of the three Charites or Graces, daughters of Zeus or Dionysus and friends of the Muses who personified Grace and Beauty and particularly favoured the art of poetry. In Greek 'Aglaia' means 'the bright one', and in the course of the play the radiance or light associated with the heroine's name is shown to have its deepest roots in death and darkness, thus confirming the teaching that Apollonian clarity and order are grounded in Dionysiac dark and chaos.

The first act is set in a sunny room from which the sound of the sea can be heard. Aglaya, blissfully happy, is dressed in white, while Anna is in black. Aglaya attaches some roses to Anna's hair and tries to add some red poppies. Anna resists, and puts the poppies in Aglaya's hair instead. At this point Aglaya recalls a picture of a bird bringing poppies in its beak to the dying Beatrice; she is clearly thinking of the painting by Dante Gabriel Rossetti entitled 'Beata Beatrix', although she does not refer to it by name. The poppies symbolize the knowledge of death into which she is to be initiated.[72]

We learn that Aleksei and Aglaya used to exist in a world of abstract harmony, symbolized by Aleksei counting the stars – an attempt to create order out of cosmic chaos. Anna, however, has introduced Aleksei into the world of passion, referred to as a whirlwind (vikhr'). The significance of these images is hinted at by Anna in a speech to Aleksei: 'You thought that the stars would save you both from the smoky whirlwind of life where the harmony of lines is broken and the circular dance of numbers is a wild dance of death and passion and chance.'[73]

The second act takes place at sunset by the edge of the sea. Aglaya's world of radiant harmony has been shattered by her discovery of Aleksei's infidelity, and she is now roaming by the sea for the fifth day, trying to come to terms with her suffering. She would like to sing her old song, the 'song about fidelity, about simple and faithful love', but her past world has been destroyed and she now refers to her love as 'crucified' (raspyata).[74] She has entered the second stage of the Dionysiac cycle: the initial excess of ecstasy has given way to the experience of sacrificial suffering.

The third and final act unfolds at night on the deck of a ship at sea. Aglaya is clothed in black; through her suffering she has reached a deeper understanding of mystical love and rejected her previous world of closed harmony. Two images are used throughout the play to symbolize the old world: the 'iron ring' and the 'dead mirror'. Aglaya now prays fervently 'that there should be no iron ring for two people, that there should be no dead mirror for the world'.[75]

Aleksei is dying and gives his ring to Aglaya who triumphantly proclaims: 'Here is the marriage of two people, a sacrifice on the flaming altar of universal Love! . . . To the ocean of Love – our rings of love!' As the sun rises Aleksei dies. Aglaya throws their rings into the sea and declares: 'One must not grudge the dear, tight little rings. Let the rings be a gift to the Inflamer!'[76] The old song is lost and a new song has been sung. After a final life-affirming speech Aglaya also dies.

From this brief summary it is plain that Aglaya's spiritual development reflects all the essential elements of the Dionysiac cycle as defined by Ivanov. It is grounded in the experience of sexual love, and embodies the cycle of ecstasy leading through sacrifice to renewed ecstasy. Aglaya must transcend the narrow feeling of earthly love which she holds for Aleksei in order to embrace the wider principle of Dionysiac mystical love. The closed ring of her marriage is broken by the introduction of a third person, and this leads to the experiences of suffering, sacrifice and ultimately of death which enable her to make the transition from sexual love to Dionysiac Eros.

This cycle is evidently closely modelled on Ivanov's and Lidiya Dimitrievna's perception of their own experience. Ivanov regarded their relationship as a stormy Dionysiac renewal which enabled him to break free of the closed ring of his marriage. Many of Aglaya's speeches on love in *Rings* directly echo lines from his poetry. The central metaphor of the ring, for example, is borrowed from his poem 'Suspiria', part of which is quoted as an epigraph to the play:

> Дар золотой в Его бросайте море
> Своих колец:
> Он сохранит в пурпуровом просторе
> Залог сердец . . .   (*SS* 1, 703)

> Throw into His sea the golden gift
> Of your rings:
> He will preserve in the purple expanse
> The hearts' pledge . . .

These lines are later paraphrased by Aglaya in the words quoted above which she pronounces when she throws the rings into the sea. Her formulation of the principle of Dionysiac Eros is also reminiscent of Ivanov's style: 'Life is a flaring up, and death. And from their impulse something new is born.'[77]

In his introductory essay 'New Masks' Ivanov welcomes Lidiya Dimitrievna's play as a return to the true Dionysiac roots of tragedy, and discusses its action in terms of the mystic cycle of ecstasy, sacrifice, death and resurrection. He defines the Dionysiac principle embodied in the play as the 'widening of the individual "I" until it reaches its universal infinity through the deepening of personal suffering' (SS 1, 79), and comments on the way in which this idea is reflected in the transition from the closed room to the open sea. Ordered, harmonious and faithful love such as Aglaya knew at the beginning of the play is like a closed room, shut off from the secrets of the universe. Only through pain or sacrificial suffering can one escape the limitations of this kind of love and gain access to mystical union with the eternal Dionysiac spirit of the universe, symbolized by the wide open sea.

The method illustrated by *Rings* is entirely amoral and independent of any fixed code of ethics. In a speech to Anna, Aglaya explains that it does not matter *how* one lives, as long as one is open to the transforming flame of mystical love. Two people may love each other, or three; everything is equal before love which is the only judge and the only absolute, admitting no other criteria or moral imperatives.[78]

Ivanov dwells on this aspect of the play's meaning at some length, quoting twice from this speech of Aglaya's and from his own poem 'Suspiria' to illustrate the amoral, sacrificial nature of Dionysiac Eros (SS 1, 79–81). In this context he discusses the question of how man, a finite individual, can best transcend his limitations and adopt the method of Dionysiac Eros, and points to the example of Dante's mystic journey as a possible answer:

The Blessed St Francis of Assisi and St Clare were, it seems, in love: and, after casting a glance at each other, they separated so as to sink in the ocean of divine Love. But more often the path to mystical purification leads through Dante's 'dark wood', and the crucifixion of love takes place on the cross of Sin.   (SS II, 81)

Ivanov argues that although some great mystics or saints may be able to transcend personal love through a voluntary act of separation and thereby achieve direct union with the divine spirit of mystical love, this path is only open to a select few. Most people must first pass through a physical stage in which the experience of sin is linked to suffering; in this way their love is 'crucified' (Aglaya's term) and its divine dimension is released. Ivanov identifies this stage of the mystic way with Dante's dark wood, linked to the experience of sinful and suffering love.

And yet Dante's dark wood is an area of sin which, like the *Inferno*, leads nowhere. It would be wrong to deduce from the structure of the *Commedia* that one can only reach Paradise by passing through the dark wood and Hell. At the beginning of the *Commedia*, Dante is entirely *lost* in the dark wood;[79] he is only rescued from it by an act of divine intervention from above, not through any internal cyclical mechanism leading from sin through suffering to purification.

In taking up Dante's image of the dark wood, Ivanov alters its meaning to make it fit within the Dionysiac cycle of a mystic method which is not bound to moral law. He introduces a sacrificial dimension into the experience of sin of which the *selva oscura* is traditionally an emblem. This transforms the experience of sin into a way of the cross, a path of suffering which leads to an ultimate goal. A similar interpretation of the image of the dark wood occurs in Ivanov's poem 'La Selva Oscura', discussed below.

This type of distortion clearly derives from the poet's wish to presente Dante as a model of his syncrétic Dionysiac–Christian ideal. By adapting Dantesque images, Ivanov succeeds in making them reflect the main tenets of Dionysiac Eros: the link with the experience of potentially sinful physical love, and the consequently amoral character of the resulting mystic journey. His interpretation of the image of the dark wood serves to give licence to the experience of sin as the first stage of the mystic journey within a recognized Christian context. Dante's spiritual experience is accordingly assimilated into the framework of the mystic journey determined by Dionysiac Eros, as defined by Ivanov in his writings and illustrated by Lidiya Dimitrievna's play *Rings*.

PART II

TEXTS AND TRANSLATIONS

5

Dantesque images in Ivanov's poetry

PILOT STARS

The opening section of Ivanov's first collection of poems, *Pilot Stars* (1902), is headed 'The Impulse and the Limits' (*Poryv i grani*). As the title suggests, it deals with the twin aspects of the Dionysiac mystic experience: the soul's impulse (*poryv*) or urge to self-transcendence, and the limits (*grani*) which it encounters in its striving to overcome its boundaries. Three poems in this section are of particular interest and deserve detailed discussion: 'The Spirit' ('*Dukh*'), 'La Selva Oscura' and 'At the Coliseum' ('*V Kolizee*'). Each of these poems uses imagery drawn from Dante's *Commedia* to illustrate different aspects of the Dionysiac experience.

'The Spirit'

'The Spirit' ('*Dukh*') is an early poem by Ivanov which treats the subject of mystical love by describing the spiritual journey of the soul through the cosmos. It reads as follows:

> L'Amor che muove il Sole e l'altre stelle
> Dante, *Parad.* XXXIII

Над бездной ночи Дух, горя,
Миры водил Любви кормилом;
Мой дух, ширяясь и паря,
Летел во сретенье светилам.

И бездне – бездной отвечал;
И твердь держал безбрежным лоном;
И разгорался, и звучал
С огнеоружным легионом.

137

Любовь, как атом огневой,
Его в пожар миров метнула;
В нем на себя Она взглянула
И в Ней узнал он пламень свой.   (*SS* i, 518–19)

L'Amor che muove il Sole e l'altre stelle
Dante, *Parad.* xxxiii

Over the abyss of night the Spirit, burning,
Moved the heavenly bodies with the helm of Love;
My spirit, spreading and hovering,
Flew to meet the luminaries.

And it responded to the abyss – with an abyss;
And it held the firmament in its boundless spread;
And it flared up and resounded
With the fire-bearing legion.

Love, like a fiery atom,
Hurled it into the fire of the heavenly bodies;
In it She saw herself –
And in Her it recognized its own flame.

Ivanov has deliberately chosen to place his description of the soul's mystic journey within the framework of Dante's ascent through the heavenly spheres, and to present the moving force behind this journey as Dante's Amor. The epigraph appended to the poem makes this quite explicit from the outset. It is Dante's most celebrated reference to Amor, the final line of the *Commedia* (*Par.* xxxiii, 145). It occurs at the climax of the poet's mystic journey when a vision of the divine spirit behind the universe is granted to him by heavenly grace in a final flash of revelation. At this moment he experiences the feeling that his desire and will to attain this vision are equally balanced and revolved like an evenly spinning wheel by 'the Love which moves the sun and the other stars'.

Kenelm Foster has described this line as one of the clearest expressions in Dante's works of the idea that the soul's natural love of God leads to a kind of union with the universe. He writes: 'Love is "spiritual union", and this "union" with the Creator implies and requires a certain union with his manifestation which is the cosmos.'[1] Dante's journey through the heavenly spheres of Paradise represents a form of spiritual union with the cosmos which culminates in his soul becoming like the stars and planets, a passive vessel filled with and revolved by divine love, the power through which God moves the universe.

The Dantesque context established by the epigraph is then developed by Ivanov in the course of the rest of the poem through further images drawn from the *Commedia*. In the first verse he dwells on the association which Dante made between the love which moves the universe and the Holy Spirit. Following the Christian tradition, Dante regarded love as the principal attribute of the Third Person of the Holy Trinity; indeed, in the *Commedia* he refers to the Holy Spirit simply as the 'primo amore' ('primal love' – *Inf.* III, 6). Ivanov takes up Dante's association in the lines 'the Spirit . . . / Moved the heavenly bodies with the helm of Love' (*Dukh* . . . / *Miry vodil Lyubvi kormilom*). These echo the epigraph and are also a close paraphrase of Dante's lines about 'uno Dio / . . . che tutto 'l ciel move, / . . . con amore' ('one God . . . who . . . moves all the heavens with love' – *Par.* XXIV, 130–3).

These Dantesque lines have been combined by Ivanov with images of Biblical origin. The opening line of the poem echoes the Biblical verse understood by Christian commentators as the first reference to the Holy Spirit: 'And the earth was without form, and void; and darkness was upon the face of the deep. And the Spirit of God moved upon the face of the waters' (*Zemlya zhe byla bezvidna i pusta, i t'ma nad bezdnoyu; i Dukh Bozhii nosilsya nad vodoyu* – Genesis 1.2). In his poem Ivanov has replaced the word 'darkness' (*t'ma*) from his Biblical verse with the word 'night' (*noch'*), following the naming of the darkness as night which occurs a few lines later in the Bible: 'And God called . . . the darkness . . . Night' (*I nazval Bog . . . t'mu noch'yu*). This combination of images serves to emphasize the cosmic dimension of Dante's mystic journey by setting it against the background of the Biblical account of creation.

In the second part of the verse Ivanov changes the subject from the Holy Spirit to his own spirit which he implicitly likens to a bird by using the verbs 'spreading' (*shiryayas'*) and 'hovering' (*parya*), usually associated with the movement of a bird in flight.[2] Here he is echoing an image from the concluding lines of *Paradiso* immediately preceding the epigraph where Dante refers to his own 'penne' ('wings' – *Par.* XXXIII, 139) as a metaphor for the power of his spirit to sustain the final stages of the upward flight.

The general movement of the verse from the divine spirit which moves the universe to the individual pilgrim's spirit rising through the heavenly spheres is also very Dantesque in character. In the opening lines of *Paradiso*, for example, Dante makes a similar transition from the glory of God who moves the universe to the position of his own spirit among the heavenly spheres (*Par.* I, 1–5).

These Dantesque associations are further reinforced by Ivanov's choice of imagery. This is directly based on the two most characteristic types of images used throughout the *Paradiso* to describe the spirits of the blessed: images of light or burning, and of singing. Ivanov's terms 'burning' (*gorya*), 'flared up' (*razgoralsya*), 'with the fire-bearing legion' (*s ogneoruzhnym legionom*), 'fiery atom' (*atom ognevoi*), 'fire of the heavenly bodies' (*pozhar mirov*), 'flame' (*plamen'*) and 'resounded' (*zvuchal*) all echo the vocabulary of *Paradiso*.

Dante's symbolic use of light imagery derives from his association of the Holy Spirit with burning, following the Biblical description of the Holy Spirit descending like fire on the disciples at Pentecost (Acts 2.3). Referring to this event he describes the Holy Spirit as 'l'ardente Spirto' ('the fiery Spirit' – *Par.* XXIV, 138). In *Paradiso* the burning of the Holy Spirit as an expression of its attribute of divine love is transferred to the spirits of the blessed who also burn or radiate light. The reciprocal love of the Creator and His creation is conveyed through the intensity of their burning or radiance. In the sphere of the moon, for example, Piccarda tells Dante that the affections of the spirits of Paradise are 'kindled' ('infiammati') only in the pleasure of the Holy Spirit (*Par.* III, 52–3). Later, in each of the three circles of the sphere of the sun, the spirits are depicted as flashing lights which wheel in circles and sing to express their joy (*Par.* X, 64–6; XIII, 28–9; XIV, 23–4). Dante refers to the lights of the third circle as the 'true sparkling of the Holy Spirit' ('Oh vero sfavillar del Santo Spiro!' – *Par.* XIV, 76).

Ivanov evidently had a special interest in the light imagery of *Paradiso*. His archive in the Manuscripts Department of the Lenin Library contains a number of sheets of notes on the *Commedia*, including a brief comparison of the *Purgatorio* and the *Paradiso* entirely in terms of their light imagery. *Paradiso* is described as follows: 'almost without contours, music, the play and movement of light and fires, and the sparkling of colours; the dancing of flames, the harmonies of the stars'. In another section of the notes dealing specifically with the *Paradiso*, he has copied out certain passages of particular interest. Significantly, most of these are connected with Dante's use of light imagery. They include, for example, the description of Dante's ascent with Beatrice and the comparison of their entry into the sphere of the moon with the way in which a ray of light enters water (*Par.* II, 19–22, 31–45); Ivanov also quotes the passage in which Beatrice explains to Dante how light, flames and love are all an expression of the soul's greater or lesser apprehension of the eternal light (*Par.* V, 1–12).[3]

Ivanov's familiarity with the significance of Dante's light imagery is clearly reflected in 'The Spirit'. The images of light which he uses in this poem all convey the same basic idea as Dante's imagery: the mutual love between the Creator and His creation, between the Holy Spirit (*Dukh*) and the individual spirit (*dukh*). Accordingly the poem describes a full circle; it begins with an evocation of the divine love which informs creation and moves the universe; then it follows the soul's flight through the heavenly spheres; and finally it returns to its point of departure by describing the consummation of the soul's union with the divine love which first set it in motion. The last verse of the poem returns the reader to the ideas of the final passage of *Paradiso* alluded to in the epigraph; with its sense of perfect cosmic balance, it shows that the order of the cosmos is a reflection of the order of divine love; each movement of creation, whether of the cosmic spheres or of an individual soul, is a manifestation of the divine love which moves the universe. The moment of union and of mutual recognition is close to the revelation which Dante experiences at the end of *Paradiso* when his love and divine love become one. It conveys the sensation described by Beatrice to Dante; that each of the spirits of Paradise feels to a greater or lesser extent the eternal breath ('sentir piu e men l'etterno spiro' – *Par.* IV, 36); here 'l'etterno spiro' refers to the Holy Spirit, to God as Love.

If, however, one looks more closely at Ivanov's poem, it is not difficult to see that the basic ideas which it conveys are not inherently Dantesque; they have been clothed in Dantesque imagery, but derive primarily from the Dionysiac and to a lesser extent from the Solovyovian elements of the poet's concept of mystical love.

Typically, it is the cosmic dimension of the epigraph from Dante which Ivanov has chosen to develop as a way of illustrating his own understanding of the essence of Dionysiac mysticism: that the

individual soul (the microcosm) should break forth from its boundaries ('the impulse and the limits') to merge with the cosmos or
divine spirit of the universe (the macrocosm). Writing about Nietzsche in his work on the religion of Dionysus, he defined this state of
religious ecstasy as the 'metaphysical merging with the unity of the
cosmos and with the soul of the suffering world'.[4] It is this principle
of Dionysiac interaction between the microcosm and the macrocosm which forms the true basis of much of the imagery of 'The
Spirit'.

Whereas Dionysiac Eros is a cyclical method, independent of
any dogmatic structure or external authority, Dante's Amor is a
measured force, controlled by divine grace and dependent on a
fixed system of moral purification. Ivanov has taken up Dantesque
images which in their original context reflect these characteristics
of Amor, and absorbed them into the framework of his Dionysiac
ideas. This process of assimilation or transposition has led to
certain types of distortion, deriving directly from the fundamental
differences between the two concepts of mystical love.

One area of divergence relates to the question of the dependence of the individual spirit on divine grace in the mystic journey.
Throughout the *Commedia* Dante emphasizes the complete indispensability of divine grace. At the beginning of his journey he only
manages to escape from the dark wood with the help of divine
intercession. Similarly, at the very end of his journey, he is granted
the strength for his final vision by divine grace; in the concluding
passage of *Paradiso* from which the epigraph to 'The Spirit' is
taken, he stresses the fact that the wings of his spirit were too weak
to be able to sustain the final vision without divine aid.

It follows from Dante's recognition of the total dependence of
the created world on divine grace that the *Commedia* is marked by
a strong sense of hierarchy and fixed structure. Since the movements of the planets as well as of men are controlled by a single
power, Dante's universe is an essentially stable one: his ascent
through the heavenly spheres takes the form of an ordered,
measured progression, each stage of which is controlled by divine
guidance, administered through divinely appointed intermediaries
such as Virgil, Beatrice or St Bernard.

In 'The Spirit', however, the presentation of the mystic journey
is entirely different, corresponding to Ivanov's view of the cyclical,
chaotic nature of Dionysiac Eros. In Lidiya Dimitrievna's play,

Rings, Anna condemned the counting of the stars as a vain pursuit, since the movement of the cosmos can only be grasped in its Dionysiac chaotic essence, not through any fixed abstract system of calculation. Her view closely echoes a passage in Ivanov's work on the religion of Dionysus which conveys the same idea: 'One can measure and reckon the movement of the luminaries without understanding the religious significance of their Dionysiac dance.'[5]

The movement of the spirit and of the planets in Ivanov's poem is much closer to this ideal of a chaotic Dionysiac dance than to Dante's ordered vision. The pilgrim spirit does not rise through the spheres; it is *hurled* (*Ego ... metnula*) into the cosmos. There is no sense of hierarchy or of the humility of the created soul before its Creator. The flight of the spirit is described as a feat of the individual will ('My spirit ... / Flew to meet the luminaries') (*Moi dukh ... / Letel vo sreten'e svetilam*) without reference to the factor of divine grace. The individual spirit and the divine spirit are presented on one level, and this is constantly underlined by structural and verbal parallelisms. Like the cosmos, the individual spirit carries its own infinity or 'abyss' (*bezdna*) within it, and is able to encompass the infinity of the cosmos; this is diametrically opposed to the constant emphasis which Dante places on the inadequacy and limitations of his powers. In this respect 'The Spirit' is far closer to the confident and bold tone of Baudelaire's poem 'Elévation', which also describes the upward flight of the spirit, than to any work by Dante.[6]

In the last verse of his poem Ivanov emphasizes the reciprocal interaction and mutual love between the Creator and the created spirit, and carries these ideas far beyond the implications of the final lines of Dante's *Paradiso*. There Dante's soul was moved by love; the height of its achievement consisted in it becoming a perfectly *passive* vessel to be acted upon by divine love. In Ivanov's poem, by contrast, the individual spirit is the initiator of actions; at the climax of its mystic union with the divine spirit it is qualified by an active verb – 'recognized' (*uznal*) – and held up to divine love as an equal mirror.

Within this general context, it is not surprising that the Dantesque images of light and burning discussed above also have their deepest roots in Ivanov's concept of Dionysiac Eros. In the *Paradiso* Dante reserves these images for the description of the beatitude of the saintly souls whom he encounters; he does not apply

them to himself. In 'The Spirit', however, they are entirely transferred to the relationship between the individual pilgrim's spirit
and the Holy Spirit, and used to evoke the ecstatic experience of
mutual burning which is the essence of Dionysiac Eros.

There are many examples of Dionysiac imagery of light and
burning in the works of both Ivanov and his wife. Lidiya Dimitrievna's play, *Rings*, draws extensively on images of burning flames
and consummation, and Ivanov's poem 'Suspiria' refers to the
spirits who accept the Dionysiac sacrifice as 'seeds ... of the
universal fire' (*vselenskogo pozhara* / ... *semena – SS* I, 703), a
phrase which closely echoes the 'fire of the heavenly bodies'
(*pozhar mirov*) described in 'The Spirit'.

The fundamentally Dionysiac character of Ivanov's burning
imagery is well illustrated by 'Torches' ('*Plamenniki*' – *SS* I,
548–50), a poem from the section of *Pilot Stars* headed 'To Dionysus' which abounds in images of burning stars, suns and spirits. It is
named after an unfinished novel by Lidiya Dimitrievna, and carries
an epigraph from this work which presents a cosmic vision of the
interaction of spirits and divine love in terms closely paralleled by
'The Spirit':

There will be a world, similar to the world of light spirits, each of which
rejoices with its own individual bright impulse. With a bright love they
rejoice amidst the beauty of shining worlds, burning with life – with the
love of one Sun, of one God-Beginning; and in this love the lone impulses
merge together and return to the Beginning-God, to the source of love.
This is a new world and a new round of love, and to this I will say Yes, and
through this Yes it will come into being.   (*SS* I, 548)[7]

This passage shows that the images of burning spirits and love
which are presented in a Dantesque context in 'The Spirit' are in
fact closely related to purely Dionysiac ideals.

Another aspect of the difference between the Dionysiac and
Dantesque concepts of love concerns the moral dimension of the
mystic journey. In Ivanov's poem the pilgrimage of the spirit is
depicted in purely mystic terms, without any reference to the moral
element. Furthermore, there is even a hint at the idea that the
mystic path may lead through darkness as well as light. This can be
seen in particular from the use of the word 'abyss' (*bezdna*), a term
which is uncharacteristic of Dante and carries a distinctly Nietzschean flavour. The idea of the abyss is introduced in a Biblical
context in the first line of the poem, associated with night, the

realm of darkness. It is then taken up again in a quite different context in the first line of the second verse; here we are told that the poet's spirit responds to the abyss of the night, mentioned above, with its own abyss (one assumes also of darkness). This part of the poem is very evocative of Tyutchev's cosmology with its emphasis on cosmic chaos and on the dark abyss of the soul and of the night.[8] The implication is that darkness and night, with their connotations of sinfulness, are a fundamental source of mystic energy.

In this sense 'The Spirit' reads like a poetic illustration of Ivanov's thesis that the deepest roots of mysticism (and therefore of all religion) lie in chaos and darkness. In his work on the religion of Dionysus he wrote that 'the mystic principle in the development of mankind's comprehension of the world is all the more indispensable, vital and true, the more deeply its roots sink into primeval chaos and ancient night'.[9] In 'The Spirit', by placing Dantesque images alongside images of primeval chaos and night, the poet has succeeded in projecting an image of Dante as a mystic of dark and chaotic Dionysiac tendencies, rather than as a traditional Christian thinker bound by the dogma and moral order of the Catholic church. Although the epigraph and imagery of the poem create the impression of a work about Dantesque Amor, it is clearly in fact a poem about Dionysiac Eros. This becomes particularly clear if one compares it to a later poem by Ivanov, 'The Firmament' ('Nebosvod' – CA, SS II, 378–9); here, very similar imagery is used in the context of an explicit address to the god Eros who is described as the force which draws the individual spirit to the 'abyss' (bezdna), 'dark' (mrak), 'whirlwind' (vikhr') and chaos (khaos) of the cosmos.

If the poet's essential subject in 'The Spirit' is Dionysiac Eros, one might well wonder why he chooses to describe it through Dantesque images relating to Amor. The reason undoubtedly lies in his desire to present Dante as an example of his syncretic spiritual ideal, as a proof that Christianity can encompass the essence of Dionysiac mysticism. The creation of poetic texts in which Dantesque images were assimilated into a Dionysiac context served as a way of lending substance to this ideal.

Although the Dionysiac element of Ivanov's spiritual ideal dominates the poem, one can also sense the presence of a few Solovyovian ideas. The 'Spirit' of Ivanov's poem bears a definite resemblance to Sophia who was also likened to a bird and identified with the Holy Spirit hovering over the dark waters at the time of creation by Solovyov in his work on Russia and the universal church. More specifically, Ivanov's description of the interaction of the individual spirit with the Spirit of the universe, although fundamentally Dionysiac, is also related to his understanding of the way in which the individual spirit communicates with Sophia through love. In a later essay on Solovyov he paraphrased the philosopher's ideas on love in terms which are very evocative of the imagery of 'The Spirit'. He wrote that the individual could only transcend his boundaries and dissolve his existence in the wider existence of the other through love: 'The act of love, and only of love, which regards the other not as an object but as a second subject, is an act of faith and of will, an act of life, an act of salvation, a return to the Mother who carries both of us (my *I* and my *you*) in her bosom, a form of communion with the mysterious activity of the World Soul who weaves the single living fabric of the universe's body' (*SS* III, 304).

In the light of this passage Ivanov's poem can be read as a description of the return of an individual spirit to the World Soul, leading to a dissolving of the barriers between the *I* and the *you* (the 'spirit' and the 'Spirit' in Ivanov's terms). It illustrates the way in which the poet drew on Dantesque images to convey a concept of mystical love which was primarily grounded in Dionysiac Eros but also indirectly linked to Solovyov's teaching on the love of Sophia.

In his later prose writings Ivanov returned to the final line of the *Paradiso* which he had chosen as an epigraph to 'The Spirit', and expounded his understanding of its meaning in some detail. These passages are of considerable interest; in many ways they serve as extended prose commentaries on the poem and fulfil the role of the 'scholia' which the literary critic Evgeny Anichkov felt were necessary for a full understanding of Ivanov's poetry.

One of the principal passages of this kind occurs in an important essay of Ivanov's, written in 1912, 'Thoughts on Symbolism' (*SS* II, 604–12). An entire section of this essay is devoted to a detailed analysis of Dante's line. The poet first quotes it, dividing it into three stressed parts – 'L'Amór / che muove il Sóle / e l'altre stélle' – and then comments: 'In this concluding line of Dante's "Paradise" images turn into myth, and wisdom is taught through music' (*SS* II, 607).

The meaning of this statement is then developed. According to Ivanov, the 'music' or rhythm of the line causes it to fall into a natural division between three 'high' points ('Amór', 'Sóle', 'stélle') and two 'low' points ('muove', 'altre'). The 'high' points are bright and blinding and identified with the Apollonian vision; the 'low' points are dark and undefined and linked to Dionysiac chaos: 'In the intervals between the shining outlines of these three ideas, night yawns. Music is embodied in a visible form; the Apollonian vision rises up above the gloom of Dionysiac unrest . . . In this way the starry firmament imprints itself on the soul, boundlessly and masterfully' (*SS* ii, 607).

The pilgrim's soul is lost in contemplation of this vast cosmic spectacle. However, it is not left without guidance. Above it a priest proclaims: 'Wisdom! You see the movement of the shining firmament, you hear its harmony: know then that this movement is Love. Love moves the Sun and the other Stars' (*SS* ii, 607).

The soul is not just a passive witness to these sacred words; it is able to recreate within itself the full force of their inner symbolic meaning. In Ivanov's words:

The stunned soul does not simply take in or merely echo the prophetic word: it discovers within itself and from mysterious depths painlessly gives birth to its own restorative inner word. A mighty magnet magnetizes it, and it itself becomes a magnet. The universe unfolds within it. That which it sees above itself overhead opens wide within it down below. And Love is in the soul – for the soul already loves. 'Amor' . . . – at this sound which asserts the magnetism of the living universe, the soul's own molecules arrange themselves magnetically. And in the soul are the sun and the stars and the murmur of consonant spheres moved by the power of the divine Mover. The soul sings its own melody of love in harmony with the cosmos, just as Beatrice's melody resounded in the poet's soul when he was uttering his cosmic words.   (*SS* ii, 607–8)

For Ivanov the last line of the *Commedia* is not simply an example of aesthetic perfection, it is a symbolic line which is divinely poetic and acquires the force of myth because of the deep significance which it holds for the pilgrim's soul. It is a triumph of synthesis in which the symbol of love ('Amor') is transformed into myth through the action of the verb 'muove'. Ivanov refers to this as the '*myth-making* crowning of the symbol' (mifotvorcheskoe *uvenchanie simvola* – *SS* ii, 608); it represents the highest, ideal form of symbolist art. In religious or metaphysical terms, he concludes, the line is a perfect example of theurgic art, and proves the identity of true symbolism with theurgy.

Ivanov's opening statement has now been clarified – Dante's symbolic images turn into myth when paired with a verb with Dionysiac connotations, and the musical rhythm of the line teaches us the wisdom that love, arising out of the Dionysiac dark, moves the universe.

In many ways, the analysis provided in this passage confirms the interpretation of Ivanov's use of Dantesque images in 'The Spirit' suggested above. First, there is the characteristic desire to introduce elements of Dionysiac darkness into Dante's final vision of the light (although this is quite inconsistent with the significance of the revelation of the essence of the Holy Trinity which occurs at the end of *Paradiso*). Ivanov's reading of the line introduces a certain dynamism into the soul's mystic union with God which remains until the very end an attempt to rise from the Dionysiac dark to the Apollonian heights. This corresponds to Ivanov's understanding, originally based on Nietzsche's teaching, that a Dionysiac reality always underlies the Apollonian surface.

The darker side of the soul's flight to the stars was also introduced into 'The Spirit', as was the Dionysiac emphasis on self-transcendence achieved through a complete merging of the microcosm with the macrocosm – another feature which Ivanov underlines in his prose analysis of the final line of *Paradiso*. The Sophiological elements of 'The Spirit' are also present in the prose passage which once more relates the Love which moves the universe to the idea of wisdom or Sophia. Dante's text is interpreted in terms of Dionysiac and Solovyovian concepts, in order to present the medieval poet as a theurgic artist or poet of Sophia, whose symbolist art contains elements of the universal art of Dionysiac myth.

A few years later, in an essay on Scriabin written in 1915, Ivanov returned to these thoughts again, citing Dante's line to illustrate the idea that Love requires the artist to serve it and to reveal its mysteries to the world. This is the basis for an understanding of the theurgic function of art; according to Ivanov, Dante regarded Virgil as a theurgic artist, and was himself one of the prophets of the mystic Rose (*SS* III, 178–9).

Remarkably, Ivanov continued to develop the ideas which he had first expressed in a condensed poetic form in 'The Spirit' over a period of almost fifty years until a few years before his death. In a late essay written in 1947, 'Il simbolismo e la grande arte', he once more quoted Dante's line to show how a symbolic image could be transformed into myth through the action of a verb. In his view, this type of symbolist–mystical art was the ideal form of universal art, originally found in Dionysiac tragedy, to which mankind would eventually return.[10]

'La Selva Oscura'

'La Selva Oscura' is placed almost immediately after 'The Spirit' in the same section of *Pilot Stars* entitled 'The Impulse and the Limits'. In many respects these two poems form a pair, illustrating opposite extremes of the mystic experience. If 'The Spirit' describes the 'impulse' (*poryv*) or flight of the spirit to the heavens and the consummation of its mystic journey, 'La Selva Oscura' concentrates on the 'limits' (*grani*) of man's earthly condition and describes the state of suffering striving which precedes the upward flight. Ivanov has chosen to place these two extremes of the spiritual experience within the framework of Dante's journey, and has underlined this by his choice of the opening and closing lines of the *Commedia* as epigraphs to the two poems.

The text of the poem is as follows:

> Nel mezzo del cammin di nostra vita...
> Dante

> О, дольний мрак! О, дольний лес!
>   И ты – вдали – одна ...
> Потир земли, потир небес
>   Испили мы до дна.

> О, крест земли! О, крест небес!
>   И каждый миг – 'прости'!
> И вздохи гор, и долго – лес.
>   И долго – крест нести!

> Все горы, за грядой гряда;
>   Все черный, старый лес.
> Светлеет ночь. Горит звезда
>   В дали святой небес.　　　　　*(SS* i, 521–2)

Nel mezzo del cammin di nostra vita . . .

Dante

O earthly dark! O earthly wood!
And you – in the distance – alone . . .
The chalice of the earth, the chalice of the heavens
Has been drained by us to the end.

O cross of the earth! O cross of the heavens!
And every instant – 'farewell'!
And the sighs of the mountains, and for so long the wood.
And for so long – carrying the cross!

Still the mountains, ridge after ridge;
Still the black old wood.
The night grows light. A star is burning
In the holy distance of the heavens.

To illustrate certain aspects of man's spiritual condition, Ivanov
has created a symbolic landscape consisting of three different
elements. These are all presented in the first verse of the poem.
The first two elements, the mountains and the dark wood, are
closely associated. They are both part of the material world and
evoke the two different paths which man may follow in his attempts
to transcend his earthly rise towards the stars, while the dark wood
symbolizes his tendency to sink or descend into the abyss. Both
these elements create an impression of monotonous familiarity;
'still' (*vse*) is twice repeated, the mountain ridges are endless and
the wood is old. The earthly world appears to be unending and
inescapable by whichever route is chosen.

The third element, the star burning in the sky, is described in the
second half of the verse. It is on an altogether different plane, high
in the heavens and far from the earthly world. It represents the
transcendent guiding absolute to which the spirit aspires. It shines
at the hour before dawn when night is lifting and spiritual darkness
is giving way to light. Its burning radiance contrasts with the
blackness of the wood, and its distance and holiness set it apart
from the long-familiar surroundings of the earthly world.

The appearance of this star at the hour before dawn suggests that
it is the morning star, the planet of Venus, regarded as the guiding
spirit of love.[11] In an adjacent poem entitled 'Morning Star'
('*Utrennyaya zvezda*' – *SS* I, 524–5) Ivanov describes this star as the
'herald of Dawn' (*vestnitsa Zari*) or 'icon-lamp of the near
morning' (*Utra blizkogo lampada*); it is the 'sister of the earthly

world' (*Mira dol'nego sestra*) which it guides through prayer. As in 'La Selva Oscura' it is singled out as a lone star; in both poems, it is addressed with the words 'you alone' (*ty odna*).

The association of this star with love is developed in another adjacent poem, 'Submissiveness' ('*Pokornost*'' – *SS* I, 523–4). Here a person is walking through a dark wood in the evening gloom; a star appears in the heavens (the evening star is the same planet as the morning star) and is addressed in the following words:

> Светило братское, во мне зажгло ты вновь
> Неутолимую, напрасную любовь!   (*SS* I, 523)

> Brotherly luminary, once again you have set alight within me
> An insatiable, vain love!

Given these close parallels, it seems likely that the star in 'La Selva Oscura' represents a transcendent absolute which is specifically associated with the kindling and guiding of man's feeling of love or Eros.

In the first half of the second verse the three elements of the first verse are repeated in a more condensed form. The first line sums up the essence of man's condition on earth, the 'earthly dark' (*dol'nii mrak*) (in another poem, 'The Firmament' ('*Nebosvod*'), man is referred to as a 'son of the earthly twilight' (*syn dol'nikh sumerek*) – *SS* II, 378), while the second line evokes the star, once more stressing its distance and therefore inaccessibility. The repeated use of the exclamation 'O' as well as the fact that the star is now addressed directly in the second person introduces a more personal, emotive note to the landscape.

This personal note is further developed in the second half of the verse with the introduction of the subject 'we', recalling the use of the word 'nostra' in the epigraph. This subject is said to have drained both the chalice of the earth and the chalice of the heavens. In 'Submissiveness' Ivanov used the phrase 'we are fated to drain three cups' (*nam ispit' tri chashi suzhdeno* – *SS* I, 524), echoing Christ's words in Gethsemane.[12] Here the word 'chalice' (*potir*) carries similar associations. The chalice, as the vessel in which the transubstantiation of wine into the blood of Christ takes place during the celebration of the Eucharist, implies an experience of suffering which leads to the transformation or spiritualization of the earthly and fleshly. The two chalices link up with the two elements of the landscape already mentioned – the mountains

and the dark wood – and suggest the two paths for the transcendence of the earthly world which these represent. The chalice
of the earth is the descent into the dark wood, and the chalice of
the heavens is the attempt to ascend the mountain towards the
stars. The lines convey the impression that the two paths through
which the transformation of the earthly world might be achieved
have been embarked on and exhausted – but to no avail. Both
paths are chalices, associated with suffering, precisely because they
are unending, unresolved.

A similar use of the image of the two chalices occurs in another
poem from the same collection, written in terzinas, 'The Sphinx'.
Here Oedipus is addressed with words which imply an association
between the chalice of the earth and the experience of sin:

> 'О, ты, до дна земли потир испивший,
> Ты, рок греха подъявший без вины   (*SS* 1, 658)

> 'O you who have drained the chalice of the earth to the end,
> You who have taken up a sinful fate without being guilty

A few tercets further on, the chalice of the heavens is associated
with the stars in words spoken by the narrator:

> И я воззрел ... Из бледного потира
> Святых небес лиется звездный свет   (*SS* 1, 659)

> And I looked on ... From the pale chalice
> Of the holy heavens flows a starry light

The stars, as in 'La Selva Oscura', are presented as transcendent
guiding absolutes. Oedipus declares:

> Се, кормчих звезд горят над вами цели.   (*SS* 1, 660)

> Behold, the goals of the pilot stars burn above you.

In the third verse of 'La Selva Oscura' the two chalices become
crosses of the earth and of the heavens, suffering paths which lead
through sacrifice to the transcendence of the physical. Both paths
involve suffering because of the constant and painful awareness of
separation. As the second line of the verse conveys, each instant is
an instant of parting or farewell. The distance from the ultimate
goal, the star, is felt acutely, and both ways involve the continuous
loss of the phenomena of a transient, mortal world.

The poem concludes with a final evocation of the first two

elements of the landscape; the mountains sigh (the frustrated aspiration to transcend by rising) and the wood goes on for ever (the earthly, material and sinful world cannot be shaken off). Both paths are crosses which must be borne for a long time with no apparent promise of release towards mystical union with the stars. The lack of a final reference to the star emphasizes the painful inaccessibility of the goal; it has retreated further into the distance.

The repetition of the rhyme between 'wood' (*les*) and 'heavens' (*nebes*) highlights the fundamental alternatives open to man – the path of the earth or the path of the heavens. Both involve suffering and remain unresolved. The sense of the earthly world as an unending, inescapable prison is underlined by the phonetic similarity of the words for 'earthly' (*dol'nii*) and 'long' (*dolgo*), each repeated twice.

As in 'The Spirit', Ivanov has sought to present the spiritual experience which he is describing within the framework of Dante's journey. In this case he has turned to the very beginning of the poet's journey as related in the first canto of the *Inferno*. He has taken the epigraph and the title of his poem from this source, and also the three elements of his spiritual landscape – the dark wood, the mountains and the star. The opening lines of the *Inferno* describe how Dante emerges from a dark wood in a valley and finds himself at the foot of a hill. When he looks up he sees that the summit of the hill is clothed in the beams of the planet which leads man straight on every road. This planet is the sun, a symbol of God, the transcendent guiding spirit. The time is the beginning of the morning at sunrise. Dante tries to climb the hill, but his way is barred by three wild animals who force him back towards the dark wood.

These elements are echoed in Ivanov's poem. The image of the dark wood is taken up directly, and the hill is alluded to in the reference to the mountains. The star, although it is not the sun, represents a source of light among darkness (in both texts it is growing light) and is a guiding spirit of love. Furthermore, one can perhaps see an allusion to the valley in which Dante's dark wood is located in the expression *dol'nii les* ('earthly wood'); the adjective *dol'nii* is derived from the Russian word for 'valley' (*dol*) and means 'of the valley' as well as 'earthly' or 'terrestrial'.

These are surface similarities, however, involving the repetition of images but not necessarily in their original meaning. The relation of Ivanov's presentation of the dark wood to Dante's use of the image is a complex one. The image has been taken up in its original sense but is then developed in a different direction which is not compatible with Dante's intent.

In so far as Ivanov has taken up the negative connotations of Dante's image, he has remained faithful to it. Dante's *selva oscura* has been variously interpreted by commentators over the years as a symbol of man's sinful nature in this life, of the earthly material world in which he is trapped. Dante's attempts to escape the dark wood and climb the hill are initially thwarted. Ivanov's poem conveys precisely this sense of man's frustrated striving to escape the earthly material world of which he is a prisoner. The wood appears to be unending and the mountains are unsurmountable; he is denied direct access to the star.

In this respect the image of the dark wood presented in the poem is closely related to an unpublished fragment of autobiographical prose which Ivanov composed in August 1893 during his period of residence in Rome, shortly after his first meeting with Lidiya Dimitrievna. This passage is of considerable interest for it shows that the state of sinfulness represented by the *selva oscura* was not just a literary abstraction for Ivanov, but a real category which he applied to his own life. The passage was begun at night and starts with a description of the night, the moon and the stars. The poet records his desire for self-improvement and sense of happiness and new resolve despite the fact that his past offers no basis for hope, containing only reasons for bitter repentance. But, he adds, he is already suffering from his past sins; his punishment lies in the fact that he is so far from his goal. In terms reminiscent of Solovyov's views on Christianity he writes that the earthly life must not be rejected but transformed; this principle strengthens his resolution to overcome his own sinful nature. The part of the passage written at night ends with a prayer to God to give him strength for this task.

The next day, he added the following paragraph:

To make the movements of my soul pure and harmonious, to banish inner chaos from the soul, to achieve inner freedom – this is what I long for above all. If I could win these moral blessings, it seems to me that I would see the light and the path to the next, supreme goal. – Nel mezzo del cammin di nostra vita mi ritrovai per una selva oscura, che la diritta via era smarrita.[13]

Here the *selva oscura* is presented as a purely negative image of sinfulness. It is a stage which is clearly differentiated from the mystic path to the stars and which must be left behind. There is no implication that the sinful life is a form of sacred suffering which will of its own accord lead to the light.

In his poem, however, Ivanov has gone beyond the negative connotations of Dante's image and developed these in a positive direction. Since the Dionysiac ideal of self-transcendence through Eros was not bound by moral strictures, it could be sought through any type of experience, pure or sinful, so long as it carried the necessary sacrificial character. This idea runs like a leitmotif through many of the poems of *Pilot Stars*. It is expressed concisely in one of the poems adjacent to 'La Selva Oscura' entitled 'The Starry Sky' (*'Zvezdnoe nebo'*). Here Ivanov describes the heart's equal desire for initiation through the way of the stars and the way of the depths:

> Сердце ж алчет части равной
> В тайне звезд и в тайне дна:
> Пламенеет, и пророчит,
> И за вечною чертой
> Новый мир увидеть хочет
> С искупленной Красотой.   (*SS* 1, 526)

> But the heart hungers for an equal share
> In the mystery of the stars and in the mystery of the depths:
> It flames and prophesies,
> And beyond the eternal line
> Yearns to see a new world
> With redeemed Beauty.

The poem ends on a Sophiological note, teaching that either path will lead to a vision of redeemed Beauty (Ivanov followed Solovyov in associating Beauty with Sophia, as is clear, for example, from his poem 'Beauty').

In his next book, *Transparency*, Ivanov formulated the same thought more daringly in a poem called 'The Cross of Evil' (*'Krest zla'*). The idea of the poem is based on the fact that two thieves' crosses stood next to Christ's cross at the crucifixion. From this the poet draws the conclusion that sin and evil are also part of the sacrificial cycle leading to redemption:

> И Грех – алтарь распятья,
> И Зла Голгофа есть! . . .

Вблизи креста Христова –
Два жертвенных креста:
Свет таинства простого
Как изъяснят уста?   (*SS* i, 744)

And Sin is an altar of crucifixion,
And there is the Evil of Golgotha! . . .

Near Christ's cross
Were two sacrificial crosses:
How can lips explain
The light of this simple mystery?

The unusual concept of the 'cross of evil' was discussed by the critic M. Bakhtin in a lecture which he gave on Ivanov in the 1920s. A student who attended the lecture recorded the following note: 'How should one understand the combination of the symbol of evil with the cross? It means that the cross is the beginning of every form of life, of every form of coming into being. . . . Everything which comes into being – and everything living comes into being – communes with the cross. And not only good communes, but also evil, particularly evil.'[14]

This idea was a fairly radical one, and Ivanov was afraid that the censors would not accept the poem for publication.[15] A very similar idea was expressed by him in the passage already quoted from his essay of 1904, 'New Masks'. Here he took up the image of the *selva oscura* to illustrate the concept of sacrificial sin as an alternative method of mystic self-transcendence: 'But more often the path to mystical purification leads through Dante's "dark wood", and the crucifixion of love takes place on the cross of Sin' (*SS* II, 81). The dark wood is clearly identified with the 'cross of Sin' (*krest Grekha*), the same cross as the one described in 'The Cross of Evil'.

'La Selva Oscura' appears to offer the same choice of paths through the heavens or through the depths as 'The Starry Sky' and the passage from 'New Masks'. The image of the dark wood is developed in precisely the same way as in the passage quoted above. The dark wood is a symbol of sin; it is transformed into the 'chalice of the earth' which Ivanov also associated with sin as is clear from Oedipus's words in 'The Sphinx'. Finally, it becomes the 'cross of the earth', an image closely linked to the 'cross of Sin' described above. This completes the cycle from sin through sacrificial suffering to the promise of mystic union.

This passage from sin to the implication of redemption contained in the image of the cross is clearly incompatible with the meaning of the *selva oscura* in its original Dantesque context. At the very beginning of the *Commedia* Dante comes to his senses and *leaves* the dark wood. Although he tells us that he had spent some time there, he does not dwell on this period of his life at all, except to say that the memory of it renews his fear, for it was as bitter as death. The time spent in the wood is not described because it is only indirectly relevant to the story of the poet's spiritual development. In the wood Dante was entirely lost and could make no progress. His journey could only begin when he realized the condition of sin and ignorance into which he had fallen and emerged from it. The experience of the *selva oscura* is a negative prelude to his journey, but not in any way an intrinsic stage of it. The distinction between the dark and the light is drawn rigidly; the *selva oscura* is bereft of the light of divine guidance, it is the place 'dove 'l sol tace' ('where the sun is silent' – *Inf.* I, 60), and Dante can only see the sun *after* he has left it.

Ivanov has however done away with this firm distinction in his poem. He has telescoped the action of *Inferno* I in such a way that the experience of the *selva oscura* and the vision of the star are presented alongside each other, in juxtaposition rather than in succession. In this way he introduces the possibility of a transcendent goal which can be perceived from within the dark wood and allows the experience of sin to assume a direction and become a path to follow or cross to be borne. The dark wood accordingly becomes more purgatorial than infernal in character.[16] It is no longer a stage which lies outside the framework of the mystic journey, but an integral part of the mystic experience which is dwelt on at length. In this respect, with its emphasis on intense suffering, it is closer to the 'dark night of the soul' described by St John of the Cross. This approach to the image of the dark wood was later further developed by Ivanov in some of the poems of *Cor Ardens*, considered below.

'La Selva Oscura' confirms the general tendency outlined earlier: Ivanov takes up Dantesque images but alters the nature of their moral dimension to bring them within the amoral Dionysiac cycle of mystical love. The experience of sin which the dark wood represents acquires a sacrificial dimension which allows it to become a first stage of the mystic way.

'At the Coliseum'

'At the Coliseum' ('*V Kolizee*') is placed in the same section of *Pilot Stars*, shortly after 'The Spirit' and immediately before 'La Selva Oscura'. It is of interest for a number of reasons; unlike the previous poems considered, it is directly related to the circumstances of Ivanov's personal life, and takes up Dantesque images within this context in an allusive rather than explicit manner; these create an undercurrent of meaning in the poem, without taking the form of epigraphs or open references.

The text of the poem is as follows:

> Great is their love, who love in sin and fear
> > Byron

> День влажнокудрый досиял,
> Меж туч огонь вечерний сея.
> Вкруг помрачался, вкруг зиял
> Недвижный хаос Колизея.

> Глядели из стихийной тьмы
> Судеб безвременные очи ...
> День бурь истомных к прагу ночи,
> День алчный провождали мы –

> Меж глыб, чья вечность роковая
> В грехе святилась и крови, –
> Дух безнадежный предавая
> Преступным терниям любви, –

> Стеснясь, как два листа, что мчит,
> Безвольных, жадный плен свободы,
> Доколь их слившей непогоды
> Вновь легкий вздох не разлучит ...   (*SS* I, 521)

> Great is their love, who love in sin and fear
> > Byron

> The damp-haired day had finished shining,
> Sowing evening fire among the clouds.
> Round about darkened, round about yawned
> The motionless chaos of the Coliseum.

Out of the elemental darkness stared
The timeless eyes of fates ...
We saw a day of languorous storms through to the threshold of
   night,
A day of craving we spent –

Among the blocks of stone whose fateful eternity
Was sanctified in sin and blood –
Submitting our despairing spirit
To the criminal thorns of love –

Clinging together like two leaves which,
Weak-willed, the avid prison of freedom drives along,
Until a light gust of the bad weather which united them
Parts them once again ...

The poem describes the evening which Ivanov spent with Lidiya Dimitrievna in the Coliseum during their three-day reunion in Rome in March 1895. This occasion was the climax of Lidiya Dimitrievna's visit and came to serve as a symbolic image of the new intensity which the lovers' relationship reached during this time. In her subsequent letters to Ivanov, Lidiya Dimitrievna frequently recalled the occasion; in June 1895, for example, she wrote: 'and Rome and the Coliseum ... all this brought about a strange sort of change in me'; in November of the same year she added: 'and I recall the Coliseum on the evening of our first closeness in Rome'.[17]

At this stage both Ivanov and Lidiya Dimitrievna regarded their love as a criminal, dark passion, an adulterous violation of the Christian sanctity of marriage. However, they also viewed it as a prelude to spiritual rebirth and new mystical insights, following their belief that sin could be transformed into the first stage of the mystic way through its sacrificial, suffering dimension.

These elements – sin, suffering and a hint at redemption – are all reflected in 'At the Coliseum'. Ivanov has achieved this by setting up a fruitful interaction between two sets of imagery. He has made use of images related to Dante's description of the plight of the two sinful lovers, Francesca and Paolo, and set these against the background of the Coliseum. By cleverly exploiting to the full the nature of this setting in order to bring out its twin sinful and sacrificial aspects, he has managed to invest the sinful passion of the lovers with a sacrificial element.

The incident of Francesca and Paolo occurred in Dante's youth and made a great impression on him. Francesca da Polenta of Ravenna was married to Giovanni Malatesta, the crippled son of the Lord of Rimini. Giovanni's younger brother, Paolo, who was also married, became Francesca's lover. Giovanni discovered them together and killed them both. The sin of allowing sexual passion to override the sanctity of marriage thus culminated in bloodshed and death. As Francesca tells Dante: 'Amor condusse noi ad una morte' ('Love brought us to one death' – *Inf.* v, 106); earlier she referred to herself and the other carnal sinners as 'noi che tignemmo il mondo di sanguigno' ('us who stained the world with blood' – *Inf.* v, 90).

Dante places Francesca and Paolo together with the sinners of carnal love in the second circle of Hell, described in *Inferno* v. The first half of this canto is taken up with a description of the setting and of the torment to which the sinners are subjected. In the second half Dante summons Francesca and Paolo to his side, and Francesca describes the course of her unhappy passion to him.

Ivanov has echoed a number of features of Dante's canto in his poem. He has adopted the same type of structure, starting with a description of the setting, and then focusing on the particular plight of the lovers against this background. Within the framework of this general structural parallel, he has taken up elements of Dante's imagery relating both to the setting and to the description of the lovers.

The darkness of the setting is stressed in both texts. Dante describes the darkness of the air in the second circle several times with phrases such as 'loco d'ogne luce muto' ('a place mute of all light' – l. 28), 'l'aura nera' ('the black air' – l. 51), 'l'aere maligno' ('the malignant air' – l. 86) and 'l'aere perso' ('the black air' – l. 89). In Ivanov's poem, evening is giving way to night, and the threatening darkness of the Coliseum is emphasized by the words 'darkened' (*pomrachalsya*), 'yawned' (*ziyal*), 'darkness' (*t'ma*) and 'night' (*noch'*).

The parallel can, however, be taken further. It is grounded in the basic metaphor which is used in both texts to convey the lovers' complete lack of resistance to their passion. Both pairs of lovers are compared to something very light, blown about and entirely controlled by a strong wind. In the second circle of the *Inferno* the carnal sinners are buffeted by a vicious, stormy wind which gives them no rest: 'La bufera infernal, che mai non resta, / mena li spirti con la sua rapina' ('The hellish hurricane, never resting, sweeps along the spirits with its rapine' – ll. 31–2), 'così quel fiato li spiriti mali / di qua, di là, di giù, di sù li mena' ('so does that blast the sinful spirits; hither, thither, downward, upward, it drives them' – ll. 42–3). Dante multiplies the variations of this central image – the lovers' lightness on the wind and their powerlessness to resist its gusts convey their full submission to the chaotic destructive whirlwind of their passion. Francesca and Paolo are locked together in their torment as they were in life: Dante singles them out from the other carnal sinners as 'que' due che 'nsieme vanno, / e paion si al vento esser leggieri' ('those two that go together and seem to be so light upon the wind' – ll. 74–5). When he summons them 'per quello amor che i mena' ('by that love which leads them' – l. 78), they fly to him and Virgil 'si tosto come il vento a noi li piega' ('as soon as the wind bends them to us' – l. 79).

In a similar fashion, Ivanov compares his lovers to leaves, buffeted by the wind. He renders the Italian verb 'mena' ('sweeps', 'drives'), used by Dante several times during his description of the wind, by the Russian verb *mchit* ('drives along'). He also empha-sizes the way the lovers are locked together by the wind through the words 'clinging together' (*stesnyas'*) and 'the bad weather which united them' (*ikh slivshei nepogody*). Here, however, at the end of the poem, he adds an extra touch, a reference to the lovers' future separation, perhaps alluding to Lidiya Dimitrievna's departure from Rome almost immediately after the evening in the Coliseum.

In both texts, the lovers' full surrender to their passion requires the abnegation of their will to resist. Francesca stresses her passivity when she tells Dante: 'Amor . . . / mi prese . . . / ancor non m'abbandona' ('Love . . . seized me . . . it does not leave me even now' – ll. 103–5). Ivanov's lovers are 'weak-willed' (*bezvol'nye*), completely controlled by the 'avid prison of freedom' (*zhadnyi plen svobody*) – the freedom of their passion is a prison because it demands their whole being and allows them no escape or rest.

Ivanov has also taken up the tone of Francesca's description of her love. In both cases, a retrospective account of past events is delivered by one voice which speaks for two in the 'we' form. The tone of each account is personal and nostalgic, as well as restrained and elliptic. Francesca gives only a few vivid details which provoke the imagination to further thought. Her concluding phrase 'quel giorno piu non vi leggemmo avante' ('that day we read no further in it' – l. 138) is echoed by Ivanov's threefold repetition of the word 'day', insisting on the fatal day of surrender, and particularly by the lines 'we saw a day of languorous storms through to the threshold of night, / A day of craving we spent' (*Den' bur' istomnykh k pragu nochi, / Den' alchnyi provozhdali my*).

However, the context in which Ivanov has set these Dantesque images is quite different from the original. Whereas Dante roundly condemned excessive carnal love and Francesca and Paolo as representatives of this sin, Ivanov regarded sexual love as closely linked to his ideal of Eros. In his poem, he has deliberately set the couple's experience of love against a background which carries associations of martyrdom in order to bring out its sacrificial dimension. He has not simply described a romantic occasion against a suitably romantic backdrop; he has drawn a carefully implied parallel between the spiritual values with which he invests the Coliseum and his own personal drama.

A clear insight into Ivanov's understanding of the symbolic significance of the Coliseum can be derived from 'The Coliseum' ('*Kolizei*' – *SS* I, 621), a poem from the cycle of Italian sonnets in *Pilot Stars* which is closely related to the imagery and ideas of 'At the Coliseum'. The sonnet describes a vision of the Coliseum at night; the stadium appears to be filled with the shades of ancient Romans who are staring transfixedly at a cross in the centre of the arena on which Christ is crucified. The historical background to this image is summarized by Ivanov in a note (*SS* I, 860). The Coliseum was venerated by Christians as a place where the blood of Christian martyrs, persecuted for their faith by pagan Romans, had been shed. In recognition of this, Pope Benedict XIV who held office during the mid-eighteenth century dedicated the Coliseum to the Passion of Christ and arranged for a large cross to be erected in the centre of the arena. This cross remained in position until it was taken down in 1874, less than twenty years before Ivanov's first visit to Rome. For Ivanov therefore, the juxtaposition of the shades of the ancient Romans with the figure of Christ on the cross served as a potent image for the continuity between sin and Christian redemption, united through suffering, which was fundamental to his spiritual outlook.

In 'At the Coliseum', the description of the theatre carries the same twin associations of sin and redemption. Many of the same images are used in both poems. In 'The Coliseum' Ivanov refers to the 'dark' (*mrak*) of the Coliseum, to its 'masses' (*gromady*), to its arches which he compares to 'eyes' (*ochi*), and to the 'bloody orgies' (*krovavye orgii*) which took place on its site. These terms are echoed in 'At the Coliseum' – 'darkened' (*pomrachalsya*), 'blocks' (*glyby*), 'eyes' (*ochi*), 'blood' (*krov'*). The earlier part of the description of the setting in the first six lines of 'At the Coliseum' stresses the dark, pagan and sinful aspects of the Coliseum through expressions such as 'darkened' (*pomrachalsya*), 'yawned' (*ziyal*), 'motionless chaos' (*nedvizhnyi khaos*) and 'out of the elemental darkness' (*iz stikhiinoi t'my*). The Christian redemption of these attributes through martyrdom and sacrifice is alluded to in the latter part of the description (ll. 9–10) which refers to the eternal spiritual value of the stones of the Coliseum, sanctified through sin and blood. These lines illustrate the same passage from sin (*grekh*) through suffering and blood (*krov'*) to redemption and sanctification (*svyatilas'*) as that conveyed by the more explicit imagery of 'The Coliseum'.

These features of the Coliseum have been carefully interwoven with the description of the lovers through a clever use of structural parallelism. A close look at the poem reveals the perfect symmetry with which the themes of the Coliseum and the lovers have been dovetailed together. If the theme of the Coliseum is designated by the letter 'a' and the theme of the lovers by 'b', the poem's structure can be represented as follows:

verses:	I	2	3	4
theme of each line:	aaaa	aa/bb	aa/bb	bbbb

The description of the Coliseum (a) occupies the first verse and the first couplets of the two central verses, while the lovers' situation (b) is described in the second halves of the central verses and in the final verse. The two themes are therefore most tightly interwoven in the alternating four couplets of the two central verses (aa/bb aa/bb), and it is here that the attributes of the Coliseum most closely merge with the description of the lovers. The first half of the second verse evokes the dark, sinful aspect of the Coliseum, and leads on to a couplet describing the sinful, stormy passion of the lovers which leads them to the threshold of night. The first half of the third verse, however, with its allusion to the sacrificial redemption of the Coliseum's stones, prepares for the fourth couplet in which the lovers' situation acquires a new dimension of martyrdom and implied redemption. The phrase 'criminal thorns of love' (*prestupnym terniyam lyubvi*) directly echoes the earlier 'was sanctified in sin and blood' (*v grekhe svyatilas' i krovi*) (a link underscored by the rhyming scheme). In Christian art and literature thorns are traditionally viewed as a symbol of martyrdom as well as of sin because of their association with the crown of thorns (*venets iz ternii*) with which Christ was crowned by the Roman soldiers before the crucifixion (Matthew 27.29). Here, the reference to the 'criminal thorns of love' (*prestupnye terniya lyubvi*) implies that the lovers' passion, while sinful, is also associated with an experience of martyr-like suffering which may lead to redemption, in the same way as the stones of the Coliseum were sanctified through sin and bloodshed.

In this way Ivanov has succeeded in transforming the sinful passion of carnal love into a source of mystic energy. This is in keeping with his view that Eros is an absolute which transcends all moral imperatives and can justify the experience of sin. The line from Byron appended to the poem as an epigraph expresses precisely this idea. It sounds remarkably like one of Francesca's blind maxims on the nature of love and its absolute power.[18] In many ways 'At the Coliseum' provides a poetic illustration of the idea which formed part of the poet's own experience and which he later formulated in his prose essay, 'New Masks' – that the path to mystic purification may lead through Dante's dark wood, and that love is often crucified on the cross of sin. The lovers described in the poem and indirectly associated with Francesca and Paolo are not condemned sinners but passionate martyrs, travelling to the same goal as St Francis and St Clare but by a different route. Later and more explicit examples of Ivanov taking up images connected with Francesca and Paolo and the whirlwind of sexual passion occur in some of the sonnets of the 'Golden Veils' cycle, considered below.

TRANSPARENCY

Ivanov's second collection of verse appeared in April 1904, published by Skorpion under the direction of Bryusov. Most of the poems in the book were written during the summer of 1903 while

Ivanov was living in Switzerland. As a result the collection is far
more unified in spirit and tone than *Pilot Stars*. It has a clearly
defined central theme, the concept of transparency, described in
one of the opening poems as the ideal state of the physical world
when the material shell which envelops it becomes transparent to
the eye, and the divine essence inherent in it is clearly revealed:

> Прозрачность! улыбчивой сказкой
> Соделай видения жизни,
> Сквозным – покрывало Майи!   (*SS* I, 738)

> Transparency! Into a smiling tale
> Turn the appearances of life,
> Make the veil of Maya – translucent!

The notion of transparency played an important role in medieval
philosophy and in the works of Dante, and Ivanov turned to these
sources for the illustration of his ideal, both in the poems of
Transparency and in his later prose works. An exposition of
Dante's understanding of the idea of transparency can be found in
his philosophical treatise, the *Convivio*. Here, the varied degrees
of divine goodness in the material world are likened to the way in
which the light of the sun is diversely received by different bodies.
Some, such as gold and precious stones, have such a large measure
of the 'clearness of the transparent' ('chiaritade di diafano') that
they become luminous in the light of the sun; some, like mirrors,
have such 'purity of transparency' ('purita del diafano') that they
cannot be contemplated without difficulty; others, like the earth,
are so completely without transparency that they receive but little
of the light (*Con.* III, vii, 2–5).

The gradual transition from darkness to light throughout the
Commedia is a direct result of this understanding. In the spheres of
Paradiso, the greater the degree of holiness or of receptivity to
divine goodness, the greater is the emphasis placed upon the
brightness of the surroundings and the transparency of the spirits
of the blessed. In *Transparency*, Ivanov has adopted the same
principle and made ample use of symbolic images of crystal, dia-
monds, mountains, sun, moonlight, pure air and stars to conjure
up a vision of the transparency or spirituality of the material world.

Ivanov was particularly interested in the application of the
concept of transparency to the sphere of aesthetics. In his view, the
relationship between spirit and matter in the created universe is

paralleled by the relationship between form and matter in a work of art. Here again, he turned to the medieval philosophers in search of support for his argument. In a late essay entitled 'Thoughts on Poetry' (1938) he declared that the problem of the nature and significance of artistic form had been clearly resolved in the Middle Ages, and quoted a definition of beauty attributed to Aquinas or one of his desciples to prove his point: 'Beauty is defined as the "shining of form" distributed throughout the proportionately arranged parts of a material substance (resplendentia formae super partes materiae proportionatas).' He explains that the concept is to be understood in the scholastic sense of the term, based on Aristotle's teaching; it is the creative, active principle or idea which gives shape or actuality to formless matter or potentiality. The form of a work of art is thus related to the idea of divine beauty, whereas its material aspect consists of the raw material of language, sound or stone from which it is made. The more 'transparent' the form, the more clearly the divine beauty which it embodies is revealed: 'The shining of form signifies the complete triumph of form over inert matter ... The symbol of shining serves as a reminder that beauty in the earthly world is a reflection, dulled by the natural medium but radiant nevertheless, of the supersensual shining of divine beauty' (SS III, 667).

In an earlier essay on Scriabin's view of art (1915), Ivanov related this notion of 'shining' or 'transparency' of form directly to Dante:

Medieval thinkers ... if they occasionally reflected on aesthetic theory, would speak of 'transparentia formae', i.e. of how in a work of art the material substance becomes translucent, transparent (skvozit, oprozrach-nivaetsya) and reveals the divine essence to the eye (vzoru), – or, in the words of Dante, of how the divine 'Love which moves the sun and the other stars' compels the artist to serve it and to reveal its secrets to people.

(SS III, 178–9)

The artist's service to divine love requires the creation of 'transparent' forms which make the divine essence inherent in the material world plainly visible to the human eye. The word 'eye' (vzor) is a key one in this context – how does the human eye see through the material, substantial shell of this world to perceive its divine essence? What type of vision does this necessitate? For the artist the challenge is a dual one: he must not only seek to acquire this type of vision but must also strive to impart it to others through the creation of transparent images.

Several poems in *Transparency* deal with different aspects of this problem. Given the fact that Ivanov related his ideal of 'transparent vision' to Dante and the Middle Ages, it is not surprising to find that in a number of these poems he turned to Dante as a source of terminology for the description of visual perception.

'Gli spiriti del viso'

This sonnet deals with the relationship between the physiology of visual perception and mystical vision within the general context of the ideal of transparency.

Есть духи глаз. С куста не каждый цвет
Они вплетут в венки своих избраний;
И сорванный с их памятию ранней
Сплетается. И суд их: *Да*, иль: *Нет*.

Хоть преломлен в их зрящих чашах свет,
Но чист кристалл эфироносных граней.
Они – глядят: молчанье – их завет.
Но в глубях дали грезят даль пространней.

Они – как горный вкруг души туман.
В их снах правдив явления обман.
И мне вестят их арфы у порога,

Что радостен в росах и солнце луг;
Что звездный свод – созвучье всех разлук;
Что мир – обличье страждущего Бога.   (*SS* 1, 785)

There are spirits of the eyes. They will not weave every flower
From the bush into the garlands of their selection;
And the plucked flower with their early memory
Intertwines. And their judgement is *Yes* or *No*.

Although the light is refracted in their seeing cups,
Yet the crystal of their ether-bearing facets is pure.
They look: silence is their bidding.
But in the depths of the distance they dream of a vaster distance.

They are like a mountain mist around the soul.
In their dreams the deception of phenomena is true.
And their harps tell me at the threshold

That the meadow is joyful under dew and sun;
That the starry vault is the accord of all separations;
That the world is the outer appearance of a suffering God.

The tone of the poem is self-consciously Dantesque. The choice of the sonnet as a verse form already evokes an association with Dante, particularly in the Russian literary tradition as a result of Pushkin's famous 'Sonnet' of 1830, beginning with the line 'Stern Dante did not disdain the sonnet . . .' (*Surovyi Dant ne preziral soneta* . . .).[19] This association is further developed in the poem by the use of a deliberately halting form of syntax, composed of short, fragmentary statements reminiscent of the structure and style of some of the sonnets of the *Vita Nuova*.

These Dantesque features can be found in other sonnets by Ivanov, such as ' "Transcende te ipsum" ', discussed in chapter 3, and also placed in the 'Sonnets' section of *Transparency* alongside 'Gli spiriti del viso'. However, in the case of 'Gli spiriti del viso' the link with Dante is made quite explicit by the phrase used as the title of the poem, first in Italian, and then in the text, translated into Russian as *dukhi glaz* ('spirits of the eyes'). Dante uses this phrase on several occasions in the course of the *Vita Nuova* to refer to the spirits which control his faculty of vision; these belong to the general category of the 'spiriti sensitivi' ('spirits of the senses'), which are all governed by a ruling 'spirito animale' ('spirit of the senses'), one of the three principal forces of life in the body whose seat is in the brain (*VN* II, 4–6).

The references to the spirits of vision in the *Vita Nuova* tend to follow a standard pattern. They usually occur in the context of a vision of Beatrice; on these occasions the figure of Amor appears to Dante and drives away all his spirits of the senses, including his spirits of vision, leaving him bereft of his faculties and entirely in the power of love. At the very beginning of the *Vita Nuova* the spirits of vision are informed by their boss, the spirit of the senses, that they have caught their first glimpse of Beatrice who is to be their principal source of joy (*VN* II, 5). Subsequently Dante describes how Love would drive away his spirits of the senses and take the place of his 'deboletti spiriti del viso' ('frail spirits of vision') whenever Beatrice was about to greet him (*VN* XI, 2). Later, the same spirits, now reduced to mere 'spiritelli', lament loudly that they would have been able to enjoy the sight of the miraculous Beatrice, had they not been ousted from their rightful place by Love (*VN* XIV, 5–6).

Dante's 'spiriti del viso' are clearly therefore no more than a personification of his faculty of vision. He describes them with humour; they are locked in a constant and unsuccessful battle with Amor, and are endowed with their own emotions and with the capacity to talk and complain when dissatisfied.

Ivanov's spirits of vision are altogether more solemn creatures. Unlike Dante's spirits, they neither talk nor complain – 'silence is their bidding' (*molchan'e – ikh zavet*) – but spend most of their time dreaming of a world beyond visual appearances and passing judgement on the phenomena of this world. These features are quite uncharacteristic of Dante's spirits of vision whose role does not extend beyond the faculty of straightforward visual perception. Although for Dante there is a connection between visual perception and judgement (in *Monarchia* I, xii, 3 he defines judgement as the link between apprehension and appetite), the two faculties remain quite separate. This is clear from the analysis of the link between visual perception and love which he provides in the central cantos of *Purgatorio*. Here he describes the way in which the faculty of visual apprehension receives an impression from outside and displays it within; if the mind then turns to it, this inclination is love (XVIII, 22–7). The passage from the first stage to the second is made with the aid of man's innate 'virtu che consiglia' ('faculty that counsels' – XVIII, 62) or 'libero arbitrio' ('free will' – XVIII, 74) which enable him to judge and choose how far he should allow the feeling of love to develop.

For Dante the moment of visual perception is therefore quite distinct from the subsequent stages of choice and judgement which are the responsibility of entirely different faculties of the soul. Ivanov's spirits of vision, although they share the same name as Dante's spirits, appear to combine the functions of spirits of vision with those of other faculties, and are clearly of a quite different nature. The poet has made use of Dante's terminology, but invested it with different associations.

A clue to the real rather than apparent nature of Ivanov's spirits of vision can be found in a sonnet entitled 'Aspects' ('*Aspekty*') which occurs a few pages after 'Gli spiriti del viso' in *Transparency* (*SS* I, 789–90). This poem forms part of a cycle of five sonnets addressed to various friends whom Ivanov met during his years abroad in the early 1900s. The last two poems of the cycle, 'La faillite de la science' and 'Aspects', are both dedicated to V. N.

Ivanovsky (1867–1931), a philosopher who was a frequent visitor at
Ivanov's home in Châtelaine in 1903 and 1904.[20] The two friends
held diametrically opposed views; whereas Ivanov's approach
tended to be emotional and intuitive, Ivanovsky's views were
founded on scepticism and strict logic. Ivanov, however, detected a
contradiction between his friend's rationalism in matters of philosophy and his love of poetry, and alluded to this ironically in his
two poems. In the first, he declares that Dante, not Hume, is
Ivanovsky's true mentor: 'Your mentor is no longer Hume – but
"stern Dante"' (*Uzhe nastavnik tvoi – ne Yum, – 'surovyi Dant'* –
SS I, 789), quoting Pushkin's famous description of Dante. In the
second poem, 'Aspects', he discusses their differing approaches to
the question of 'aspects', a philosophical term which he uses to
refer to a particular method of religious knowledge. He links the
concept of aspects to Dante's spirits of vision, addressing them as
'spirits of the eyes (as Dante would have said)' (*dukhi glaz (skazal
by Dant)*) and describing them as the 'intellects of perceiving
pupils' (*zenits vozzrevshikh intellekty*).

These last two phrases confirm what has already been established: that Ivanov intended the phrase *dukhi glaz* to refer
specifically to Dante's 'spiriti del viso', and that he attributed an
intellectual capacity to these organs of visual perception. However,
the poem's association of these spirits of vision with the concept of
aspects is new and adds an important dimension to the significance
of Ivanov's spirits of vision.

To understand the nature of this connection, it is necessary to
turn to another source, dating from about the same time. Ivanov's
work on the religion of Dionysus, based on the lectures which he
gave in Paris in 1903, contains an illuminating discussion of aspects
which in many ways serves as a prose gloss on the two sonnets
under discussion.

In the concluding section of this work, Ivanov wrote that religious feeling, like music, defies rational analysis. Its essence is
incompatible with any form of dogmatic morality, and cannot be
reduced to a classified system of fixed truths or statements.[21] This
belief naturally affected his understanding of the nature of religious knowledge. If religion is the domain of the emotions rather
than of the intellect, the same must be true of all forms of religious
knowledge: these stem from the heart, not from the mind. This led
Ivanov to introduce the concept of aspects to refer to the non-

dogmatic forms of perception and knowledge which are possible within a mystical form of religious experience. As he wrote: 'The sphere of emotions and the sphere of aspects – these were (to the exclusion of dogma and morality) the primordial property of religion ... Religion, by its very essence, does not claim to be a normative instance of knowledge; but its emotional sphere necessarily determines the *aspect* of the object of knowledge.'[22]

Ivanov then offers an explanation of the way in which the aspect of an object is determined. It is the result of a process of perception which involves three stages. The first of these is the associative stage of perception, the second is the stage of choice at which certain elements of the perceived object are selected and others are discarded, and the third is the stage of evaluation which, through the exercise of the will, leads to the confirmation (*utverzhdenie*) or negation (*otritsanie*) of the perceived object. The three stages are summarized as follows: 'Association, choice and evaluation create the psychological medium in which phenomena are inevitably refracted before they enter our consciousness.'[23]

The aspect of an object is therefore that which is retained after this three-fold process of perception has taken place. It bridges the gap between perception and religious knowledge, and reveals the Dionysiac essence of the universe. In Ivanov's words:

It is precisely the aspect, not dogma, which mediates between religious feeling and knowledge.

And here is the aspect of the world in the light of the religion of Dionysus: the world is the outer appearance of a suffering deity [*mir – oblich'e bozhestva stradayushchego*].[24]

The last part of this quotation is almost identical to the final line of 'Gli spiriti del viso'. It is clear that in Ivanov's understanding, the *dukhi glaz* or 'spiriti del viso' are the organs of visual perception which, equipped with the necessary spiritual and intellectual faculties, carry out the three-fold process of perception which determines the aspect of an object and through this the Dionysiac essence of the universe.

Returning to Ivanov's poem, one can now see how it illustrates this process. In the first verse, the three stages of perception are described (out of sequence) – first, choice (not every flower is picked), then association (through memory), and finally evaluation ('And their judgement is *Yes* or *No*') (*I sud ikh*: Da, *il'* Net).

These are the three stages which the *dukhi glaz* pass through, and which determine the aspect of an object.

The second verse dwells on the idea that although human vision is necessarily imperfect, it nevertheless retains the capacity for deep mystical insight. The pure light is broken – 'refracted' (*prelomlen*) echoes the phrase 'phenomena are inevitably refracted' (*yavleniya neobkhodimo prelomlyayutsya*) quoted above – when it passes through the convex pupils of the eyes, but the edges of the eyes remain pure like crystal (capable of 'transparent' vision). The spirits of vision therefore look beyond the aspects of phenomena to the higher reality which lies behind these; this forms the substance of their dreams.

In the third verse Ivanov compares the spirits of vision to a mountain mist surrounding the soul. The idea behind this image is alluded to by Deschartes in her comments on *Transparency*. She writes that the ideal medium for the vision of the mystical essence of objects to take place in should be transparent, and yet at the same time not quite transparent ('the medium ... must refract the ray') (*sreda ... dolzhna prelomlyat' luch*) or the mystical essence will remain invisible (*SS* 1, 63).

In this sense, the mountain mist created by the spirits' dreams of a higher reality sets the illusory nature of appearances in its correct and 'true' perspective. In 'The Religion of Dionysus' Ivanov commented: 'One can give oneself up to world sorrow over universal suffering, and fail to recognize in this suffering the features of suffering Dionysus and crucified Christ. The aspects of a single essence may be varied.'[25] Ivanov's spirits of vision do not commit this error; first they determine the aspect of the universe through their particular type of vision, and then they look through this aspect to the Dionysiac essence which lies beyond it. In the final verse of the poem, they see the happiness of the universe but realize that the apparent harmony of the heavens is only achieved through countless separations, and that the universe is but an outer shell under which lies one reality – the suffering essence of God, whether of Dionysus or Christ.

The poem also contains certain Sophiological allusions. These become particularly clear if one compares it to the vision of Beauty or Sophia described in 'Beauty' (*SS* 1, 517). The words 'distances' (*dali*), 'mountains' (*gory*), 'crystal' (*kristal*), 'dream' (*son*), 'gods' (*bogi*), 'proved true' (*opravdali*), 'ether' (*efir*), 'see' (*zret'*), 'world' (*mir*), 'joyfully' (*radostno*), 'flower-bearing' (*tsvetonosnyi*), 'Yes' (*Da*) which occur in 'Beauty' are all closely echoed in 'Gli spiriti del viso', emphasizing the point that the vision of the suffering essence of the universe is also a vision of Sophia, the divine principle inherent in the material world which the eye must strive to perceive through 'transparent' vision.

Ivanov's spirits of vision fulfil a role which is clearly very different from that of Dante's 'spiriti del viso'. He has taken up a straightforward term denoting no more than ordinary visual perception, and applied it to his own understanding of a complex process of spiritual perception which determines the aspect of the universe in the light of its Dionysiac and Sophiological essence. This adaptation of Dante's terminology once more creates the impression that Dante shared the peculiar Dionysiac and Sophiological view of the universe propounded by Ivanov.

COR ARDENS I

The poems which Ivanov wrote after the appearance of *Transparency* were collected together in his fourth major book, *Cor Ardens*. This work grew up over a number of years by stages. Ivanov first referred to it in a letter to Bryusov of July 1905,[26] but it was not until six years later that it was finally published in two separate volumes. Its contents reflect a substantial period of the poet's life: the last year of his residence in Switzerland (from his 1904 spring trip to Russia until his final return to St Petersburg in 1905), his life in the tower and relations with Gorodetsky and Sabashnikova in 1906, the death of Lidiya Dimitrievna in 1907, and the subsequent growth of his attachment to Vera, culminating in the summer of 1910.

This was a time of tremendous upheaval in the poet's life during which his spiritual outlook underwent important new developments. The central pivotal event of the period was the death of Lidiya Dimitrievna, and this is reflected in the division of *Cor Ardens* into two parts; the first part comprises three books consisting almost entirely of poems written before the death, while the second includes a further two books, composed in 1908 and 1910, which had not formed part of the original plan. Ivanov's approach to Dante in the second part of the work differs quite considerably from that adopted in the first, and this change of emphasis will be traced in the poems discussed below. The poems in this section are taken from the first part of *Cor Ardens* (an early poem of 1904 addressed to Bryusov and the 1906 cycle of sonnets dedicated to Sabashnikova), and in the next section from the two books of the second part, 'Love and Death' and 'Rosarium'.

'Mi fur le serpi amiche'

This poem forms part of an early dialogue in verse between Bryusov and Ivanov and should be considered in the context of their relationship. After their first meeting in Paris in the spring of 1903, the two poets embarked on a busy correspondence which included the regular exchange of recent poems as an alternative form of communication. Bryusov undertook to publish Ivanov's second collection of verse, *Transparency*, which appeared in 1904. After his spring visit to Russia, Ivanov returned to Switzerland and resumed his correspondence with Bryusov. The poem under consideration was written towards the end of the year in November 1904 in response to a poem which Bryusov had sent him a few days earlier. Both poems therefore belong to the end of Ivanov's period of residence abroad, after the firm establishment of his friendship with Bryusov but before his permanent return to Russia in 1905.

Bryusov's poem was entitled 'Again my soul is split . . .' (*'Opyat' dusha moya raskolota . . .'*).[27] It was written at a time of personal crisis, prompted by the complications surrounding the poet's triangular relationship with Nina Petrovskaya and Andrei Bely. Bryusov sent it to Ivanov on 21 November 1904, and wrote in an accompanying note that it was intended to serve the purpose of a letter; elsewhere he referred to it as a photograph of the current state of his soul.[28] It is essentially a confession of the poet's surrender to the forces of darkness. He writes of his descent into an abyss ('I fell into the depths of existence') (*Upal v provaly bytiya*) where he is met by a group of spirits of the dead 'On the ashes of the site of an old fire, / In the smoke of a final conflagration' (*Na peple starogo pozharishcha, / V dymu poslednego ognya*). The spirits triumphantly claim him as their own:

'Ты – наш! – вскричали в дикой нежности, –
Ты наш! и в безднах вечно будь!
Свободный дух предай мятежности,
Тропы лазурные забудь!'

'You're ours! – they exclaimed with savage tenderness –
You're ours! and be in the abysses forever!
Submit your free spirit to storminess,
Forget the azure paths!'

The poet willingly gives himself up to the torment, finding a
perverse pleasure in the burning flames:

> И мне от жгучей боли весело,
> И мне желанен мой костер

> And I'm full of joy from the burning pain,
> And I desire my fire.

Ivanov responded by sending his poem, 'Mi fur le serpi amiche',
to reach Bryusov by his thirty-first birthday on 1 December. In a
letter written shortly afterwards, he explained that his poem was
also intended to be read as an expression of his state of mind:
'Since your poems, those snake bites, those burning hymns, are a
substitute for your letters, you for your part will be able to understand what I grasp from my poem ('Mi fur le serpi amiche') which I
hope you received on your birthday.'[29]
Bryusov was very taken with the poem. At the end of the month
Ivanov wrote to him again, expressing his pleasure and surprise at
his friend's reaction and discussing the arrangements for the
poem's publication in the 1905 almanach of *The Northern Flowers*.
He wished his poem to be printed with a dedication to Bryusov,
providing the latter agreed.[30]
The poem was later included in the first volume of *Cor Ardens*;
Ivanov placed it in 'Arcana', the first section of the second book
'Speculum Speculorum', both of which, like the poem itself, were
dedicated to Bryusov.[31]
The text of the poem is as follows:

MI FUR LE SERPI AMICHE

Dante, *Inf.* xxv, 4

Валерию Брюсову

> Уж я топчу верховный снег
> Алмазной девственной пустыни
> Под синью траурной святыни;
> Ты, в знойной мгле, где дух полыни, –
> Сбираешь яды горьких нег.

В бесплотный облак и в эфир
Глубокий мир внизу истаял ...
А ты – себя еще не чаял,
И вещей пыткой не изваял
Свой окончательный кумир.

Как День, ты новой мукой молод;
Как Ночь, стара моя печаль.
И я изведал горна голод,
И на меня свергался молот,
Пред тем как в отрешенный холод
Крестилась дышащая сталь.

И я был раб в узлах змеи,
И в корчах звал клеймо укуса;
Но огнь последнего искуса
Заклял, и солнцем Эммауса
Озолотились дни мои.

Дуга страдальной Красоты
Тебя ведет чрез преступленье.
Еще, еще преодоленье,
Еще смертельное томленье, –
И вот – из бездн восходишь ты!   (*SS* II, 290–1)

MI FUR LE SERPI AMICHE

Dante, *Inf.* xxv, 4

To Valery Bryusov

Already I tread the topmost snow
Of a diamond virgin desert
Under the blue of a mournful heaven;
You, in the sultry darkness where wormwood's spirit is,
Gather the poisons of bitter pleasures.

The deep world below has melted away
Into insubstantial cloud and ether ...
But you have not yet held out hope for yourself,
And by prophetic agony have not carved out
Your final idol.

Like Day, you are young with recent torment;
Like Night, my sorrow is old.
I too have known the hunger of the furnace,
And the hammer fell upon me

Before the steaming steel
Was baptized in indifferent cold.

I too was a slave in the knots of the snake,
And in spasms called for the stigma of a sting;
But the fire of the final ordeal
I charmed, and by the sun of Emmaus
My days were gilded.

The arc of suffering Beauty
Leads you through transgression.
One more, one more trial to overcome,
One more mortal agony –
And behold – out of the abyss you rise!

The poem is built on a contrast between the description of two
different states – that of the narrator, the 'I' of the poem (linked to
Ivanov) and that of the person addressed as 'you' (linked to
Bryusov). Whereas the first three verses each consist of two
unequal parts, describing the two different states, the last two
verses each refer to one state only, first Ivanov's, then Bryusov's.

Ivanov contrasts his present state with Bryusov's present state
(verses 1 and 2), but draws a comparison between his past and
Bryusov's present (verse 3 and the first two lines of verses 4 and 5),
and implies a further parallel between his present and Bryusov's
future (the last three lines of verses 4 and 5). Ivanov has passed
through the stage of the burning abyss which Bryusov is now
experiencing, and has emerged into the cool, ethereal regions of a
higher realm. He assures Bryusov that his experience will follow
the same pattern, and that he too will eventually rise out of the
abyss.

Ivanov has deliberately referred back to a number of the images
which Bryusov used in his poem. He has taken up the image of the
abyss where torment is by fire in phrases such as 'in the sultry
darkness' (v znoinoi mgle), 'the hunger of the furnace' (gorna
golod), 'the fire of the final ordeal' (ogn' poslednego iskusa), 'out
of the abyss' (iz bezdn), and, like Bryusov, has contrasted these
images with a higher, heavenly region (Ivanov's phrases 'I tread'
(topchu) and 'under the blue' (pod sin'yu) echo the 'azure paths'
(tropy lazurnye) which the spirits of the dead enjoined Bryusov to
forget).

These two sets of imagery create a topography or spiritual

landscape in which reference to Dante is clearly invited. Although Bryusov's poem contains no explicit Dantesque imagery, its insistence on the experience of the abyss and on torment by fire, contrasted with heavenly regions, creates the type of context in which Dante was commonly invoked as a figure of the poet who descended into the abyss and rose from it to higher regions; this is the case, for example, in Bryusov's later poem of 1907, 'To the Poet' ('*Poetu*'), where the poet is commanded to be like Dante and allow the flame of the underworld to burn his cheek.

Not surprisingly, therefore, Ivanov has drawn on Dantesque imagery in his poem – this enables him to set Bryusov's experience of the abyss in a new context, implying that it forms part of a journey with a direction which will lead to future redemption. If, as is discussed in chapter 6 below, Ivanov and Bryusov were both considering working on a joint translation of the *Commedia* at this time, these references to Dante acquire an additional level of significance, for Bryusov was to translate the *Inferno* and Ivanov the *Purgatorio* and *Paradiso*.

The Dantesque images occur mainly in the fourth verse of the poem, and are explicitly related to their source by the poem's title, 'Mi fur le serpi amiche' ('the serpents were my friends'), a direct quotation from *Inferno* xxv, 4. Cantos xxiv and xxv of the *Inferno* deal with the sin of thievery and the manner of its punishment in the seventh ditch of the eighth circle of Hell. The thieves are condemned to run naked, with their hands bound behind their backs by a coiled serpent whose head and tail are knotted together at the front of the sinner's body (xxiv, 94–6). In this way they are deprived of the use of their hands in the after-life, as a punishment for having misused them during their life on earth.

In this circle Dante witnesses a memorable scene. One of the sinners is stung in the nape of the neck by a serpent. He immediately catches fire and burns until he is reduced to ashes. Then the dust miraculously draws together of its own accord, and the sinner resumes his former shape, reborn from his ashes like the phoenix (xxiv, 97–108). This cycle of destruction and rebirth makes it possible for the sinner's torment to be eternally renewed through the sting of the serpents.

The sinner attacked in this way turns out to be Vanni Fucci, a much despised contemporary of Dante's described as 'a man of blood and rage' (xxiv, 129). He is shamed by Dante witnessing his plight, and takes his revenge in two ways. First he implies that Dante may never emerge from Hell ('se mai sarai di fuor da' luoghi bui' – 'if ever you escape from these dark regions' – xxiv, 141), and then he delivers an unpleasant prophecy about Florence, specifically designed to wound Dante's feelings ('E detto l'ho perché doler ti debbia!' – 'And I have said this that it may grieve you!' – xxiv, 151).

At the beginning of the next canto, Vanni Fucci rounds off his venomous speech by raising his hands in an obscene gesture and blaspheming God. At this point a serpent coils itself about his neck, to prevent him from further speech, and another knots itself about his arms, holding them back from further movement (xxv, 1–9). When this happens Dante makes the comment which Ivanov has chosen as the title of his poem – from this time forth, the serpents were his friends. He feels this way because the serpents were not only carrying out the divine scheme of vengeance, but had also, in this instance, inflicted punishment on a particular enemy of his.

A close look at the imagery of the fourth verse of Ivanov's poem reveals a number of links with Dante's description of the punishment of the thieves. The poet announces that he too was a slave, bound in the knots of the serpent, and called for the final sting which would release him from his torment. This sting, according to Dante's text, would cause him to burst into flames, and perhaps with reference to this image, Ivanov adds that he nevertheless succeeded in charming the fire of this final trial, and achieved a true and lasting resurrection (unlike the resurrection of Dante's sinners who are only reborn for new torment). The reference to the sun of Emmaus in this context serves to inscribe the poet's experience within a Christian framework – Ivanov's final redemption and the lesson which it carries for Bryusov are implicitly compared to Christ's appearance at Emmaus to two of his disciples after his crucifixion and resurrection from the dead; this was to confirm the teaching that the Messiah would enter into his glory after having first passed through a stage of suffering (Luke 24. 13–26).

The passage from the image of the coils of the snake ('I too was a slave in the knots of the snake') (*I ya byl rab v uzlakh zmei*) to the gold of the sun ('and by the sun of Emmaus / My days were gilded') (*i solntsem Emmausa / Ozolotilis' dni moi'*) occurs elsewhere in Ivanov's poetry of this period. When 'Mi fur le serpi amiche' was

first published in *The Northern Flowers* in 1905, it formed part of a
cycle entitled 'Snakes and Suns' ('*Zmei i solntsa*').

One of the other poems of this cycle, 'Resurrection' ('*Vozrozhdenie*'), placed immediately before 'Mi fur le serpi amiche' in *Cor Ardens*, uses the same images of snakes' coils and golden suns to illustrate the Dionysiac cycle linking death and sin to resurrection and redemption; the snake is traditionally a Biblical emblem of sin, and therefore of death, but its self-renewing scales hint at the idea of new life, conveyed more fully by the image of the sun. A couplet from the poem states that those who worship snakes and suns are able to perceive the 'secret wingedness of the depths' (*sokrovennaya krylatost' glubiny* – *SS* II, 290), a phrase which could well serve to summarize the basic message of 'Mi fur le serpi amiche'.

In 'Mi fur le serpi amiche' Ivanov has exploited the surface similarity between these images of snakes and suns, clearly of Dionysiac origin, and Dante's description of the snakes in *Inferno* XXIV and XXV, also associated with coils, burning flames and a resurrection of sorts (the Phoenix-like rebirth of the sinner). The Dantesque images have been divorced from their original context and assimilated into the Dionysiac meaning established by the text of the poem. The way in which this process of redefinition takes place is well illustrated by one particular example concerning two phrases with Dantesque associations which change their meaning when transposed to the new context.

The first of these phrases, 'Mi fur le serpi amiche', is used as the title of the poem and is a direct quotation of the words spoken by Dante in the *Inferno* when he witnesses the divine punishment of sin. The second phrase, 'I too was a slave in the knots of the snake' (*I ya byl rab v uzlakh zmei*), is not a quotation from Dante but sounds as if it could well be derived from the same canto. If, however, this were the case it could only be spoken by a sinner such as Vanni Fucci who had undergone the torment of the seventh ditch; it could not be attributed to Dante since he experienced neither the sin nor its punishment.

In Ivanov's poem, however, the original meaning of the two phrases is substantially altered. They are presented alongside each other as the utterances of a single voice (both are related to the central 'I' or narrator of the poem). This creates the impression that the Dante whose voice speaks in the first phrase – and who merely witnessed the sin – had in fact also experienced it – he was not only friends with the serpents but had also been trapped in their coils. In fact, in the overall context of the poem, the opening quotation from Dante loses its original meaning, associated with the poet's approval of the divine punishment of sin, and reads more like an open confession of past complicity in sin.

In this way, by merging the concepts of spectator of sin and actual sinner, Ivanov implies that the sinner of his poem will emerge from the dark of the abyss to the light of redemption, in the same way as Dante, the witness of sin, passed out of *Inferno* to the spheres of *Paradiso*. And yet this teaching ignores the moral message of the *Commedia* – Dante is only able to emerge from the *Inferno* because he is free of its sins, whereas the sinners like Vanni Fucci who are imprisoned in the coils of the serpents have no hope of redemption.

The transition from sin to redemption is made possible by the special emphasis placed upon the suffering dimension of sin. Throughout the poem, allusions to sin (through reference to the darkness and phrases such as 'you gather the poisons of bitter pleasures' (*sbiraesh' yady gorkikh neg*) alternate with evocations of the accompanying suffering, agony (*pytka*) and torment (*muka*). In the last verse these two threads merge to convey the final message – that the path of suffering ('the arc of suffering Beauty' – *duga stradal'noi Krasoty*) leads through sin ('through transgression' – *chrez prestuplenie*) to redemption ('And behold – out of the abyss you rise' – *I vot – iz bezdn voskhodish' ty*). The Christian idea of *suffering* as a path to redemption, illustrated by the reference to Emmaus, has been combined with the Dionysiac view that *sin* can also lead to redemption, through its suffering dimension. The Dantesque imagery in the poem helps to bridge the gap between these two essentially incompatible views. It places sin within the context of a journey with an ultimate purpose leading to redemption. Although in their original context these images referred only to the *knowledge* or *understanding* of sin, in Ivanov's poem they appear to endorse the view that the path to spiritual enlightenment may lead through the *experience* of sin. In this respect 'Mi fur le serpi amiche' is very similar to some of the poems discussed above such as 'La Selva Oscura' or 'At the Coliseum'; it makes use of Dantesque imagery to lend a Christian purgatorial quality to sin.

The poem also provides an interesting reflection of Ivanov's personal experience. It was written at a time when the poet's initial

sense of sin as a dark demonic force had given way to a new
understanding of suffering sin as a possible path to mystic growth.
In his poem Ivanov is inviting Bryusov to forego the deliberate
dwelling on sin which is reflected in the latter's poem and to adopt
the wider perspective on the experience of the abyss which Ivanov
has reached. He is dissociating himself from the younger poet's
overtly decadent stance by underlining that he has progressed
beyond this stage and by pointing the way forward for future
development.

Ivanov's prediction that Bryusov would emerge from the abyss
was in some sense fulfilled. In September of the following year,
Bryusov experienced a feeling of spiritual and artistic renewal
which he described to Ivanov in terms which deliberately echo the
imagery of 'Mi fur le serpi amiche':

I feel myself dying in one part of my soul and reviving in another. Reviving
in that part which you know best. I am working a great deal, as I haven't
worked for a long time ... I am printing my *Stephanos* in which you will
find many new things. In general, in my work I feel a fresh vitality,
strength, a sense that everything is possible – the wingedness of a bright
morning when it is so easy to reach what I was vainly striving for both in
the flaming evening and the will-less night.[32]

These feelings were short-lived, however. After the publication
of *Stephanos* in December 1905, Bryusov experienced a sense of
anti-climax and felt that he had reached the end of a road. He did
not choose to follow Ivanov along the path of a flight to higher
spiritual regions. His position remained linked to the old school of
Russian Symbolism with its primarily aesthetic principles taken
over from the French movement. He did not espouse the religious
or theurgic view of art which Ivanov and the younger Symbolists
were trying to promote. In this respect Ivanov's poem marks a
significant turning-point in the poets' relations which is indicative
of the wider split between the two strands of Symbolism which was
taking place at the time. These differences are hinted at in the
poem but there is still sufficient common ground for a dialogue to
take place. By the following year, after the revolution of 1905, the
poets' differences became more pronounced and their paths diver-
ged altogether.

'Golden Veils'

The cycle of seventeen sonnets entitled 'Golden Veils' ('*Zolotye zavesy*') was inspired by Ivanov's relationship with Margarita Sabashnikova at the end of 1906 and beginning of 1907. It was first published in 1907 in the literary almanach of Ivanov's publishing house Oraea; later, in a shorter version reduced to sixteen sonnets, it was republished in *Cor Ardens* alongside the poems connected with Gorodetsky (these had also already appeared under separate cover in 1907 in *Eros*, Ivanov's third book of verse). Together, the two sets of poems formed the third and final book of the first part of *Cor Ardens*. This arrangement highlighted the parallelism between the two affairs and their role in Ivanov's life; it reflected their importance as a culminating stage in the poet's cult of Eros before the death of Lidiya Dimitrievna in 1907 and the transition to the poems of the second part of *Cor Ardens*. In order to set the two affairs within the framework of the wider understanding of their significance brought about by the death of Lidiya Dimitrievna, Ivanov composed a new epigraph in 1911 dedicated to Diotima; this was strategically placed at the beginning of the third book, immediately after the earlier epigraph of 1906 which had accompanied the first publication of *Eros* in 1907:

ЗНАЕШЬ И ТЫ, ДИОТИМА, КОМУ ТВОЙ ПЕВЕЦ ЭТИ МИРТЫ,
   ИВОЙ УВЕНЧАН, СВИВАЛ: РОЗЫ ВПЛЕТАЛИСЬ ТВОИ
В СМУГЛУЮ ЗЕЛЕНЬ ЖЕЛАНИЙ И В ГИБКОЕ ЗОЛОТО
   ПЛЕНА.
   РОЗОЙ СВЯТИЛА ТЫ ЖИЗНЬ; В РОЗАХ К БЕССМЕРТНЫМ
УШЛА.
   МСМХІ   (*SS* II, 362)

YOU TOO, DIOTIMA, KNOW FOR WHOM YOUR SINGER, CROWNED WITH
   WILLOW,
   WREATHED THESE MYRTLES: YOUR ROSES WERE PLAITED
INTO THE DARK GREEN OF DESIRES AND THE SUPPLE GOLD OF CAPTIVITY.
   WITH A ROSE YOU SANCTIFIED LIFE; IN ROSES YOU WENT AWAY TO
THE IMMORTALS.
   МСМХІ

The cycle 'Golden Veils' is prefaced with its own epigraph, taken from Petrarch: 'Di pensier in pensier, di monte in monte / Mi guida Amor . . . ' ('From thought to thought, from mount to mount / I am guided by Love . . .'). These are the opening lines of a *canzone*

from the 'Sonetti e canzoni in vita di Madonna Laura' which describes the various images of Laura which arise in the poet's mind as
he wanders through different landscapes, far from his beloved.[33]
Ivanov's choice of epigraph serves to place the experience of
erotic–mystical love described in his cycle within the context of the
tradition of love poetry established by Dante and continued by Petrarch. His allegiance to this tradition is further emphasized by the
use of the form of the sonnet, and by the obscure, visionary nature
of the imagery which prevails throughout the cycle.

In life as well as in Ivanov's poetry, Margarita Sabashnikova was
also linked with the works of Petrarch. She was called Amori by
both Ivanov and her husband, Voloshin – a name which carries
Petrarchan associations; in a number of poems, including the
canzone from which the epigraph to 'Golden Veils' is taken,
Petrarch refers to his beloved, Laura, as Amor.[34]

Ivanov's cycle describes the various stages of initiation in the
mystic journey of two lovers guided by Eros. In a succession of
visions and dreams, the figure of Eros leads the lovers through
several veils (*zavesy*) until they reach a final stage of spiritual
illumination. Given the nature of this subject, and the context
established by the epigraph to the cycle, it is not surprising to find a
number of Dantesque images in the cycle. These are mainly connected with the description of the lovers, who are compared to
Francesca and Paolo, and with the structure of their spiritual
journey which, like Dante's, progresses from the dark wood to the
light of Paradise. Ivanov's approach to these two areas of Dantesque imagery is generally very similar to that reflected in 'La Selva
Oscura' and 'At the Coliseum', as can be seen from a few
examples.

From the very first lines of the opening sonnet, the experience of
Eros is established as one of suffering and martyrdom:

Лучами стрел Эрот меня пронзил,
Влача на казнь, как связня Севастьяна;   (*SS* II, 384)

With rays of arrows Eros pierced me,
Dragging me to my execution, like the captive Sebastian.

Within this context Ivanov turns to the figures of Francesca and
Paolo as examples of martyred lovers. The first explicit reference
to Dante's lovers occurs in the third sonnet of the cycle:

Во сне предстал мне наг и смугл Эрот,
Как знойного пловец Архипелага.
С ночных кудрей текла на плечи влага;
Вздымались перси; в пене бледный рот . . .

'Тебе слугой была моя отвага,
Тебе, – шепнул он, – дар моих щедрот:
В индийский я нырнул водоворот,
Утешного тебе искатель блага.'

И, сеткой препоясан, вынул он
Жемчужину таинственного блеска.
И в руку мне она скатилась веско . . .

И схвачен в вир, и бурей унесен,
Как Паоло, с твоим, моя Франческа,
Я свил свой вихрь . . . Кто свеял с вежд мой сон?   (*SS* II, 385)

In a dream Eros appeared to me naked and swarthy,
Like the swimmer of the sultry Archipelago.
From nocturnal curls moisture flowed onto his shoulders;
His bosom rose; his pale mouth was in foam . . .

'My courage was your servant,
For you – he whispered – a gift of my munificence:
I dived into an Indian whirlpool,
A seeker of comforting good for you'.

And, girded with a string-bag, he took out
A pearl of mysterious radiance.
And it rolled into my palm heavily . . .

And caught up in the whirlwind, and carried away by the storm,
Like Paolo, my Francesca, with yours
I wove my whirlwind . . . Who blew the dream from my eyelids?

The appearance of the figure of Eros to the poet in a dream is clearly modelled on the descriptions of the lordly figure of Amor who appears to Dante in a series of dreams or visions recorded in the *Vita Nuova*.[35] Eros presents the poet with a pearl (a symbol of Margarita, as noted earlier). After receiving this gift the poet compares himself to Paolo, swept away with Francesca in the whirlwind of their shared passion. The Dionysiac whirlwind (*vikhr'*) alluded to in the leaf and wind imagery of 'At the Coliseum' is here explicitly related to the 'bufera infernal' ('the hellish hurricane') which blows Francesca and Paolo about in the second circle of the *Inferno*.

Needless to say, the Dantesque elements in this sonnet are presented in a manner which is totally uncharacteristic of Dante. In a review published in *Vesy* in 1907, Bely expressed strong criticism of Ivanov's cycle, and singled out this particular sonnet for a biting attack as an example of the poet's indiscriminate syncretic blending of images and words from unrelated cultures:

The swarthy figure of Hellenic Eros dives into the Indian Ocean for Mr Ivanov in search of a pearl, a whirlpool envelops Mr Ivanov in Greece, like Paolo and Francesca, and sweeps him along, while he declares to us that he has '*woven his own whirlwind*' himself. It is good that Mr Ivanov weaves his own whirlwinds himself, but unfortunate that he weaves them out of just any old geographical and historical images. Is not Mr Ivanov's own verbal 'whirlpool' a trifle over-bold when he launches himself from India and Greece simultaneously into Slavonic philology ('whirlpool' [*vir*] is a Slavonic word), becoming like Paolo and Francesca, buffetted about in ... perhaps in the world of a philological whirlpool? Oh no: Paolo and Francesca flew about in an underworld of true passion, and not in a world of imaginary philological eroticism.[36]

Bely's criticisms strike rather close to the bone. Ivanov's cult of Eros sometimes appeared artificial, and his syncretic approach to other cultures did lead to a number of distortions. However, he would no doubt have defended himself against Bely's accusations by arguing that the features under attack were part of a deliberate method designed to reflect the confused and undefined nature of his relationship with Sabashnikova.

Imagery related to Francesca and Paolo also occurs in a number of other sonnets of the cycle. Although it is no longer explicitly linked to the names of Dante's lovers, the connection remains obvious. The fifth sonnet, for example, opens with a description of the two lovers dreaming on a bed. The second verse continues:

> Воздушных тел в божественной метели
> Так мы скитались, вверя дух волне
> Бесплотных встреч, – и в легкой их стране
> Нас сочетал Эрот, как мы хотели.   (*SS* II, 386)

In the divine blizzard of airy bodies,
So we wandered, entrusting our spirit to a wave
Of incorporeal meetings – and in their light country
Eros united us as we wished.

The image of lovers caught in a whirlwind of light bodies and giving themselves up to the driving force of love is evidently inspired by Dante's description of the condition of Francesca and Paolo. Similar imagery is used again in the thirteenth sonnet:

> В слиянных снах, смыкая тело с телом,
> Нам сладко реять в смутных глубинах
> Эфирных бездн, иль на речных волнах,
> Как пена, плыть под небом потемнелым.
>
> То жаворонком в горних быстринах,
> То ласточкой по мглам отяжелелым –
> Двоих Эрот к неведомым пределам
> На окрыленных носит раменах . . .   (*SS* ii, 390)

> In interfused dreams, pressing body to body,
> It is sweet for us to hover in the troubled depths
> Of ethereal abysses, or in river waves,
> Like foam, to swim under a darkened sky.
>
> Now like a lark in the mountain rapids,
> Now like a swallow through the weighty gloom –
> Eros carries two to unknown frontiers
> On his winged shoulders . . .

The fusion of the lovers and the sweetness of their passion are evoked in terms reminiscent of *Inferno* v. The comparison of Eros to a lark or swallow carrying the lovers on its wings is also indirectly related to the imagery of this canto. Dante compares the carnal sinners driven by the blast of the infernal wind to starlings, carried along in a broad flock on their wings (*Inf.* v, 40–2). When he summons Francesca and Paolo to his side, they fly to him like doves, with wings poised and motionless, borne by their will through the air (ll. 82–4). In both these images, the lovers are compared to birds, swept along by the force of their passion. Ivanov has retained the elements of Dante's comparison, but transferred the image of the bird to Eros, the passion which drives the lovers.

The cycle culminates in a vision of the two lovers being led out of a dark wood towards the light by Eros. The penultimate sonnet describes the lovers' vain attempts to leave the trackless thicket until Eros, heralded by the sound of pipe music, arrives to be their companion; he guides them out of the dark wood (*sumrachnyi les*) to the light, drawing back veil after veil before them:

Когда уста твои меня призвали
Вожатым быть чрез дебрь, где нет дорог,
И поцелуй мне стигмы в руку вжог, –
Ты помнишь лик страстной моей печали ...

Я больше мочь посмел, чем сметь я мог ...
Вдруг ожили свирельной песнью дали;
О гроздиях нам птицы щебетали;
Нам спутником предстал крылатый бог.

И след его по сумрачному лесу
Тропою был, куда, на тайный свет,
Меня стремил священный мой обет.

Так он, подобный душ вождю, Гермесу, –
Где нет путей и где распутий нет, –
Нам за завесой раздвигал завесу.

(*SS* II, 391)

When your lips called me
To be a guide through the jungle where there are no roads,
And when a kiss burnt stigmata into my hand –
You remember the countenance of my passionate sorrow ...

I dared to be able to do more than I was able to dare ...
Suddenly the distance came to life with the song of a reed-pipe;
Birds twittered to us about clusters;
A winged god appeared to us as a companion.

And the trace he left through the dark wood
Was a path to which, towards a mysterious light,
My sacred vow directed me.

Thus he, like the leader of souls, Hermes –
There where there are no ways and no partings of the ways –
Lifted back veil after veil for us.

In the concluding sonnet, the last of the golden veils is lifted back, and the wood where the lovers were lost parts to reveal a fertile garden. The poet has arrived in Paradise and undergone a complete spiritual resurrection:

Единую из золотых завес
Ты подняла пред восхищенным взглядом,
О Ночь-садовница! и щедрым садом
Раздвинула блужданий зыбкий лес.

Так, странствуя из рая в рай чудес,
Дивится дух нечаянным отрадам,
Как я хмелен янтарным виноградом
И гласом птиц, поющих: 'Ты воскрес'.   (*SS* II, 391–2)

A single one of the golden veils
You lifted before delighted eyes,
O Night-gardener! and with a lavish garden
Parted the shifting wood of wanderings.

Thus, roaming from paradise to paradise of wonders,
The spirit marvels at the unexpected delights,
In the same way as I am intoxicated by the amber grapes
And by the voice of birds singing: 'You are risen'.

Very similar imagery is used in the final verse of another poem
from the first part of *Cor Ardens*, 'De Profundis'. Here the poet
prays for deliverance from the depths of a dark wood to a god who
is more powerful than the Sun (a traditional Christian image for
God the Father). This god, from his vantage point in the transparent heavens and from the other side of the veils which obscure the
poet's vision, will be able to send light down into the dark wood
and rescue the poet from his predicament:

В родной прозрачности торжественных небес, –
Я жду, – из-за моих редеющих завес,
    Единосущней, соприродней,
Чем ты, о зримый свет, источнику чудес
Вожатый озарит блужданий темный лес:
    К нему я звал из преисподней.   (*SS* II, 237)

In the dear transparency of the exultant heavens –
I wait – from the other side of my dwindling veils,
    A guide who is closer in essence and in nature
Than you, o visible light, to the source of wonders,
Will illuminate the dark wood of wanderings:
    To him I called from the depths.

Like the figure of Eros in 'Golden Veils', the god addressed in this
poem – referred to simply as 'the guide' (*vozhatyi*) – has the power
to lead the pilgrim soul from darkness to light.

'Golden Veils' and the stage of Ivanov's life to which it belongs
represent a peak point in the poet's cult of Eros and, within this
context, in his assimilation of Dantesque images of love into the
framework of a Dionysiac mystic journey, inspired by an amoral

experience of Eros. Ivanov has used Dantesque images to imply
the exact opposite of their original meaning – in his cycle sexual
love is no longer a possible barrier to spiritual development but a
direct means to its attainment. The carnal passion of the lovers
associated with Francesca and Paolo, far from condemning them to
eternal torment in Hell, becomes a force closely linked with Eros
which enables them to pass from the dark wood to Paradise and to
embrace all the stages of Dante's spiritual journey. Dionysiac Eros
has taken on the role of Dante's Amor, without shedding its
association with carnal love.

After the 'Golden Veils' cycle, references to Francesca and Paolo
become noticeably rarer in Ivanov's work, apart from one significant exception. This is the translation of D'Annunzio's play,
Francesca da Rimini, which Ivanov undertook with Bryusov
between the end of 1907 and the summer of 1908 at the request of the
actress Vera Komissarzhevskaya.[37] The original play is a typical *fin
de siècle* piece of writing and presents a decadent glorified picture of
the lovers' passion. This emphasis is reflected in the translation but
was by then no longer so typical of Ivanov's approach to Dante.
During the period following Lidiya Dimitrievna's death in October
1907, the poet's interest in Dante underwent a considerable change
and his preoccupation with Dantesque images of sin and of carnal
love gradually lessened. A later isolated couplet on Paolo and
Francesca which he included in the fifth book of *Cor Ardens*,
'Rosarium', composed in the summer of 1910, reflects this development; it portrays Dante's lovers as representatives of a fiery passion,
but does not extol them and is considerably more restrained in tone:

ПАОЛО И ФРАНЧЕСКА
Юноше красную розу дала чрез решетку невеста:
Два запылали костра, плавя железный закон.   (*SS* II, 503)

PAOLO AND FRANCESCA
The bride gave the youth a red rose through the grille:
Two fires flared up, melting the iron law.

COR ARDENS II

The Fourth Book: 'Love and Death'

The poems from *Cor Ardens* considered so far have all been taken
from the first part of the work, composed between 1904 and 1907.

Ivanov originally regarded his collection as complete by this stage. In June 1906 he wrote to Bryusov that he would be sending him the completed manuscript of *Cor Ardens* in the near future. He finally did so, after extensive further correspondence, at the end of July 1907.[38] At this stage his work consisted of just three books, 'Cor Ardens', 'Speculum Speculorum' and 'Eros', forming what later became the first part of *Cor Ardens*.

The two books which subsequently came to form the second part of *Cor Ardens* were unplanned additions which initially arose quite independently as new books in their own right. After Lidiya Dimitrievna's sudden death in October 1907, Ivanov began to develop ideas for a new book. In June 1908 he recorded in his diary that he had already begun work on a new collection of poems, to consist of a series of *Canzoni* and sonnets (*SS* II, 772). In the following month he wrote to Bryusov that he was about to leave for the Crimea and was writing a new book of poems (*SS* II, 695). At the beginning of November he wrote again to inform Bryusov that he had returned from the Crimea to the tower in time for the anniversary of Lidiya Dimitrievna's death, and now planned to embark on a new life of hard work. He felt full of renewed faith in the value of a religious approach to life, and had almost finished writing his book of poems, now referred to as 'Love and Death' (*'Lyubov' i Smert''*) and described as '*canzoni* and sonnets dedicated to the departed one'.

Ivanov was anxious to publish his new poems as soon as possible; he referred to this as a 'moral need ... to mark the anniversary of the departure of her to whose name they are dedicated'. He therefore planned to publish them immediately, as a separate book, unless there was a chance that *Cor Ardens* would be ready by December. In this case he would prefer to include 'Love and Death' in *Cor Ardens* as a fourth book, since it would greatly improve the architectural balance of the work and enhance the meaning of its title.

In his reply Bryusov insisted that Ivanov should include his new poems in *Cor Ardens* and not publish them separately.[39] Ivanov did not however, finish preparing the proofs of the book in its new form until August 1909, and was then overcome by a crisis of deep indifference which lasted throughout the winter of 1909 to 1910 and prevented him from handing over the completed manuscript to the publishers.[40] In the early summer of 1910 he wrote a new series of poems which he decided to include in *Cor Ardens* as a fifth book, entitled 'Rosarium'. It was only at this point, before travelling to Italy to join Vera in the summer of 1910, that he handed in the manuscript of the entire work, now in five books and divided into two parts; these appeared in two separate volumes in 1911.[41]

The fourth book of *Cor Ardens*, 'Love and Death', therefore consists of the poems which Ivanov composed between June and November 1908 to express his feelings over the death of Lidiya Dimitrievna in the previous year. This tragic event forced him to come to terms in real life with theories which he had previously espoused in a somewhat more abstract form. The two principal sources of his ideal of mystic love – the religion of Dionysus and the teachings of Solovyov – both called for the spiritualization of earthly love. According to the first system, this was to be achieved by embracing the Dionysiac cycle, leading from an initial abundance of life through death to the creation of new life. According to Solovyov's teachings, love should transcend the physical object of its affections and rise to a higher, purely spiritual level.

The death of Lidiya Dimitrievna gave Ivanov an opportunity to implement these ideals more fully, and to further identify his experience of love with the works of Dante and Petrarch. Previously, he had turned to these works for images of love or sin connected with the mystic journey; now, however, the parallel between his experience and their's was far closer. Dante and Petrarch had both suffered the loss of their beloved and striven to express their experience in artistic forms. Like Beatrice and Laura, Lidiya Dimitrievna had died an early death and, like Dante and Petrarch, Ivanov was faced with the challenge of learning to love her image in a purely spiritual way. 'Love and Death' is the record of his response to this challenge. Not surprisingly, given the similarity of circumstance, it is closely modelled on Dante's *Vita Nuova* and on Petrarch's 'Sonetti e canzoni in morte di Madonna Laura'. Both these works record the poet's intense love of a woman during her life-time, the suffering caused by her death, and the attempt to overcome this suffering through a new, more spiritual form of love. For the first time Ivanov turned to these works not just as a source of images, but also in order to imitate their structure. In later years he took this process even further by translating parts of both works.

Ivanov's conscious intention to model his new book on Dante and Petrarch is clear from his first reference to the project in his diary. On 13 June 1908 he resumed his diary after a break of six years and recorded a dream in which Lidiya Dimitrievna appeared to him, crowned him with a golden wreath, handed him a golden lyre, and instructed him to 'sing the last songs' (*Poi poslednie pesni – SS* II, 772). The next entry in the diary, written two days later, begins with the following passage:

42 sonnets and 12 *canzoni* should at the very least go into my future book 'sub specie mortis', in accordance with the number of years of our life and of our shared life together. Yesterday I finished the first *canzone* which moved Marusya to tears as well as Kuzmin, whose eyes lit up. Yesterday I wrote a sonnet about swans. In all, there are so far three sonnets for the book. K[uzmin] suggests writing a connecting text in prose following the model of the 'Vita nova'.   (*SS* II, 772)

The idea of writing a book of lyrics consisting of *canzoni* and sonnets is clearly an attempt to imitate the structure of Dante's *Vita Nuova* and of Petrarch's 'Sonetti e canzoni in morte di Madonna Laura'. Ivanov's attention to the symbolic value of numbers is also typical of both poets. Dante, for example, arranged the sonnets and *canzoni* of the *Vita Nuova* in a symmetrical pattern based on the numbers 1, 3, 9 and 10, and associated three and nine (symbolic of the Holy Trinity) with the circumstances of his love for Beatrice, their ages when they first met, the hour and day of Beatrice's death and many other factors. In similar fashion, Ivanov planned to include forty-two sonnets in his work (to correspond to the years of his life from 1866 to 1908) and twelve *canzoni* (to correspond to the years of his life shared with Lidiya Dimitrievna, from the decisive meeting in the Coliseum of 1895 to Lidiya Dimitrievna's death in 1907).

Ivanov did not in fact carry out this early plan. In its final form his book consists of three *canzoni* between which cycles of sonnets are arranged in different numerical groupings; the most common grouping is the one adopted by Dante in the *Vita Nuova* – a cycle of ten sonnets – which in Ivanov's case takes the form of an introductory sonnet followed by a cycle of nine sonnets. The collection also contains a *sestina* and an epilogue.

The *canzone* to which Ivanov refers in his diary remained the first *canzone* of the book, as originally planned. It is entitled 'The Great Bell to a pilgrimage ...' ('*Velikii Kolokol na bogomol'e* ...') and is prefaced by the opening section of Petrarch's first *canzone* on Laura's death, 'Che debbo io far? Che mi consigli,

Amore? . . . ' ('What should I do? What do you advise me, Love? . . . ' – *SS* II, 396). The parallel with Petrarch is further developed in the poem which exactly reproduces the structure of the Italian *canzone*, beginning with a reference to the death of the beloved, continuing with a description of the poet's suffering, and concluding with a *tornata* addressed to the *canzone*.

Kuzmin's suggestion that Ivanov should follow the model of the *Vita Nuova* and compose prose passages connecting the poems of 'Love and Death' and explaining their meaning is of particular significance. There is an interesting parallel here with Blok's later project of 1918 to remodel the *Verses about the Beautiful Lady* in the manner of the *Vita Nuova*. Blok did not complete his project, nor did Ivanov take up Kuzmin's suggestion, but both ideas are nevertheless evidence of the authors' sense of affinity between their works and the *Vita Nuova*. Had Ivanov followed Kuzmin's suggestion, or carried out the plan which he entertained at one stage of including earlier poems written before Lidiya Dimitrievna's death in his book, it would have borne an even closer resemblance to the *Vita Nuova* which incorporates earlier poems from Dante's youth as well as later ones.[42]

From the point of view of its composition and form, Ivanov's book bears a closer resemblance to Petrarch's 'Sonetti e canzoni in morte di Madonna Laura' than to the *Vita Nuova*, as it consists only of poems written after the death of the poet's beloved and does not contain a prose commentary. However, its general mood and the feelings which it expresses are closely related to Dante's work in a number of ways. This can be seen both from the poems of the book and also from certain passages of the diary which Ivanov was keeping at the time. These can in a sense be compared to the prose passages of the *Vita Nuova*; they supply the background to the poems and clarify the experiences which gave rise to them. In some cases they reveal a deep affinity between the emotions which Ivanov experienced after the death of Lidiya Dimitrievna and those recorded by Dante in the *Vita Nuova* after the death of Beatrice. Ivanov was evidently aware of this parallel; when he began his diary on 13 June 1908 he adopted a style reminiscent of the opening of the *Vita Nuova*; just as Dante refers to his intention to copy the meaning ('sentenzia') of the experiences preserved in his memory into his little book ('libello'), so Ivanov refers to his diary as a sacred little book (*svyataya knizhechka*) in

which he will record his experiences (*zapisyvat' perezhivaemoe* –
SS II, 771).

A more striking example of this parallel occurs in the next diary
entry, dated 15 June 1908. After outlining the plan of his new book
(the passage quoted earlier), Ivanov continued to describe a dream
or vision of Lidiya:

I saw Lidiya with enormous swan's wings. In her hands she was holding a
glowing heart [*pylayushchee serdtse*] of which we both partook: she –
painlessly, and I – with pain from the fire. Before us lay Vera, apparently
lifeless. Lidiya placed the fiery heart [*ognennoe serdtse*] from which we had
eaten into her breast, and she revived; but, losing her senses and with a
dagger in her hands, she attacked us both in a fury and, clinging to Lidiya,
kept saying about me: 'Is he mine?'. Then Lidiya took her in her arms, and
I saw her, absorbed into the glassy transparent breast of her mother.

(*SS* II, 772)

    Ivanov's account of his dream closely echoes a passage from the
third chapter of the *Vita Nuova* in which Dante describes a vision
of Beatrice. The figure of Amor appears to Dante, holding the
sleeping Beatrice in his arms. In one of his hands he holds 'una cosa
la quale ardesse tutta' ('an object which was burning all over'); he
tells Dante that this is his heart ('Vide cor tuum' – 'Behold your
heart'), and wakens Beatrice in order to make her eat part of the
glowing heart ('questa cosa che . . . ardea' – 'the object which . . .
was burning'). He then enfolds Beatrice in his arms and ascends
with her to the heavens. Dante wakes up in anguish and composes
a sonnet about his dream in which he refers to his heart as a 'core
ardendo' ('burning heart').
    The two dreams are remarkably similar. In Ivanov's dream
Lidiya Dimitrievna appears in place of Amor, holding a glowing
(*pylayushchee*) or fiery (*ognennoe*) heart which she consumes part
of with Ivanov. Vera, like Beatrice, lies motionless, but revives
when the glowing heart is placed in her breast. In the same way as
Dante's dream seems to indicate that Beatrice is to possess his
heart, Ivanov's dream suggests that Vera will take over from
Lidiya Dimitrievna and rule the poet's heart (Ivanov was already
obsessed with this thought by this date). Lidiya Dimitrievna's final
gesture – gathering Vera into her arms – recalls the way in which
Amor gathers Beatrice into his embraces, and perhaps in a similar
way hints at the future death of the poet's beloved.
    Ivanov evidently knew this particular passage of the *Vita Nuova*

3 The frontispiece of *Cor Ardens*, 1911

closely; in fact he subsequently translated it and made it the basis of one of his essays on Symbolist aesthetics.[43] It may well also have served as one of the sources of the title *Cor Ardens*. Dante uses the verb 'ardere' ('to burn') twice in the prose part of the passage to describe his burning heart, and the phrase 'core ardendo' (the Italian version of 'cor ardens') occurs in the sonnet. Whether or not Ivanov had this in mind when he first chose the title *Cor Ardens* (already in use by June 1906) is open to question;[44] however, it does seem likely that he became aware of the association after the death of Lidiya Dimitrievna, if not before, and intended it to be made by others. This is clear from the new dedication to Lidiya Dimitrievna which he composed after her death (*Cor Ardens* had originally been dedicated to Bryusov);[45] it is placed after the title page of the first book and reads as follows:

БЕССМЕРТНОМУ СВЕТУ
ЛИДИИ ДИМИТРИЕВНЫ
ЗИНОВЬЕВОИ-АННИБАЛ

ТОЙ, ЧТО, СГОРЕВ НА ЗЕМЛЕ МОИМ ПЛАМЕНЕЮЩИМ СЕРДЦЕМ,
СТАЛА ИЗ ПЛАМЕНИ СВЕТ В ХРАМИНЕ ГОСТЯ ЗЕМЛИ.

(SS ΙΙ, 225)

TO THE IMMORTAL LIGHT
OF LIDIYA DIMITRIEVNA
ZINOVEVA-ANNIBAL

TO SHE WHO, AFTER BEING CONSUMED ON EARTH BY MY FLAMING HEART,
FROM FLAME BECAME LIGHT IN THE HOUSE OF THE GUEST OF THE EARTH.

These lines read like a condensed paraphrase of the passage from the *Vita Nuova* described above. Like Beatrice, Lidiya Dimitrievna has left this earthly world for the heavens, consumed by the fire of Ivanov's love for her, compared – as in the case of Dante's love for Beatrice – to a burning heart; *plameneyushchee serdtse* ('flaming heart'), the phrase used in the dedication, is the Russian translation of *Cor Ardens* which Ivanov gives on the title page of his work as a sub-title.

The fact that Ivanov has used the phrase in its Latin form adds two further dimensions to the significance of his title. Firstly, it relates it to the liturgy of the Catholic church where the term 'cor ardens' is frequently used to refer to the sacred hearts of Jesus and the Virgin Mary, or to symbolize the religious fervour which ignites the hearts of the faithful.[46] There are many poems in the second part of *Cor Ardens* which use the image of the heart in this sense. The sacred hearts of Jesus and Mary are also frequently depicted in Christian iconography; Jesus's heart is usually surrounded by thorns, and Mary's by roses. This tradition is reflected in the dramatic frontispiece which Konstantin Somov designed for *Cor Ardens* in 1907.[47] It portrays a flaming heart surrounded by wreaths of purple roses intertwined with thorns, thus combining the symbolic motifs of both Jesus and Mary.

The second dimension of the title is a Biblical one. The phrase 'cor ardens' occurs in the Vulgate where it is used in this precise form by two of the apostles to describe the way their heart burnt within them when Christ spoke to them on the road to Emmaus: 'nonne *cor* nostrum *ardens* erat in nobis . . . ?' ('did not our heart burn within us . . . ?' – Luke 24. 32). At the time of this meeting the apostles did not recognize the resurrected Christ who spoke to them about the stage of suffering which would precede the revelation of his glory, as foretold in Scripture.

An entire section of the first book, 'Cor Ardens', entitled 'The Sun of Emmaus' ('*Solntse Emmausa*') is devoted to this subject. One of its poems, 'The Road to Emmaus' ('*Put' v Emmaus*' – *SS* II, 264) ends with a direct paraphrase of the incident described in the Bible, including the reference to the burning heart. The last line of the poem, 'And the heart breathes and burns . . .' (*I serdtse – dyshit i gorit . . .*), closely echoes the Russian translation of the Biblical verse 'did not our heart burn within us . . . ?' (*ne gorelo li v nas serdtse nashe . . . ?*). The coincidence between this paraphrase of the Biblical reference to 'cor ardens' and Ivanov's title is clearly not accidental, particularly if one considers that 'The Road to Emmaus' was first published in 1906, the year in which Ivanov chose his title.

As well as these Latin associations, there is also a further Greek dimension to the title which Ivanov draws attention to in a second dedication, placed immediately after the first dedication at the beginning of the section 'Ecce Cor Ardens':

> ТОЙ,
> ЧЬЮ СУДЬБУ И ЧЕЙ ЛИК
> Я УЗНАЛ
> В ЭТОМ ОБРАЗЕ МЭНАДЫ
> "С СИЛЬНО БЬЮЩИМСЯ СЕРДЦЕМ"

ΠΑΛΛΟΜΕΝΗΣ ΚΡΑΔΙΗΝ
– КАК ПЕЛ ГОМЕР –

КОГДА ЕЕ ОГНЕННОЕ СЕРДЦЕ
ОСТАНОВИЛОСЬ   (SS II, 225)

TO SHE
WHOSE FATE AND WHOSE FACE
I RECOGNIZED
IN THIS IMAGE OF A MAENAD
'WITH PALPITATING HEART'
ΠΑΛΛΟΜΕΝΗΣ ΚΡΑΔΙΗΝ
– AS HOMER SUNG –

WHEN HER FIERY HEART
STOPPED

Here the burning heart, translated as 'fiery heart' (*ognennoe serdtse*), belongs to Lidiya Dimitrievna and is linked by Ivanov to the 'palpitating heart' of a Maenad sung by Homer. The Greek phrase quoted by Ivanov occurs in the *Iliad* where it is used to describe Andromache in a state of passionate emotion. Hector, her husband, has just been killed, and Andromache, hearing the screams of Hecuba, Hector's mother, begins to suspect the worst. 'With palpitating heart' she rushes from the house 'like a mad woman'.[48] After she discovers the truth, the world goes black as night before her eyes and she falls into a dead faint. When she finally recovers her senses, she delivers a passionate lament on the death of her husband.

The analogy which Ivanov draws between Andromache in this situation and Lidiya Dimitrievna at the moment of her death is based on the two women's shared intensity of passion for their husbands; in both cases this excess of passion reaches its climax at the moment of its association with death, and resolves itself through a form of self-transcendence or oblivion (death in the case of Lidiya Dimitrievna, or a dead faint in the case of Andromache). Ivanov's analogy serves to underline the Dionysiac nature of Lidiya Dimitrievna's passion and death; like Andromache's passion, it can be understood in terms of the Dionysiac mystical principle at the heart of the universe, 'a force which tries to find freedom from its own excess through suffering and death', or as an illustration of Ivanov's words from another part of his work on the religion of Dionysus: 'where love awakens, the self dies'.[49]

The image of the burning heart is a typical example of Ivanov's syncretic use of imagery. It functions on several different levels which all have one thing in common: the idea of passionate love and its intrinsic connection with suffering and death. Andromache's heart beats stronger when she hears of her husband's death, the apostles' hearts are set alight by their love of Christ when they hear him speak of the mysteries of death and resurrection, the hearts of Jesus and Mary are emblems of their suffering love, and Dante's heart is consumed with love of Beatrice, intensified by the presentiment of her death. In this way, through the image of the burning heart, Ivanov succeeds in uniting the worlds of pagan antiquity, Biblical Christianity, Catholic liturgy and medieval love poetry.

The Dantesque dimension of Ivanov's title is particularly important because it relates the abstract symbol of the burning heart to the personal biography of the poet with whom Ivanov identified his own experience. When Ivanov tried to persuade Bryusov to include the poems of 'Love and Death' in *Cor Ardens*, one of his arguments was that the inclusion of these poems would make the use of his title for the whole book much more appropriate (*umestno*).[50] Here he clearly had in mind the Dantesque aspect of his title's meaning which he felt would be well brought out by the imagery of his new collection.

'Golden Sandals'

In the poems of 'Love and Death' Ivanov's association of his experience with Dante's works generally takes the form of thematic echoes, sometimes highlighted by the use of overtly Dantesque images. Some typical examples occur in the series of 'triptychs' or cycles of three sonnets which are placed after the third and final *canzone* of the book. 'Roses', the first of these triptychs, concludes with a sonnet in which Ivanov describes the same struggle taking place within himself as the one which engaged Dante in the *Vita Nuova*: the attempt to love his beloved in a purely spiritual way after her death, transcending all desire for a physical dimension to love. The first two verses read as follows:

> С порога на порог преодолений
> Я восхожу; но все неодолен
> Мой змеевидный корень, – смертный плен
> Земных к тебе, небесной, вожделений.

И в облаке пурпуровых томлений
Твой недоступный образ мне явлен
Во мгле пещер, чей вход запечатлен
Сезаму нег и милости молений.   (*SS* II, 435)

From threshold to threshold of trials overcome
I ascend; but still have not overcome
My snake-like root – the mortal prison
Of earthly longings for you, o heavenly one.

And in a cloud of purple languors
Your inaccessible image is revealed to me
In the darkness of caves whose entrance is sealed
To the sesame of pleasures and the sweetness of prayers.

This theme is taken up with explicit reference to Dante in 'Golden Sandals', the closing triptych of the book. The three sonnets are linked by the image of the golden sandals, symbolizing the possibility of communication between this world and the world of spirits (the image is perhaps borrowed from Hermes whose winged sandals enabled him to be the messenger of the gods and to mediate between the upper and the lower worlds). At the end of each sonnet *dalei* ('distances') is rhymed with *sandalii* ('sandals'), a device which emphasizes the link between the sandals and the distant heavens.

The first sonnet describes the famous apparition of the Virgin Mary to a peasant-girl at Lourdes. Her path from the heavens is marked by the traces of her golden sandals, and roses flower under her feet. The next two sonnets deal with different aspects of Ivanov's relationship with the spirit of Lidiya Dimitrievna after her death, and compare this directly to Dante's relationship with Beatrice. The image of the golden sandals here refers to Lidiya Dimitrievna's ascent to the heavens and possible descent to the poet's dark wood. The juxtaposition of these two sonnets with the opening sonnet about the Virgin Mary underlines Ivanov's allegiance to the tradition of love poetry established by Dante and Petrarch in which the spiritual love of the beloved after her death is a preparation for the pure love of the Virgin Mary.

The text of the second sonnet of the triptych is as follows:

Когда б я знал, что в темном море лет
Светила роз моих, дробясь, дрожали –
Отражены, как письмена скрижали,
Замкнувшей в медь таинственный завет;

Когда б я знал, что твой грядущий свет
Они за склон заране провожали,
Откуда тень за тению бежали
В угрюмый лес, где Беатриче нет:

Златых кудрей, меж кипарисов черных,
Печалию тех смугло-желтых роз
Я б не венчал! Земле моей покорных,

Я б алых роз искал, и пьяных лоз! . . .
Я б не сковал тебе для райских далей
Из золота любви моей сандалий!   (*SS* II, 440–1)

If I had known that in the dark sea of years
The luminaries of my roses, fragmented, were trembling –
Reflected like the characters of a tablet
Enclosing in copper a mysterious testament;

If I had known that they were accompanying
Your future light behind the slope prematurely,
From where shadow after shadow ran
To the gloomy wood where Beatrice is not:

I would not have crowned your golden curls among the black
    cypresses
With the sorrow of those dark yellow roses!
I would have searched for submissive to my earth

Scarlet roses and drunken vines! . . .
I would not have forged for you for the heavenly distances
Sandals out of the gold of my love!

The poem is difficult to interpret because of the compression of
its syntax and allusive nature of its imagery. Some of the symbols
which it uses are not clearly defined and remain open to several
different interpretations. The following notes therefore do no
more than suggest a possible reading of the poem.

The first two verses introduce a hypothetical condition (if the
poet had known in advance that his beloved was going to die), and
the last two verses describe the different course of action which the
poet would then have adopted. The 'luminaries' of the poet's
roses, which are the subject of the main subordinate clauses in both
quatrains, refer to the guiding spirit or higher symbolic meaning of
the roses with which the poet had crowned his beloved on an
earlier occasion. Because these 'luminaries' know the transcendent

meaning of earthly phenomena, they are compared to the characters engraved on a copper tablet which carries a secret message. Their reflection in the sea of time reveals their knowledge of a shaky and fragmented future. The meaning of this complex image becomes a little clearer in the next verse. The luminaries were destined to accompany Lidiya Dimitrievna behind the slope of a hill to her premature death (the image of her 'future light' refers to her spiritual presence, revealed after death); after this, all brightness was lost, and only shadows ran back to the earthly world, compared to a dark wood bereft of the light of Beatrice.

If Ivanov had been able to foresee this course of events, he would not have crowned his beloved with the yellow roses associated with these luminaries, nor would he have forged the sandals which enabled her to escape to heaven. The first tercet gives the impression of referring to a specific incident in the poet's past. It seems likely that Ivanov is recalling the occasion described in his poem of 1895, 'The Funeral Rites in Memory of Dionysus'. During a visit to the ancient theatre of Dionysus at Fiesole, he crowned Lidiya Dimitrievna as a new Maenad with a wreath of roses and ivy. This gesture was symbolic of the mission with which he then entrusted her – to overcome death and revive Dionysus from his winter sleep. The attempt was a failure, however, and the poem ends on a melancholy and despondent note.

Certain features of this poem are echoed in the sonnet from 'Golden Sandals'. In both poems the scene described takes place against a background of cypresses, and the act of crowning the beloved with a wreath of roses is associated with sorrow (*v'pechali* – 'in sorrow' – is rhymed with *venchali* – 'we crowned' – in the earlier poem, and different forms of the same words (*pechaliyu, venchal*) occur in the later poem). The sorrowful character of the roses is due to their unfulfilled potential as a symbol of spiritual revival. Later, in the light of Lidiya Dimitrievna's death, the symbol comes to be regarded as wholly inappropriate. If the poet had known that his beloved would die, he would have chosen red roses and drunken vines, symbolic of the Dionysiac, earth-bound cycle of love, death and suffering. These images would have been more consonant with the course of events, leading from love through death to suffering, than the promise of a spiritual triumph over death implied by the gift of the golden sandals and yellow roses.

There is a further dimension to the symbolism of the yellow and red roses which fits in well with the Catholic imagery of 'Love and Death' and with the preceding sonnet about the Virgin Mary. In the Catholic tradition the devotion of the rosary, epitomizing the lives of Christ and the Virgin Mary, is divided into three chaplets known as the Joyful, Sorrowful and Glorious Mysteries. Each of these chaplets is symbolized by a wreath of different roses. White roses represent the Joyful Mysteries (concerned with events from the Annunciation to the Finding of the Child Jesus in the Temple), red roses represent the Sorrowful Mysteries (from the Agony in Gethsemane to the Crucifixion) and yellow or gold roses represent the Glorious Mysteries (from the Resurrection and Ascension of Christ to the Assumption and Coronation of the Virgin Mary).

According to this symbolic tradition, red roses are connected with sorrowful events on earth relating to suffering and death, while yellow roses refer to spiritual, non-earthly events, epitomizing the triumph of life over death, or of spirit over flesh. It is probable that Ivanov intended to allude to this aspect of the rose in his poem. Had he known that his beloved was destined for death, he would not have chosen yellow roses, symbolic of life after death, but red roses, symbolic of death and suffering. Symbols traditionally associated with the cult of the Virgin Mary are thus transferred to the poet's beloved.

The mood of despair prevalent in this sonnet arises because the poet is unable to make contact with the spirit of his beloved. Her death appears final, and there is no possibility of communication between the two worlds. The dark wood is bereft of the light of her spiritual presence, and the golden sandals on which she rose to the heavens do not seem able to bring her back down to earth.

This pessimistic mood is dispelled in the final sonnet of the triptych which takes up many of the same images and redefines them in the light of the poet's new mood of optimism.

Благословен твой сонм, собор светил,
Невидимых за серебром полдневным!
В годину слез, на торжестве плачевном,
Мне Бог Любви твой свет благовестил.

Благословен Вожатый, кто мостил
Твой путь огнем нежгучим и безгневным!
Он телом тень твою одел душевным
И ног твоих подошвы озлатил.

Я видел сны; я ведал откровенья;
Я в злате роз идущей зрел тебя:
Твои шаги – молитв златые звенья,

Ты движешься, пылая и любя . . .
Сойди ж в мой лес из недоступных далей
На золотых лугах твоих сандалий!   (*SS* II, 441)

Blessed be your throng, assembly of luminaries,
Invisible behind the midday silver!
At the time of tears, at the mournful solemnity,
The God of Love brought me tidings of your light.

Blessed be the Guide who paved
Your path with an unburning and unfierce fire!
He clad your shadow in a spiritual body
And gilded the soles of your feet.

I had dreams; I experienced revelations;
I beheld you walking in the gold of roses:
Your steps are golden links in a chain of prayers,

You move, glowing and loving . . .
Come on down into my wood from the inaccessible distances
On the golden meadows of your sandals!

Here the poet is once more granted visions of his beloved in her full glory, surrounded by golden roses symbolic of the Glorious Mysteries. He anticipates her descent into his wood which is no longer described as dark or gloomy, and regards her golden sandals as a positive symbol of her desire to communicate with him, rather than as a negative symbol of her disappearance to heaven.

Many aspects of the poem echo the early Italian poets. The first part of the sonnet with its repetition of the injunction 'Blessed . . .' (*Blagosloven* . . .) is very evocative of Petrarch's sonnet 'Benedetto sia 'l giorno e 'l mese e l'anno . . .' ('Blessed be the day and the month and the year . . .').[51] Other features of the poem are overtly Dantesque. Ivanov notes the anniversary of Lidiya Dimitrievna's death in the same way as Dante does in chapter XXXIV of the *Vita Nuova*. He refers to his visions and dreams of his beloved (chapters XXXIX and XLI of the *Vita Nuova* describe visions of Beatrice after her death in glory in the heavens), and implores her to descend into his dark wood; this recalls the beginning of the *Inferno* in which Virgil tells Dante how Beatrice descended to the

underworld to ask him to help Dante escape from the dark wood
(*Inf.* II, 52–120). During this passage Beatrice's eyes are compared
to shining stars ('Lucevan li occhi suoi piu che la stella' – 'Her eyes
were more resplendent than the stars' – l. 55) and she tells Virgil
that she was moved to descend to the underworld by Divine Love
('amor mi mosse' – 'Love moved me' – l. 72). These details are
taken up by Ivanov in his sonnet and applied to Lidiya Dimitrievna
– her image is also associated with the light of the stars, and her
path is similarly paved by Divine Love.

In these two poems Ivanov is deliberately casting his visions and
dreams of Lidiya after her death in terms reminiscent of Dante's
works, using the sonnet form of the *Vita Nuova* and portraying
Lidiya as a Beatrice figure on whom the poet depends for his
spiritual salvation. The dark wood is no longer an ambivalent
image for the lovers' shared experience of Eros, but the symbol of
a negative condition from which the poet hopes to be saved by a
new, spiritual version of his beloved. This marks a significant
transition in Ivanov's work from physical to spiritual love, brought
about, as with Dante, by the death of the poet's beloved.

The Fifth Book: 'Rosarium'

The fifth and final book of *Cor Ardens*, 'Rosarium, Verses on the
Rose' ('Rosarium. *Stikhi o roze*') was mainly written during the
summer of 1910 before Ivanov travelled to Italy to join Vera in
Rome. A few poems, composed later in the year and in 1911, were
subsequently added to the collection. The book carries a dedication to Vera ('To our one and only Vera' – *SS* II, 448) and neatly
rounds off the structure of *Cor Ardens* which, in its final form,
articulates the stages of Ivanov's spiritual development, as he
perceived it, modelled on the Dionysiac cycle. The initial abundance of life is reflected in the poems of the first part which deal
with images of Eros and of sin; this then gives way to the second
stage of suffering and death described in 'Love and Death', and
finally leads to the new lease of life or spiritual resurrection which
Ivanov found in his understanding of Vera's role as Lidiya Dimitrievna's successor.

'Rosarium' was conceived as a work of conclusion and synthesis
in which the various strands of *Cor Ardens* would be drawn
together to illustrate the poet's composite spiritual ideal. In 'Love

and Death' Ivanov had conveyed this ideal through poems closely based on his personal experience. 'Rosarium' achieves a similar purpose, but through a network of generalized, impersonal imagery centred on the symbol of the rose. The fact that the rose was a major symbol in both the classical and the Christian traditions made it an ideal vehicle for the expression of the poet's syncretic ideal. In pagan antiquity the rose was celebrated as a symbol of physical beauty linked to the cult of death, and the rose in the Christian tradition, particularly in medieval times, was revered as a symbol of suffering love and martyrdom, associated with Christ, the Virgin Mary and various saints. These twin classical and Christian connotations are reflected in Ivanov's choice of title. In classical Latin a 'rosarium' is a rose garden, while in medieval Latin the word has three meanings: it may refer to a wreath of roses, or to the series of devotions on the lives of Christ and the Virgin Mary, known as a rosary, or to the string of beads used for keeping count during the recitation of these devotions (also known as a rosary).

In his collection Ivanov has built up a complex network of poems dealing with these different manifestations of the rose. There are numerous poems on the rose in classical times, such as 'The Rose of Dionysus' ('*Roza Dionisa*' – *SS* II, 462), devoted to the rose as a symbol of Dionysiac Eros, or 'Rosalia' ('*Rozalii*' – *SS* II, 490), a sonnet on the Roman spring festival during which the spirits of the dead were invoked and their tombs decorated with fresh roses. These pagan celebrations of the rose alternate with accounts of the rose's role in the lives of various Christian saints and with imitations of French medieval verse or sonnets in the Petrarchan and Dantesque style. Through this constant interplay of images, Ivanov is able to create a poetically unified universe in which the classical and Christian traditions are presented side by side as harmonious manifestations of a single underlying essence.

Many of Ivanov's allusions to the rose are highly obscure and would not be intelligible to the ordinary reader without reference to the explanatory notes provided by the poet. The main source quoted by Ivanov is a lengthy essay on the poetics of the rose by the literary critic and historian Aleksandr Veselovsky. This work first appeared in 1898 and includes sections on the rose in classical antiquity, in Christianity and in Russian popular poetry.[52] In its structure, argument and illustrations, it closely echoes an earlier and more substantial work by Charles Joret, *La rose dans l'anti-quité et au moyen âge*, published in Paris in 1892.[53] Although Ivanov does not refer to this work in his notes, it seems likely that he was also familiar with it, as some of his poems are based on instances of the cult of the rose which occur in Joret's work but not in Veselovsky's. Ivanov's poem on Saint Elizabeth is a typical example; it reproduces a passage on Saint Elizabeth from Joret's work down to the minutest detail.[54]

Both Joret and Veselovsky analyse the way in which the Christian tradition took over the rose of pagan times and transformed it into a central symbol of the new faith. In this respect their works are concerned with a problem similar to the one which preoccupied Ivanov and caused him to turn to the rose – the nature of the relationship between pagan antiquity and Christianity. However, although Joret and Veselovsky provide examples of the continuity between the two traditions by pointing out survivals of purely pagan motifs in the Christian rose, they are primarily concerned with showing that the Christian rose came into being as a reaction against the pagan rose and represented a new departure. As Veselovsky wrote in his essay: 'the rose blooms more fully for us than it did for the Greeks; it is not only the flower of love and of death, but also of suffering and of mystical revelation.'[55]

Ivanov's emphasis is different. In keeping with his spiritual ideal, he wishes to underline that the rose of Christianity is deeply rooted in the pagan tradition and cannot be divorced from it. The desire to unify these two worlds through the symbol of the rose is the principal drive behind 'Rosarium', and this is clearly spelt out in the first poem of the book, 'Ad Rosam', an address to the rose which serves as an opening manifesto or prologue to the collection.

'Ad Rosam'

Тебя Франциск узнал и Дант-орел унес
В прозрачно-огненные сферы:
Ревнуют к ангелам обитель нег – Пафос –
И рощи сладостной Киферы.

Но твой расцветший цвет, как древле, отражен
Корней твоих земной отчизной:
Ты, Роза милая, все та ж на персях жен,
И та ж под сенью кипарисной.

Таинница Любви, твоя печать горит
　　На бледном хладе саркофага;
И на снегах твоим дыханьем говорит
　　Мечу завещанная сага.

В алмазно-блещущем и голубом снегу
　　Она властительно напевна;
И снится рыцарю : в дубраве на лугу
　　Сном непробудным спит Царевна ...

О Роза дремная! Кто, мощный паладин,
　　Твой плен глубокий расколдует?
Кто, лирник избранный, найдет глагол один
　　И пеньем сферы согласует?

Кто с корнем цвет сроднит? Чей взор не помрачен
　　Волшебным куревом Киферы?
Плывут в морях глава и гусли. Рассечен,
　　Но трижды жив триглав Химеры.

Кто б не был ты: Геракл, иль в облаке Персей,
　　Убийца ль Гидры иль Медузы, –
Тебя зовут у волн, где солнце пел Орфей,
　　Над Розой плачущие Музы!　　　　　　(*SS* II, 449–50)

Francis recognized you and Dante the eagle carried you off
　　To the transparent fiery spheres:
Jealous of the angels are the abode of pleasures – Paphos -
　　And the groves of sweet Cythera.

But your full-bloomed flower, as of yore, is reflected
　　In the native soil of your roots:
You, sweet Rose, are still the same on women's bosoms,
　　And the same under the cypresses' canopy.

Confidante of Love, your stamp burns
　　On the pale cold of the sarcophagus;
And among the snows with your breath speaks
　　The saga bequeathed to the sword.

On the diamond sparkling and blue snow
　　It is powerfully melodious;
And the knight dreams: in a grove in a meadow
　　The Princess sleeps in a sound sleep.

O slumbering Rose! Who, mighty paladin,
   Will break the spell of your deep prison?
Who, chosen lyrist, will find a single language
   And harmonize the spheres through song?

Who will link the bloom to the root? Whose vision is not obscured
   By the magic incense of Cythera?
A head and psaltery float at sea. Cut through,
   But thrice alive is the triple-head of the Chimaera.

Whoever you may be: Hercules, or Perseus in a cloud,
   The killer of the Hydra or of Medusa –
You are summoned at the waves where Orpheus sang the Sun
   By the Muses who mourn the Rose!

Bryusov's comments on Ivanov are particularly apt in relation to this poem: 'He deals with such questions in his verses as ordinarily are treated in close-reasoned prose, but even while deciding them he remains a poet.'[56] 'Ad Rosam' advances a complex intellectual argument which relates to the fields of philosophy of culture, religion and aesthetics. And yet it does not do this in the manner of prose, spelling out each stage of the debate clearly. The discussion is conducted through a series of frequently obscure and allusive images drawn from Greek mythology and the works of Veselovsky and Joret. It is left to the reader to work out their place within the argument and to supply the missing links between them.

Kuzmin pinpointed this difficulty in his review of the first part of *Cor Ardens*. He wrote that some of Ivanov's poems, like the *canzoni* of Guido Cavalcanti (the famous Florentine poet and friend of Dante), require a special philosophical and metaphysical commentary. This is not due to any lack of clarity in the poet's ideas or imprecision in his language, but results from the 'rich compression' (*nasyshchennaya szhatost'*) of thought and expression in his poetry, and from his habit of skipping from one image to the next, without making plain the logical link which underlies the transition.[57]

This is certainly true of 'Ad Rosam'. Although Ivanov has provided a note to his poem, it is brief and inadequate. A much fuller commentary is required, not only to elucidate some of the more obscure images, but more importantly to clarify their relation to the central argument.

The poem falls into three parts, starting with an outline of the problem of the split between the two faces of the rose, continuing with examples of different manifestations of the rose throughout the ages, and finally concluding with an appeal to poets to restore the rose to its former unity.

The first verse describes the rift which has occurred between the rose as a symbol of spiritual love and the rose as a symbol of earthly love. Significantly, the problem is presented in terms of the break between the two traditions which Ivanov wished to reconcile – medieval Christianity and pagan antiquity. The Middle Ages are represented by two Italian mystics and poets, St Francis and Dante. St Francis's link with the rose is dealt with in detail in two other poems of 'Rosarium' entitled 'Roses at Subiaco' ('Rozy v Subiako' – SS II, 497–8). These relate how red roses sprang from the blood of St Francis when he threw himself on thorns at Subiaco to mortify his flesh. This allusion to the rose as a symbol of suffering and martyrdom paves the way for Dante's image of the rose as a symbol of the complete transformation of flesh into spirit. In the final cantos of the *Paradiso*, Dante uses the image of a white rose to describe the Empyrean, the realm of 'transparency' or pure spirit which is the innermost circle of God's presence, filled with the ranks of the redeemed who, like so many flame-coloured and golden petals, rejoice in the divine light emanating from the centre of the rose.

For Dante, therefore, the rose has become an image of the heavenly love between the Creator and his created. For this reason Ivanov compares him to an eagle in upward flight who has removed the rose from earth and transported it to the heavens, transforming it into a symbol of spiritual love. The guardians of the rose as a symbol of earthly love are left behind, feeling bereft and jealous. For them, the rose was sacred to Aphrodite, the goddess of beauty and love and mother of Eros whose cult flourished on the island of Cythera and at Paphos on the island of Cyprus. These places were renowned for their temples, dedicated to Aphrodite, from which the smoke of daily sacrifices and incense constantly rose.[58]

This jealousy is misplaced, however, because the link between the heavenly rose and the earthly rose cannot be broken, even though at times it may be obscured. The full bloom of Dante's celestial rose grew from earthly roots and remains connected to these. To prove the point, the poem continues with a series of examples of different manifestations of the rose in its twin guises throughout the ages. In classical antiquity the rose was a symbol of love (linked to a woman's beauty) or of death (the shade of cypresses).[59] It always retained a spiritual dimension, and knew the secrets of love and the mysteries of death, as is shown by the roses carved on Roman sarcophagi or strewn over the tombs of the dead during the spring festival of 'Rosalia'; according to Joret and Veselovsky, these roses testified to the enduring love pledged by the living to the souls of the dead which were temporarily revived each spring.[60]

From the Middle Ages onwards, following the tradition established with the *Roman de la Rose* and the literature of courtly love, the rose became the conventional symbol of the beloved lady or ultimate goal of the knight's quest. Ivanov gives two examples of this symbolic usage; the rose in Nordic sagas as an image of the final goal of the heroic adventure, and the rose in the tale of the Sleeping Beauty which – as he explains in a note – is essentially a legend about the rose (*SS* II, 812).

This last example enables the poet to make a clear transition to the final part of his poem. The Sleeping Beauty, waiting to be woken from her deep sleep by the knight, becomes an image for the rose, caught in a magic spell, waiting to be released from its captive state and restored to its former glory by a poet. Ivanov asks who will take on this task – who will reestablish the lost link between the flower and the root, between heaven and earth, between the spiritual and the physical? The task is doubly difficult because most people's vision has been clouded by the smoking altars of Cythera – false forms of the cult of Aphrodite which obscure the goddess's true nature.

This part of the poem can be clarified by reference to various other sources. A few years earlier, in 1908, in an essay on the two major tendencies prevalent in contemporary symbolism, Ivanov introduced the term 'false Aphrodites' to designate the forms of symbolism which he opposed. In his view, although the artists and poets of the Middle Ages and Pre-Renaissance (of whom Dante was the leading representative) had sought after true spiritual beauty ('Aphrodite of the Heavens'), later artists from the Renaissance onwards had attempted to bring the heavenly Aphrodite down to earth and incarnate her in physical forms. This had led to a form of false idealism, based on a pagan sensuality divorced from any spiritual dimension, and to the creation of artistic norms which

Ivanov and the other religious Symbolists, ranged on the side of Dante and the Middle Ages, were trying to reverse (*SS* II, 544).

In another passage, taken from an undated archival fragment of prose, Ivanov discusses the reasons for this post-medieval decline directly in terms of the rose's symbolic value. Although, as he writes, 'the Mystic Rose on the Cross of the Earth ... was the sacred idea of the Middle Ages', this ideal failed to take root in the individual's consciousness. It needed to gather more 'weight' or 'flesh' but, in the course of this process, the physical element grew increasingly resistant to spiritualization, and eventually 'the secret seal of the union between Christ and the Earth' was lost: 'The Rose broke away from the Cross, and the Mystic Rose became an earthly rose, and the Cross of the Earth – of Golgotha – became a cross of the distant heavens.' This was the point at which the gradual process of decline initiated by the Renaissance set in.[61]

In Ivanov's symbolic language, the image of the rose flowering from the cross represents the transformation of earthly love into a spiritual form of love through the process of suffering. This was the ideal achieved by Dante, and described by Ivanov at the beginning of 'Ad Rosam' in terms of the transition from St Francis's mortification of the flesh to the celestial rose of *Paradiso*. After the loss of this ideal, the physical and the spiritual had gone their separate ways, leading on the one hand to a form of abstract spirituality, no longer related to the transformation of physical experience (the cross in the distant heavens), and on the other hand to a physical world bereft of a spiritual dimension (the mystic rose reduced to an earthly rose).

In a further essay, 'Thoughts on Symbolism' (1912), written shortly after 'Ad Rosam', Ivanov uses imagery closely related to this poem in order to define the task of true symbolism:

It is more characteristic of true symbolism to depict the earthly, than the heavenly: not the strength of the sound but the power of the echo is important for it. A realibus ad realiora. Per realia ad realiora. True symbolism does not break away from the earth; it wishes to combine the roots and the stars and grows up into a starry flower out of its close, native roots. It makes no substitutions for things and, when speaking of the sea, means the earthly sea, and, when speaking of snowy heights ... means the peaks of earthly mountains.   (*SS* II, 611–12)

In an excursus appended to this essay in 1914, Ivanov defined Dante as a true Symbolist in precisely this sense (*SS* II, 613). The

214

Texts and translations

full bloom of Dante's celestial rose described at the beginning of
'Ad Rosam' is like the starry flower which grows from its native
roots, advanced as the model for contemporary Symbolists. False
versions of symbolism, not based on the divine, have led present
art back into a prison cell world of illusion and dream. The task of
the present artist is to rouse poetry from its dreamy torpor and free
its innermost soul (*SS* II, 612).

In 'Ad Rosam' Ivanov regards this task as so formidable that he
compares it to the Chimaera, a three-headed fire-breathing
monster which terrorized the inhabitants of Lycia until it was
finally defeated by Bellerophon with the aid of the winged horse
Pegasus, a favourite of the Muses. To meet a challenge of this
magnitude, a new hero of the stature of the great heroes of classical
antiquity is required, a figure like Hercules who killed the nine-
headed Hydra, or Perseus who cut off Medusa's head and escaped
unharmed, rendered invisible by Pluto's helmet. In the previous
verse the wording of Ivanov's plea for a chosen poet capable of
harmonizing the spheres through song and language had already
suggested Orpheus, the poet-hero whose exploits in life were
matched by his achievements in art. Through the magic of his
poetry and song, Orpheus succeeded in charming the upper and
the lower worlds. On land, the woods, the rocks and the creatures
of the wild would follow him, bewitched by his art. When he
descended to the underworld in an attempt to retrieve Eurydice
from her premature death, the king and queen of the shades were
spellbound by the words which he sang to the music of his lyre.

This allusion to Orpheus is then made explicit in the next verse
through the reference to the head and psaltery floating at sea.
After the second loss of Eurydice, Orpheus wandered unconsol-
able, spurning the attentions of all women. The Ciconian women, a
people of Thrace who inhabited the coastal regions by the Hebrus,
were jealous of his indifference and, gripped by a Dionysiac
frenzy, took their revenge by tearing his body to pieces. They cast
his head and psaltery into the Hebrus, and from here these were
carried out to sea and borne across to Lesbos, the next great seat of
lyric poetry. Ivanov's reference to this episode seems to suggest a
question: Orpheus no longer lives, who will now take over his
craft?

The final verse of the poem portrays the Muses, lamenting the
loss of the rose and calling out for a new poet to restore it to its

former glory by the shores where Orpheus had sung the Sun. This concluding association of the death of the rose with the death of Orpheus requires some explanation. It derives from the author's understanding of Orpheus as the prototype of the ideal artist who combines the experience of the Dionysiac depths with Apollonian clarity of expression. Ivanov regarded the myth of Orpheus – his descent into the realm of the shades and return to the upper world – as an embodiment of the Dionysiac cycle leading from dark to light, from death to life. In 'Ad Rosam' he alludes to both these aspects of Orpheus. The Dionysiac dimension is implicit in the description of Orpheus as having sung the praises of 'the Sun', a common image in Ivanov's poetry for Dionysus with whom the Orphic mysteries were closely connected.[62] The reference to the manner of Orpheus's death also emphasizes the poet's link with the god of suffering. In an earlier poem from *Transparency* entitled 'Orpheus Dismembered' (*'Orfei rasterzannyi'* – *SS* I, 801–4), the death of Orpheus, torn apart by Maenads, is directly compared to the death of Dionysus who, according to one version of his legend, was torn apart in his youth by the Titans and then reborn.[63] Furthermore, in the cult of Dionysus, the animal or human sacrifice was identified with the god whose passion it echoed. According to this principle, which Ivanov terms 'the mystery of the identity of the sacrifice with the god', Orpheus, sacrificed by the Maenads, becomes one with Dionysus.[64]

The other, Apollonian aspect of Orpheus relates to his art and is brought out in the poem by the reference to the Muses. Orpheus's mother was Calliope, the Muse of epic poetry, and according to some versions of this legend, his father was Apollo. He received his lyre from Apollo, and was instructed in his craft by the Muses whom Apollo, following tradition, had stolen from Dionysus. After Orpheus's death, the Muses buried his limbs at the foot of Mount Olympus, and the lyre with which he had descended into the underworld became a constellation in the heavens – a tribute to Apollo.

These two facets of Orpheus's character explain why Ivanov has linked him to the rose. Both share the characteristic of belonging to two worlds, the upper and the lower, the light and the dark. This is explicitly given as the reason for their association in another poem of 'Rosarium', 'The Poet' (*'Poet'* – *SS*, II, 498–9). Although Orpheus is not named in this poem, it is clear from the imagery that he is the poet who is being addressed. The poem first describes how the Muses instructed him in his art and rewarded him with the attributes of laurel and ivy. The figures of the three Charites are then introduced. These were the daughters of Aphrodite by Zeus or Dionysus, regarded in earliest times as the companions of Dionysus, and later of Aphrodite. They were closely associated with the Muses with whom they lived on Olympus, and particularly favoured the art of poetry. In Ivanov's poem they take a rose, described as the 'divine flower of Aphrodite enthroned' (*bozhestvennyi tsvetok prestol'noi Afrodity*), and add it to the poet's symbolic attributes of laurel and ivy. The reason for this new gift is clearly stated – it is because Orpheus, who illuminated the night, had sung of the light of the nether regions on earth ('Because you sang of the rays of the earth's depths ...' – *Zato chto nedr zemnykh ty pel ... luchi*).

The linking of the loss of the rose with the death of Orpheus in 'Ad Rosam' also emphasizes that the rose is a symbol of art which exists only in so far as it is created by an artist. With the passing of Orpheus, the prototype of the artist who could unite the two worlds, the rose has faded and lost its power as a symbol binding heaven to earth. If a new Orpheus were to come into being, the rose would be reborn. The dependence of the rose on its creator is underlined by the fact that the poem starts by addressing the rose as 'you' ('Francis recognized you' – *Tebya Frantsisk uznal*), but ends by transferring this address from the rose to the poet who is called upon to create a new rose ('You are summoned ... By the Muses' – *Tebya zovut ... Muzy*). Ivanov's poem is consequently far more than a meditation on two aspects of the rose's significance; it is an appeal, centred on the image of the rose as a symbol of art, for a new generation of religious Symbolists to take over from Dante or Orpheus and create a new art form, based on a synthesis of heaven and earth.

'Ad Rosam' presents a challenge which Ivanov has in a sense attempted to answer himself in the poems of 'Rosarium'. The opening poem provides an illustration of his technique for creating a 'single language' (*glagol odin*), composed of syncretic images, in order to reconcile heaven and earth. The parallels which are drawn between the rose of Aphrodite and the rose of Dante, or between the heroes of classical antiquity and the knights of the Middle Ages, serve to bring these different worlds together within the framework of a single, poetically unified text. This technique is used throughout the collection to achieve a harmonious synthesis or balance of the various manifestations of the basic tension between flower and root introduced in 'Ad Rosam' – whether between heaven and earth, light and dark, Christian and pagan, Apollonian and Dionysiac, or spirit and flesh.

An important dimension of this tension, also reflected in the collection, is the Sophiological one. The union of the spirit and the flesh through Sophia which Solovyov advocated was central to Ivanov's spiritual ideal, and many instances of the rose in his poems carry overtly Sophiological connotations. In a poem of 1892 Solovyov had in fact already used the image of the rose's flower and roots to convey the ideal interdependence of spirit and flesh represented by Sophia:

> Свет из тьмы. Над черной глыбой
> Вознестися не могли бы
> Лики роз твоих,
> Если б в сумрачное лоно
> Не впивался погруженный
> Темный корень их.[65]

> Light from darkness. Above the black mass
> The heads of your roses
> Would not be able to rise
> If their dark buried root
> Did not sink itself
> Into the gloomy soil.

Ivanov knew this poem well, and paraphrased these lines in the light of his view of Dionysiac Eros as the root of all true spiritual love in his essay on Solovyov. This tribute was written in 1910, the year during which most of the poems of 'Rosarium' were composed, and it is quite possible that Ivanov conceived 'Ad Rosam' as an extension of Solovyov's original image. For Solovyov, just as the flower cannot exist without the root, so light cannot exist without darkness. Ivanov makes the same point, using the image of Dante's heavenly rose for the flower and of Aphrodite's earthly rose for the roots. He takes the point further, however, and argues that this link has been obscured and must be reestablished. Here he is following the teachings developed in Solovyov's prose writings which called for a renewal of the link between the spirit and the flesh and urged poets to serve Sophia by creating art forms which would achieve this purpose. In other poems of 'Rosarium' such as 'Rosa in Cruce' or 'Rosa Sophia' (*SS* II, 493–4 and 502) Ivanov uses the image of the rose in this sense to reflect its close association with Sophia.

The quest for the rose which Ivanov undertakes in 'Rosarium' can therefore be interpreted on many different levels. On the one hand, on an aesthetic level, it can be seen as an image of the poet's quest for the creation of a new type of true Symbolist art which, like Dante's flower blooming from earthly roots, would reflect the ideal transformation of the physical into the spiritual. On the other hand, the quest may also be read as an allegory of the lover's search for a higher, spiritual form of love, in which the earthly beloved could lead on to Sophia or the Virgin Mary. This aspect of the quest is only hinted at in 'Ad Rosam' (through the image of the Sleeping Beauty), but is more fully developed in other poems of the collection, such as 'Crux Amoris', discussed below. In particular, some of the later poems of 'Rosarium' take up the image of the rose surrounded by snow from 'Ad Rosam' in order to hint at the revival of the poet's love for Lidiya Dimitrievna through Vera.[66]

'Crux Amoris'

The 'Sonnets' section of 'Rosarium' includes a group of three poems, 'Crux Amoris', 'Crux Florida' and 'Rosa in Cruce', which each deal with differing aspects of the connection between the cross and the rose. The imagery of these poems, as suggested by their Latin titles, is closely related to the tradition of Biblical exegesis developed by the Catholic church and reflected in its liturgy.

The first of the sonnets, 'Crux Amoris', reads as follows:

> 'Amor e cor gentil son una cosa'...
> Тебе разоблачилась, Алигьери,
> Любви земной и временной потери
> Богоявленная апофеоза.
>
> Цвети же, сердце, жертвенная роза!
> Их четверо, свершителей мистерий;
> И семь мечей, у роковых преддверий,
> В тебя войдут, о Rosa Dolorosa!

Испытаны священные мерила,
Оправдана премудрость каждым словом;
Кто любит, видит смерть – и любит дале.

Узнай, жених, невесту в покрывале!
Благоухай, любовь, в венце терновом!
Слетит пчела собрать, что ты творила.   (*SS* II, 492–3)

'Amor e cor gentil son una cosa'. . .
To you was unveiled, Alighieri,
The divinely revealed apotheosis
Of earthly love and temporary loss.

Flower then, o heart, sacrificial rose!
There are four of them, of the perpetrators of the mysteries;
And seven swords, at the fatal threshold,
Will pierce you, o Rosa Dolorosa!

The sacred measures have been tested,
Wisdom is justified by every word;
Whoever loves, sees death – and continues to love.

Recognize, bridegroom, the bride in the veil!
Smell sweet, love, in a crown of thorns!
The bee will fly down to gather what you have created.

The central theme of the poem, summarized in its title, is the concept of the 'cross of love'. This ultimately refers back to the lesson of the crucifixion which teaches that earthly love can only be transformed into its higher spiritual form through suffering and death. This is the path which all true love must embrace, following the example of Christ. The idea is advanced in the poem through imagery related to the Biblical account of the crucifixion, and Dante is presented against this background as a poet who applied the eternal truths of the crucifixion to his own experience and understanding of love.

The poem begins with a direct quotation of the opening line of the sonnet from chapter xx of the *Vita Nuova*, 'Amore e 'l cor gentil sono una cosa . . .' ('Love and the noble heart are one thing . . .'); Ivanov has omitted two syllables from the original line to make it fit within his metrical scheme. This line is one of Dante's most famous statements on the nature of love as the natural instinct of the noble heart. It is in fact a close paraphrase of the opening line of a *canzone* by the Bolognese poet Guido Guinizelli, 'Al cor

gentil rempaira sempre amore . . . ' ('Love will always repair to the
noble heart . . . '). Guinizelli was the most illustrious of the Italian
poets prior to Dante who regarded him as his father and teacher in
poetry and referred to this particular *canzone* as an important
influence on the formation of his doctrine of courtly love.[67] In his
sonnet, Dante first paraphrases Guinizelli's celebrated line, then
attributes it to its author, referred to simply as 'il saggio' ('the wise
one'), and finally continues to expound its meaning. He argues that
love and the noble heart go together, like reason and a reasoning
mind, because love is always present as a potential force in the
heart. The second part of the sonnet describes how this potential is
made actual – all that is required is the sight of a wise woman's
beauty, and love will be awoken from its dormant slumber.

This sonnet was in fact translated by Ivanov a few years later
when he was working on his translation of the *Vita Nuova*. Here he
closely follows the pattern of the original sonnet. First he quotes its
opening line, then he attributes it to its author, and finally he
elaborates on its significance. In this way he emphasizes his sense
of forming part of a single chain of poets of love; he has received
and taken over the tradition from Dante, just as Dante did from
Guinizelli.

In his commentary on Dante's line, Ivanov goes beyond its
original significance (which bears no relation to the themes of
death or resurrection) and places it within the wider context of the
Vita Nuova. This work traces the development of Dante's love for
Beatrice from the poet's initial dependence on her physical presence to his later purely spiritual love for her after her death.
Accordingly, Ivanov describes Dante as a visionary to whom the
transcendent meaning of earthly love and of death as a form of
temporary loss was revealed. The phrase 'divinely revealed apotheosis' (*bogoyavlennaya apofeoza*) introduces an idea of release
from life and ascension to higher spheres normally associated with
deities, and hints at the link which is developed in the rest of the
poem between Beatrice and the figures of Christ, Mary and
Sophia.

In the second verse Ivanov moves on from the description of
Dante's love for Beatrice to images connected with the suffering
love of Christ and the Virgin Mary. This transition is consonant
with the various levels of meaning associated with the title of the
collection, *Cor Ardens*. The burning heart is an image of Dante's

love for Beatrice, and also of the sacred hearts of Jesus and Mary. Not surprisingly, therefore, the Dantesque reference to the heart as a symbol of love which Ivanov quotes in his first verse is succeeded by a reference to the sacred heart of Mary.

This transition also mirrors the development of Dante's own experience of love, as recorded in the *Vita Nuova*. As the poet's understanding of his love for Beatrice progresses, he gradually comes to interpret it more frequently in terms of the eternal truths taught by Scripture. In chapter xxiv he identifies Beatrice with Christ, implying a parallel between her future destiny and the death and resurrection of Christ. Later, when Beatrice dies, he writes that she has been called to join the Blessed Queen, the Virgin Mary (chapter xxviii). Ivanov takes his lead from these associations. He follows the movement of Dante's thoughts, and raises his eyes from the contemplation of Beatrice to the figure of the Virgin Mary. If Beatrice is seen as a Christ-figure, then the parallel can be taken one step further, and Dante's love for Beatrice can be likened to the love of the Virgin Mary for Christ – a prototype of the lesson which Dante has mastered, that love of a physical person can be transcended by faith in life after death and spiritual love.

This is the analogy which Ivanov has developed in the second verse of his sonnet. He addresses the sacred heart of Mary, the ultimate symbol of suffering love, and compares it to a sacrificial rose (*zhertvennaya roza*). This comparison is based on the tradition of referring to Mary as a rose and depicting her heart encircled by a wreath of roses. In the works of St Bernard and in Dante's *Paradiso* (xxiii, 73–5) Mary is described as a rose, and in certain prayers of the Catholic liturgy such as the Litany of the Blessed Virgin she is addressed as the 'Mystic Rose'. At the end of the verse the image of the sacrificial rose is taken up again with the Latin phrase 'o Rosa Dolorosa', a device which underlines the liturgical associations of the poem's symbolism.

The poet prophesies that Mary's heart will be pierced by seven swords. This is a reference to the Seven Dolours (as in 'Rosa Dolorosa') or Sorrows of Mary, a tradition derived from the Biblical account of Simeon's prophecy to Mary. When Mary brought the infant Jesus to the temple, Simeon spoke to her of her son's troubled future and prophesied that her soul would be pierced by a sword (Luke 2. 15). According to Christian tradition, this prophecy was subsequently fulfilled at the moment of the crucifixion when Mary stood at the foot of the cross and witnessed the suffering and death of her son. Later, the tradition was elaborated and expanded into a fuller version which consisted of seven sorrows, ranging from the original prophecy of Simeon to the crucifixion, deposition and entombment of Christ. These sorrows were commemorated in various liturgical prayers such as the Rosary of the Seven Sorrows, recited by members of the Order of Servites, and the medieval hymn 'Stabat Mater Dolorosa', the title of which is echoed by Ivanov's address to Mary as a 'Rosa Dolorosa'. They also gave rise to the tradition of representing the heart of Mary pierced by seven swords.[68]

In his sonnet Ivanov echoes the tone of Simeon's original prophecy and hints at the time of its future fulfilment through the phrase 'at the fatal threshold' (*u rokovykh preddverii*). This phrase can be interpreted either literally, as referring to the site of the crucifixion outside Jerusalem – 'without the gate' (*vne vrat*) as stated in Hebrews 13. 12 – or figuratively, as an allusion to the significance of the crucifixion as a fatal prelude to death and resurrection.

The identity of the four 'perpetrators of the mysteries' referred to in this context is more problematic. It is most probable that they represent the soldiers who crucified Christ. In John 19. 23 we read that after the crucifixion the soldiers divided Christ's garments into 'four parts, to every soldier a part'. From this one can deduce, as Ivanov appears to do, that there were four soldiers present at the crucifixion. The actions which they perform (the flagellation, scourging and crucifixion of Christ, the dividing of his garments and piercing of his side with a spear) are referred to as mysteries because of their sacred, hidden significance as the fulfilment of Scriptural prophecies. Significantly, the soldiers' division of the garments into *four* parts and the presence of the Virgin Mary at the foot of the cross are both only mentioned once in the Bible and in almost immediate succession (John 19. 23 and 25). Ivanov's association of the two images may derive from this Biblical precedent.

The third verse consists of three precisely worded pronouncements. The wisdom of Simeon's prophetic words, the 'sacred measures' laid out in Scripture, have been tested and proven true through their fulfilment in the events of the crucifixion and resurrection. The law that love leads through death to further love is fixed forever as an eternal truth, as the course of Dante's love for

Beatrice illustrates. The first two dicta in this verse are reminiscent of the Biblical declarations which often accompany the narration of events regarded as the fulfilment of earlier prophecies. The second one, 'Wisdom is justified by every word' (*Opravdana premudrost' kazhdym slovom*) is in fact a close paraphrase of the Biblical verse 'But wisdom is justified of all her children' (*I opravdana premudrost' vsemi chadami ee* – Luke 7. 35).

The final verse contains several different allusions. The first injunction – that the bridegroom should recognize his bride in her 'veil' – is open to a number of interpretations, depending on the meaning which one attributes to the word 'veil' (*pokryvalo*); this term is ambiguous in Russian and can refer either to a marriage veil or to a shroud. If the line is read in conjunction with the statement in the previous line about the need to love beyond death, it may signify that a person should recognize his beloved even after her death as his true betrothed, still in her marriage veil, and continue to love her spiritual image. Or the covering may refer to a shroud, in which case the line would mean that the bridegroom should recognize and continue to love his bride in her death shroud. Ivanov may have intended the ambiguity to remain unresolved in order to emphasize that the bride's marriage veil is also a shroud, for the course of earthly love leads through death to further love. The bridegroom must understand that death is present in love and recognize the connection between the two.

The line can also be read on a figurative level. Ivanov subscribed to the tradition developed by Dante and Solovyov according to which the physical love of a mortal woman could be transcended by a higher form of spiritual love devoted to a divine female being. Following this tradition, the veiled bride of 'Crux Amoris' can be interpreted as a figure of Sophia or the Virgin Mary. In the first case, the bride's veil would refer to the material world in which the divine essence of Sophia is enveloped, and could also allude to Sophia's role as bride of mankind. The line can then be read as an expression of Solovyov's teaching on the meaning of love: the bridegroom must recognize the divine spark inherent in the woman he loves and understand that his true bride is not the earthly woman of his affections but Sophia. This interpretation fits in well with the 'divinely revealed apotheosis' of the first verse (Sophia being the divine essence of earthly phenomena, revealed to man by

God) and with the more explicit reference to wisdom (*premu-drost'*) in the third verse.

Alternatively, the bride can be understood as a reference to the Virgin Mary who is often represented with a veil (*pokrov*), symbolizing her powers of protection and intercession on behalf of humanity. This interpretation is perfectly compatible with the Sophiological reading of the poem; Sophia and the Virgin Mary were frequently merged into a single composite figure, and Ivanov's tendency to associate them is particularly marked in many of the sonnets adjacent to 'Crux Amoris'. In 'Rosa in Cruce', for example, allusions to the poet's personal experience of love are interwoven with Catholic imagery relating to the Virgin Mary and with a reference to Sophia, described as the 'wise Woman' (*mudraya Zhena – SS* II, 493–4).

There is a further entirely allegorical dimension to the meaning of the line. In the Christian tradition, the terms 'bridegroom' (*zhenikh*) and 'bride' (*nevesta*) are frequently used to denote Christ and his church. This usage goes back to Biblical precedent; the words 'He that hath the bride is the bridegroom' (*Imeyushchii nevestu est' zhenikh*) are spoken by St John the Baptist to describe Christ (John 3. 29), and in St Paul's Epistle to the Ephesians men are urged to love their wives as Christ loved the church (Eph. 5. 25).

In 'Crux Amoris', the terms 'bridegroom' (*zhenikh*) and 'bride' (*nevesta*) are written without capital letters, and thus retain an ordinary human dimension compatible with the personal level of meaning of the poem – the poet's love for his dead beloved and Dante's love for Beatrice. However, the allegorical dimension of the terms cannot be ignored. It is reinforced by the structural parallel between this line and the following one: 'Smell sweet, love, in a crown of thorns' (*Blagoukhai, lyubov', v ventse terno-vom*!). Both lines follow a similar syntactical pattern (a verb in the imperative followed by a vocative address); this establishes a parallel between the bridegroom of the first line and 'love in a crown of thorns', a phrase which immediately calls to mind the figure of Christ who is often referred to as love incarnate and appears to Pilate in a crown of thorns (*v ternovom ventse* – John 19. 5).

The line therefore hints at the mystic marriage between Christ and Sophia (a figure of the church), symbolizing the ideal union between the Spirit and the Flesh which man should strive to emulate. It returns the reader to the Biblical prototypes of love set out in the second verse of the poem; in both cases the crucifixion is advanced as the model of suffering love.

This allegorical reading is supported by the imagery of a later poem by Ivanov, 'Tender Mystery' ('*Nezhnaya taina*'), written in the summer of 1912. Here the poet represents the universe as a marriage (*brak*) between the created world (*tvoren'e*), described as the bride (*nevesta*), and a Bridegroom (*Zhenikh*) in a wreath (*venets*) who is clearly a figure of Christ. The mystery or 'tender secret' of this union is symbolized by a rose (*SS* III, 30).

In the course of 'Crux Amoris' love is presented through several different images. In the opening line, borrowed from Dante, it is identified with the heart. Then, in the second verse, this heart becomes the heart of the Virgin Mary and is compared to a sacrificial rose, an emblem of suffering love. In the final verse, love appears in a crown of thorns and is linked, as already mentioned, to the person of Christ. The sacred heart of Jesus is traditionally depicted as surrounded by a wreath of thorns; here it is implicitly compared to a flowering rose (thus also sharing certain features with the heart of the Virgin Mary described earlier in the poem) and commanded to exude its fragrance from amidst the thorns. This command exactly parallels the earlier injunction to the heart of Mary to flower at its peak moment of suffering. The lesson of both images is summarized in the final promise that a bee will fly down to collect the honey which the rose (representing the suffering heart or love) has created. This image is taken from an earlier poem in the 'Roses' triptych of 'Love and Death' where bees fly down to gather honey and tell a fading rose, symbolic of the poet's heart, that their sting will revive it and make it flower once more. This poem ends with the line 'Flower then, o heart, sacrificial rose!' ('*Tsveti zhe, serdtse, zhertvennaya roza!*' – *SS* II, 435), used again in 'Crux Amoris', and teaches the same lesson that love, through suffering, will lead to spiritual wealth, just as the rose, when stung by a bee, will flower and produce honey.

The idea was closely related to Ivanov's personal feelings after the death of Lidiya Dimitrievna. He was convinced that he should continue to love her image through Vera, and that the more suffering his love caused him, the greater its reward would be. During Easter week of 1910 (just before the period when most of the poems of 'Rosarium' were written), he recorded a long passage in his diary about the need to 'crucify oneself with Christ' (*soraspi-nat'sya Khristu*) and take on the wounds of the world so as to transform it. Then, he writes, roses will spring out of the wounds, bees will fly out of the decaying flesh, and a new transparent vision of the true essence of the world will be reached (*SS* II, 807).

A similar biographical motif clearly underlies the ideas expressed in 'Crux Amoris'; Ivanov is advocating that his love for Lidiya after her death should follow the course of Dante's love for Beatrice, modelled on the suffering love of Christ and Mary; then it will flower like a rose and produce honey. One of the most persistent images for this idea throughout the sonnets of 'Rosarium' is that of the cross which flowers into a rose. The cross is an emblem of the poet's earthly suffering and search, and the rose represents his reward, the revelation of his beloved's true image. The quest for the rose undertaken in 'Rosarium' thus becomes an image for the poet's quest for his beloved after her death. Many years later Ivanov wrote that 'under every one of life's roses lies a cross out of which the rose has flowered' (*SS* III, 386). In the poems of 'Rosarium', as in 'Crux Amoris', he is intent on revealing the cross or path of suffering which must precede the flowering of the rose.

'Crux Amoris' is an example of the much fuller and more harmonious fusion of Dantesque, Solovyovian and Dionysiac images which Ivanov achieved with particular success in the later poems of *Cor Ardens*, written in the light of the new understanding brought about by the death of Lidiya Dimitrievna. Dante is advanced as the representative of the doctrine that love can lead through death to a higher form of spiritual love. This idea is primarily related to the Biblical truths of the New Testament, while its Dionysiac and Sophiological dimensions, although still present, are much less obtrusive; they are no longer in the foreground, but form part of the poem's network of secondary allusions. The combination of Dante with Biblical and liturgical imagery is much more harmonious than the earlier attempts to synthesize Dante and Dionysus. The connotations of sin and darkness which frequently accompanied the Dionysiac aspect of Ivanov's spiritual ideal in his earlier works have now almost entirely disappeared. The cross of love leads through death, but it is no longer identified with the 'cross of sin' which Ivanov had advocated as a mystical path for lovers in his essay of 1904, 'New Masks'.

In this respect, 'Crux Amoris' reflects a change which Evgeny

Anichkov, the literary critic and medieval scholar, described as Ivanov's transition from the Old Testament of Dionysus to the New Testament of Dante and Petrarch, from the personal experience of Eros to the more universal path of Amor. The old elements of the poet's spiritual ideal have not disappeared, but they are now much more fully assimilated into a predominantly Christian context. As Anichkov pointed out, in this way Ivanov escaped the conflict between sexual love and universal love which dominated the thinking of Tolstoy and Dostoyevsky; in reconciling both forms of love he was following the tradition established by the medieval poets of love and further developed in his own time by Vladimir Solovyov.[69] His dual allegiance to both stages of this tradition can be clearly discerned in the imagery of 'Crux Amoris'.

Ivanov appears to have taken a similar view of his own development. In 1915 he wrote a poem entitled 'Purgatory' (*'Chistilishche'*) in which he reviewed his past in terms of Dante's spiritual experience. He described the early stages of his development as a series of 'burnt years' (*sgorevshie leta*); experiences which he took for pleasures at the time were in fact purgatorial torments which had led him through a tortuous labyrinth to a new state of spiritual refinement:

Лишь ныне я понял, святая Пощада,
Что каждая лет миновавших услада
В устах была мед, а во чреве полынь
И в кущу глядело безумье пустынь.

Я вижу с порога высоких святилищ,
Что вел меня путь лабиринтом чистилищ,
И знаю впервые, каким палачам
В бесчувственном теле был отдан я сам;

Каким причастился я огненным пыткам,
Чья память смывалась волшебным напитком, –
Затем, чтобы в тихом горении дней
Богач становился бедней и бедней. (*SS* III, 548)

Only now have I understood, O holy Mercy,
That every sweet pleasure of years gone by
On the lips was honey, but in the womb was wormwood,
And the madness of the desert was staring into the shelter.

I see from the threshold of high sanctuaries
That I was led by a path through a labyrinth of purgatories,

And I know for the first time to what torturers
I myself in an unfeeling body was given over;

What fiery torments I partook of,
The memory of which was washed away by a magic drink –
So that in the quiet burning of days
The rich man should become poorer and poorer.

Although Ivanov still clings to the view that the dark wood of sin
can be a purgatorial experience, he now regards this stage as part
of the past which he has left behind him. His new perception of the
past brings him more closely in line with Dante's view of man's
spiritual journey, and explains why his treatment of Dantesque
images in the later poems involves substantially less distortion than
before – a development which has been traced throughout the
poems discussed in this chapter.

6

Ivanov's translations of Dante

THE SYMBOLIST BACKGROUND

The activity of translation has played a particularly important role in the development of the Russian literary tradition from its very inception; it has served as one of the major channels of expression for the intensity of Russia's interest in the West and desire to overcome the barrier of cultural isolation from Europe. Through translation, a work of foreign literature would be incorporated into the Russian tradition, and come to be regarded as an original creation in its own right. When, for example, Gnedich's translation of Homer's *Iliad* appeared in 1829, Pushkin greeted it as a new *Russian Iliad* which would take its place within Russian literature as a major influence: 'At last the translation of the *Iliad* which we have been waiting for so impatiently and for so long has appeared! ... A Russian *Iliad* is before us. We are embarking on a study of it so as to give our readers a report in due course on a book which is bound to have so important an influence on our native literature.'[1]

Translators in Russia have accordingly often enjoyed a particular reverence; their work is not regarded as secondary in status to original literary activity, but as equally important. Many of Russia's most gifted poets and writers have made substantial contributions to Russian literature through translations. Zhukovsky's translation of the *Odyssey* or Pasternak's translations of Shakespeare are classic examples.

A remarkable efflorescence of activity in the sphere of translating took place in Russia from the end of the nineteenth century onwards. This tendency became particularly pronounced during the Symbolist period. As a movement, Russian Symbolism was syncretic in its approach to other cultures, and one of the principal means which it adopted to assimilate the legacy of other cultures was translation. The Symbolists translated extensively, and it is symptomatic of the spirit of the times that a number of publishing houses launched special series of world literature in translation at the beginning of the twentieth century. In 1901 the Brockhaus and Efron publishing house initiated their famous series 'The Library of Great Writers' under the editorship of S. A. Vengerov. The third publication of this series, the collected works of Byron, included new translations by Symbolist poets such as Bryusov, Blok, Yurgis Baltrushaitis and Vyacheslav Ivanov.[2] The Okto publishing company ran a series entitled 'The Library of European Classics', edited by A. E. Gruzinsky. In 1910 the publishers Mikhail and Sergei Sabashnikov founded a series called 'Monuments of World Literature';[3] several Symbolists did translations for this series which maintained an extremely high standard. The publishers formulated their aims in a set piece which was appended to many of their publications; this provides a clear expression of the general attitude of the period towards translation as the major channel through which the spiritual influence of a foreign culture can best be received and disseminated: 'So be it – a translation can never be a substitute for the original. But throughout the ages the spiritual life of cultured nations has only been really deeply influenced by those works of foreign genius which became accessible to them through translation.'[4]

The younger Symbolists' interest in Dante naturally led them to try their hand at translating the poet. All the publishing houses' series mentioned above were at some stage linked with these ventures. The fact that numerous translations of Dante were already available did not act as a deterrent. Since the end of the eighteenth century Dante's works had begun to appear in Russian translation, and by the middle of the nineteenth century D. E. Min had embarked on his monumental version of the *Commedia*, completed by the time of his death in 1885 but not published until the beginning of the twentieth century. This was a time of peak popularity for Dante in Russia, largely as a result of the spread of the cult of Dante and the Middle Ages initiated by the pre-Raphaelites in England. Among the Symbolists of the older generation, Merezhkovsky and Balmont translated excerpts from Dante, and during the decade from 1892 to 1902 new translations of the poet's works multiplied like mushrooms.[5]

The younger generation of Symbolists inherited this rich corpus of translations – altogether, nine of the *Inferno*, six of the *Purgatorio*, five of the *Paradiso*, and two of the *Vita Nuova*. However, although they were naturally influenced by their predecessors' image of the Italian poet, their own approach developed along very different lines. Those who were inclined towards religion tended to regard Dante primarily as a spiritual teacher and possible source for an aesthetics of religious symbolism. As poets, they were more interested than most of their predecessors in Dante's language and versification. It was no longer enough simply to have a 'Russian Dante', as, for example, Min's translations provided; it was necessary to have a new Russian *Symbolist* Dante who would reflect all the characteristics with which the Symbolists invested their image of the poet. This could be achieved most effectively through a new translation which would establish the medieval poet firmly within the Russian Symbolist tradition.

Among the Symbolists of the second wave, Ellis, Sergei Solovyov, Bryusov and Ivanov were all engaged in translations of Dante's works at various stages of their literary careers. Their versions reflect the general mood of the times as well as each poet's individual approach. The example of Ellis (the pseudonym of L. L. Kobylinsky, 1879–1947) is extremely typical in this respect. He was the first of the younger Symbolists to translate Dante, and published his versions of substantial fragments of the *Commedia* and the *Vita Nuova* over a period of ten years, from 1904 to 1914. His first attempts appeared in *Immorteli*, a two-volume anthology of foreign poetry in translation which he produced in 1904.[6] This work clearly reflected the Symbolists' desire to appropriate other cultures through translation. It included a large section on Dante composed of translations and original poems written in a pseudo-Dantesque vein. The resulting image of Dante is decadent and heavily influenced by the author's enthusiasm for Baudelaire and the other late nineteenth-century poets of France and Belgium represented in the collection.

Two years later, however, this purely aesthetic image of Dante was replaced by a new one, tinged with religion and philosophy. In 1906 Ellis published an article entitled 'The Wreath of Dante' in the literary–philosophical almanach *Free Conscience (Svobodnaya sovest')*.[7] The same issue of the almanach carried part of Vladimir Solovyov's work on Russia and the universal church; not surprisingly, the image of Dante presented in Ellis's translations and accompanying commentary is strongly coloured by the Russian philosopher's teachings. Beatrice is portrayed as a figure of Divine

Wisdom or Sophia, capable of providing all the answers to the mystical searchings of the age.

In the following year, Ellis decided to translate the *Vita Nuova*.[8] The project was never completed, but part of it survives in the proofs of his first book of poetry, *Stigmata*, published in the same year as *Cor Ardens* (1911).[9] The translations from the *Vita Nuova* which appear in these proofs are of extremely poor quality and perhaps for this reason were discarded from the final version of the book.

Ellis's last major publication on Dante before he left Russia was an article entitled 'The Teacher of Faith' which appeared in 1914 in the newly formed Danteana section of the late Symbolist journal *Trudy i dni*.[10] It was written to counter the current vogue for erotic or theosophical readings of Dante, and insisted on the poet's primary role as a representative of traditional Christianity, quoting several passages from *Purgatorio* and *Paradiso* in support of this view. It was published alongside a major article by Ivanov on Symbolist aesthetics which, like Ellis's piece, based its argument on a text from Dante quoted in the author's translation.

One can see from these examples that Ellis was constantly refashioning his image of Dante in the light of his current beliefs, whether these were decadent, Sophiological or more conventionally Christian. Translation was an important tool in this process; it enabled him to establish a text which supported the image of the poet which he was promoting at each stage.

The other Symbolists who translated Dante did not go through such extreme changes of world-view, but they did share with Ellis the tendency to interpret and present Dante in terms of their own beliefs. Sergei Solovyov, for example, followed the pattern set by his uncle Vladimir Solovyov, and developed his interest in Dante in close connection with his religious inclinations and growing attraction to Catholicism. For him, Dante was primarily the supreme representative of the Catholic tradition. In 1913 he declared that 'the entire spiritual force of Catholicism embodied itself in the majestic image of Dante'.[11] Typically, his contribution to the Dante celebrations held in 1921 took the form of a public lecture on Dante and Catholicism.[12] After the revolution he became a Russian Orthodox priest, and then converted to Catholicism of the Greco-Roman rite in 1923, taking up the post of vice-exarch of Catholics of this rite a few years later.[13] In this respect his interest in Dante has much in common with that of Ivanov whose conversion to Catholicism around the same time was also the culmination of many years' fascination with Dante and the Middle Ages.

Sergei Solovyov's archive in Moscow contains various materials on Dante including translations of his works,[14] but these are inaccessible as the archive is still officially closed to researchers. There is evidence from other sources that Solovyov translated a sonnet from the *Vita Nuova* in 1903,[15] and that many years later, at the beginning of the 1930s, he was one of three translators commissioned by the Academia publishing house to prepare a new version of the *Commedia*. Mikhail Lozinsky was to translate the *Inferno*, Sergei Shervinsky the *Purgatorio*, and Solovyov the *Paradiso*.[16] However, in 1931 Solovyov was arrested in connection with his religious activities, and after his release he spent several periods in psychiatric care until his death in 1942 in a mental hospital in Kazan.[17] In 1934 Lozinsky was still not sure whether Solovyov was continuing to participate in the translation, but soon after this date it must have become clear that he had withdrawn from the project which was eventually completed singlehandedly by Lozinsky between 1936 and 1942.[18] This new translation superseded all previous ones and established itself as the standard Russian version of the *Commedia*.

Bryusov did not affiliate himself with the religious Symbolists, and is therefore in a quite different category from Ellis, Sergei Solovyov and Ivanov. However, over a period of sixteen years, from 1904 to 1920, he was also intermittently involved in translating Dante and, curiously enough, even cooperated with Ivanov in a projected translation of the *Commedia*. This plan originated with S. A. Vengerov who wished to include Dante in the 'Library of Great Writers' series which he edited for the Brockhaus and Efron publishing house.[19] In 1904 he inquired if Bryusov would like to take part in a new translation of the *Commedia*, and probably also approached Ivanov at the same time with a similar proposal. Bryusov's response was enthusiastic, and he began work on the *Inferno* immediately. However, at the end of 1905, the project was dropped by the publishers, and not taken up again until 1920 when Bryusov and Ivanov were once more commissioned by Vengerov to translate different parts of the *Commedia* for the same publishing house. Ivanov's involvement in the project will be discussed in greater detail below.

During the intervening years Bryusov made several attempts to interest various other publishers in his translation of the *Inferno*. None of these approaches were successful, however, and his translation of the first canto of the *Inferno* – the only substantial fragment of his work to have survived – was not published until 1955.[20] His version is of remarkably high quality, clear and faithful to the original, without the sort of ideological distortion or woolliness of language which marred the attempts of Ellis.

It is clear from this brief survey that translating Dante was a fairly commonplace activity among the Symbolist poets: over a period of thirty years, from the beginning of the century through to the 1920s and 1930s, Ellis, Sergei Solovyov and Bryusov were all intermittently working on new versions of the Italian poet's works. This is the background against which Ivanov's translations must be considered. They are very much a phenomenon of their age, and yet at the same time they reflect the idiosyncratic views of their author. In translating Dante, Ivanov was not only seeking to bring him into the Russian Symbolist tradition, he was also trying to incorporate him into the framework of his own spiritual outlook as one of the corner-stones of his world-view. His translations, like any other, are necessarily an act of interpretation, and reveal the way in which he saw Dante and wished to present him to others.

Over a period of several years Ivanov worked on translations of parts of Dante's three major works, the *Vita Nuova, Convivio* and *Divina Commedia*, in the order of their composition. None of these translations was completed, and only a fragment from the *Vita Nuova* was published during his life-time. The rest of the evidence survives in the form of manuscripts and unpublished correspondence, scattered among the poet's archival papers in Moscow and Rome. In the following sections each of these translation projects will be considered in turn, starting with an outline of its background, and continuing with the text of the translation, followed by an analysis of its most characteristic features.[21]

VITA NUOVA

At one stage or another of their development, all of Ivanov's projected translations of Dante's works were linked with the Sabashnikov brothers' publishing house and the new series which they set up in 1910, 'Monuments of World Literature'. The original plan for this series provides for five sections, covering classical antiquity, Russian literature, world classics and the European Renaissance. Dante's name figures twice in the plan as one of the main authors whose works were to be represented in the series.[22]

Ivanov first became involved with the series in 1911 as a translator of the Greek classics. On 6 April 1911, Mikhail Sabashnikov sent him a letter spelling out the conditions for his translation of Aeschylus's tragedies. He was to translate the trilogy of the *Oresteia* by 1 May 1912, and the remaining tragedies by 1 May 1913. Ivanov also undertook to translate poems by Alcaeus and Sappho for the series, and completed the first part of this task by the spring of 1912; in February 1913, Sabashnikov accepted his offer of further translations from Sappho.[23]

Having thus established himself as one of Sabashnikov's translators in the field of classical antiquity, Ivanov sought to widen his scope and turned to the translation of Dante's works. The reasons for this were partly economic; as he wrote to Sabashnikov from Rome on 20 January 1913, he found that he worked better in Italy than in Russia, and therefore wished to prolong his stay beyond the autumn, for longer than originally planned. This decision entailed sacrificing the income from a course of lectures which he would have read in St Petersburg, had he returned to Russia. He was therefore looking for more work as a translator to finance his extended stay. In his letter, he made the following suggestions:

As for poetic translations, I am attracted and even inspired by a great deal which would fit into your programme quite naturally. I am not just speaking of poets of classical antiquity. I would be happy, for example, at some point to translate Dante's *Purgatory* and particularly his *Paradise*, his *New Life*, and in the field of classical antiquity to show that I can provide a faithful and harmonious rendering of Aristophanes.[24]

The preference which Ivanov expresses for the *Vita Nuova* and those parts of the *Commedia* dealing with purely transcendent, spiritual matters parallels the general development of his interest in Dante, as traced in the previous chapter through his poetry. Early poems such as 'La Selva Oscura', 'At the Coliseum', 'Mi fur le serpi amiche' or 'Golden Veils' tended to concentrate on images connected with sin and its punishment, drawn from the *Inferno*, whereas the later verse, written after the death of Lidiya Dimitrievna, reflects the influence of the *Vita Nuova, Purgatorio* and *Paradiso* much more strongly. It is not surprising, therefore, to find that these were the particular works which Ivanov felt drawn to translating in 1913.

Although Sabashnikov did not take up Ivanov's offer of a translation of part of the *Commedia*, he did react positively to the idea of the *Vita Nuova*. On 10 March 1913 he sent off a definitive reply to Ivanov's proposal in the form of a letter and a contract which Ivanov signed and returned to him on 21 April.[25] The contract repeated the agreement which Ivanov had concluded two years previously with Sabashnikov to translate all of Aeschylus's tragedies, and added to this the translation of the *Vita Nuova* and of further poems by Sappho. According to the terms of the contract, Ivanov took it upon himself to complete all these translations in the order of his choice within the next two years, submitting his translations of Sappho at the earliest possible date for inclusion in the anthology *Alcaeus and Sappho* which was already being printed.

Ivanov sent his additional translations of Sappho to Sabashnikov from Italy in the spring of 1913,[26] and his translation of *Agamemnon*, the first part of the trilogy of the *Oresteia*, was completed on 1 June 1913 in Rome and received by Sabashnikov in Moscow at the end of the month.[27] However, he did not keep to the contract's deadline as far as Aeschylus's other tragedies and the *Vita Nuova* were concerned. The complete translation of the *Oresteia* was only ready for printing in 1916, and Ivanov's autobiographical letter, written in Sochi in January and February 1917, reveals that his main current occupation at that time was still working on his translations of Aeschylus and the *Vita Nuova* (*SS* II, 22). In 1917 the building of the Sabashnikov publishing house was severely damaged by fire; this caused the printing of the *Oresteia* to be abandoned, and the *Vita Nuova* project may well also have been dropped at this stage for the same reason. Although in 1926 Ivanov returned once more to the question of Sabashnikov publishing his translation of the *Oresteia*, he did not raise the topic of the *Vita Nuova* again in his correspondence with Sabashnikov.[28]

Ivanov's interest in translating the *Vita Nuova* continued in the years which he spent at the University of Baku (1920–4). During this period he introduced an Italian language course for beginners into the university curriculum.[29] One of his former students, the critic, Viktor Manuilov, attended this course and recalls that Ivanov used the *Vita Nuova* as his basic language-teaching text during the second semester; the students would read aloud and translate from the *Vita Nuova* into Russian, and their teacher would correct their Italian pronunciation and improve their translation.[30] It is possible that the choice of the *Vita Nuova* for this purpose was linked with Ivanov's own interest in translating the work, and that he wished to use the class as a forum for discussing techniques of translation.

After this point, there is no more evidence of Ivanov working on his translation of the *Vita Nuova*. It is difficult to say whether or not he ever completed it, for only fragments of it have survived, and it is not clear whether these constitute the whole of his work on the translation or just a part of it. It seems likely, however, given the lack of coherence among the fragments, that they only represent a part of the work carried out.

The surviving passages come from six different chapters of the *Vita Nuova*. Only one of these (from chapter III) was ever published; it forms the basis of Ivanov's celebrated essay on the aesthetics of Symbolism, 'On the Limits of Art', first written and delivered as a lecture in 1913, and printed in the newly formed Danteana section of *Trudy i dni* in the following year.[31]

Apart from this passage, all the other surviving fragments of Ivanov's translation are in the Manuscripts Department of the Lenin Library in Moscow. In Ivanov's archive, there is a sheaf of eight foolscap sheets, boldly headed in the poet's handwriting 'Dante: *The New Life*'.[32] These sheets contain the draft of an introductory note on the significance of the *Vita Nuova*, and the text of Ivanov's translations of the following passages: chapter I, in which Dante announces his intention to recount the events which occurred after the beginning of his new life and their meaning; the first half of chapter V, which contains an account of the way in which, when Dante was sitting in church staring at Beatrice, the people present mistook the object of his gaze for another woman who was sitting in between him and Beatrice; the sonnet from chapter VII (of which Ivanov gives four different versions), describing the poet's distress at the departure of this lady (who had served as a cover for the object of his true love), and detailing the trials and torments of love; the whole of chapter XX, in which Dante tells how a friend of his requested him to write a sonnet treating of love, and then gives the text of the sonnet which he wrote and a prose explanation of its meaning; and finally, the whole of chapter xxi, in which Dante describes how he wished to write more on the subject of love, and how Beatrice, by the effect of her eyes and gaze, was capable of evoking love not merely in people in whom love was dormant, but also in those from whom love was totally absent; a sonnet on this subject, followed by a prose explanation of its meaning, concludes the chapter.

The first three passages are pencilled in a rough draft, whereas the last two passages (chapters xx and xxi) are written out in ink in a much more polished final version. The text of the sonnets from these last two chapters is given below; since these translations are finished versions rather than rough drafts, they provide a useful basis for the analysis of Ivanov's manner of translation, studied in conjunction with the published fragment from chapter iii.

The sonnet from chapter xx beginning 'Amore e 'l cor gentil sono una cosa ...' ('Love and the noble heart are one thing ...') is rendered as follows:

> Любовь и сердце высшее - одно:
> Был прав мудрец, сих слов провозвеститель -
> С душой разумной разум разлучить иль?
> Не разлучить и тех двоих равно.
>
> Природою влюбленною дано
> Царю-Амуру сердце, как обитель.
> И долго ль, нет ли, спит в чертоге житель;
> Настанет срок - подвигнется оно.
>
> Женой смиренномудрою предстанет,
> Взор мужеский пленяя, Красота.
> Желание родится. Не устанет
>
> Тревожить сердце нежная мечта,
> Доколе не разбудит властелина.
> Так и жене достойный лишь мужчина.

The next translation is of the sonnet from chapter xxi beginning 'Ne li occhi porta la mia donna Amore ...' ('My lady bears Love in her eyes ...'):

> Любовь сама в очах мадонны светит;
> И на кого воззрит, - преображен.
> К идущей мимо каждый притяжен;
> Но обомрет, кого она приветит.

Потупит взор, кто взор небесный встретит;
Укором тайным в сердпе пристыжен,
Поник гордец. Как чтить ее? Из жен
Участливых, какая мне ответит?

Кто слышал дивной тихие слова,
Так помыслов смиренномудрых сладость [;][33]
Блажен царицу видевший едва.

Кому ж цвета ее улыбки радость,
Любовь чудо знает, что ни изречь
Устами нельзя, ни памяти - сберечь.

A comparison of Ivanov's translations with the original text rapidly reveals a number of minor but significant distortions and inaccuracies. By 1913, the year in which the contract for the translation of the *Vita Nuova* was signed, Ivanov had already spent many years residing in Italy, and his knowledge of Italian was fluent. It was not therefore a question of his failing to catch the meaning of the original; it was much more a matter of deliberate adaptation, designed to bring Dante more firmly into the orbit of Symbolist attitudes by 'rewriting' the text of his works. The main tendency which emerges from the translations is one which is endemic to the nature of Symbolism, and derives from the movement's view of the role of the Symbolist artist in society and the nature of his art. Ivanov's ideas on this subject can be found in two essays which he wrote in 1904, 'The Poet and the Rabble' and 'Athena's Spear' (*SS* 1, 709–14 and 727–33). His spiritual and artistic golden age was the classical world of Ancient Greece when man had been in touch with the mystical essence of the universe and 'great art' (*bol'shoe iskusstvo*) had flourished in the form of universal myths. This ideal unity of man and the universe had, however, been broken, and in the present day 'great art' was no longer possible. Man could only strive to create 'lesser art' (*maloe iskusstvo*) of which one particular type would eventually lead him back to the ideal of universal art. This was 'art of the cell' (*keleinoe iskusstvo*), a form of art in which the artist acknowledged the fatal split between himself and the world, and retired to meditate in solitude in order to create an intuitive, personal, and mystical art whose symbols would be the seeds of future myths.

The present stage of Symbolist art was identified by Ivanov with 'art of the cell'. In this scheme Dante played an extremely important role. On the one hand, he was held up as the last true representative of 'great art'; the Middle Ages were seen as the final period in history when a collective, unified spirit had informed a society and its culture (*SS* I, 710 and 730). On the other hand, his art was also seen to contain features of 'art of the cell', and as such was presented to the Symbolist as a model to imitate in order to travel the path back to ideal universal art. This is the reason why Ivanov chose the following lines from *Purgatorio* (xxvII, 88–90) as the epigraph to his first collection of poetry, *Pilot Stars*:

> Poco potea parer li del di fuori
> Ma par quel poco vedev'io le stelle
> Di lor solere e piu chiare e maggiori.   (*SS* I, 513)

> Little of the outside could be seen there,
> but through that little I saw the stars
> brighter and larger than their wont.

For Ivanov these lines expressed the spiritual stance of the Symbolist artist, looking out from his isolation to the transcendent spiritual truths of the universe which for the moment might simply be private symbols, but would eventually become universal myths. In 'Athena's Spear' he cited these lines once more, referring to them as the 'symbol of the mystical soul' of 'art of the cell' (*SS* I, 729). Later, Blok took up the epigraph in his essay on the poetry and aesthetics of Ivanov, and used it to justify the isolation and obscurity of Symbolist verse which would eventually, in his and Ivanov's view, lead to a purer art of universal myth.[34]

While Symbolism was still at the stage of 'art of the cell', the process of artistic creation was naturally viewed as one in which the poet retired from the crowd to meditate on his own before producing a work of art which would be obscure and unintelligible to the masses. In 'The Poet and the Rabble', Ivanov linked this view of artistic creation to two poems by Pushkin, 'The Poet' ('*Poet*') and 'The Poet and the Crowd' ('*Poet i tolpa*') (originally entitled 'The Rabble' – '*Chern'*'):

Tragic is the genius who has not yet discovered himself, and who has nothing to give the crowd, because for new revelations (and it is only granted to him to speak of new matters) his spirit moves him to retire first with his god. In deserted silence, in a secret sequence of visions and sounds which are useless and unintelligible to the crowd, he must wait for the 'blowing of a fine chill' and the 'epiphanies' of his god. He must take his seat on an inaccessible tripod so that he can later, endowed with new clarity of vision, 'bring to the trembling people prayers from the lofty heights' . . . And the Poet withdraws – 'for sweet sounds and prayers'. The split has taken place.

> He runs, wild and austere,
> Full of sounds and confusion,
> To the shores of deserted seas,
> Into wide rustling forests.

This is the source of the artist's isolation – a fundamental feature of the recent history of the spirit, – and of the consequences of this feature: the attraction of art to esoteric exclusiveness, the subtlety and refinement of the 'sweet sounds', and the estrangement and introspectiveness of the solitary 'prayers'.   (SS I, 771)

It is natural, given this view of the creative process, that when Ivanov came to start work on his translation of the Vita Nuova, he should have been struck by the analogy between his own views and Dante's account of the way he used to write poetry. In particular, chapter III of the Vita Nuova provided a strong parallel. In this chapter, Dante describes his encounter with Beatrice when out on a walk; her greeting made him so happy that he retired to his room to reflect in solitude upon the experience. Here he has a dream in which he sees a vision of Amor holding a figure wrapped in a crimson sheet whom he recognizes as Beatrice; Amor wakes the sleeping Beatrice and makes her eat Dante's glowing heart which he holds in his hand. Amor's happiness then changes to sorrow, and he departs. Dante awakens in anguish from his dream, reflects upon it, and then composes a sonnet in which he describes his vision and asks other poets to interpret it for him.

The clear sequence of events recorded in this passage – moving from an initial experience to withdrawal for solitary meditation, followed by a vision which culminates in the artistic creation of a poem which is not comprehensible to all – was seen by Ivanov as the perfect illustration of his own theory of artistic creation. He had experienced similar visions, such as the one recorded in his diary entry of 15 June 1908 (discussed in the previous chapter) and had also written poetry as a result. He therefore decided to incorporate Dante's passage into his essay of 1913 on the creative process, 'On the Limits of Art' (SS II, 628–51). Here he argues that artistic creation is a two-fold process, involving an initial stage of ascent (voskhozhdenie), requiring the poet's isolation and culminating in a moment of spiritual revelation, followed by the poet's descent (*niskhozhdenie*) from these heights to impart his vision to the people through an intelligible artistic form. The essay begins with almost the whole of chapter III of the *Vita Nuova*, quoted in Ivanov's own translation (*SS* II, 628–9). Ostensibly this text is presented as an objective source from which the argument is then derived. In reality, however, the situation is rather more complex. Ivanov first selected the text because it overlapped in some respects with his own ideas. He then adapted it in such a way as to make it fit more closely with his aesthetic theories, using translation as a technique for remodelling the text to prepare the ground for the argument developed in the second part of the essay.

To illustrate this 'remodelling' process, one can take the sentence in which Dante describes how he retired to his room after experiencing the joy of Beatrice's greeting. The original text reads: 'presi tanta dolcezza, che come inebriato mi partio da le genti, e ricorsi a lo solingo luogo d'una mia camera, e puosimi a pensare di questa cortesissima' ('I was filled with such sweetness that, as if intoxicated, I went away from the people, and withdrew to the solitude of one of my rooms, and began to think about this gracious lady.' Ivanov has translated this as follows: *ya ispytal takuyu sladost', chto, kak p'yanyi, ushel iz tolpy. Ubezhav v uedinenie svoei gornitsy, predalsya ya dumam o milostivoi* ('I experienced such a feeling of sweetness that, as if intoxicated, I went away from the crowd. After running away to the solitude of my chamber, I gave myself up to thoughts of the gracious one'). There are a number of significant alterations in this translation which derive directly from Ivanov's view of the creative process. First, instead of 'da le genti' ('from the people'), he writes *iz tolpy* ('from the crowd'). This change has no foundation in Dante's text; Beatrice is accompanied by two other women, and no other people are mentioned in the chapter. Ivanov has clearly introduced the idea of the crowd to make the text more consonant with his interpretation of Pushkin's poems (the word 'crowd' (*tolpa*) occurs twice in the passage quoted above from 'The Poet and the Rabble'). Secondly, he has translated 'ricorsi' ('I withdrew') as *ubezhav* ('after running away'); as well as changing the form of the verb, he has also changed its meaning – from simply withdrawing to running. This again is clearly to bring Dante's text closer to Pushkin's poem 'The

Poet' from which Ivanov had quoted the line 'He *runs*, wild and austere' (Bezhit *on, dikii i surovyi*) in support of his argument. Finally, instead of the straightforward Italian word 'camera' ('room'), which in Russian would be *komnata*, we have the unusual and archaic term *gornitsa*, a chamber. The added emphasis which this word places on seclusion is evidently designed to evoke an association with the idea of the cell (*kel'ya*) to which the Symbolist poet repairs to create 'art of the cell' (*keleinoe iskusstvo*).

By dint of introducing these small changes of emphasis, Ivanov succeeds in making a passage from Dante's *Vita Nuova* read like a manifesto for his own brand of Symbolist aesthetics.

At the end of the passage quoted above from 'The Poet and the Rabble', Ivanov defended the right of contemporary Symbolist art to be esoteric and veiled. This characteristic of Symbolist art was directly linked by both Ivanov and Blok to Dante as a representative of 'art of the cell'. The Symbolists' desire to view Dante as a precursor of their own spiritual outlook caused them to regard him as a Symbolist in their own understanding of the term: as an obscure, inaccessible artist. This led to some considerable distortion of Dante. To the medieval mind, the transcendent world was a reality which could be experienced in a direct way; the mysteries of life after death could be described by Dante in terms of a real journey, conveyed through lucid, visual images. For the Symbolists, however, the transcendent world was something much more distant and abstract, to be recovered through an act of the imagination and intellect, rather than simply apprehended as a reality; its mysteries could only be intuited from a distance and hinted at through vague images whose very obscurity was designed to safeguard their esoteric nature.

Because of this approach, the Symbolists tended to invest Dante with an uncharacteristic aura of otherworldliness and obscurity. It is for this reason that Ivanov made so much of Dante's plea to the reader to note 'la dottrina che s'asconde / sotto 'l velame de li versi strani' ('the doctrine that is hidden under the veil of the strange verses' – *Inf.* IX, 62–3). Around 1890 he appended these lines as an epigraph to his long and highly obscure poem written in terzinas, 'The Sphinx' (*SS* I, 643). Many years later, in an essay of 1936 on symbolism, he quoted them again as an example of the conviction held by all poets of true, 'eternal' symbolism, such as Dante and Goethe, that the divine never manifests itself without a veil, but always appears in a shrouded, inaccessible form (*SS* III, 655).

These views led Ivanov to endow his translations of Dante with an obscurity and complexity which are characteristic of his own language, but not of the original. This tendency is to some extent a feature of all Russian translations of Dante; it derives from the attempt to match medieval Italian by creating a deliberately archaic form of Russian, full of church Slavonicisms and obsolete expressions, which ignores the fact that Dante's language is very much lighter in tone and closer to the modern idiom. In the case of the Symbolists this tendency became even more marked. Throughout Ivanov's translations the simple and straightforward is replaced by the complicated; archaic or obsolete terms are used in place of normal, everyday words, and simple sentence structure gives way to more involved syntax. The overall effect of these changes is to present Dante as a difficult writer with a heavy, rhetorical style – whereas Dante was the first to insist, in his famous letter to Can Grande, that the *Commedia* is written in a 'humble' rather than elevated style.[35]

Ivanov's translation of some of the terms referring to speech in the *Vita Nuova* seems to be designed to make the function of language appear more obscure than it is in reality. In chapter III, the 'parole' ('words') spoken by the lordly figure who represents Love become *glagoly*, an obsolete term for *slova*, 'words'; a straightforward Italian word becomes archaic and ponderous in the Russian translation. The simple phrase 'lo dir presente' ('these present words') which occurs in the sonnet of this chapter becomes *svitok sei* ('this scroll') in Ivanov's rendering, introducing classical and esoteric connotations which are entirely foreign to the original. In the same way, in the sonnet from chapter XX quoted above, the rhetorical *sikh slov provozvestitel'* ('the proclaimer of these words') replaces the straightforward 'in suo dittare pone' ('tells in his rhyme').

The general language of the original is also changed for the same purpose. In chapter III, Dante uses the verb 'apparve' ('appeared') for the appearance of Beatrice; Ivanov translates this as *predstala* which has a much more ceremonial majestic resonance to it. The simple 'in mezzo a' ('between') becomes *promezh*, an unusual version of *mezhdu* ('between') which would have been a more obvious translation. When Dante seems to see a cloud in his room, he writes factually: 'me parea vedere ne la mia camera una nebula di colore di fuoco' ('I seemed to see in my room a cloud the colour of fire'); this becomes *budto zastlalo gornitsu ognetsvetnoe oblako* ('as if a fire-coloured cloud had obscured the chamber'); the verb *zastlalo* ('obscured') is entirely absent from the original, and reveals Ivanov's typical desire to add extra connotations of veiled obscurity to Dante's text. In the same way, when Amor departs, Dante writes at the end of the sonnet in the same chapter: 'appresso gir lo ne vedea piangendo' ('then I saw him depart, weeping'); this is rendered by Ivanov as *I s plachem vzmyl v nadzvezdnye kraya* ('And, weeping, he flew up to the celestial regions'), which introduces an unusual verb generally reserved for birds (*vzmyt'*) in place of the simple Italian verb, and gratuitously adds a typically Symbolist abstract reference to the celestial regions.

Ivanov's translation of the sonnet from chapter xx contains similar features. The simple Italian conjunction 'tanto . . . che' ('for so long that') is rendered by the archaic Russian *dokole* ('until'). Dante's 'spirito d'Amore' ('spirit of Love') – which has a quite precise meaning for the medieval mind – becomes a vague reference to a 'master' (*vlastelin*).

Two further details are equally revealing of Ivanov's approach to Dante. Both are linked to his interpretation of Beatrice. First, there is the tendency to present her as a sensual rather than purely spiritual figure. This follows on naturally from the view that the Dionysian cult of Eros is the essence of all religious experience and has been absorbed into the Christian concept of love. Dante's Amor accordingly acquires the features of Dionysian Eros, and the portrayal of Beatrice, as the object of these feelings, is correspondingly affected. In chapter III of the *Vita Nuova* Dante has a vision of Amor bearing Beatrice on his arms, and feeding her Dante's heart. The original text reads: 'Ne le sue braccia mi parea vedere una persona dormire nuda, salvo che involta mi parea in uno drappo sanguigno leggeramente' ('In his arms I seemed to see a person sleeping naked, apart from seeming to be lightly wrapped in a crimson cloth'); Ivanov renders this as *I budto na rukakh ego spyashcheyu vizhu zhenu naguyu, edva prikrytuyu tkan'yu krovavo-aloyu* ('And I seemed to see a naked woman sleeping in his arms, barely covered by a blood-red cloth'). The difference between these two passages is small but significant; whereas Dante has Beatrice fully but lightly covered, Ivanov presents her as *scarcely* covered. Similarly, in the sonnet, the Italian reads 'e ne le bracchia avea / madonna involta in un drappo dormendo' ('and in his arms he held / my lady wrapped in a cloth and sleeping'), while the Russian becomes *I Gospozhu, pod legkim pokryvalom, / V ob''yatiyakh vladyki vizhu ya* ('And I see my Lady, under a light covering, / In the embraces of the master'). Again, the same added emphasis on the lightness of the covering recurs, and Beatrice is found in the *embraces* of a ruler, rather than simply carried in the arms of Amor.

The sensual touch conferred upon Beatrice through these details of the translation prepares for the analysis of the passage which Ivanov develops in the rest of the essay. He argues that the process of artistic creation originates in a moment of erotic enjoyment which leads to a stormy wave of Dionysiac feeling; this in turn gives rise to the Dionysiac epiphany or vision. The flash of mystic insight which inspires all true art therefore arises from the experience of Eros (*SS* II, 630). He then attempts to illustrate this in terms of Dante's passage. Beatrice's appearance and her greeting to the poet provide the initial moment of erotic enjoyment, and provoke the intense feeling of blissful sweetness which constitutes the stage of the Dionysiac epiphany. The sensual features previously associated with Beatrice in the translation make this interpretation of the passage more plausible.

The second detail concerns the association of Beatrice with Sophia. One can sense the influence of Solovyovian ideas on the language which Ivanov has used in his translations of the sonnets from chapters XX and XXI. In the first sonnet, 'Amore e 'l cor gentil sono una cosa . . .', Dante describes the way in which the potentiality of love, always dormant in the heart, is made actual by the sight of the beauty of a wise woman ('saggia donna'). Ivanov had already set the opening line of this sonnet in a Sophiological context in his poem 'Crux Amoris', composed some three years earlier. Here he extends this interpretation to the rest of the sonnet by subtly altering the text of the original through his translation. He renders the line about a beautiful and wise woman appearing before the eyes of a man with the words *Zhenoi smirennomudroyu predstanet, / Vzor muzheskii plenyaya, Krasota* ('In the guise of a wise and humble woman, Beauty / Will appear, captivating man's gaze'). Beauty here is not the physical beauty of a wise woman, as in

Dante's text, but an abstract, personified Beauty which will manifest itself to man in the guise of a 'wise woman'. The use of the poetic *zhena* rather than *zhenshchina* for 'donna' ('woman') suggests a link between this 'wise woman' and Sophia. Solovyov used the term *zhena* to refer to Sophia whom he identified with the 'woman clothed in the sun' (*zhena, oblechennaya v solntse*) of Revelation; this link subsequently became a commonplace among the Symbolists, including Ivanov, who refers to it in his essay on Solovyov (*SS* III, 302).

Ivanov loses the subtle transition from visual perception to the feeling of love which is so important in the original. Instead of describing this process on a simple, literal level, he takes us into a symbolic, abstract realm in which Beauty appears to man as a wise woman evocative of Sophia. In this respect his translation is very reminiscent of his earlier poem, 'Beauty', in which the figure of Beauty is also clearly identified with Sophia and appears to man in the guise of a woman.

The next sonnet from chapter XXI deals directly with Beatrice, and in his translation Ivanov describes her with a term usually applied to Sophia. To express the idea that the person who sees Beatrice is blessed, Dante writes 'è laudato chi prima la vide' ('blessed is he who first sees her'); Ivanov translates this as *Blazhen tsaritsu videvshii edva* ('Blessed is he who has barely glimpsed the queen'), substituting for the simple pronoun 'la' ('her') the word 'queen' (*tsaritsa*). For the Symbolist poets, this term had special connotations, deriving from its use in Solovyov's Sophiological poems as a way of referring to Sophia. It would be quite out of character for Dante to describe Beatrice by any such term. In the *Commedia* he refers to her as his 'donna', and reserves the term 'regina' ('queen') for the Virgin Mary.

Furthermore, in the immediately preceding line, Ivanov introduces another word which is absent from the original. Dante's phrase 'Ogne dolcezza, ogne pensero umile' ('All sweetness, every humble thought'), referring to the thoughts and emotions which arise in the heart of a person who hears Beatrice speak, is translated as *pomyslov smirennomudrykh sladost'* ('the sweetness of wise and humble thoughts'). Ivanov has added to the quality of humility the idea of wisdom, the main attribute of Sophia and her seekers. These two additions lend a distinctly Solovyovian aura to the depiction of Beatrice in this sonnet.

In these translations, therefore, Dante is subtly redefined in terms of Ivanov's spiritual outlook and Symbolist aesthetics; he emerges as a writer who has retired from the crowd in order to compose obscure, archaic verse, devoted to a Beatrice who combines sensual features with Sophiological ones.

CONVIVIO

The next translation of a work by Dante in which Ivanov became involved was a joint project; in 1914 he cooperated with the philosopher Vladimir Frantsevich Ern (1881–1917) in a translation of the *Convivio* which the Sabashnikov publishing house was interested in printing. The project was never completed, and only survives in the form of a manuscript text of the translation of the first half of the work, located in the Sabashnikov archive of the Manuscripts Department of the Lenin Library in Moscow. Although the text is entirely in Ern's hand, only the prose part of the work is in his translation; the *canzone* which occurs at the beginning of the second book was translated by Ivanov.[36]

The friendship of Ivanov and Ern dates back to 1904 when the two writers first met each other while abroad, towards the end of Ivanov's period of residence in Switzerland. After Ivanov returned to Russia, Ern was one of the first guests to attend the regular Wednesday gatherings at the tower where he frequently stayed when visiting St Petersburg.[37] The idea of doing a joint translation of the *Convivio* probably first took form several years later when both writers found themselves living in Rome and became particularly close friends. In the late autumn of 1912 Ivanov and his family moved from France to Rome where they remained until their departure for Russia the following autumn. Ern had been living in Italy since 1911, based mainly in Rome. In December 1912 he moved back from his country retreat near Rome to the city, and stayed there until his return to Russia in May 1913.[38] He was therefore together with Ivanov in Rome throughout the period from January to May 1913 when Ivanov began his correspondence with Sabashnikov about the possibility of undertaking new translations of Dante's works and signed the contract for the translation of the *Vita Nuova*. Ern would certainly have followed these negotiations with interest, and it is quite possible that at this stage Ivanov may have suggested to Sabashnikov that he should also

consider publishing a translation of the *Convivio* which, unlike
the *Vita Nuova* and the *Commedia*, had never previously been
fully translated into Russian. It would have been natural for Ern,
a professional philosopher, to take on the prose parts of the
treatise, but to leave the verse to Ivanov with his reputation as a
poet and experience of translating verse. A similar venture was
undertaken by Ivanov for the same series with the literary critic
and historian Mikhail Gershenzon (1869–1925). In 1914 they
worked together on a translation of Petrarch's works, published
in 1915. Ivanov translated the poetry, and Gershenzon did the
prose.[39]

There are several reasons connected with Ivanov's and Ern's
religious and philosophical interests which explain why they were
attracted to Dante and the *Convivio* in particular. On a general
level, there was the fervent, almost mystical love of Italy which
they shared with a number of other Russians of their generation.
When Ivanov first visited Rome in 1892, he was quite overwhelmed. He poured out all his impressions in a long poem
entitled 'Laeta' which he sent from Rome to his friend A. M.
Dmitrievsky in Russia. Unlike Ovid who lamented the bitterness
of exile in *Tristia*, he wrote about the joy of discovering a second
homeland:

Рим – всех богов жилищем клянусь! – мне по сѐрдцу обитель:
  Цели достигнув святой, здесь я, паломник, блажен.
....
Родине верен, я Рим родиной новою чту.   (*SS* I, 636, 638)

Rome – I swear by the home of all the gods! – is an abode to my liking:
  Having reached my holy goal, here I, a pilgrim, have found bliss.
....
Faithful to my homeland, I honour Rome as a new homeland.

Similar feelings were recorded by him over thirty years later
when he returned to Rome after leaving Russia in 1924. The cycle
of 'Roman Sonnets' ('*Rimskie sonety*') opens with the following
lines:

Вновь арок древних верный пилигрим,
В мой поздний час вечерним 'Ave Roma'
Приветствую как свод родного дома,
Тебя, скитаний пристань, вечный Рим.   (*SS* III, 578)

> Once again a faithful pilgrim of the ancient arches,
> In my late hour, with an evening 'Ave Roma'
> I greet you like the roof of my own home,
> You, the haven of my wanderings, eternal Rome.

Ern expressed his delight at being in Italy in a letter he wrote to his friend, the literary historian and critic Aleksandr Sergeevich Glinka (1878–1949), soon after settling in Italy in 1911:

It's nice to be in Italy – it is a kind of second homeland for us. I feel as if my soul has set off on a series of wanderings, and is travelling through unknown lands and sailing over unknown seas, and yet its path [*put'*] is clear. And from afar the homeland somehow seems particularly dear and glimmers with a kind of starry glory.

The next year, he echoed the same sentiments in another letter to his friend:

We have become terribly attached to Italy and even now it is already hard for us to think that we will soon be leaving – perhaps we will never return here again. It is a unique country, the noblest and most brilliant in Europe. It seems to me that for the Russian soul, Italy is a second homeland.[40]

This sense of Italy as a second homeland with a special spiritual meaning for Russians underlay both Ivanov's and Ern's fascination with Dante as Italy's chief poet. It was linked for both of them with a strong interest in the relationship between the religions of both nations, Russian Orthodoxy and Catholicism. Whereas Ivanov moved from a childhood upbringing firmly grounded in his native faith to an increasing interest in Catholicism, culminating in his conversion of 1926, Ern was much more strongly wedded to the Russian Orthodox tradition. He came from a family of German origin, and took up Russian Orthodoxy in a rather militant fashion, being particularly opposed to the rationalist elements of Catholicism. In his letters to Glinka from Italy he expresses constant criticisms about Catholics, and approves only of those who turn to the Russian Orthodox church for spiritual inspiration. In one letter, he contrasts the soberness of Greek and Russian saints with what he describes as the 'drunkenness' of their Catholic counterparts.[41] In another, he describes at length a meeting with a Catholic priest whom he had befriended on an earlier occasion in a train; he calls him a 'good, pure soul' because he was very interested in Russia, had started to learn Russian, and was planning to travel to Russia. Encouraged by this example, he continues with a report on his recent meeting with the Italian theologian, A. Palmieri, renowned for his interest in Russian Orthodoxy:

Generally speaking, among the Catholics one does come across some good people. They are sincerely amazed at the religiousness of Russians and of Slavs in general, which is undoubtedly greater than in the West, and some of them are beginning to look towards the distant, defamed and stigmatized East with hope and expectation. Recently I saw Palmieri; he knows Russian and has made a magnificent scholarly study of the whole of Russian theological and philosophical literature. He considers it to be *extremely rich* and most remarkable, and thinks that the official Roman Church's indifferent attitude to orthodoxy is stupid.[42]

In her memoirs of this period, Lidiya Ivanova recalls Ern's daily visits to her father in Rome; apparently, the main subject of their lengthy discussions was Catholicism – for which Ivanov offered an apologetic – and Orthodoxy – defended by Ern.[43] For both writers, translating the *Convivio* fitted in well with their general interest in promoting the dialogue between the two churches; it was a means of incorporating a work of Catholic philosophy into the Russian Orthodox tradition with a view to either Catholicizing the latter or Russianizing the former.

Ern also shared Ivanov's view of the metaphysical nature of true culture. In *The Struggle for Logos (Bor'ba za Logos)*, published in 1911, he took up Ivanov's ideas on the alienation of the modern artist from the world around him; like Ivanov, he saw classical antiquity and the Middle Ages as periods in history when the artist had still been at one with his environment. To recover this lost unity, he advocated a restoration of the ideal harmony between culture and the church which had prevailed in the Middle Ages.[44] In this attempt to restore culture to its religious Christian roots, Dante, as the chief representative of medieval art, was obviously an important model for Ern, in the same way as he was for Ivanov.

Within this general framework Ern's perception of Dante was strongly influenced by the ideas of two nineteenth-century Italian ontologist philosophers whose works he had been studying in Italy during the period before he began work on the *Convivio*. His interest in these philosophers was perhaps partly related to the fact that both, although ordained priests, had gone through periods of ill-favour with the Catholic church and had had their works put on the index. Significantly, Dante played an important role in both authors' systems. Antonio Rosmini-Serbati (1797–1855) turned to medieval scholastic philosophy as a source for some of his ideas; his reference to Dante in this context was quoted by Ern in his book on Rosmini, published in 1914. Vincenzo Gioberti (1801–52) was the subject of Ern's next major work of 1916. He was a Dante scholar who regarded Dante as a great philosopher of the Platonic school of ontologism, and interpreted the *Convivio* as a masterful expression of this tradition. Ern discusses these views at length and quotes a passage from the *Convivio* which Gioberti cites as his motto for a universalistic approach in philosophy.[45]

All these factors contributed to Ern's and Ivanov's joint interest in translating the *Convivio*. Although the idea may well have originated in Rome in 1913, it seems unlikely that much work was done on it until the following year. After leaving Italy in May 1913, Ern returned to his home-town in the Caucasus, Tiflis, and settled down to work full-time on his dissertation which he was under great pressure to complete as soon as possible. In February 1914 he was nearing the end of his task and wrote to Glinka that he expected to be able to travel to Moscow and submit his thesis in another two months. His next letter was written in Moscow on 26 May, the day after handing in his dissertation. He was staying with Ivanov, and one of the highlights of his visit so far had been their trip to the Trinity Monastery of St Sergius at Sergiev Posad (the seat of the Theological Academy) to witness Florensky defending his dissertation. Ivanov and the priest Pavel Florensky (1882–1952) were close friends at this time, and a few days later Florensky came to stay with Ivanov for a couple of 'nights', as Ern put it in his letter, since the two friends apparently slept all day and talked through the night.[46]

The contact is significant because there is a letter of this period in Florensky's private archive which reveals that the question of whether or not a translation of the *Convivio* by Ivanov and Ern would be commissioned by the Sabashnikov publishing house for the 'Monuments of World Literature' series was still undecided by mid-May 1914.[47] Soon after this juncture, however, the matter must have been resolved, for there is clear evidence that Ern spent the following summer working on the translation.

During the summer of 1914 Ivanov and Ern both left Moscow for different destinations. Ivanov travelled to Petrovskoe, a small village on the river Oka, where he stayed with his Lithuanian friend, the Catholic poet Yurgis Baltrushaitis (1873–1944). Ern returned to the Caucasus and rented a dacha in Anapa, a coastal resort not far from Novorossiisk. It was here that he evidently began work on his translation of the *Convivio*. On 8 July he wrote a letter to Ivanov, composed in a curious mock-Dantesque style which evidently had the status of a private language between the two writers:

I inform you that Anapa is an extremely nasty little town with a charming sea-scape which is most conducive to reflections on Aphrodite of the Heavens, to translating the *Convivio* and to writing the 'Letters about the Name of God' – just what is needed for my 'kidneys' and my sinful soul. Furthermore, I inform you that yesterday I sent off by registered post the *Convito* and the 25 roubles which a certain great gentleman slipped into my side-pocket with great consideration when I was leaving the home which had sheltered me with such unlimited hospitality in the days of my Moscow wanderings. It is necessary to say that my heart is filled to the brim with the deepest gratitude, and that all the details of my sweetest sojourn in that Arcadia of friendship are inscribed in the book of my memory in letters of gold.[48]

The general tone of this letter recalls Dante's effusive expressions of gratitude to Can Grande, the famous lord of Verona who provided him with generous hospitality and patronage during his exile, a fact which Dante acknowledged by dedicating the *Paradiso* to him. The last sentence of the passage quoted was originally written in Italian; its style ('nel libro della memoria mia siano scritti con lettere d'oro tutti dettagli del mio soavissimo soggiorno ...') deliberately echoes the opening of the *Vita Nuova* in which Dante declares his intention to record the words which are written in the book of his memory.

The *Convito* which Ern mentions in his letter is most likely to be an Italian edition of the work (not his translation) – either Ivanov's copy which Ern had borrowed and is now returning, together with the 25 roubles, or Ern's own copy which he is lending Ivanov. In either case, the fact that he is taking the trouble to post it to Ivanov at his holiday retreat suggests that it was needed by his friend for work on his part of the translation over that summer.

A few days later Ern wrote to Glinka, outlining his current work projects. These included two sets of letters on religious topics (the dispute over the name of God and Ern's impressions of Christian Rome), destined for the periodical press, and the translation of the *Convivio*, about which he writes the following:

Thirdly, I am translating Dante's *Convivio* for the Sabashnikovs. This translation is my only source of income for the whole autumn. In all likelihood not one of those projects will be finished by the autumn. I am somewhat torn between them, but on the other hand all three projects are extremely close to my heart and I experience a feeling of bliss when translating Dante, and when delving into the debate over the name of God, and when recalling my impressions of Rome.

The outbreak of the First World War interrupted the letter which was only resumed after an interval of over a month on 21 August:

As was to be expected, I did not manage to complete any of the projects which we mentioned. I only translated half of Dante, and both sets of letters have ground to a halt because the advent of war has brought about an upheaval in the world of journals and I do not know which of them still exist and which have stopped existing.[49]

Shortly afterwards, in September 1914, Ern moved back to Moscow where he rented a room in Ivanov's flat on Zubovsky Boulevard. He remained in this flat until his death from tuberculosis in May 1917, and spent much time 'in great friendship and great spiritual closeness' with Ivanov and his family.[50] However, the two friends never returned to their translation of the *Convivio*. The manuscript which is in the Sabashnikov archive corresponds to the part of the work which Ern had completed by the end of August 1914; the fact that it is entirely in his handwriting suggests that he already had Ivanov's translation of the *canzone* with him at that time and incorporated it into his final manuscript. The project may have been abandoned for any one of several reasons – perhaps Sabashnikov backed out of the agreement as in the case of the *Vita Nuova*, or perhaps it was due to the pressure of other work or to Ern's poor state of health. After Ern's death, Ivanov wrote a number of poems dedicated to his memory. Not surprisingly, these draw extensively on Dantesque imagery, reflecting the deep interest which both friends shared in Dante.[51]

At the beginning of the *Convivio*, Dante describes the subject of his book; it will consist of fourteen *canzoni* and their exposition in prose; the *canzoni* themselves may be a little obscure, but each one will be followed by a detailed exposition in prose, designed to elucidate its literal and allegorical meaning (*Con.* I, i, 14–15). Dante did not in fact finish the *Convivio*, and out of the projected fourteen *canzoni*, only three were written. In its final form the

Convivio consists of four tractates. The first describes the general purpose of the work, and defends various aspects of it, such as the use of the Vulgate rather than Latin; each of the remaining three tractates consists of a *canzone* followed by an extensive commentary in prose. The part of the *Convivio* which Ern and Ivanov translated (the first half, i.e. tractates I and II) only contains one *canzone*, placed at the beginning of the second tractate, 'Voi che 'ntendendo il terzo ciel movete ...' ('O you who move the third heaven by intellection ...'), and this is the text which Ivanov translated.

It is worth noting at the outset that the *Convivio*, according to Dante's own definition of its subject, is based on a relationship which interested Ivanov greatly, and which he associated with Dante; this is the relationship between a profound spiritual experience, its expression in poetry, and the subsequent interpretation of this poetic record in prose. In his introductory note to his translation of the *Vita Nuova* Ivanov laid particular stress on this aspect of the work; his comments are entirely devoted to a discussion of the relationship between the poems of the *Vita Nuova* and the prose passages which describe the biographical origin of the poems and interpret their meaning. A few years earlier he had considered adapting this method for use in his own writing; after the death of Lidiya Dimitrievna, Kuzmin suggested to him that he should write a prose commentary to accompany the poems of 'Love and Death', following the model of the *Vita Nuova*.[51]

Although Ivanov did not take up this suggestion, the way of thinking which is laid bare in the poetry–prose structure of the *Vita Nuova* and the *Convivio* was clearly one with which he felt a particular sense of affinity. It was in perfect harmony with the two sides of his nature – the mystical–poetic and the rational–philosophic. Sergei Bulgakov made a special point of comparing him to Dante in this respect, using the term 'poet-thinker' of both writers. Ivanov's friend, the poet Vladimir Pyast, recorded a similar comment; when he visited the tower in September 1905 with Ern, he observed: 'Vyacheslav was divided: with Ern he was a philosopher, with me a poet.'[52]

At the end of the *canzone* which Ivanov has translated, Dante draws a distinction between the rational sense of the poem, which may not be clear to all, and its poetic beauty. Ern has in some sense taken on the role of the rational philosopher, explaining the sense of the poem in the prose commentary which he has translated; his translation is excellent, very close to the original and lucid in style. However, the *canzone* is by no means limited to the mystical, poetic side of reality; it explores the tension between the irrational and rational sides of man by describing the struggle which is taking place in Dante's heart between his love for Beatrice, who is no longer living, and his new love for another woman. The poet used to be consoled by thoughts of Beatrice in the heavens, but a new thought now comes to him and banishes these reflections by bidding him look at another woman. While Beatrice represents the contemplative, mystical way which leads through faith to truth, the second lady, as Dante explains in his prose commentary, represents Philosophy, the path which leads through rational understanding based on the evidence of the senses to truth (*Con.* II, xv, 3). These are two complementary aspects of wisdom, truth revealed to man from above, or truth searched out by man on earth, the mystic way and the philosophical way.

The *canzone* thus dramatizes, both through its explicit subject and through the tension in its form between poetic beauty and rational sense, an inner debate between the mystical and the rational aspects of man's soul. This theme held a place of special importance in Ivanov's world-view and is presented by him in a characteristic way in his translation.

The text of Ivanov's translation of 'Voi che 'ntendendo il terzo ciel movete . . .' is as follows:

О вы, чей разум движет сферу третью!
Услышьте тайный помысл мой сердечный!
Зане другим сказать бы я не мог
Столь новых дум. Свод неба быстротечный
Влекомый вами, жизнь мою, как сетью,
Своим круговращением увлек.
Итак сколь долу горестен мой рок,
Достойно вам поведаю, благие
И мудрые бесплотные! Молюсь
Внемлите вы, какой тоской томлюсь
И как душа стенает и какие
Ей прекословя, речи говорит
Тот дух, чей звездный лик меж вас горит.

Бывало сумрак сердца оживляла
Небесная мечта. Ее державе
Владыки вашего святил я в дань.

Жену я видел в лучезарной славе.
Столь сладко горний свет мечта являла [,]
Что дальнюю душа рвалася грань
Переступить. Но враг подъемлет брань.
Душа бежит гонителя. Владеет
Мной деспот новый, и волнует грудь.
Он на жену другую мне взглянуть
Велит. 'Кто зреть спасенье вожделеет', –
Так шепчет он – 'пусть в очи смотрит ей
Коль не страшится вздохов и скорбей ['].

Но с помыслом губительным враждует
Умильная мечта, что говорила
Мне о жене, увенчанной в раю.
Душа, чью боль она заворожила,
Осиротев[,] мятется и тоскует,
Утешную зовет мечту свою.
Корит глаза: 'Разлучницу мою
В который час [,] мятежные [,] узрели?
И вас она? О новой сей жене,
Ослушные [,] не верили вы мне!
Мечи для душ таких, как я, горели
В очах убийственных. Я не могла
Те очи скрыть от вас – и умерла!'

– 'Нет, ты не умерла, но ужаснулась
Внезапности, душа, и возроптала' –
Ей молвит некий друг, любви посол:
[–'] Прекрасную узрев, иной ты стала.
Преобратясь, почто же содрогнулась,
И малодушный страх в тебя вошел?
Смири мятеж и победи раскол!
Сколь мудрая приветно величава,
Сколь благочестна, кротости полна!
Отныне госпожа твоя – она.
Окресть ее чудес столь многих слава [,]
Что скажешь ты: "Вотще была борьба [,]
Господь любви, се аз, твоя раба!" ['.]

О песнь моя! согласным одобреньем
Принять могущих весть твою – немного[;]
Твой смысл доступен, ведаю, не всем.
Коль темная ведет тебя дорога
Ко встрече с равнодушьем и бореньем [,]
Утешься, и кому глагол твой нем [,]

Ответствуй на вопрос его: зачем?
Твое вещанье странно и неясно?
– 'Пусть весть темна, но я ль не сладкогласна?'

From the point of view of form, Ivanov's translation is faithful to the original. It keeps exactly to the number of lines of Dante's *canzone* – four parts of thirteen lines each, followed by an *envoi* or *tornata*, as Dante calls it, of nine lines. Ivanov has used iambic pentameters throughout, and has successfully reproduced Dante's rhyming scheme.

However, formal perfection in a translation can sometimes only be achieved at the expense of exactitude of meaning; there are instances in Ivanov's version where a line or phrase has been added in quite gratuitously, without any basis in the original, evidently to make up an extra line or to preserve the rhyming scheme. For similar reasons, there are some omissions.

As in the case of the *Vita Nuova* translation, these changes generally reflect features of Ivanov's own spiritual outlook. There is the same tendency to prefer the complicated to the simple. On the syntactical level, this takes the form of the introduction of *enjambements*. Although these do not occur in the original, Ivanov introduces them seven times in the course of his translation (at the end of ll. 4, 9, 15, 19, 21, 23 and 40), thereby creating considerably more tension in the text. He also introduces complicated inversions of natural word order; one can contrast, for example, the complexity of the first two lines of the *envoi* in the Russian version (nearly every word is put in a different order from the expected one) with the simplicity and straightforward sentence structure of the original:

Canzone, io credo che saranno radi
color che tua ragione intendan bene

My song, I think they will be few
who clearly understand your meaning

On the lexical level Ivanov introduces numerous archaisms; *zane* (l.3), an archaic word for 'since') is just one of several possible examples.

The most characteristic feature of the translation is the treatment of the theme of the relationship of man to the cosmos. This was one of the corner-stones of Ivanov's world-view. There is some justification for introducing it into the translation, since the original *canzone* opens with an address to the angelic intelligences who move the third sphere (Venus, the planet of love) which is held responsible by the poet for the state in which he finds himself. Dante thus does link his own state to the activities of the cosmos. However, in the translation, this link acquires a quite different resonance.

For Ivanov, the essence of the mystical experience was the act of self-transcendence, the breaking of the soul's boundaries. In this way, man, the microcosm, could achieve a form of mystical union with the universe, the macrocosm. These ideas were influenced by Nietzsche, and frequently affected Ivanov's portrayal of Dante's universe. In 'The Spirit', for example, he projected his own Dionysiac vision of the universe on to Dante's. The melodramatic post-Romantic flavour of this poem's depiction of the individual's soul, scooped up and hurled into the cosmic wheeling of the planets, has little in common with Dante's measured ascent through the heavens of Paradise. A similar tendency is reflected in some of the distortions of Ivanov's translation of 'Voi che 'ntendendo ...'. Lines 4–6 can be taken as an example. In Italian they read as follows:

> El ciel che segue lo vostro valore,
> gentili creature che voi sete,
> mi tragge ne lo stato ov'io mi trovo.

> The heaven that follows your power,
> noble creatures that you are,
> draws me into the state in which I find myself.

For the simple 'el ciel' ('the heaven') Ivanov has substituted *svod neba bystrotechnyi* ('the fast-flowing vault of the sky'), introducing the idea of vast cosmic spaces filled with movement; furthermore, *vlekomyi* ('moved') implies a stronger force than 'segue' ('follows'); *kak set'yu, / Svoim krugovrashcheniem* ('as if with a net, by its circular whirling') is a complete addition on the poet's part, contributing further to the idea of swirling, inevitable movement. These additions have been made at the expense of Dante's charming phrase 'gentili creature che voi sete' ('noble creatures that you are'), and of the important idea of the 'valore' ('power') of the angelic intelligences, as well as of the state in which Dante finds himself.

Whereas for Dante the starry spheres are a part of the real world, on which they exert a controlled influence, for Ivanov they are abstractions, *blagie / I mudrye besplotnye* ('blessed and wise incorporeal beings' – ll. 8–9). Ivanov's translation of 'un spirto . . . / che vien pe' raggi de la vostra stella' ('a spirit . . . that comes on the rays of your star' – ll. 12–13) as *Tot dukh, chei zvezdnyi lik mezh vas gorit* ('That spirit whose starry countenance burns among you') completely misses the point of the original; in medieval cosmology the rays of a planet were seen as the means by which its influence was transmitted to earth, as Dante explains in some detail in his prose commentary to the *canzone* (*Con.* II, vi, 9). Ivanov's translation substitutes for this precise concept a vague undefined image.

Similarly, in the second stanza, the soul's simple direct statement 'Io men vo' gire' ('I wish to go there too') is replaced by a lengthy paraphrase: *Stol' sladko gornii svet mechta yavlyala [,] / Chto dal'nyuyu dusha rvalasya gran' / Perestupit'* ('So sweetly did the heavenly light appear in the dream, That my soul longed to cross the distant limit'). This paraphrase introduces characteristic Ivanovian themes: the abstract concept of the 'heavenly light' (*gornii svet*) (its counterpart, the notion of the 'earthly world' (*dol'nii mir*) was also gratuitously introduced by Ivanov in l. 7) and the idea of the soul bursting to transcend its limitations ('longed' (*rvalasya*) and 'limit' (*gran'*) directly echo the title of the section of *Pilot Stars* entitled 'The Impulse and the Limits' ('*Poryv i grani*')).

The vision of the cosmos which Ivanov presents in his translation is quite different from that conveyed by the original; instead of a sense of real celestial bodies, we have abstractions; instead of an organized system of influences, we have a chaotic universe in perpetual Dionysiac motion. Typically, different forms of the word *myatezh* ('restlessness', 'storminess') are introduced by Ivanov at three points during the *canzone* (ll. 31, 34 and 46) although they do not occur in the original.

However, to Ivanov's credit, apart from distortions of this type which result directly from his own world-view, there are several points in his translation which show a close knowledge of the meaning which Dante intended his text to carry. It is clear from various details of the translation that Ivanov made extensive use of Dante's prose commentary as a guide to the best way of translating the *canzone*. As an example, one can take the second line of Dante's poem, 'udite il ragionar ch'è nel mio core' ('listen to the speech in my heart'), rendered into Russian as *Uslysh'te tainyi pomysl moi serdechnyi!* ('Hear the secret thought of my heart'). At first glance, this may seem inaccurate – why has Ivanov replaced the precise indication of 'nel mio core' ('in my heart') with the vaguer adjective *serdechnyi* ('of the heart'), and why has he added the adjective *tainyi* ('secret'), implying a degree of mystery which does not appear to be in the original? The translation is, however, based on the interpretation which Dante gives to the line in his commentary: '*Udite il ragionar* lo quale *è nel mio core*: cioè dentro da me, chè ancora non è di fuori apparito. E da sapere è che in tutta questa canzone, secondo l'uno senso e l'altro, lo "core" si prende per lo secreto dentro, e non per altra spezial parte de l'anima e del corpo' ('*Listen to the speech* which is *in my heart*: that is to say inside me, which has not yet appeared on the outside. One should know that in this entire *canzone*, according to one meaning and the other, the "heart" is taken to be the secret within, and not any other special part of the spirit or body' – *Con.* ii, vi, 2). In the light of Dante's explanation of the meaning of 'nel mio core' ('in my heart') as 'lo secreto dentro' ('the secret within'), Ivanov's translation seems well in character with the full meaning intended in the original.

These details of translation reflect a characteristic combination of scholarly knowledge and understanding of the original text, together with a generous measure of poetic license in the adaptation of this text to the author's spiritual outlook.

DIVINA COMMEDIA

According to the poet and literary historian Ilya Golenishchev-Kutuzov (1904–69), Ivanov was involved in a plan for a new translation of the *Commedia* at the beginning of the century. Bryusov was to translate the *Inferno* and Ivanov was responsible for the *Purgatorio* and *Paradiso*.[53] Golenishchev-Kutuzov recalls Ivanov telling him of this project when they met in Rome in the summer of 1928. Ivanov may have been referring to the translation of the *Commedia* which Vengerov wished to include in the 'Library of Great Writers' series published by Brockhaus and Efron. We have already seen that Bryusov worked on a translation of the *Inferno* for Vengerov from 1904 until the collapse of the project at the end of 1905. Ivanov was in close contact with Bryusov at this

time, and, like Bryusov, had already done some translations of
Byron for the same series; he may well, therefore, have also been
invited by Vengerov to take part in the Dante project.

However, apart from Golenishchev-Kutuzov's recollections,
there is no further evidence of Ivanov working on a translation of
the *Commedia* at this stage. Several years later in 1913, he wrote to
Sabashnikov with a proposal that he should translate the *Vita
Nuova*, *Purgatorio* or *Paradiso* for the 'Monuments of World
Literature' series. Sabashnikov took up the first part of the proposal, but did not respond to the second. Ivanov did not then
return to the idea of translating the *Commedia* until 1920. The first
indication of his plan occurs in a letter of 12 May 1920 which he
addressed to the Society of Lovers of Russian Literature. After
announcing his plan to travel abroad in order to work on three
projects – the completion of his translation of Aeschylus's tragedies, a monograph on Aeschylus, and the translation of the *Commedia* – he appealed to the Society to lend him its official support in
order to facilitate his access to foreign book collections and
academic circles.[54]

Since the winter of 1919 to 1920, the health of Ivanov's wife had
been very poor, and the family had made several attempts to
secure permission to travel abroad. In early 1920 a travel permit
was authorized by Lunacharsky, and the day of departure was fixed
for May. This explain's Ivanov's reference to his imminent departure for abroad. The trip was cancelled, however, and Ivanov
remained in Russia for another four years. According to several
indications, he spent the summer of 1920 working on his translation of the *Commedia*.

Firstly, in Ivanov's Rome archive, there is a copy of a contract
for the translation of the *Commedia*, drawn up on 14 May 1920
(exactly two days after the letter to the Society was written)
between Ivanov and the Brockhaus and Efron publishing house.[55]
The translation may have been commissioned at this particular
time because of the impending six-hundred-year anniversary of
Dante's death, due to fall in September 1921. The contract consists
of nine clauses specifying the conditions under which the work is to
be executed. Ivanov undertook to translate the *Commedia* into
Russian in two versions, verse and prose, and to provide necessary
notes and commentaries to his translation. He was to finish both
versions within three years from the date of completion of con-

tract, and in any case not later than 31 December 1923, submitting one part of the translation each year. The document is stamped and signed by A. Perelman, a representative of the Brockhaus and Efron publishing house's management.

Two further sources reveal that Ivanov was working on his translation during the following month. The first comes from the record kept by Feiga Kogan (1891–1974) of the poetry classes given by Ivanov from late February to early August 1920 under the auspices of the Moscow State Institute of Declamation.[56] The classes were used by Ivanov as a forum for discussing poetry (his own as well as his students'), and for lecturing on the techniques of versification. At the fifteenth meeting of the circle (around 20 June) he read out four sonnets from his new cycle 'De Profundis Amavi'. Kogan commented that she could sense Dante's influence on the poems. Ivanov agreed, and added that he had in fact always felt a great sense of affinity with Dante and was currently working on him (a reference to his translation of the *Commedia*, as Kogan notes in her record). This is an interesting example of Ivanov acknowledging the close inter-relationship between his poetry and translations, and the importance of Dante in both spheres.

Further light on the translation is shed in the *Correspondence from Two Corners* (*Perepiska iz dvukh uglov*), first published in 1921. This book contains the letters which Vyacheslav Ivanov and his friend Mikhail Gershenzon wrote to each other from opposite corners of a room which they were sharing in a sanatorium near Moscow during the summer of 1920. In their letters they conducted an intense philosophical debate about the role of culture in civilization. The fourth letter of the exchange, written by Gershenzon between 19 and 30 June, reveals that Ivanov was then working on a translation of Dante's *Purgatorio*:

Now I am writing in your presence, while, lost in quiet reflection, you try to smooth out through thought the stiff, age-old folds of Dante's terzinas, in order to then, with an eye on the model, fashion their likeness in Russian verse ... And after dinner we shall lie down, each on our own bed, you with a sheet of paper, I with a little leather-bound book, and you will begin to read to me your translation of 'Purgatory' – the fruits of your morning's work, and I will compare and argue. And now again, as on previous days, I will drink in the thick honey of your verse, but will also experience again the familiar aching sensation.

Oh, my friend, swan of Apollo! Why is it that feeling was so strong, why was thought so fresh and the word so significant – then, in the fourteenth

century, and why are our thoughts and feelings so pale, our speech as if
laced with cobwebs?   (*SS* III, 387)

The two friends clearly have a well-established daily pattern
which they have been following for some time. This was not the
first occasion they were working together on a translation from the
Italian classics; in 1914 Ivanov had translated various sonnets for
the edition of Petrarch's works which Gershenzon was preparing
for Sabashnikov's 'Monuments of World Literature' series.

Gershenzon accurately distinguishes two stages in Ivanov's
translating method: first the complete intellectual understanding of
the meaning of Dante's verses, and then the recreation of something new within the Russian tradition. His description of his
friend's technique is not, however, just an introductory scene-
setting piece of preamble; it is an integral part of his argument
against the poet's tendency towards cultural obscurity and in
favour of a return to an earlier simplicity of spirit. He sees in the
relationship between the original text of Dante's work and
Ivanov's translation a concentrated expression of the gulf between
the clarity and directness of the medieval world-view and the
obscurity of the modern mind, cluttered with the cultural heritage
of many centuries. In Ivanov's translation, Dante's language
becomes heavy and obscure; although Gershenzon may experience
a feeling of intoxication from the 'thick honey' of his friend's verse,
it nevertheless renews his feeling of painful oppression over the
state of modern culture. In his desire to divest Dante of Symbolist
obscurantism and return him to the direct simplicity of the medieval outlook, Gershenzon was anticipating the polemical, anti-
Symbolist tendency of Mandelshtam's *Conversation about Dante*
(*Razgovor o Dante*) (1933).[57] His comments reflect the characteristic importance which could be attached to a translation from
Dante as the expression of an entire spiritual outlook, and the way
in which such a translation could assume a central role in the
crucial post-revolutionary polemics over the relation of man to his
cultural heritage.

In the passage cited, it is no longer Ivanov's translation of the
Commedia which is being referred to, but just the *Purgatorio*. The
poet's commitment to a translation of the *Commedia* appears to
have changed from one of total responsibility – as envisaged in the
contract described above – to one of partial responsibility. This
becomes clear from a letter which S. A. Vengerov wrote to

Bryusov on 5 July, about seven weeks after the contract between Ivanov and the Brockhaus and Efron company had been drawn up. The letter reveals that Bryusov was also working with Ivanov on the translation of the *Commedia* commissioned by Brockhaus and Efron. Vengerov has evidently known this for some time, but has only just learnt of Bryusov's further agreement to translate Goethe's *Faust* for the same publishers (he heard from A. F. Perelman, the member of the publishing house whose signature appears on the contract for Ivanov's translation of the *Commedia*). He expresses his pleasure at the news, and continues to inquire about Bryusov's progress:

How is your work advancing? Are you working on both Goethe and Dante at the same time or concentrating on one of them? Could you let me know what state your translations are in? If you have something which is ready, this would give me grounds for reproaching Vyach. Ivanovich for his slowness. As I have written to both you and Vyach. Ivanovich, I have no doubt that his translation will be a major literary event, but it is difficult to believe in the real fulfilment of this event. Vyach. Ivanovich works extremely slowly and, while firmly relying on you, the publishers take a very gloomy view of the second part of the translation of the 'Divine Comedy'.[58]

This indicates a return to the cooperative type of translating venture originally envisaged by Vengerov for the same publishing house in 1905. It is not altogether surprising to find Bryusov joining forces with Ivanov again. Since the failure of the original project, Bryusov had shown remarkable persistence in his attempts to get his translation from the *Commedia* published, approaching Vengerov once more on the matter in 1915, and trying other publishers as well in 1913 and 1917. In 1920, he came into frequent contact with Ivanov as a result of the setting up of a Literary Department within the People's Commissariat for Education (Lito Narkomprosa). Lito began functioning in February 1920, with Lunacharsky at its head and Bryusov as its deputy director. It then founded a Literary Studio which, commencing on 24 May 1920, organized a series of lectures and seminars for about a hundred students. Bryusov and Ivanov both worked together at this time as regular lecturers for the Literary Studio. Bryusov was also the editor of Lito's official publication, *Khudozhestvennoe slovo*, and included in the journal's first issue Ivanov's 'Winter Sonnets' and his own favourable review of Ivanov's long poem *Infancy* (*Mladenchest-*

vo).[59] Against this background it is not difficult to see how the decision to work together on a joint translation of the *Commedia* could have arisen.

It is not stated in Vengerov's letter exactly which parts of the *Commedia* Bryusov and Ivanov were responsible for, but it seems reasonable to assume that Bryusov was translating the *Inferno* for which he had always expressed a clear preference in previous negotiations with the Brockhaus and Efron publishing house. The 'second part' referred to as Ivanov's responsibility could be either the *Purgatorio*, or the *Purgatorio* and the *Paradiso* together. Since no mention is made of the involvement of any other translator, the latter possibility seems most likely.

The references in the current periodical press confirm the general picture that Ivanov and Bryusov were engaged on translations of the *Commedia* at this time. In 1921, for example, *Kazanskii bibliofil* informed its readership that Ivanov and Bryusov were preparing new verse translations of the *Commedia* for the Dante Jubilee celebrations due to take place in September 1921. In Italy, the prominent Slavist Ettore Lo Gatto announced that Ivanov – described as one of the greatest of contemporary Russian poets – was about to publish a translation of the *Purgatorio*.[60]

Neither translation ever appeared however. Although the Brockhaus and Efron publishing house continued to function until 1929, after Vengerov's death in September 1920 its interests developed in a different direction, and it dropped its plans for new translations of Dante and Goethe. Both these projects appear to have passed into the hands of Vsemirnaya Literatura, founded in 1918 by Maksim Gorky and run by A. N. Tikhonov (whom Bryusov had previously approached in 1917 over the publication of his translation of *Inferno* I). Bryusov and Ivanov were both close associates of the publishing house, and may well have put forward their own translation projects for possible publication.[61] This was certainly the case with Bryusov's translation of *Faust* which was brought out in 1928 by Gosizdat, the publishing house which absorbed Vsemirnaya Literatura in 1925.[62] There is also evidence that the question of the *Commedia* was considered by Vsemirnaya Literatura. It was raised – but unsuccessfully – at a meeting of the publishing house in 1923. K. I. Chukovsky, one of the principal editors, was present at the discussion and recorded it in his diary on 13 February:

Tikhonov gave a talk about the broadening of our aims. He wants to include Shakespeare, Swift, and Latin and Greek classics in the list of books planned for publication. But because we have to get this publication plan through the editorial section of Gosizdat, we had to attach suitable forms of recommendations to each author, for example:

Bocaccio – the struggle against the clergy.
Vasari – brings art closer to the masses.
Petronius – a satire of the Nepmen etc.

But for the Divine Comedy we just could not think up a suitable form of recommendation.[63]

Although Vsemirnaya Literatura had originally been conceived as an independent part of Gosizdat, founded in May 1919, relations between the two factions had already badly deteriorated by the end of 1920; at the end of 1924, Tikhonov was fired from his post as director, and by early January 1925 Vsemirnaya Literatura was officially liquidated and absorbed into Gosizdat. Many of the publishing house's plans moved with Tikhonov to Academia, of which Tikhonov eventually became director.[64] This appears to have been the case with the project to publish a translation of the *Commedia* which, as already noted in connection with Sergei Solovyov, next surfaced in Academia's 1930 plan. In 1938 Academia was absorbed into Goslitizdat which finally brought out Lozinsky's translation of the three parts of the *Commedia* between 1939 and 1945.[65] Lozinsky's translation was thus in a sense the culmination of a process which had been set in motion by Bryusov and Ivanov many years earlier. It is a fitting symbol of this chain of succession that Lozinsky's collection of books on Dante which he used when working on his translation should contain a copy of the *Commedia* which originally belonged to Ivanov; this copy was presented by Ivanov to his friend the historian I. M. Grevs in Rome in 1892, and Grevs later passed it on to Lozinsky.[66]

The project therefore survived, but what of Ivanov's translation? After Vera's death in August 1920, the poet left Moscow for the south, travelling first to Kislovodsk and then to Baku. During his first year at the University of Baku, he gave a course of lectures on Dante and Petrarch.[67] According to some sources, he also continued working on his translation of the *Commedia*. One of his students from this period, Moisei Semyonovich Altman, remembers hearing him speak of his translation of part of the *Commedia*. Another former pupil, Viktor Andronikovich Manuilov, accompanied the poet on his last trip from Baku to Moscow in 1924. He recalls Ivanov showing him the manuscript of his translation of various passages from the *Commedia* shortly before his departure for Italy.[68]

After Ivanov's emigration, there are only a few isolated references to his translation of the *Commedia*. Golenishchev-Kutuzov recalls him reading a canto of the *Paradiso* in his translation when they met in Rome in 1928. In 1929 Maksim Gorky tried to arrange for Ivanov's translation of the *Inferno* to be published in Russia. Ivanov had visited Gorky at his Sorrento home a few years earlier, and Gorky evidently had a vested political interest in supporting Ivanov as a Soviet citizen resident abroad.[69] Nothing came of the suggestion, however, and after this point references to the translation peter out.

Although the various references to Ivanov's translation of the *Commedia* which we have encountered suggest that he was working on translations on all three *cantiche* at different times, there is no textual evidence to support this. The only part of the translation which has survived is located in the poet's Rome archive, together with the Brockhaus and Efron contract for the translation of the *Commedia*. It consists of four sheets of manuscript in the poet's hand, headed 'Purgatory. First Canto', and comprising ll. 1–67 of the opening canto of *Purgatorio*. These are written out in ink with very few corrections added, and the impression is that of a final version. Although the manuscript is not dated, the translation is most likely to date from the summer of 1920, when Gershenzon records helping his friend with his translation of the *Purgatorio*. The final text (incorporating the poet's corrections and with his numbering of the lines) is given below.

1   Для плаванья на благостном просторе
     Подъемлет вдохновенье паруса:
     Жестокое мой челн покинул море.

4   Пою второго царства чудеса,
     Где дух, от скверн очистившийся, станет
     Достоин вознестись на небеса.

7   Здесь мертвая поэзия воспрянет:
     Коль ваш, святые Музы, я пророк.
     Во весь свой рост Каллиопея встанет

10 Со звоном, чтò Пиерия сорòк
    В отчаянье поверг: напела лира
    Соперницам безумным горький рок.

13 Цвет сладостный восточного сафира,
    По первый круг сгущаясь в вышине
    Чистейшего, прозрачного эфира,

16 Опять целил и нежил очи мне,
    Так долго мертвым воздухом, без света,
    Дышавшему в исхоженной стране.

19 Любови благосклонная планета
    Гасила Рыб-сопутниц, веселя,
    Прекрасная, свой край лучом привета.

22 Направо свод сияньем убеля,
    Меж звезд искрились ясные четыре;
    Их знал Адам и первая земля.

25 Тех пламеней нет радостнее в мире.
    О Север, вдовый, южный их узор
    Не блещет на твоей ночной порфире.

28 Уж Колесницы не мерцал собор
    На супротивном полюсе вселенной,
    Куда нескоро перевел я взор.

31 Мне старец предстоял достопочтенный,
    Маститой убоялся я красы,
    Как пред отцом робеет сын смиренный.

34 Делились на две ровных полосы,
    На грудь сбегая, с длинною брадою,
    Ручьем черносеребряным власы.

37 Он осиян был силою святою
    Звезд четырех, как будто бы в упор
    Взирал на солнце прямо пред собою.

40 'Кто вы? Слепой реке наперекор,' –
    Он рек, честнóе зыбля оперенье, –
    'Как, узники, бежали на простор?

43 Кто в долах тьмы давал вам уверенье
    Стези надежной? Из темницы вон
    Лампады чьей вело вас озаренье?

46   Что ж? Преисподней попран ли закон
     Иль отменен уставом свыше новым?
     Запретен осужденным сей притон.'

49   Касаньем рук, бровей движеньем, словом
     Наставник мой вложил мне в мысль совет
     Склонить колени пред судьей суровым.

52   Сам речь держал: 'Моей тут мысли нет.
     Сошедшая с небес в мои юдоли
     Жена святая мне дала завет:

55   Сего путеводить. Но так как боле
     Ты хочешь знать о путниках, – изволь:
     Мой долг твоей послушествовать воле.

58   Он смерти не вкусил еще; но столь
     Безумно жил он, что во тьме греховной
     Блуждал на шаг от гибели, – доколь

61   Я не был послан благостью верховной
     С ним разделить глубоких странствий труд:
     Иной тропы нет в мир ему духовный.

64   Я показал ему проклятый люд;
     Пусть узрит ныне, коих очищает,
     К спасенью предназначенных, твой суд.

67   Повествовать мне время воспрещает [.]

From the formal point of view the translation is faultless; Ivanov
has created an unbroken succession of iambic pentameters with
alternating masculine and feminine rhymes. However, as before,
there is a general tendency to complicate the original. *Enjambements* are introduced where there are none in the original (at the
end of ll. 5, 9, 54, 58 and 60); in many cases these are particularly
noticeable because they link the end of one tercet to the beginning
of the next. Strangely enough, Ivanov is here acting in defiance of
his own principles; at the poetry classes which he ran in 1920, he
devoted some time to explaining the correct manner of construc-
tion of terzinas, and stipulated that each tercet should be a self-
contained unit, not running over into the next one.[70]
   Natural word order is also replaced by more complicated syntax;
one can compare, for example, ll. 19–21 of Ivanov's translation
with the same lines in the original:

Lo bel pianeto che d'amar conforta
faceva tutto rider l'oriente,
velando i Peschi ch'erano in sua scorta.

The fair planet that prompts to love
was making the whole East smile,
veiling the Fishes that were in her train.

Ivanov inverts the order of the last two lines of this tercet, and
introduces additional interruptions of the natural flow of words (by
removing 'bel' (*prekrasnaya*) from the subject which it qualifies in
the first line to the third line, where it is awkwardly interposed
between the verb and its object).

Unusual archaic words are substituted for simple ones; the
expression *na suprotivnom polyuse* ('at the opposite pole') is used
for 'a l'altro polo' ('to the other pole' – l. 29); when Cato is
described, 'diss'' ('said') becomes *rek* ('uttered'), and 'movendo
quelle oneste piume' ('moving those venerable plumes') becomes
chestnoe zyblya operen'e ('causing his venerable plumage to ripple'
– l. 41); unusual verbs like *popran* ('flouted' – l. 46) for 'rotte'
('broken') or *poslushestvovat'* ('to do the bidding' – l. 57) create a
sense of archaic obscurity which is absent from the original.

Ivanov also tends to replace vivid concrete images with abstract
paraphrases which make the meaning of the original much harder
to grasp. One need look no further than the first tercet of the canto
for an example of this. Dante's text reads as follows:

Per correr miglior acque alza le vele
omai la navicella del mio ingegno,
che lascia dietro a sé mar sì crudele;

To course over better waters
the little bark of my genius now hoists her sails,
leaving behind her a sea so cruel;

Dante's picture of the little boat of his poetic genius preparing to
traverse the calmer waters of Purgatory is one of the most celebrated images of the *Commedia*. Ivanov has made the point of the
image extremely hard to grasp; he has replaced the literal phrase
'miglior acque' ('better waters') with the abstract paraphrase *na
blagostnom prostore* ('on the blessed expanse'), and he has also
dropped the image of 'la navicella del mio ingegno' ('the little bark
of my genius') and reduced this to the single word *vdokhnoven'e*
('inspiration'). It is consequently much more difficult for the reader

272 Texts and translations

to make the connection between the images of the two seas, one cruel, one better, and Dante's poetic genius as a boat which must traverse these two seas, although this connection is crystal clear in the original.

Apart from this move towards increased abstraction and complexity, there are further characteristic types of distortion in Ivanov's translation. One of these is the tendency to place additional emphasis on the darkness of sin, contrasted with the transcendent realm. Ivanov replaces the simple 'si purga' ('is purged') with the much stronger *ot skvern ochistivshiisya* ('after cleansing itself of all defilement' – l. 5), echoing the language of the Bible (Ezek. 36.25; 2 Cor. 7.1). In the same way, when Virgil is describing Dante's past life to Cato, Ivanov adds the words *vo t'me grekhovnoi / Bluzhdal* ('in sinful darkness he wandered' – ll. 59–60) to his speech, whereas in the original there is just a brief reference to Dante's past 'folly'. Similarly, in ll. 10–12 of his translation, Ivanov contracts an entire line of the original 'seguitando il mio canto con quel suono' ('accompanying my song with that strain') into two words *so zvonom* ('with the sound'), thus making his translation very difficult to follow, and then introduces one-and-a-half lines of purely gratuitous additional material: *napela lira / Sopernitsam bezumnym gor'kii rok* ('the song of the lyre brought a bitter fate to the mad rivals') – the themes of madness and of inevitable fate were close to Ivanov as a result of his interest in Greek myths and Dionysian passion, and they are here imposed on Dante's text.

Dante's vision becomes less natural and more fantastic in Ivanov's version; whereas Dante simply announces his intention to sing of the second realm, Ivanov adds a reference to its *chudesa* ('wonders' – l. 4). Cato's first appearance is unduly melodramatic in Ivanov's rendering; 'vidi presso di me un veglio solo' ('I saw close to me an old man alone') is replaced by the more archaic *Mne starets predstoyal dostopochtennyi* ('a venerable elder stood before me' – l. 31), 'degno di tanta reverenza in vista' ('worthy in his looks of so great reverence') becomes *Mastitoi uboyalsya ya krasy* ('I took fright at his venerable beauty' – l. 32) and the simple idea of the natural reverence a son owes his father is replaced by the image of a humble son quailing before his father (l. 33). The same additional aura of trembling fear and melodrama which accompanied the appearance of *Amor* in the third chapter of the *Vita Nuova* discussed above is here applied to Cato.

In the same *Vita Nuova* passage Ivanov introduced his concept of the poet as a Pushkinian, prophet-like figure, retiring from the crowd to have visions and write poetry. In his translation of *Purgatorio* I, he does this once more. Dante writes 'o sante Muse, poi che vostro sono' ('O holy Muses, since I am yours'); Ivanov adapts this to reflect his own Symbolist aesthetics: *Kol' vash, svyatye Muzy, ya prorok* ('As yours, holy Muses, I am a prophet' – l. 8).

The translations of Dante which Ivanov embarked on in the 1910s represent the culmination of a process of interpretation and adaptation which began in the late 1880s and can be traced through his understanding of the religion of Dionysus and of the concept of Sophia and through the Dantesque images in his poetry. In his translations the poet succeeded in creating a text which embodied many of the features with which he endowed the figure of Dante in his religious philosophy and aesthetics. Dante is advanced as the carrier of a syncretic form of mysticism, based on the Dionysian ideal of Eros and involving an ecstatic experience of self-transcendence, in which elements of sin could play a significant role. The image of Beatrice becomes part-erotic, part-Solovyovian in character. The transcendent realm is viewed as an esoteric domain which can only be hinted at in veiled terms, and Dante is presented in this context as an obscure, complex poet who anticipates in his verse the fundamental tenets of Symbolist aesthetics. In this sense Ivanov's translations more than bear out Dostoevsky's contention that a Western poet cannot fail to become a *Russian* poet when transplanted to Russia. In his versions Dante becomes a Russian *Symbolist* poet, a final vindication of his claim, cited as an epigraph to this book: 'And so – Dante is a Symbolist!'

Notes

Unless otherwise stated all references to the works of V. I. Ivanov are to the *Collected Works, Sobranie sochinenii* (hereafter *SS*), ed. D. V. Ivanov and O. Deschartes (Brussels, 1971–). In both the text and the notes these are given in the following form: *SS*, followed by the volume number (roman numerals) and page reference (arabic numerals).

INTRODUCTION

1 The image of Jacob's ladder occurs in Ivanov's letter of 15 July 1920 to M. O. Gershenzon in *Perepiska iz dvukh uglov, SS* III, 412.
2 Fyodor Stepun, 'Wjatscheslaw Iwanow. Der russische Europäer', in *Mystische Weltanschauung. Fünf Gestalten des russischen Symbolismus* (Munich, 1964), 208, and *Vstrechi* (Munich, 1962), 141.
3 Osip Mandelshtam, *Sobranie sochinenii v trekh tomakh*, ed. G. P. Struve and B. A. Filippov, 3 vols., second edition (Washington and New York, 1967–71), II, 486.
4 Ibid., II, 487.
5 Ibid., II, 257.
6 See the record of Bakhtin's lectures on Ivanov in M. M. Bakhtin, *Estetika slovesnogo tvorchestva*, ed. S. G. Bocharov and S. S. Averintsev (Moscow, 1979), 374–83, and Bakhtin's comments on Ivanov's work on Dostoevsky in M. Bakhtin, *Problemy poetiki Dostoevskogo* (Moscow, 1963), 12–14.
7 Quoted by R. L. Jackson in his introduction to *Vyacheslav Ivanov: Poet, Critic and Philosopher*, ed. Robert Louis Jackson and Lowry Nelson, Jr (New Haven, 1986), 7.
8 See, for example, Z. G. Mints, 'O "Besedakh s poetom V. I. Ivanovym" M. S. Altmana', M. S. Altman, 'Iz besed s poetom Vyacheslavom Ivanovichem Ivanovym (Baku, 1921 g.)', N. V. Kotrelyov, 'Vyach. Ivanov – Professor Bakinskogo Universiteta', in *Uchenye zapiski Tartuskogo gos. universiteta, Vypusk 209, Trudy po russkoi i slavyanskoi filologii, XI, Literaturovedenie* (1968), 297–303, 304–25, 326–39. Ivanov's relations with Bryusov and Blok are covered in 'Perepiska s Vyacheslavom Ivanovym (1903–1923)', ed. S. S. Grechishkin, N. V. Kotrelyov and A. V. Lavrov, in *Literaturnoe nasledstvo*

(hereafter *LN*), vol. 85, *Valery Bryusov* (Moscow, 1976), 428–545; E. L. Belkind, '*Blok i Vyacheslav Ivanov*', in *Tartuskii Gosudarstvennyi Universitet, Blokovskii sbornik II* (Tartu, 1972), 365–84; '*Blok v neizdannoi perepiske i dnevnikakh sovremennikov (1898–1921)*', in *LN* vol. 92, book 3 (1982), 153–539.

9 Vyacheslav Ivanov, *Stikhotvoreniya i poemy*, with an introductory article by S. A. Averintsev, ed. R. E. Pomirchy (Leningrad, 1976).

10 Carin Tschöpl, *Vjačeslav Ivanov. Dichtung und Dichtungstheorie* (Munich, 1968); James West, *Russian Symbolism. A Study of Vyacheslav Ivanov and the Russian Symbolist Aesthetic* (London, 1970); F. Malcovati, *Vjačeslav Ivanov: Estetica e Filosofia* (Florence, 1983); Johannes Holthusen, *Vjačeslav Ivanov als symbolistischer Dichter und als russischer Kulturphilosoph* (Munich, 1982).

11 Vladimir Markov, 'Vyacheslav Ivanov the Poet: A Tribute and a Reappraisal', in *Vyacheslav Ivanov: Poet, Critic and Philosopher*, 50.

12 Sergei Averintsev, 'The Poetry of Vyacheslav Ivanov', in *Vyacheslav Ivanov: Poet, Critic and Philosopher*, 40–1.

13 Ilya Serman, 'Vyacheslav Ivanov and Russian Poetry of the Eighteenth Century', in *Vyacheslav Ivanov: Poet, Critic and Philosopher*, 205.

14 *Polnoe sobranie sochinenii F. M. Dostoevskogo*, 12 vols. (St Petersburg, 1894–5), x, part 1, 204–5.

15 See Turgenev's short story, first published in 1849, '*Gamlet Shchigrovskogo uezda*'.

16 Mandelshtam, '*V raznogolositse devicheskogo khora . . .*', in *Sobranie sochinenii v trekh tomakh*, I, 58–9.

17 Many writers and artists of the early twentieth century, including Ivanov and Mandelshtam, stayed at the Crimean home of the poet Maksimilian Voloshin (1877–1932) in Koktebel. Typical feelings about the Crimea are expressed by Voloshin in a letter to Ivanov of 1907. He attributes everything vague and unclear in their relationship to St Petersburg, and urges Ivanov and his wife to come and join him in the Crimea where he has rediscovered his 'ancient clarity': 'We must all live together in this land where it is fitting for poets to live, where there is a real sun, real bare earth and a real Odyssean Sea' (*SS* II, 809). For Mandelshtam the Crimea embodied the Hellenic spirit. See his poems '*Zolotistogo meda struya iz butylki tekla . . .*' (1917) and '*Feodosiya*' (1920).

18 Letter from Gogol to M. P. Balabina [April 1838], quoted in P. Muratov, *Obrazy Italii*, 2 vols. (Moscow, 1911–12), I, 8.

19 The history of Dante's reception in Russia has been outlined by a number of scholars. The period from 1798 to the 1950s is covered by N. G. Elina in '*Dante v russkoi literature, kritike i perevodakh*', *Vestnik istorii mirovoi kul'tury*, 1/13 (1959), 105–21. This article was supplemented by the research of M. P. Alekseev who traced the first references to Dante in Russia from 1757 through to the beginning of the nineteenth century in his article '*Pervoe znakomstvo s Dante v*

Rossii', in *Ot klassitsizma k romantizmu. Iz istorii mezhdunarodnykh svyazei russkoi literatury*, ed. M. P. Alekseev (Leningrad, 1970), 6–62. The findings of both scholars were incorporated into the book by I. N. Golenishchev-Kutuzov, *Tvorchestvo Dante i mirovaya kul'tura*, ed. I. V. Golenishcheva-Kutuzova and V. M. Zhirmunsky (Moscow, 1971). There is also a major bibliography of references to Dante in Russia from 1762 to 1972 which includes an introductory survey: V. T. Danchenko, *Dante Alig'eri. Bibliografichicheskii ukazatel' russkikh perevodov i kriticheskoi literatury na russkom yazyke 1762–1972*, ed. M. P. Alekseev (Moscow, 1973).

20 *Tsvetochki Frantsiska Assizskogo* (Fioretti). *Legenda*, tr. O. S., *Novyi put'* (hereafter *NP*), 1904, April, May, June and July issues. In 1913 Musaget published a new translation by A. P. Pechkovsky in book form.

21 See G. P. Fedotov, *The Russian Religious Mind*, 2 vols. (Cambridge, Mass., 1946 and 1966) and Nicolas Zernov, *Eastern Christendom: A Study of the Origin and Development of the Eastern Orthodox Church* (London, 1961), chapters VII, IX and XI.

22 Andrei Bely, *Vospominaniya ob Aleksandre Aleksandroviche Bloke* (Letchworth, 1964), 36–7.

23 See the materials on Dante, including notes on the *Commedia* and the text of a draft lecture on Dante, Petrarch and Bocaccio, in Ivanov's archive in the Manuscripts Department of the Lenin Library, GBL, *fond* 109. While at the University of Baku, Ivanov lectured on Dante and Petrarch from 1920 to 1921 (Kotrelyov, 326).

24 Sergei Bulgakov, 'Sny Gei', in *Tikhie dumy (Iz statei 1911–15 gg.)* (Moscow, 1918; reprinted Paris, 1976), 135–45 (138).

25 E. Anichkov, *Novaya russkaya poeziya* (Berlin, 1923), 44–5.

26 Valery Briusov, 'Russia', *The Athenaeum*, 4 July 1903, 24.

1. IVANOV'S DIONYSIAC IDEAL AND DANTE

1 See *'Avtobiograficheskoe pis'mo'* (hereafter *'AP'*), 1917, *SS* II, 5–22 (11–12). The information on Ivanov's early life and education in this chapter has mainly been drawn from this letter, clarified by O. Deschartes's introduction to Ivanov's collected works (*SS* I, 5–227), and supplemented by V. Ivanov's *'Avtobiografiya'*, 14 December 1904, GBL, *fond* 109.

2 In his autobiography of 14 December 1904 (GBL, *fond* 109), Ivanov wrote the following about his two years at the University of Moscow: 'I received a prize for my success in classical languages, although I worked almost exclusively on history!'

3 Ivanov's dissertation was eventually published under the title *De societatibus vectigalium publicorum populi romani* (St Petersburg, 1910).

4 See Vyacheslav Ivanov, *'Religiya Dionisa'* (hereafter *'RD'*), *Voprosy zhizni* (hereafter *VZh*), 7 (1905), 122–48 (141).

5 Ivanov recorded this transition in his autobiography of 1904: 'In my Berlin period his works [those of V. Solovyov], together and in equal measure with the creations of Dostoevsky and Schopenhauer, exerted a powerful influence on the world-view which I had formed, just as towards the end of the same period I was particularly influenced by Nietzsche' ('*Avtobiografiya*', 14 December 1904, GBL, *fond* 109).

6 See Richard D. Davies, 'Nietzsche in Russia, 1892–1917: A Preliminary Bibliography, Part 1', *Germano-Slavica*, 2, no. 2 (1976), 107–46 (111).

7 See Ivanov's preface to his dissertation *Dionis i pradionisiistvo* (Baku, 1923), v. In 1903 Ivanov agreed to Bryusov's proposal that he should translate his (Ivanov's) 'favourite book', *The Birth of Tragedy out of the Spirit of Music*, for an edition of Nietzsche's works planned but not produced by the Skorpion publishing house. See Ivanov's letters to Bryusov of 16 November and 25 December 1903, in *LN* vol. 85: 441 and 445.

8 See, for example, V.P. Preobrazhensky, '*Fridrikh Nitsshe. Kritika morali al'truizma*', *Voprosy filosofii i psikhologii* (hereafter *VFP*), 15 (1892), 115–60. This article is prefaced by a note from the editors defending their decision to publish an article about Nietzsche despite his heretical anti-Christian views.

9 See '*Ellinskaya religiya stradayushchego boga*' (hereafter '*ER*'), *NP*, 2 (1904), 48–78 (62–3).

10 In the preface to his Baku dissertation Ivanov reiterated the same points in greater detail, discussing the inadequacy of Nietzsche's interpretation of the spirit of Dionysus from the point of view of its religious, mystical content and of its link with Christianity. See *Dionis i pradionisiistvo*, v–vii.

11 See the letters exchanged by Bryusov and Ivanov between May and December 1903 in *LN*, vol. 85: 435–6 and 442.

12 Vyacheslav Ivanov, '*ER*', *NP*, 1 (1904), 110–34; 2 (1904), 48–78; 3 (1904), 38–61; 5 (1904), 28–40; 8 (1904), 17–26; 9 (1904), 47–70; '*RD*', *VZh*, 6 (1905), 185–220; 7 (1905), 122–48.

13 '*ER*', *NP*, 1 (1904), 110.

14 '*RD*', *VZh*, 7 (1905), 122 and 136.

15 Ivanov's interest in linking Dionysus and Christianity was not an isolated phenomenon. The question of the links between the Dionysiac religion and Christianity was much discussed at the beginning of the twentieth century (see H. Jeanmaire, *Dionysus. Histoire du culte de Bacchus*, Paris, 1951, 478). One of the earliest modern scholars to have investigated the psychology of Dionysus and commented on some of its connections with Christianity was Erwin Rohde. His work, *Psyche. The Cult of Souls and Belief in Immortality amongst the Greeks* (London, 1925) first appeared in German between 1891 and 1894. Ivanov's particular contribution was to advocate this synthesis as the spiritual ideal for his age; in this respect he was continuing the tradition

established by the German Romantics Hölderlin and Novalis. See Max
L. Baeumer, 'Nietzsche and the tradition of the Dionysian', in *Studies
in Nietzsche and the Classical Tradition*, ed. J. C. O'Flaherty, T. F.
Sellner and R. M. Helm (Chapel Hill, 1976), 165–89 (166–72).

16 '*ER*', *NP*, 9 (1904), 47.
17 '*ER*', *NP*, 1 (1904), 112 and 2 (1904), 48.
18 '*ER*', *NP*, 9 (1904), 51.
19 '*ER*', *NP*, 3 (1904), 61.
20 '*RD*', *VZh*, 7 (1905), 141.
21 '*ER*', *NP*, 5 (1904), 35.
22 '*ER*', *NP*, 2 (1904), 64.
23 '*RD*', *VZh*, 7 (1905), 137.
24 '*RD*', *VZh*, 7 (1905), 140.
25 '*ER*', *NP*, 2 (1904), 59.
26 '*RD*', *VZh*, 7 (1905), 134–6 and '*ER*', *NP*, 1 (1904), 117.
27 '*RD*', *VZh*, 7 (1905), 142 and '*ER*', *NP*, 1 (1904), 115.
28 '*ER*', *NP*, 2 (1904), 58–9.
29 See '*ER*', *NP*, 2 (1904), 60–4. The same scheme in its broad outlines is
   adopted by a modern classical scholar, Hugh Lloyd-Jones, in 'Nietzsche and the Study of the Ancient World', in O'Flaherty *et al.*, 1–15
   (4).
30 See Domenico Comparetti, *Vergil and the Middle Ages*, tr. E. F. M.
   Benecke (London, 1895), particularly 79–80 and 166–8.
31 See Edward Moore, *Studies in Dante. First Series: Scripture and
   Classical Authors in Dante* (Oxford, 1896); reprinted with new introductory matter, ed. C. Hardie (Oxford, 1969).
32 All quotations and translations from the *Commedia* have been taken
   from Dante Alighieri, *The Divine Comedy*, tr. with a commentary by
   Charles S. Singleton, second printing with corrections, 3 vols. (Princeton, 1977). Singleton has used the text established by Giorgio Petrocchi
   in his authoritative critical edition of the *Commedia*.
33 All quotations from the *Convivio* and the *Monarchia* have been taken
   from the following editions: *Il Convivio*, ed. G. Busnelli and G. Vandelli, second edition, 2 vols. (Florence, 1953–4); *Monarchia*, ed. P. G.
   Ricci (Milan, 1965).
34 See David Knowles, *The Evolution of Medieval Thought* (London,
   1962), 221–3 and 255–68 and R. W. Southern, *The Making of the
   Middle Ages* (London, 1967), particularly 164–77.
35 See Moore, 4 and Lorenzo Minio-Paluello, 'Dante's Reading of Aristotle', in *The World of Dante. Essays on Dante and his Times*, ed. Cecil
   Grayson (Oxford, 1980), 61–80 (64).
36 See, for example, the punishment of pride on the first terrace of
   Purgatory (*Purg.* x, 34–96 and xii, 25–63).
37 See the excerpt from Aquinas's *Summa Theologica* quoted in the
   commentary on *Purgatorio* vii, 31 in Dante Alighieri, *La Divina
   Commedia*, with Scartazzini's commentary revised by G. Vandelli,

twenty-first edition (Milan, 1979), 356; also, the commentary on the same line in Charles S. Singleton's edition of *The Divine Comedy*, II, Part 2. *Commentary*, 141.

38 *The 'Summa Contra Gentiles' of Saint Thomas Aquinas*, tr. English Dominican Fathers, 5 vols. (London, 1924–9), The Fourth Book (1929), 3.

39 See Comparetti, 99–103.

40 Most of the scholarly works dealing with Dante's relation to pagan antiquity express similar conclusions. See Augustin Renaudet, *Dante humaniste* (Paris, 1952), Paul Renucci, *Dante: Discipline et juge du monde gréco-latin* (Paris, 1954) and Eugenio Garin, *Medioevo e rinascimento: Studi e ricerche* (Bari, 1954). Of these authors, Renaudet, who views Christianity as a continuation and fulfilment of pagan antiquity rather than as a rupture, is most inclined to stress Dante's sympathy with pagan antiquity. He still points out, however, Dante's total condemnation of the orgiastic forms of ancient cults and of the Bacchic rites (156–7). Renucci and Garin place greater emphasis on the religious limitations of Dante's and the medieval attitude to pagan antiquity.

41 See Wjatscheslaw Iwanow, 'Vergils Historiosophie', *Corona*, Heft 6 (1931), 761–74 (761–2), originally composed in German.

42 See '*RD*', *VZh*, 7 (1905), 133 and 136.

43 See '*ER*', *NP*, 2 (1904), 60.

44 See '*ER*', *NP*, 2 (1904), 48.

45 For a discussion of the diminished importance of Bacchic images during the Middle Ages, see Caroline Houser, *Dionysos and his Circle: Ancient through Modern* (Cambridge, Mass., 1979), 15–16. See also Jean Seznec, *La survivance des dieux antiques* (London, 1940) for an account of Bacchic images in the Renaissance.

46 References in order: *Inf.* xx, *59; Purg* xviii, 91–6; *Par.* xiii, 25–7.

47 Etienne Gilson, *The Spirit of Medieval Philosophy*, tr. A. H. C. Downes (London, 1936), 443.

48 It is interesting in this context to consider the ideas raised by Eugen Biser in 'Between *Inferno* and *Purgatorio*: Thoughts on a Structural Comparison of Nietzsche with Dante', tr. Cheryl L. Turney, in O'Flaherty *et al.*, 55–70.

49 See Ivanov's essay of 1904, '*Poet i chern*'', *SS* I, 710.

50 '*Mysli o poezii*', *SS* iii, 650–72 (655–6).

51 See '*ER*', *NP*, 9 (1904), 65–7.

52 In the *Aeneid* (iii, 22–43) Virgil describes Aeneas's attempts to tear off the shoots of a tree on his way to Italy; the shoots drip blood and the voice of Polydorus, the son of Priam, issues forth, begging Aeneas to desist for he is buried under the trees which have grown up over his grave.

53 Friedrich Nietzsche, *The Birth of Tragedy and The Case of Wagner*, tr. Walter Kaufmann (New York, 1967), 130 (Section 21).

54 Ovid, *Metamorphoses*, tr. Mary M. Innes (Harmondsworth, 1981), 43–4.

2. VLADIMIR SOLOVYOV AND DANTE

1 '*Ob upadke srednevekovogo mirosozertsaniya*', in *Sobranie sochinenii Vladimira Sergeevicha Solovyova* (hereafter *SS V.S. Solovyova*), ed. M. S. Solovyov and G. A. Rachinsky, 9 vols. (St Petersburg, 1901–7), VI, 347–58 (354, 356).
2 Ibid., VI, 353.
3 '*Chteniya o bogochelovechestve*', in *SS V. S. Solovyova*, III, 1–168 (106).
4 Ibid., III, 106–7.
5 Vladimir Soloviev, *La Russie et l'Eglise Universelle*, second edition (Paris, 1906), 242. A translation by G. A. Rachinsky of the third part of this work, entitled '*Troichnoe nachalo i ego obshchestvennoe prilozhe-nie*', was published in the almanach *Svobodnaya sovest'. Literaturno-filosofskii sbornik. Kniga pervaya* (Moscow, 1906), 204–94. This was followed by the publication of the complete work in Russian: Vladimir Solovyov, *Rossiya i vselenskaya tserkov'*, tr. from the French by G. A. Rachinsky (Moscow, 1911).
6 *La Russie*, 260–4.
7 V. S. Solovyov, '*Smysl lyubvi*', VFP, 14 (1892), 97–107; 15 (1892), 161–72; 1/16 (1893), 115–28; 2/17 (1893), 130–47; 21 (1894), 81–96.
8 '*Smysl lyubvi*', in *SS V. S. Solovyova*, VI, 364–418 (405). It is interesting to note that Solovyov does not use the term 'Sophia' in 'The Meaning of Love'.
9 Ibid., VI, 404.
10 Ibid., VI, 405.
11 Ibid.
12 Ibid.
13 Ibid.
14 Ibid., VI, 372.
15 Ibid., VI, 378.
16 Ibid.
17 Ibid., VI, 376.
18 Ibid., VI, 378–9.
19 Ibid., VI, 376.
20 Vladimir Solovyov, *Stikhotvoreniya*, ed. S. M. Solovyov, seventh edition (Moscow, 1921), 170–9.
21 Ibid., 170, 177, 179.
22 Ibid., 62–3.
23 See '*Na zare tumannoi yunosti*', a short story which first appeared in *Russkaya mysl'* in 1892, and was republished in *Pis'ma Vladimira Sergeevicha Solovyova*, ed. E. L. Radlov, 3 vols. (St Petersburg, 1908–11), III (1911), 283–98.

24 See K. Mochulsky, *Vladimir Solovyov. Zhizn' i uchenie* (Paris, 1936), 34–6.
25 Ibid., 88, 104.
26 Ibid., 195–201.
27 Vl. Solovyov, *Pis'ma*, ed. E. L. Radlov (St Petersburg, 1923), 150–2.
28 See Mochulsky, 258–60. The correspondence of Anna Schmidt and V. Solovyov was published by S. Bulgakov with an introductory essay in *Iz rukopisei A. N. Schmidt* (Moscow, 1916). The subject is discussed in detail by Sergei Bulgakov in '*Vladimir Solovyov i Anna Schmidt*', in *Tikhie dumy*, 71–114. Bely first met A. Schmidt in the autumn of 1901; see Bely, *Vospominaniya*, 25 and A. Bely, *Nachalo veka* (Moscow and Leningrad, 1933), 343–6. A. Schmidt visited Blok at Shakhmatovo on 12 and 13 May 1904; see Aleksandr Blok, *Zapisnye knizhki*, ed. V. N. Orlov (Moscow, 1965), 64, and Blok's description of the visit in his letter to Bely of 16 May 1904 in Aleksandr Blok, *Sobranie sochinenii v vos'mi tomakh* (hereafter Blok, *SS*), ed. V. N. Orlov, 8 vols. (Moscow and Leningrad, 1960–3), VIII, 102.
29 '*Chteniya o bogochelovechestve*', in *SS V. S. Solovyova*, III, 109.
30 '*Krasota v prirode*', in *SS V. S. Solovyova*, VI, 30–68 (32).
31 '*Obshchii smysl iskusstva*', in *SS V. S. Solovyova*, VI, 69–83 (77–8).
32 '*O liricheskoi poezii*' (1890), in *SS V. S. Solovyova*, VI, 215–40 (228, 234–5).
33 '*Pervyi shag k polozhitel'noi estetike*', in *SS V. S. Solovyova*, VI, 424–31 (429, 431).
34 '*Russkie simvolisty*', in *SS V. S. Solovyova*, VI, 504–15.
35 See the articles '*Poeziya F. I. Tyutcheva*', '*Poeziya gr. A. K. Tolstogo*' and *Poeziya Ya. P. Polonskogo*', in *SS V. S. Solovyova*, VI, 470; 481–503 (481); 619–42 (625).
36 See *SS V. S. Solovyova*, VI, 625–6 and 639.
37 Solovyov's interest in Catholicism is discussed in N. O. Lossky, *History of Russian Philosophy* (New York, 1951), 81–133, particularly 84–7.
38 *La Russie*, lvi.
39 '*Ob upadke srednevekovogo mirosozertsaniya*', in *SS V. S. Solovyova*, VI, 355–6.
40 See *Par. xxxi, 37–9*.
41 '*Velikii spor i khristyanskaya politika*', in *SS V. S. Solovyova*, VI, 1–105.
42 V. Solovyov, *Pis'ma* (1923), 22 and 26–7.
43 See Georges Florovsky, 'Vladimir Soloviev and Dante: the Problem of Christian Empire', in '*For Roman Jakobson*'. *Essays on the occasion of his sixtieth birthday* (The Hague, 1956), 152–60.
44 See Mochulsky's account of the controversy surrounding the articles in *Vladimir Solovyov*, 135–43 and S. L. Frank's comments on the subject in his introduction to *A Solovyov Anthology*, tr. N. Duddington (London, 1950), 17.
45 The Russian censors did not accept the work for publication. The first volume was published in Zagreb in 1887, and later included in *SS V. S.*

Solovyova, VI, 214–582. The titles of the unfinished second and third parts of the work were respectively '*Filosofiya tserkovnoi istorii*' and '*Zadachi teokratii*'. Part of Solovyov's work on the projected second volume was incorporated into *La Russie et l'Eglise Universelle*. For a description of the project, see Mochulsky, 164–75.

46 See '*Opravdanie dobra*' in *SS V. S. Solovyova*, VII, 1–484 (456–7).
47 See *La Russie*, 262.
48 '*Ideya chelovechestva u Avgusta Konta*', in *SS V. S. Solovyova*, VIII, 225–45 (238–9).
49 See '*O Sofianstve*', in Georgy Chulkov, *O misticheskom anarkhizme*, with an introduction by Vyacheslav Ivanov (St Petersburg, 1906), 45–68 (55).
50 See V. Rozanov, '*Iz starykh pisem. Pis'ma Vlad. Serg. Solovyova*', *Zolotoe runo*, 2 (1907), 49–59 (55).
51 Sergei Solovyov, '*Ideya tserkvi v poezii Vladimira Solovyova*', in *Bogoslovskii vestnik*, 1 (1915), 59–86 (73).
52 Solovyov's translation was first published in *Vestnik Evropy*, 8 (1886), 614–17 with a note which described it as a 'free and abridged rendering' from Petrarch. The translation was subsequently included in the various editions of Solovyov's verse, but without the original note. I have used the text published in the seventh edition of *Stikhotvoreniya* (1921), 197–201, together with the notes and variant readings supplied by the editor, S. M. Solovyov, 344–6. For the text of Petrarch's *canzone*, see *Le Rime di Francesco Petrarca di su gli originali*, ed. G. Carducci and S. Ferrari (Florence, 1920), 511–21.
53 *Le Rime*, 512.
54 *La Russie*, 262–3.
55 *Stikhotvoreniya* (1921), xiii.
56 Ibid., 197.
57 Ibid., 198.
58 Ibid., 197, 344. The second phrase is a variant provided by S. M. Solovyov in his notes to the translation.
59 Ibid., 198, 199.
60 For the text of the translation and S. M. Solovyov's note on its date and first place of publication (*Vestnik Evropy*, 6 (1886), 748), see V. Solovyov, *Stikhotvoreniya* (1921), 195 and 344.
61 See *Pis'ma V. S. Solovyova*, II (1909), 196.
62 See Vladimir Solovyov, *Stikhotvoreniya*, ed. Sergei Solovyov, sixth edition (Moscow, 1915), 223 and *Stikhotvoreniya* (1921), 196.
63 *Stikhotvoreniya* (1921), 179.
64 See Dante Alighieri, *La Vita Nuova*, ed. M. Barbi (Florence, 1932), chapters I; III, 9; XIX, 1; XLI, 1, 7. All references and quotations from the *Vita Nuova* are taken from this edition.
65 See the 'Note on the structure of the *Vita Nuova*' in Dante Alighieri, *La Vita Nuova*, tr. with an introduction by B. Reynolds (Harmondsworth, 1971), 101. Although Dante and Beatrice were in fact both

eight years old at the time of their first meeting, Dante deliberately chooses to describe their age in terms of the number nine; 'quasi dal principio del suo anno nono apparve a me, ed io la vidi quasi da la fine del mio nono' (*VN*, II, 2). The Russian Dante scholar Evgeny Gustavo-vich Braun (1866–1917) commented on this parallel between Solo-vyov's poem and the *Vita Nuova*. In 1915 and 1916, he translated the *Vita Nuova*. Opposite his translation of chapter II, he noted down a paraphrase of 'Three Meetings' and commented on the similarity between Dante's and Solovyov's accounts of an experience of child-hood love connected with the age of nine or ninth year. See E. G. Braun, '*Perevod "Novoi zhizni" Dante*', GBL, *fond* 443, *k.l, ed.khr.* 12.
66 *Stikhotvoreniya* (1921), 170.
67 Ibid., 171.

3. THE SYMBOLIST VIEW OF DANTE AS A POET OF SOPHIA

1 Bulgakov, '*Vladimir Solovyov i Anna Schmidt*', in *Tikhie dumy*, 72 and 96–8.
2 '*Avtobiografiya*', in Blok, *SS* VII, 5–16 (16). Blok mentions the date when he glimpsed Solovyov in a letter to G. I. Chulkov of 23 June 1905 (Blok, *SS* VIII, 128).
3 See Avril Pyman, *The Life of Aleksandr Blok*, 2 vols. (Oxford, 1979–80), I, 70.
4 See '*Avtobiografiya*', in Blok, *SS* VII, 14.
5 See '*Dnevniki*', diary entry dated 30 (17) August 1918, in Blok, *SS* VII, 344.
6 '*Avtobiografiya*', in Blok, *SS* VII, 13.
7 Sergei Solovyov, '*Vospominaniya ob Aleksandre Bloke*' (December 1921), in *Pis'ma Aleksandra Bloka*, with introductory articles and notes by S. M. Solovyov, G. I. Chulkov, A. D. Skaldin and V. N. Knyazhnin (Leningrad, 1925), 9–45 (12).
8 See Bely, *Vospominaniya*, 15–18.
9 See Blok's correspondence with M. S. Solovyov, ed. N. V. Kotrelyov and A. V. Lavrov, in *LN*, vol. 92, *Aleksandr Blok: Novye materialy i issledovaniya*, 4 books (Moscow, 1980–), book 1 (1980), 407–13 (409, 412).
10 See Blok's letter of 5 November 1902, M. Solovyov's reply of 21 December 1902 and the notes in *LN*, vol. 92, book 1: 409–12.
11 See S. Solovyov's letter to Blok of 5 October 1903 in Blok's correspon-dence with S. Solovyov, ed. N. V. Kotrelyov and A. Lavrov, in *LN*, vol. 92, book 1: 308–407 (342).
12 See S. Solovyov's letter to Blok of 1 September 1903 and Blok's reply of 10 November 1903 in *LN*, vol. 92, book 1: 339, 349. '*Dukhovnye osnovy zhizni*' was published in *SS V. S. Solovyova*, III, 270–382.
13 L. D. Blok, '*I byl' i nebylitsy o Bloke i o sebe*', in *Aleksandr Blok v*

vospominaniyakh sovremennikov, 2 vols. (Moscow, 1980), I, 134–87 (159).

14 See Pyman, I, 148 and 169–70.

15 Blok, *SS* I, 94.

16 See V. Zhirmunsky, '*Poeziya Bloka*', in *Ob Aleksandre Bloke* (Petrograd, 1921), 65–165 (75); K. Chukovsky, *Kniga ob Aleksandre Bloke* (St Petersburg, 1922), 28; N. Minsky, *Ot Dante k Bloku* (Berlin, 1922), and the more recent study by R. I. Khlodovsky, '*Blok i Dante (K probleme literaturnykh svyazei)*', in *Dante i vsemirnaya literatura*, ed. N. I. Balashov, I. N. Golenishchev-Kutuzov and A. D. Mikhailov (Moscow, 1967), 176–248.

17 See Blok's letter of 10 November 1903 to S. Solovyov in *LN*, vol. 92, book 1: 349, and of 23 June 1905 to G. Chulkov in Blok, *SS* VIII, 128.

18 See Blok, *SS* I, 232 and L. D. Blok, 158–9.

19 See Blok's letter to Bryusov of February 1903 in Blok, *SS* VIII, 55.

20 '*Mne bitva serdtse veselit . . .*' (15 December 1901), in Blok, *SS* I, 146.

21 See Blok, *Zapisnye knizhki*, 26, and Aleksandr Blok, *Sobranie sochinennii. Stikhotvoreniya. Poemy. Teatr*, ed. V. V. Goltsev (Moscow and Leningrad, 1929), 304.

22 See Blok's letter to S. Solovyov and the accompanying editor's note, in *LN*, vol. 92, book 1: 345–6.

23 *Zapisnye knizhki*, 21.

24 See for example chapters III, XII and XXIII of the *Vita Nuova*.

25 See Blok, *SS* I, 560.

26 '*Ironiya*', in Blok, *SS* V, 345–9 (346). Sologub's '*Nedotykomka*', from his novel *Mel'kii bes* (1906), is defined by Blok as a symbolic image of everyday vulgarity in '*Tvorchestvo Fyodora Sologuba*' (July 1907), in Blok, *SS* V, 160–3 (162).

27 Blok, *SS* III, 15–18 (15).

28 The note first appeared in A. Blok, *Sobranie stikhotvorenii. Kniga tret'ya* (Moscow, 1912); it is quoted by Orlov in his note to '*Pesn' Ada*' in Blok, *SS* III, 502.

29 Blok, *SS* V, 425–36 (433). The quotation from Bryusov is from the poem '*Poetu*' (18 December 1907), included in Bryusov's collection *Vse napevy* (1909); see Valery Bryusov, *Stikhotvoreniya i poemy*, ed. D. E. Maksimov and M. I. Dikman (Leningrad, 1961), 287.

30 *Zapisnye knizhki*, 423.

31 '*Nabrosok predisloviya k neosushchestvlennomu izdaniyu sbornika "Stikhi o Prekrasnoi Dame"*', in Blok, *SS* I, 560–1 (561). See Orlov's editorial note (Blok, *SS* I, 692) in which he also refers to L. D. Blok's account of Blok's plan to present explanations of his early verse in prose, making partial use of his letters to L. D. Mendeleeva of 1902 and 1903.

32 *Zapisnye knizhki*, 424. The date is given in the New Style, corresponding to 17 August, Old Style, the date of Blok's marriage.

33 See Blok, *SS* VII, 338–45, 346–50.

34 See Bely, *Vospominaniya*, 17. For a further description of these early meetings and conversations, see '*Vladimir Solovyov. Iz vospominanii*', in Andrei Bely, *Arabeski. Kniga statei* (Moscow, 1911), 387–94.

35 A. Bely, '*Material k biografii*' (1923), Gosudarstvennyi literaturnyi muzei, Moscow (hereafter GLM), N-v 1282, 52.

36 Ibid., 52–3 and Bely, *Vospominaniya*, 18.

37 Bely, '*Material k biografii*', GLM, N-v 1282, 56, 61, 63.

38 *Nachalo veka*, 18. See also Bely's long poem, *Pervoe svidanie* (St Petersburg, 1921), which describes his first encounter with Sophia.

39 See Bely, *Vospominaniya*, 35–6. The reference to Goethe's 'Ewig-Weibliche' is taken from the last two lines of *Faust* (Part 2): 'Das Ewig-Weibliche / Zieht uns hinan' – 'The Eternal-Feminine / draws us upwards' (*Goethes Faust*, ed. Georg Witkovski (Leiden, 1936), 388). The lines are spoken by the mystical chorus, and are connected with Margarita's soul drawing the soul of Faust upwards towards heaven after his death. The phrase 'Das Ewig-Weibliche' was used by Vladimir Solovyov as the title of a poem on the theme of Sophia which he wrote in 1898; the poem contained the well-known lines '*Znaite zhe: vechnaya zhenstvennost' nyne / V tele netlennom na zemlyu idet*' (*Stikhotvoreniya* (1921), 164). The Symbolist poets took up the phrase 'das Ewig-Weibliche' and used it to refer to Solovyov's concept of the Eternal Feminine.

40 *Vospominaniya*, 35.

41 Andrei Bely, '*O teurgii*', *NP*, 9 (1903), 100–23 (111–12).

42 A. N. Shmidt, '*Pis'mo v redaktsiyu zhurnala "Vesy" (Bryusovu V.Ya.)*', [1 November 1904], Institut mirovoi Literatury im. Gorkogo, Moscow (hereafter IMLI), *fond* 13, *op.* 3, *n.* 119.

43 A. Bely, [Review of] '*I. Skartatstsini, Dante, Peterburg 1905 goda*', *Vesy*, 11 (1905), 75.

44 See Erich Auerbach, '"Figura"', in *Scenes from the Drama of European Literature*, tr. Ralph Mannheim (New York, 1959; reprinted Gloucester, Mass., 1973), 11–76 (73).

45 *Tikhie dumy*, 97.

46 A. Bely, '*Blok: "Nechayannaya radost'"*', in *Arabeski*, 458–63 (459–60).

47 See *Nachalo veka*, 296 and A. Bely, '*Nachalo veka. Vospominaniya*' (1922–23), Berlin version, typescript, Tsentral'nyi gosudarstvennyi arkhiv literatury i iskusstva, Moscow (hereafter TsGALI), *fond* 53, *op.* 1, *ed.khr.* 27, vol. 3, chapter 9:2.

48 See S. Solovyov, '*Vospominaniya ob Aleksandre Bloke*', 13 and 45.

49 Ivanov's poem, '*Ty tsarskim poezdom nazval ...*', was dedicated to Blok and placed at the opening of his fourth collection of verse, also dedicated to Blok, *Nezhnaya taina* (1912). Blok's poem '*Vyacheslavu Ivanovu*' (18 May 1912) is in Blok, *SS* III, 141–2.

50 For a general account of Ivanov's relations with V. Solovyov, see O. Deschartes's introduction (*SS* I, 38–41) and her extended notes to

Ivanov's article on Solovyov '*Religioznoe delo Vladimira Solovyova*' (*SS* III, 746-804).

51 In his '*Avtobiografiya*' of 14 December 1904 (GBL, *fond* 109), Ivanov wrote: 'In the autumn of 1898 and spring of 1899 my poetry was published for the first time in *Vestnik Evropy* and *Kosmopolis*. This was arranged by V. Solovyov whom I met in 1895 when my early poems were given to him for his verdict.' For more detailed references, see O. Deschartes's note, *SS* I, 844-5.

52 Ivanov, '*Avtobiografiya*', 14 December 1904, GBL, *fond* 109 and '*AP*', *SS* II, 20.

53 See O. Deschartes's introduction, *SS* I, 40-1.

54 L. D. Zinoveva-Annibal, Letter to V. Ivanov of 1 August 1900, in Letters to V. Ivanov (1894-1906), GBL, *fond* 109.

55 See *SS* I, 557-8, 49-51 and 858 for the text of the poem and Deschartes's comments.

56 V. Ivanov, '*Predislovie k sborniku stikhov "Kormchie zvezdy"*, "*Kormchie zvezdy*". Korrektura', Carmel, May 1901, GBL, *fond* 109.

57 Each of the three *cantiche* of the *Commedia* ends with the word 'stelle' to emphasize the importance of relating each completed stage of Dante's spiritual journey to the ultimate goals which guide him. For a detailed study of the links between Ivanov's image of the *Kormchie zvezdy* and Dante's references to the guiding stars, see my article 'Vyacheslav Ivanov and Dante: The Image of the Guiding Stars', in *Dante i slavenski svijet*, ed. F. Čale (Zagreb, 1984), 85-106.

58 The lines are from *Purg*. XXVII, 88-90, cited in the form in which Ivanov quotes them in *Pilot Stars*.

59 See '*Tvorchestvo Vyacheslava Ivanova*', in Blok, *SS* v, 7-18.

60 See Ivanov's discussion of the correspondence between the Augustinian principle of 'transcensus sui' and earlier Platonic and ancient Greek notions of self-transcendence in 'Anima' (1933), a later version of the essay '*Ty esi*' (1907), *SS* III, 269-93 (283).

61 This parallel was noted by Chulkov. He compared the ideas on sexual love which Solovyov advanced in 'The Meaning of Love' to the emphasis which Ivanov placed on the importance of sex in mysticism in 'The Hellenic Religion'. He saw both systems as attempts to escape the confines of dogmatic Christianity in favour of a new, freer mysticism based on love. See Chulkov, *O misticheskom anarkhizme*, 60-8.

62 *SS V. S. Solovyova*, VI, 393.

63 See the last verse of Solovyov's poem, quoted on p. 217 (*Stikhotvoreniya* (1921), 112). Mochulsky describes this poem as a concentrated poetic expression of the ideas of 'The Meaning of Love' (*Vladimir Solovyov*, 198).

64 For the translation of the *Eclogue* and the accompanying note, see V. Solovyov, *Stikhotvoreniya* (1921), 193-4. The original manuscript of the translation of the *Eclogue* is dated December 1883 - 23 April 1887.

See Vl. S. Solovyov, '*Pollion. Perevod chetvertoi eklogi Virgiliya*', TsGALI, *fond* 446, *op*. 1, *ed. khr*. 12.

65 See V. Ivanov, Letter to A. Blok, 12 November 1908, Gosudarstvennaya publichnaya biblioteka im. Saltykova-Shchedrina, Leningrad, Otdel rukopisei (hereafter GPB), *fond* 77, *ed. khr*. 9.

66 Vyacheslav Ivanov, '*O znachenii V. Solovyova v sud'bakh nashego religioznogo soznaniya*' (14 December 1910) and Aleksandr Blok, '*Rytsar'-monakh*' (13 December 1910), in *Sbornik pervyi. O Vladimire Solovyove* (Moscow, 1911), 32–44 and 96–103.

67 See '*Rytsar'-monakh*', in Blok, *SS* v, 446–54 (452).

68 The text quoted above was slightly altered by Ivanov from the original text of the 1910 article for a later version entitled '*Religioznoe delo Vl. Solovyova*' published in Vyacheslav Ivanov, *Borozdy i Mezhi: Opyty esteticheskie i kriticheskie* (Moscow, 1916), 95–115. Ivanov followed Solovyov and Bely in incorporating Goethe's 'Ewig-Weibliche' into the Sophiological tradition.

69 Venceslao Ivanov, 'Gli aspetti del bello e del bene nella poesia di Puškin', in *Alessandro Puškin nel primo centenario della morte*, ed. Ettore Lo Gatto (Rome, 1937), 25–42 (32).

4. IVANOV'S IDEAL OF MYSTICAL LOVE

1 V. F. Khodasevich, *Nekropol'. Vospominaniya* (Paris, 1976), 8.

2 Ibid., 13–14.

3 For biographical details of Ivanov's relationship with L. D. Zinoveva-Annibal until 1899, see Deschartes's introduction, *SS* I, 17–36.

4 I. M. Grevs (1860–1941) taught history at the University of St Petersburg. His academic interests developed from the study of Ancient Rome to medieval history of which he eventually became professor. He was responsible for persuading Ivanov to make his first trip to Rome from Paris in 1892 ('*AP*', *SS* II, 19), and visited him in Rome later that year. When he left, Ivanov gave him as a parting present a copy of Dante's *Commedia*, ed. Brunone Bianchi (Firenze, 1890) with the inscription: 'For dear I. M. Grevs. V. I. Rome 1892. Quando fia ch'i ti riveggia? (*Purg*. 24, 75)'. The words are those which the poet Forese Donati addressed to his friend Dante when they met again on the sixth terrace of Purgatory, before their parting. The book was subsequently given by Grevs to M. L. Lozinsky, the translator of the *Commedia*, and is now in Leningrad, in the private archive of the latter's son, S. M. Lozinsky.

Grevs's interest in Dante later led him to further research on Dante and to the completion of a translation of the *Monarchia*. These materials, mostly dating from the early 1920s, are housed in Grevs's archive in the Leningrad branch of the Archive of the Academy of Sciences of the USSR (Arkhiv Akademii Nauk SSSR, Leningrad, hereafter ANSSR, *fond* 726, *op*. 1, *ed. khr*. 212–21). In 1938 Grevs wrote the commentary to M. Lozinsky's translation of the *Inferno* (Dante Alig'eri, *Bozhestvennaya komediya. Ad*, tr. M. Lozinsky, Leningrad, 1939).

5 L. D. Zinoveva-Annibal, Letters to V. Ivanov of 12 and 17 September 1894, GBL, *fond* 109.

6 Lidiya Dimitrievna announced her date of arrival in her letters to V. Ivanov of 19, 21 and 26 September 1894, GBL, *fond* 109.

7 The exact date of Ivanov's move is not known. It is possible that it is the subject of a poem in *Kormchie zvezdy* entitled '*Ustalost*'' (*SS* 1, 560) which describes a difficult emotional parting (*mig razluki tomnoi*). The manuscript of this poem in Ivanov's archive is marked 'Florence. December 1894' (GBL, *fond* 109). This may therefore be the date of Ivanov's move to Rome.

8 The envelope is addressed to Ivanov in Rome and post-marked 18 January 1895. On it Ivanov has written 'Talisman' (L. D. Zinoveva-Annibal, Letters to V. Ivanov, GBL, *fond* 109).

9 See L. D. Zinoveva-Annibal, Letters to V. Ivanov of 22, 27, 28 February and 3 March 1895, GBL, *fond* 109.

10 On 11 March 1895 Lidiya Dimitrievna sent a telegram from Florence to Rome: 'J'arrive aujourd'hui' minuit'; on 15 March 1895 she wrote again from Florence about her suffering since her parting with Ivanov seven hours earlier (GBL, *fond* 109).

11 See the discussion of this poem in chapter 5.

12 See Lidiya Dimitrievna's letter of 7 May 1895 to Ivanov, posted from Florence to Berlin (GBL, *fond* 109).

13 L. D. Zinoveva-Annibal, Letter to V. Ivanov of 12 June 1895, GBL, *fond* 109.

14 L. D. Zinoveva-Annibal, Letter to V. Ivanov of 6 May 1895, GBL, *fond* 109.

15 Nikolai Berdyaev, '*Ivanovskie sredy*', in *Russkaya literatura XX veka (1890–1910)*, ed. S. A. Vengerov, 3 vols. (Moscow, 1914–16), III, book 8: 97–100 (98).

16 The manuscript version of the poem is marked '20.21 Jan. 95, Rome' in the *Kormchie zvezdy* section of Ivanov's archive, GBL, *fond* 109. In the archive it is paired with an unpublished poem entitled 'To you alone!' ('*Tebe odnoi!*'), dated 23 January 1895. This poem is also devoted to an evocation of Ivanov's and Lidiya Dimitrievna's meetings, described in a Dionysiac light.

17 The manuscript title of the poem is given by R. E. Pomirchy in an editorial note to '*Trizna Dionisa*' in Vyacheslav Ivanov, *Stikhotvoreniya i poemy*, 454. The editor of this edition has had access to Ivanov's archive in GBL.

18 See Ivanov's description of the winter Dionysiac festivities in '*ER*', *NP*, 1 (1904), 117–24.

19 See L. D. Zinoveva-Annibal's letters to Ivanov of 21 March and 12 June 1895, GBL, *fond* 109.

20 The Romans knew Dionysus as Bacchus or Liber and celebrated the Liberalia festival (the equivalent of the Great Dionysia) every year on 17 March. See, for example, the article on Dionysus in *Real'nyi slovar' klassicheskoi drevnosti Fr. Lyubkera*, tr. V. I. Modestov, 1 (St Petersburg and Moscow, 1884), 313–16.

21 See Deschartes's note, *SS* 1, 844–5.

22 L. D. Zinoveva-Annibal, Letter to Ivanov of 3 July 1895, GBL, *fond* 109.

23 *Spisok izdanii vyshedshikh v Rossii v 1902 godu* (St Petersburg, 1903), 435 lists *Kormchie zvezdy* among the books which appeared during the week of 24 to 31 October 1902. The book had evidently been ready for some time before this date. Its proofs are stamped throughout with dates ranging from 14 August 1900 to 11 August 1901, and carry the date of 1901 on the title page (GBL, *fond* 109). Some copies were printed with the date of 1902, others with the date of 1903 (see Deschartes's note, *SS* 1, 858).

24 Valery Bryusov, [Review of] '*Vyacheslav Ivanov. Kormchie zvezdy. Kniga liriki. Spb. 1903 g.*', *NP*, 3 (1903), 212–14.

25 Many writers have left descriptions of these meetings. See for example Berdyaev, '*Ivanovskie sredy*', the chapters '*Pervye "sredy"*' and '*Eshche o "sredakh"*' in V. Pyast, *Vstrechi* (Moscow, 1929), 44–62, 85–102, and Sergei Gorodetsky, '*Vospominaniya ob Aleksandre Bloke*', in *Aleksandr Blok v vospominaniyakh sovremennikov*, 2 vols. (Moscow, 1980), 1, 325–42 (331–3).

26 N. G. Chulkova, '*Vospominaniya o moei zhizni s G. I. Chulkovym i o vstrechakh s zamechatel'nymi lyud'mi*', typescript, GBL, *fond* 371, *k.* 6, *ed. khr.* 1 (composed in the 1950s).

27 See for example Ivanov's poem '*Tikhii Fias*' in *KZ*, *SS* 1, 641.

28 Chulkova lists these names but does not explain their significance. The source of the name Primavera is given by Sabashnikova in her memoirs, M. Woloschin, *Die grüne Schlange* (Stuttgart, 1954), 184. According to Chulkova, only three or four of these meetings were held in 1906 before they came to an end in the spring of 1907.

29 Oscar Wilde (1854–1900) was, for example, written about and translated by K. Balmont; see the translation of *The Ballad of Reading Gaol* and essay '*Poeziya Oskara Uail'da*' in K. Balmont, *Izbrannoe. Stikhotvoreniya. Perevody. Stat'i* (Moscow, 1980), 530–48 and 594–9. André Gide (1869–1951) published *Les nourritures terrestres* in 1897 and *L'immoraliste* in 1902; Ivanov's wife L. Annibal wrote a literary portrait of Gide, '*V Rayu Otchayan'ya. Andre Zhid. Literaturnyi portret*', which Bryusov published in *Vesy*, 10 (1904), 16–38.

30 S. Diaghilev and A. Benois, both editors of the journal, for example.

31 See John E. Malmstad, '*Mikhail Kuzmin: A Chronicle of His Life and Times*', in M. A. Kuzmin, *Sobranie stikhov*, ed. John E. Malmstad and Vladimir Markov, 3 vols. (Munich, 1977), III, 7–319 (96–7).

32 See the entry for 18 January 1906 in Kuzmin's diary in *LN*, vol. 92, book 2: 151.

33 See Malmstad in Kuzmin, *Sobranie stikhov*, III, 34–47 for an account of Kuzmin's trip to Italy in 1897 and interest in early Christian Rome, Italian Catholicism and St Francis, and 119–22 for an analysis of his relationship with Ivanov.

34 An example of the way in which Ivanov merged the Platonic and Persian traditions can be seen from the poem *'Pevets u Sufitov'*, composed between 1914 and 1945 (see *SS* III, 492–4 and note, 821–2). The poem presents a discussion of the nature of poetry and combines references to Hafiz with allusions to Plato's *Symposium*. For Solovyov's translations, see *'Iz Gafiza'*, in V. Solovyov, *Stikhotvoreniya* (1921), 215–20 and note, 349. Ivanov's comment was noted by F. I. Kogan in her record of the fourteenth meeting (13 June 1920) of the poetry circle run by Ivanov from February to August 1920 in Moscow. See *'Kruzhok poezii pod rukovodstvom poeta Vyacheslava Ivanova'*, 12 Sepember 1953 (IMLI, *fond* 55, *op.* 1, *n.* 6).

35 Ivanov's two poems were *'Vstrecha gostei'* (*SS* II, 738–9) and *'Gimn'*, later reprinted as part of *'Palatka Gafiza'* in *CA, SS* II, 342–3. Kuzmin's poem, *'Druz'yam Gafiza'* is in Kuzmin, *Sobranie stikhov*, III, 446–7.

36 See Malmstad's discussion of the code-names in Kuzmin, *Sobranie stikhov*, III, 710–11 and Deschartes's identification of the same code-names used by Ivanov in his diary of 1906, *SS* II, 744–50.

37 Ivanov addresses Kuzmin as Antinous in his poem *'Anakhronizm'*, dedicated to Kuzmin (*CA, SS* II, 332–3).

38 For the text of the poem, *'Kharikl iz Mileta'*, and editorial comments, see Kuzmin, *Sobranie stikhov*, III, 441–4 and 708–9.

39 See *SS* II, 744 and Ivanov's poem 'Petronius Redivivus', dedicated to Nuvel, in which he uses both code-names (*CA, SS* II, 332).

40 The magic of Somov's work is conveyed by Ivanov in the two poems which he addressed to him, *'Feierverk'* and *'Tertsiny k Somovu'* (*CA, SS* II, 312 and 325–6). The second poem is dated 1906, the year in which Somov did a portrait of Ivanov. In 1907 Somov also designed the frontispiece of *Cor Ardens*.

41 See Gorodetsky, *'Vospominaniya'*, 331–3, and S. M. Gorodetsky, *'Moi put'*, in *Sovetskie pisateli. Avtobiografii v dvukh tomakh*, ed. B. Ya. Brainina and E. F. Nikitina, 2 vols. (Moscow, 1959), I, 320–31 (322–3).

42 See Deschartes, *SS* I, 97–101.

43 S. Gorodetsky, Letter to Blok of 3 June 1906, in *LN*, vol. 92, book 1: 26.

44 For the text of the diary, see *SS* II, 744–54. Ivanov's letters to his wife of the period have not been fully published; only extracts from them are quoted by Deschartes in her commentary to the diary (*SS* II, 754–64).

45 Kuzmin kept a regular diary throughout his life. According to the archival description of the diary (now in TsGALI), the first exercise book was completed on 12 June 1906, the day before the reading at the

tower. See the introductory comments to *'Pis'ma M. A. Kuzmina k Bloku i otryvki iz dnevnika M. A. Kuzmina'*, ed. K. N. Suvorova, in *LN*, vol. 92, Book 2: 142–74 (146).

46 Vyacheslav Ivanov, *Eros* (St Petersburg, 1907). Later Ivanov republished the collection as part of the third book of *CA* (*SS* II, 362–82).

47 See Deschartes's commentary, *SS* II, 808.

48 See the extract from Kuzmin's diary, dated [21] October 1906, in *LN* vol. 92, book 2: 152.

49 Deschartes, *SS* I, 103–4.

50 See Deschartes's comments on Ivanov's cycle of sonnets *'Zolotye zavesy'*, *SS* II, 765.

51 *'Tsvetnik Or'. Koshnitsa pervaya. Sbornik liricheskii i dramaticheskii* (St Petersburg, 1907), 215–33. The cycle, reduced by one sonnet, was republished in *CA* (*SS* II, 383–92), of which it formed the third book, together with the poems of *Eros* connected with Gorodetsky.

52 *'Zolot klyuch'*, the tenth sonnet in the cycle, was dedicated to Adelaida Gertsyk; later it was taken out of the cycle and republished separately in *CA* (*SS* II, 331).

53 See Deschartes's summary of M. S. Altman's unpublished article *'Onomastika v poezii Vyacheslava Ivanova'* (*SS* II, 764–5). Altman analyses the phonology of the ninth sonnet of the cycle and shows that it is based on syllables from the name Margarita, only given in full at the end of the poem. Margarita is also associated with the symbol of the pearl (*zhemchuzhina*) which recurs throughout the cycle (in Latin 'margarita' means pearl).

54 Deschartes, *SS* II, 733.

55 See Deschartes's introduction, *SS* I, 117–20. The funeral took place on 29 October 1907 (see Blok's letter to his mother of 29 October 1907, in Blok, *SS* VIII, 217). Kuzmin, Gorodetsky and Chulkov were also present; see Evgeniya Gertsyk, *Vospominaniya* (Paris, 1973), 46.

56 See Ivanov's diary from 26 to 29 June 1909 (*SS* II, 774–9) and Deschartes's commentary (*SS* II, 808–10).

57 There are similar entries dated 26 and 27 June 1909 (*SS* II, 775, 777).

58 See Deschartes's note, *SS* II, 811–12.

59 See G. I. Chulkov, Letters to Ivanov of 21 and 27 October 1910 (NS), GBL, *fond* 109, and V. I. Ivanov, Letter to G. I. Chulkov of 25 October 1910 (NS), GBL, *fond* 371, *k.* 3, *ed.khr.* 45.

60 Chulkova, *'Vospominaniya'*, GBL, *fond* 371, *k.* 6, *ed.khr.* 1.

61 See Deschartes's introduction, *SS* I, 135–6.

62 Ibid., *SS*, I, 140–1.

63 They were accompanied on the trip by Evgeniya Gertsyk (1875–1944), the sister of the poetess Adelaida Gertsyk. She describes the marriage ceremony in her memoirs (Gertsyk, 66–7 and 71–2).

64 See Deschartes's introduction, *SS* I, 169–70.

65 For example, he describes Beatrice and the Virgin Mary in the same canto (*Par.* XXXI), but in quite different manners; his portrayal of the

Virgin Mary in her glory is entirely impersonal. The language of St
Bernard's prayer to the Virgin Mary on behalf of Dante (*Par.* XXXIII,
1–39) is also marked by restraint and is entirely free of the erotic
element sometimes associated with the cult of the Virgin Mary.
66 See for example Dante's final words to Beatrice in *Par.* XXXI, 79–90.
67 Vl. S[olovyov], '*Mistika, -tsizm*', in *Entsiklopedicheskii slovar'*, ed.
   F. A. Brokgauz and I. A. Efron, XIX (St Petersburg, 1896), 454–6.
68 See the prominent place assigned to St Bonaventura by Dante in *Par.*
   XII.
69 '*RD*', *VZh*, 7 (1905), 146.
70 Vyacheslav Ivanov, '*Novye Maski. Vstupitel'naya stat'ya*', in
   L. Zinoveva-Annibal, *Kol'tsa* (Moscow, 1904), iii–xiv. *Kol'tsa*
   appeared in September; Ivanov's article had been published separately
   a few months earlier in the July 1904 issue of *Vesy*. The present
   references to Ivanov's article are taken from the text in *SS* II, 76–82.
71 On 10 June 1903 Ivanov wrote to Bryusov from Paris that his wife was
   currently working on a three-act drama, *Kol'tsa*, of which she had
   already completed the first draft. Three months later, on 16 September
   1903 he wrote to Bryusov from Châtelaine near Geneva and asked him
   if he would accept his wife's drama, just completed, and his own
   collection of poetry, *Prozrachnost'*, for publication by 'Skorpion'
   (*LN*, vol. 85: 436–7).
72 See *Kol'tsa*, 45–6. This scene is an interesting example in Lidiya
   Dimitrievna's works of a Dantesque image being assimilated into the
   Dionysiac cycle of death and resurrection. In this case the Dantesque
   image is refracted through the Pre-Raphaelite perception of Dante,
   popularized at the turn of the century in Russia by Zinaida Vengerova
   in a series of articles entitled '*Prerafaelitskoe bratstvo*', '*Dante Gabriel'*
   Rozetti', '*Znachenie Dante dlya sovremennosti*', collected in the first
   volume of her *Literaturnye kharakteristiki* (St Petersburg, 1897). A
   more immediate source of Lidiya Dimitrievna's image may have been
   an article which was published in *Novyi put'* at the same time as Lidiya
   Dimitrievna was working on *Kol'tsa*: Rikhard Muter, '*Rossetti, Bern
   Dzhons i Uotts*', tr. Rapsod, *NP*, 6 (1903), 22–46 and 7 (1903), 38–55.
   The first part of this article included a reproduction of Rossetti's 'Beata
   Beatrix' and a discussion of Rossetti's sense of affinity with Dante's
   love for Beatrice.
73 *Kol'tsa*, 69. The image of the *vikhr'* is also used extensively by Ivanov
   in his poetry in connection with Dionysiac Eros. In his poem '*V
   Kolizee*' it is associated with the image of the stormy wind which
   mercilessly buffets Francesca and Paolo and the carnal sinners in the
   second circle of *Inferno*.
74 *Kol'tsa*, 91, 131.
75 Ibid., 139.
76 Ibid., 178, 204.
77 Ibid., 151.

78 Ibid., 182–3.
79 Dante writes clearly that he had abandoned the *true* way: 'la diritta via
    era smarrita' (*Inf.* I, 3) and 'la verace via abbandonai' (*Inf.* I, 12).

5. DANTESQUE IMAGES IN IVANOV'S POETRY

1 Kenelm Foster, *The Two Dantes and Other Studies* (London, 1977), 84.
2 In his dictionary Dal gives the following examples for *shiryat': 'shiryat'
   kryl'ya, shiroko raspuskat'. Orel shiryal po podnebes'yu, shiryal
   krylami, letya plavno, paril.'* The word occurs in the same form as in
   Ivanov's poem in *The Lay of Igor's Campaign* where it is used to refer to
   a falcon spreading its wings on the wind: '*Yako sokol na vetrekh
   shiryayas'*'.
3 V. Ivanov, Notes on the *Divina Commedia*, GBL, *fond* 109.
4 '*ER*', *NP*, 2 (1904), 64.
5 '*RD*', *VZh*, 7 (1905), 143.
6 See Charles Baudelaire, *Les Fleurs du Mal*, ed. Enid Starkie (Oxford,
   1966), 6–7. Ivanov admired Baudelaire's poetry and translated some
   poems from *Les Fleurs du Mal* in 1905 (See *SS* II, 739). These translations were later incorporated into the second book of *Cor Ardens* (*SS*
   II, 344–7).
7 Lidiya Dimitrievna's novel, '*Plamenniki*', was composed in the early
   1900s, before *Kol'tsa*. It deals with a Dionysiac theme, the myth of
   Agave who, in the company of Bacchic revellers, tore her son Pentheus
   to pieces for refusing to allow the worship of Dionysus in Thebes.
   Ivanov hoped that Bryusov would publish the novel under the Skorpion
   imprint, but the plan was never realized (see their correspondence in
   LN, vol. 85: 435–6). The manuscript of the novel is in Ivanov's archive
   in Rome.
8 The words *bezdna* and *noch'* occur regularly in Tyutchev's poetry in the
   context of the soul's desire to merge with the infinite. See, for example,
   '*O chem ty voesh', vetr nochnoi? . . .*' in F. I. Tyutchev, *Polnoe sobranie
   stikhotvorenii*, ed. V. Gippius and K. Pigarev (Leningrad, 1939), 58,
   76.
9 '*ER*', *NP*, 3 (1904), 38.
10 V. I. Ivanov, 'Il simbolismo e la grande arte', in *L'estetica e la poesia in
   Russia*, ed. Ettore Lo Gatto (Florence, 1947), 477–81 (480).
11 Dante refers to Venus as 'lo bel pianeto che d'amar conforta' (*Purg.* I,
   19).
12 Christ prays three times in Gethsemane that the cup should pass him
   by. On the second occasion his words are '*Otche Moi! esli ne mozhet
   chasha siya minovat' Menya, chtoby Mne ne pit' ee, da budet volya
   Tvoya*' (Matthew 26.42).
13 V. Ivanov, '*Dnevniki*', Loose sheet dated '*V noch' na 31 (19) Avg.
   1893*' GBL, *fond* 109.
14 See Bakhtin, *Estetika slovesnogo tvorchestva*, 379.

15 See Ivanov's letter to Bryusov of 12 October / 29 September 1903 in *LN*, vol. 85: 438.

16 The introduction of the star into the landscape of the dark wood brings the *selva oscura* close to Ivanov's characterization of the *Purgatorio* in terms of its light imagery. In his notes on the *Commedia* (GBL, *fond* 109), Ivanov described the *Purgatorio* as '*sumerki utra i vechera*'.

17 L. D. Zinoveva-Annibal, Letters to V. Ivanov of 12 June and 26 November 1895, GBL, *fond* 109.

18 Ivanov's epigraph is taken from Byron's 'Heaven and Earth: A Mystery' (Part I, scene i, line 67), composed in Ravenna in 1821. The Mystery is based on the Biblical verses from Genesis 6. 1–2 which describe the sons of God taking the daughters of men for wives. The line chosen by Ivanov as an epigraph is spoken by Anah, a woman consumed with love for an angel, Azaziel. It expresses the essence of a passion which, like that of Francesca and Paolo, defies divine law. Byron had in fact translated Francesca's account of her passion to Dante in the previous year (1820), also in Ravenna. For the text of this translation and of line 67 of 'Heaven and Earth', see *The Poetical Works of Lord Byron*, ed. Ernest Hartley Coleridge (London, 1905; reprinted 1958), 463 and 653.

19 A. S. Pushkin, *Sobranie sochinenii v desyati tomakh*, 10 vols. (Moscow, 1974–78), II, 219.

20 For information on V. N. Ivanovsky, see Deschartes's note, *SS* I, 863–4.

21 'RD', *VZh*, 7 (1905), 145–6.

22 Ibid., 146–7.

23 Ibid., 147.

24 Ibid.

25 Ibid., 143.

26 See Ivanov's letter to Bryusov of 31 July 1905 in *LN*, vol. 85: 476.

27 For the text of the poem, dated 17 November 1904, see Valery Bryusov, *Stikhotvoreniya i poemy*, 253–4. It was first published under the title '*Molniya*' in the collection *Stephanos*, which appeared in December 1905 and was dedicated to Ivanov.

28 See Bryusov's letter to Ivanov of [28] November 1904 and the accompanying editorial note in *LN*, vol. 85: 469. For the biographical background to the poem, see Joan Delaney Grossman, *Valery Bryusov and the Riddle of Russian Decadence* (Berkeley, Los Angeles, London, 1985), 272–6.

29 Ivanov, Letter to Bryusov of 2 December 1904, *LN*, vol. 85: 469.

30 See Ivanov's letter of 28 December 1904 to Bryusov in GBL, *fond* 386, *k.* 87, *ed. khr.* 2. This letter is not included in Bryusov's and Ivanov's correspondence in *LN*. Fragments from it are quoted by Deschartes in her note to 'Mi fur le serpi amiche', *SS* II, 713.

31 Vyacheslav Ivanov, *Cor Ardens. Chast' pervaya. Cor Ardens – Speculum Speculorum – Eros – Zolotye zavesy* (Moscow, 1911), 93.

32 Bryusov, Letter to Ivanov of 1 September 1905, *LN*, vol. 85: 481.
33 See Petrarca, *Le Rime* (CXXIX), 204.
34 See Voloshin's letter to Ivanov of 18 August 1907, quoted by Deschartes in *SS* II, 808–9, and Petrarca, *Le Rime*, CXXIX, l. 36 (206), CVIII, l. 2 (158) and CLXVIII, l. 1 (255).
35 See chapters III, IX, XII and XXIV of the *Vita Nuova*.
36 Andrei Bely, [Review of] ' "*Tsvetnik Or*". *Koshnitsa pervaya*. Spb. 1907', *Vesy*, 6 (1907), 66–9 (68).
37 G. D'Annuntsio, *Francheska da Rimini. Tragedia v pyati deistviyakh*, tr. V. Bryusov and V. Ivanov (St Petersburg, 1908). The original manuscript of the translation is in Bryusov's and Ivanov's handwriting; this enables one to see exactly which parts of the play Ivanov translated (G. D'Annuntsio, '*Francheska da Rimini*', with an introductory article '*Geroi tragedii v istorii*', manuscript text of the translation by V. Ya Bryusov and V. I. Ivanov, GBL, *fond* 386, *k.* 21, *ed.khr.* 7). Vera Komissarzhevskaya wrote to Bryusov on 3 November 1907 asking him to find someone who could translate *Francesca da Rimini* for her in ten days; see *Vera Fyodorovna Komissarzhevskaya. Pis'ma aktrisy. Vospominaniya o nei. Materialy*, ed. A. Ya Al'tshuller, with an introduction by Yu. P. Rybakov (Leningrad and Moscow, 1964), 166. The history of Bryusov's and Ivanov's work on the project can be traced from their correspondence in *LN*, vol. 85: 507–15 and from further unpublished letters from Ivanov to Bryusov (GBL, *fond* 386, *k.* 87, *ed.khr.* 4) and from Bryusov to Ivanov of 1908 (GBL, *fond* 109).
38 See Ivanov's letters to Bryusov of 3 June 1906 and 23 July 1907 in *LN* vol. 85: 492, 499.
39 See Ivanov's letter to Bryusov of 7 November 1908 and Bryusov's reply of 12 November 1908 in *LN*, vol. 85: 513–16.
40 See Ivanov's '*Dnevniki*' (*SS* II, 791) and his letter to Bryusov of 3 January 1910 in *LN*, vol. 85: 523.
41 In a letter to S. A. Polyakov of 3 November [1910] Ivanov wrote that the manuscript of his book had been handed over to M. F. Likiardopulo at Skorpion five months earlier (in June). He confirmed that the second part of CA should contain 'Love and Death' and the poems of 'Rosarium' which he had written that summer before leaving for Italy. This letter and Polyakov's reply of 1 December 1910 are in IMLI, *fond*, 76, *op.* 3, *n.* 80 and *n.* 8. Deschartes quotes from Ivanov's letter to Polyakov (with a slight difference in the date of the letter) in *SS*, II, 697–8. Although the second part of *CA* was printed with the date of 1912 on its title page, it appeared ahead of schedule in 1911.
42 See Ivanov's letter to Bryusov of 1 November 1908 in *LN*, vol. 85: 514.
43 '*O granitsakh iskusstva*' (1913), *SS* II, 628–51. For a discussion of Ivanov's translation of this passage, see the section on the *Vita Nuova* in chapter 6.
44 See Ivanov's letter to Bryusov of 3 June 1906 in *LN*, vol. 85: 492.
45 See Ivanov's letter to Bryusov of 1 June 1907 in *LN*, vol. 85: 498.

46 See, for example, *L'ame embrasée de l'amour divin par son union aux Sacres Coeurs de Jesus et de Marie* by the author of *L'Ame Elevée à Dieu*, ninth edition (Lyon, 1802), and the terminology used in the Litany to the Sacred Heart of Jesus in the Russian Catholic prayer-book *Gospodu pomolimsya. Molitvennik dlya russkikh katolikov*, compiled by S. L. and I. U., second edition (St Petersburg, 1912).

47 See Ivanov's letter to Bryusov of 1 June 1907 in *LN*, vol. 85: 498.

48 See Homer, *The Iliad*, XXII, 460–1. I am grateful to Dr Simon Franklin for his help in tracing this reference.

49 '*ER*', *NP*, 3 (1904), 61 and 5 (1904), 35.

50 See Ivanov's letter to Bryusov of 7 November 1908 in *LN*, vol. 85: 514.

51 See Petrarca, *Le Rime* (LXI), 90–1.

52 A. N. Veselovsky, '*Iz poetiki rozy*', in *Privet. Khudozhestvenno-nauchno literaturnyi sbornik* (St Petersburg, 1898), 1–5.

53 Joret's work is cited in the article on the rose in the Brockhaus and Efron encyclopaedia, vol. XXVI[a] (St Petersburg, 1899), 958–9.

54 Compare Ivanov's poem (*SS* II, 468–9) with Joret, 272–3.

55 Veselovsky, 2.

56 Briusov '*Russia*', 24.

57 See M. Kuzmin, [review of] 'Cor Ardens *V. Ivanova*', *Trudy i dni*, 1 (1912), 49–51.

58 This part of the poem echoes Pushkin's poem of 1827 on the rose ('*Est' roza divnaya: ona . . .*') which includes references to the cult of Aphrodite at Cythera and Paphos. See Pushkin II, 99.

59 Ivanov's line '*Ty, Roza milaya, vse ta zh na persyakh zhen*', following his reference to Paphos, echoes Pushkin's poem of 1830, '*Otryvok*': '*Ne rozu pafosskuyu,/ . . . Ya nyne poyu,/ . . . No rozu schastlivuyu,/ Na persyakh uvyadshuyu/ Elizy moei*' (Pushkin II, 256). The cypress is also used as a symbol of death in Ivanov's reference to the Roman tombs '*Gde kiparis kivaet grobovoi*' in another poem of 'Rosarium', 'Il Tramonto. Rondo', *SS* II, 486.

60 See Joret, 54, 69, and Veselovsky, 2. This part of the poem is closely echoed by lines from another poem of 'Rosarium', 'Cor Ardens Rosa. Ballada': '*Ty negi, pesen i pirov / Napersnitsa. Ty – charovnitsa / Lyubvi. Toboi tsvetet grobnitsa*' (*SS* II, 484).

61 V. Ivanov, '*Stat'ya bez nachala i kontsa*', GBL, *fond* 109.

62 See for example the '*Solntse-serdtse*' section of the first book of *CA* (*SS* II, 229–37). A poem from this section, '*Serdtse Dionisa*', contains the phrase '*serdtse Solntsa-Dionisa*' (*SS* II, 236). For a discussion of the connection between the Orphic cult and the religion of Dionysus, see '*RD*', *VZh*, 7 (1905), 130–3.

63 This legend is recounted in detail in 'The Hellenic Religion of the Suffering God' where it is said to have had a particular influence in Orphic circles; see '*ER*', *NP*, 5 (1904), 39–40.

64 Ibid., 39.

65 *Stikhotvoreniya* (1921), 112.

66 See, for example, the images of the rose's fire and the winter grave in *Palomnitsa* and the last verse of *Zimnie sumerki* (*SS* II, 510–11).

67 See Dante's words to Guido Guinizelli in *Purg.* XXVI, 97–9 and his reference to Guinizelli's *canzone* in *Con.* IV, XX, 7.

68 For other examples of Ivanov's reference to this tradition in his poetry, see '*Pod drevom kiparisnym*' in *KZ, SS*, I, 555 and '*Materinstvo*' in *NT, SS* III, 26.

69 Anichkov, 55–7.

6 IVANOV'S TRANSLATIONS OF DANTE

1 Puskhin, VI, 29.

2 *Bairon*, ed. S. A. Vengerov, 3 vols. (St Petersburg, 1904).

3 See A. L. Panina, '*Arkhiv izdatel'stva M. i S. Sabashnikovykh*', Gosudarstvennaya biblioteka im. Lenina, *Zapiski Otdela rukopisei* (hereafter *ZOR*), 33 (1972), 81–139 (91).

4 *Alkei i Safo: Sobranie pesen i liricheskikh otryvkov*, tr. Vyacheslav Ivanov (Moscow, 1914), 219.

5 For bibliographical details of Russian translations of Dante, see Danchenko, 26–45.

6 Ellis, *Immorteli. Vypusk I-i. Sh. Bodler* (Moscow, 1904); Ellis, '*Immorteli*'. *Vypusk II-i. P. Verlen, Zh. Rodenbakh, M. Meterlink, S. Pryudomm, Dante Aligieri, L. Steketti, D. Leopardi, F. Nitsshe, i drugie inostrannye poety* (Moscow, 1904). The Dante section covers pp. 79–103.

7 Ellis, '*Venets Dante*', in *Svobodnaya sovest'. Literaturno-filosofskii sbornik. Kniga pervaya* (Moscow, 1906), 110–38.

8 See his letter to E. K. Metner [March 1907], GBL, *fond* 167, *k.* 7, *ed. khr.* 4, and the publisher's announcement in *Sharl' Bodler, Tsvety zla*, tr. Ellis (Moscow, 1908).

9 Ellis, *Stigmata: Kniga stikhov* (Moscow, 1911). *Stigmata* was published by Musaget, and its proofs are in the Musaget archive, GBL, *fond* 190, *k.* 37, *ed. khr.* 6.

10 Ellis, '*Uchitel' very*', *Trudy i dni*, 7 (1914), 63–78.

11 Sergei Solovyov, '*Ellinizm i tserkov'*', *Bogoslovskii vestnik*, 9 (1913), 50–76 (55).

12 G. I. Porshnev, '*Yubilei Dante*', *Pechat' i revolyutsiya*, 3 (1921), 297–9 (297).

13 See *LN*, vol. 92, book 1: 320.

14 See the brief description of the archive's contents in *ZOR*, 38 (1977), 182–3.

15 See Blok's letter to S. Solovyov and the accompanying note in *LN*, vol. 92, book 1: 345–6.

16 Academia first included a translation of the *Commedia* in its 1930 plan of publication for 1931 without, however, specifying the translators ('*Redaktsionno-izdatel'skii plan "Academia" na 1931 g.*' (1930) GBL,

fond 384, *k.* 9, *ed. khr.* 1). The translators are first mentioned in the publisher's plan of 1932 for the period from 1933 to 1935 (*'Perspektiv-nyi plan izdatel'stva "Academia" na 1933–35 gg.'* (1932), GBL, *fond* 384, *k.* 9, *ed. khr.* 6).

17 See *'Iz vospominanii sestry Marii'*, in S. M. Solovyov, *Zhizn' i tvor-cheskaya evolyutsiya Vladimira Solovyova* (Brussels, 1977), 13–15 (14). Sister Maria writes that Solovyov's arrest interrupted his work on a new translation of the *Commedia*. The exact date of Solovyov's death is given in *LN*, vol. 92, book 1: 320.

18 See M. L. Lozinsky's letter of 27 January 1934 to the editor of the translation, A. K. Dzhivelegov (TsGALI, *fond* 2032, *op.* 1, *ed. khr.* 227). The dates of Lozinsky's work on the *Commedia* are noted on the manuscript of his translation, and were shown to me in Leningrad by his son, S. M. Lozinsky, now in possession of his father's archive.

19 In 1901, in the first publication of the series, Dante was listed as one of the authors whose works would be represented in the forthcoming volumes. See *Sobranie sochinenii Shillera v perevode russkikh pisatelei*, ed. S. A. Vengerov, 4 vols. (St Petersburg, 1904), II, inside front cover.

20 For an account of Bryusov's plan to translate the *Inferno*, see N. Sokolov, *'V. Ya. Bryusov kak perevodchik (iz pisem poeta)'*, in *Masterstvo perevoda: Sbornik statei* (Moscow, 1959), 368–88, and Svyatoslav Belza, *'Bryusov i Dante'*, in *Dante i slavyane*, ed. I. Belza (Moscow, 1965), 69–94. The text of the translation was first published in Valery Bryusov, *Izbrannye sochineniya v dvukh tomakh*, 2 vols. (Moscow, 1955) II, 19–23, and later republished with Bryusov's accompanying preface and notes in Belza's article, 81–93.

21 An abridged version of the following sections has been published as an article; see Pamela Davidson, 'Vyacheslav Ivanov's Translations of Dante', in *Oxford Slavonic Papers*, New Series, 15 (1982), 103–31.

22 M. V. Sabashnikov, ' *"Vechnye knigi"* - *pervonachal'nyi proekt serii "Pamyatniki mirovoi literatury"* ' (1910), GBL, *fond* 261, *k.* 9, *ed. khr.* 105.

23 M. V. Sabashnikov, Letters to V. I. Ivanov, 6 April 1911, 16 March 1912, 5 February 1913, GBL, *fond* 109.

24 V. I. Ivanov, Letter to M. V. Sabashnikov, 20 January 1913, GBL, *fond* 261, *k.* 4, *ed. khr.* 25.

25 M. V. Sabashnikov, Letter to V. I. Ivanov, 10 March 1913, GBL, *fond* 109. The contract is in the archive of the Sabashnikov publishing house, GBL, *fond* 261, *k.* 8, *ed. khr.* 7.

26 *Izdatel'stvo M. i S. Sabashnikovykh*, Letter to V. I. Ivanov, 8 November 1913. GBL, *fond* 109.

27 The date of completion of the translation of *Agamemnon* was marked by Ivanov on the manuscript of his translation, located in Ivanov's Rome archive, and kindly shown to me by D. V. Ivanov. M. V. Sabashnikov wrote to Ivanov that he had received this translation on 25 June 1913 (GBL, *fond* 109).

28 Ivanov summarizes the history of his translation of the *Oresteia* in his preface to the translation, written in Rome in October 1926, and located with the translation in TsGALI, *fond* 225, *op.* 1, *ed. khr.* 29. In August 1926 he wrote to M. V. Sabashnikov from Rome, requesting the latter either to publish his translation of the *Oresteia*, or to pass it on to the publishing division of Gosudarstvennaya Akademiya Khudozhestvennykh Nauk (V. I. Ivanov, Letter to M. V. Sabashnikov, 9 August 1926, GBL, *fond* 261, *k.* 4, *ed. khr.* 25). A Soviet edition of Ivanov's translation is currently being prepared by the Nauka publishing house.

29 Kotrelyov, 327.

30 Conversation with Viktor Andronikovich Manuilov, Leningrad, Komarovo, 30 April 1978.

31 In 1913, after his return from Italy to Moscow, Ivanov delivered '*O granitsakh iskusstva*' as a lecture to the Moscow Religious and Philosophical Society (see V. Ivanov, *Borozdy i mezhi*, 186). The lecture was first published in *Trudy i dni*, 7 (1914), 81–106 alongside Ellis's article on Dante '*Uchitel' very*'. The proofs of the article in the Musaget archive are dated 10 December 1913 (GBL, *fond* 190, *k.* 51, *ed. khr.* 20).

32 V. Ivanov, '*Perevod "Novoi zhizni" Dante*', GBL, *fond* 109.

33 Square brackets are used here and elsewhere to indicate punctuation or parts of words omitted from the original manuscript.

34 Blok, *SS* v, 10–11.

35 See *Epistole* XIII, 10, xxxi in *Epistole*, ed. Ermenegildo Pistelli, in *Le Opere di Dante. Testo critico della Società Dantesca Italiana* (Florence, 1921), 413–46 (439).

36 For the original manuscript, see Dante Alig'eri, '"*Pirshestvo*". *Perevod "Convivio", sdelannyi V. F. Ernom. Kantsona na str. 43–5 perevedena Vyach. I. Ivanovym*', GBL, *fond* 261, *k.* 10, *ed. khr.* 10. The actual manuscript is unsigned. The archive's catalogue and the description of the holdings of the Sabashnikov archive published in *ZOR* (Panina, 110) state that the *Convivio* is in Ern's translation, apart from the *canzone* which is translated by Ivanov. This information is based on the original *opis'* of the archive compiled by the daughter of M. V. Sabashnikov, Nina Mikhailovna Artyukhova, who handed over her father's papers to the Lenin Library.

37 In his '*Material k biografii*' (GLM, N-v 1282), Bely recorded the following entry for September 1904: '*Vskore Ern uezzhaet za granitsu, gde on vstrechaetsya s V. I. Ivanovym i tesno druzhit s nim*'. For Ern's visits to the tower, see Pyast, 49 and O. Deschartes's note in *SS* III, 833.

38 These dates can be worked out from Ern's letters to A. S. Glinka of 18 December 1911, 9 December 1912, 28 March 1913 and 20 May 1913, TsGALI, *fond* 142, *op.* 1, *ed. khr.* 313. Ern's meetings with Ivanov in Rome are described by Gertsyk (69).

39 Petrarka, *Avtobiografiya. Ispoved'. Sonety*, tr. M. Gershenzon and

Vyach. Ivanov (Moscow, 1915). Ivanov translated thirty-three sonnets. His Moscow archive contains the manuscript versions of some of his translations and a letter from M. V. Sabashnikov of 15 November 1914 with a final payment for additional sonnets translated (GBL, *fond* 109). For an excellent discussion of Ivanov's translations, see the article by Lowry Nelson, '*Translatio Lauri*: Ivanov's Translations of Petrarch', in *Vyacheslav Ivanov: Poet, Critic and Philosopher*, 162–81.

40 V. F. Ern, Letters to A. S. Glinka of 18 December 1911 and 14 July 1912, TsGALI, *fond* 142, *op.* 1, *ed. khr.* 313.

41 Ibid., Letter of 5 September 1912.

42 Ibid., Letter of 9 December 1912. The Italian theologian A. Palmieri was strongly in favour of the reunification of the churches, a subject which he also discussed with Ivanov in Rome (see Gertsyk, 68–9). For his views on Russian Orthodoxy, see his article, 'La religione dello Santo Spirito', in *Russia. Rivista di letteratura, storia e filosofia*, II, 2 (1923).

43 Lidiya Ivanova, '*Vospominaniya o Vyacheslave Ivanove*', *Novyi zhurnal*, 148 (1982), 136–60 (152).

44 Vladimir Ern, *Bor'ba za Logos* (Moscow, 1911), 351–2 and 357.

45 Vladimir Ern, *Rozmini i ego teoriya znaniya. Issledovanie po istorii ital'yanskoi filosofii XIX stoletiya* (Moscow, 1914), 100, and Vladimir Ern, *Filosofia Dzhoberti* (Moscow, 1916), 102, 104–5 and 280.

46 See Ern's letters to Glinka of 20 May 1913 (postmarked Rostov), 14 June 1913 (postmarked Tiflis), 18 February 1914 and 26 May – 1 June 1914 in TsGALI, *fond* 142, *op* 1, *ed.khr.* 313. Florensky defended his dissertation on 19 May 1914.

47 This information was provided by N. V. Kotrelyov who has had access to Florensky's private archive.

48 V. F. Ern, Letter to V. I. Ivanov, 8 July 1914, GBL, *fond* 109.

49 V. F. Ern, Letter to A. S. Glinka, 14 July – 21 July 1914, TsGALI, *fond* 142, *op.* 1, *ed.khr.* 313. Only the first of Ern's '*Pis'ma ob imyaslavii*' was published in *Itogi zhizni* (V. F. Ern, '*Okolo novogo dogmata (Pis'ma ob imyaslavii)*', *Itogi zhizni*, 19 July 1914, 4–9); after one subsequent issue on 21 August 1914, the journal stopped appearing. Ern's '*Pis'ma o khristianskom Rime*' appeared in *Bogoslovskii vestnik*, 11 (1912), 561–8; 12 (1912), 760–71; 1 (1913), 104–14; 9 (1913), 77–86.

50 V. F. Ern, Letter to A. S. Glinka, 18 May 1916, TsGALI, *fond* 142, *op.* 1, *ed.khr.* 313.

51 See '*Skorbnyi rasskaz*', '*Opravdannye*' and the last stanza of '*Derev'ya*' ('*Vladimir Ern, Frantsiska syn, – amin'!*') in *Svet vechernii*, SS III, 524–5 and 536.

52 See Bulgakov, *Tikhie dumy*, 138 and Pyast, 49–50.

53 See Golenishchev-Kutuzov, *Tvorchestvo Dante i mirovaya kul'tura*, 467–8 and 484. Golenishchev-Kutuzov lived outside Russia from the date of his father's emigration to Yugoslavia in 1920 until his return to

Moscow in 1955. He went to Italy from Yugoslavia during the summers of 1927 and 1928. According to Deschartes's note to '*Zemlya*', a poem written by Ivanov in August 1928 and dedicated to Golenishchev-Kutuzov, the latter frequently visited Ivanov in the summer of 1928 (*SS* III, 829). The two poets subsequently maintained regular contact. From 1929 to 1933 Golenishchev-Kutuzov studied at the Sorbonne in Paris. In 1930 he published an article on Ivanov, '*Lirika Vyacheslava Ivanova*' in *Sovremennye zapiski*, 43 (1930), 463–71, and in 1935 a collection of his verse entitled *Pamyat'* was published in Paris with a preface by Ivanov.

54 V. I. Ivanov, Letter to the *Obshchestvo lyubitelei rossiiskoi slovesnosti*, 12 May 1920, GBL, *fond* 207, *k*. 32, *ed.khr*. 12.

55 Copy of the contract by kind courtesy of D. V. Ivanov, Rome.

56 Kogan, '*Zapisi*', IMLI, *fond* 55, *op*. 1, *n*. 6.

57 See Osip Mandelshtam, *Razgovor o Dante* (Moscow, 1967), 21–2.

58 S. A. Vengerov, Letter to V. Ya Bryusov, 5 July 1920, GBL, *fond* 386, *k*. 79, *ed.khr*. 39. The earlier letter to Ivanov which Vengerov refers to is not among his letters to Ivanov in GBL, *fond* 109 (14, 21); these do not go beyond 1918.

59 The *khronika* section of *Khudozhestvennoe slovo. Vremennik literaturnogo otdela NKP*, ed. V. Ya. Bryusov, 1 (1920) contains a description of the Literary Studio on p. 62; the same issue published Ivanov's '*Zimnie sonety*' on pp. 10–12, and Bryusov's review of *Mladenchestvo* on p. 57.

60 M. Kovalevsky, '*Russkie perevody "Bozhestvennoi komedii"*', *Kazanskii bibliofil*, 2 (1921), 58–60 (60), and pp. 189, 192, 194 of the same issue. Lo Gatto's original article, 'La fortuna di Dante nel mondo: In Russia' (*L'Italia che scrive*, 4 April 1921, 66–70), is cited in *Russia. Rivista di letteratura, storia e filosofia*, 1, 4–5 (1921), 128 and republished as 'Sulla fortuna di Dante in Russia' in *Saggi sulla cultura russa* (Naples, 1923), 165–74 (169–70).

61 See the list headed '*Redaktsionnaya Kollegiya ekspertov*' in *Katalog izdatel'stva 'Vsemirnaya Literatura' pri narodnom komissariate po prosveshcheniyu*, with an introductory article by M. Gorky (St Petersburg, 1919), 167. Bryusov and Ivanov are also mentioned by A. N. Tikhonov in a report on the activities of the publishing house given in the following year; see A. N. Tikhonov, '*Doklad o deyatel'nosti izdatel'stva "Vsemirnaya Literatura"*', 5 April 1920, TsGALI, *fond* 2163, *op*. 1, *ed.khr*. 46.

62 Gete, *Faust*, tr. Valery Bryusov, ed. A. V. Lunacharsky and A. G. Gabrichesky (Moscow and Leningrad, 1928). In a note on p. 4, the editors state that Bryusov translated both parts of *Faust* in 1919 and 1920. They are only publishing the first part, but hope that the second part will soon appear (it was never published).

63 K. I. Chukovsky, '*Dnevnik*', 13 February [1923], K. I. Chukovsky's private archive, Moscow, Peredelkino, by kind courtesy of E.Ts. Chukovskaya.

64 I. A. Shomrakova, '*Knigoizdatel'stvo "Vsemirnaya literatura"* (*1918–1924*)' in *Kniga. Issledovaniya i materialy. Sbornik XIV* (Moscow, 1967), 175–93 (180–3 and 185).

65 Dante Alig'eri, *Bozhestvennaya komediya. Ad*, tr. M. Lozinsky (Leningrad, 1939); *Bozhestvennaya komediya. Chistilishche*, tr. M. Lozinsky (Moscow, 1944); *Bozhestvennaya komediya. Rai*, tr. M. Lozinsky (Moscow, 1945).

66 See chapter 4, note 4.

67 See Introduction, note 23.

68 Altman and Manuilov both spoke at an evening entitled '*Masterstvo poeticheskogo perevoda*', dedicated to Ivanov the translator, held at the Writers' Union in Leningrad on 19 January 1977. Altman referred to Ivanov's translation of the *Inferno*, but this may have been an error of memory. In a subsequent conversation with the present author Manuilov confirmed that he did not know which parts of the *Commedia* Ivanov had translated (Komarovo, Leningrad, 30 April 1978).

69 For Ivanov's meeting with Gorky in the late summer of 1925, see *Letopis' zhizni i tvorchestva A. M. Gorkogo*, 4 vols. (Moscow, 1958–60), III, *1917–1929*, 421 and Gorky's short memoir of 1925 in *Arkhiv A. M. Gorkogo*, VI (Moscow, 1957), 210–11. On 7 March 1929 Gorky wrote to P. S. Kogan, the president of Gosudarstvennaya Akademiya khudozhestvennykh nauk (of which he was an honorary member since 1927), requesting him to look into the question of Ivanov's Soviet pension; he also asked him if the Academy's publishing division could publish Ivanov's translation of the *Inferno* or his work on Aeschylus, and underlined the importance of supporting Ivanov as a Soviet citizen abroad (see *LN*, vol. 70, *Gorky i sovetskie pisateli. Neizdannaya perepiska* (Moscow, 1963), 213). Golenishchev-Kutuzov records that Gorky wrote to Kogan about Ivanov's translation of the *Paradiso*, the part of the *Commedia* from which he had heard the poet reading a canto in his translation (*Tvorchestvo Dante i mirovaya kul'tura*, 468). Lidiya Ivanova, on the other hand, recalls long discussions of a project which was extremely attractive to her father – the translation of the *whole Commedia* – but adds that nothing ever came of it (Lidiya Ivanova, '*Vospominaniya. Neizdannye pis'ma Vyacheslava Ivanova*', *Minuvshee. Istoricheskii al'manakh*, 3 (1987), 45–77 (57–8).

70 See the entry for the sixth meeting of the poetry circle, held on 26 March 1920, in Kogan, '*Zapisi*', IMLI, *fond* 55, *op.* 1, *n.* 6.

Select bibliography

The bibliography is divided into three main sections: Principal works by Ivanov, Works on Ivanov, and General. Within each section the entries are arranged in alphabetical order.

PRINCIPAL WORKS BY IVANOV

Sobranie sochinenii, ed. D. V. Ivanov and O. Deschartes (Brussels, 1971-). This major edition of the writer's *Collected Works* includes most of his previously published works. Four of the six projected volumes have so far been published. Earlier and original editions of Ivanov's most important publications are listed below under three headings: Poetry and drama, Prose, Translations.

Poetry and drama

Chelovek (Paris, 1939)
Cor Ardens. Chast' pervaya. Cor Ardens – Speculum Speculorum – Eros – Zolotye zavesy (Moscow, 1911)
Cor Ardens. Chast' vtoraya. Lyubov' i smert' – Rosarium (Moscow, 1912)
Eros (St Petersburg, 1907)
Kormchie zvezdy. Kniga liriki (St Petersburg, 1903)
Mladenchestvo (Petersburg, 1918)
Nezhnaya taina. Lepta (St Petersburg, 1912)
Prometei. Tragediya (Petersburg, 1919)
Prozrachnost'. Vtoraya kniga liriki (Moscow, 1904)
Stikhotvoreniya i poemy, with an introductory article by S. A. Averintsev, ed. R. E. Pomirchy (Leningrad, 1976)
Svet Vechernii, with an introduction by Sir Maurice Bowra and commentary by O. Deschartes, ed. Dimitri Ivanov (Oxford, 1962)
Tantal. Tragediya, in *Severnye Tsvety – Assiriiskie*, Almanach IV (Moscow, 1905)

Prose

Borozdy i Mezhi. Opyty esteticheskie i kriticheskie (Moscow, 1916)
De societatibus vectigalium publicorum populi romani (St Petersburg, 1910)
Dionis i pradionisiistvo (Baku, 1923)

'*Ellinskaya religiya stradayushchego boga*', *Novyi put'*, 1 (1904), 110–34; 2 (1904), 48–78; 3 (1904) 38–61; 5 (1904) 28–40; 8 (1904), 17–26; 9 (1904), 47–70
Esse, stat'i, perevody (Brussels, 1985)
Freedom and the Tragic Life. A Study in Dostoevsky, with a foreword by Sir Maurice Bowra, tr. Norman Cameron (New York, 1952)
Ivanov, Vyacheslav and M. O. Gershenzon, *Perepiska iz dvukh uglov* (Petersburg, 1921)
Po zvezdam. Stat'i i aforizmy (St Petersburg, 1909)
'*Religiya Dionisa*', *Voprosy zhizni*, 6 (1905), 185–220; 7 (1905), 122–48
Rodnoe i vselenskoe. Stat'i (1914–1916) (Moscow, 1917)

Translations

Alkei i Safo: Sobranie pesen i liricheskikh otryvkov, tr. Vyacheslav Ivanov (Moscow, 1914)
D'Annuntsio, G., *Francheska da Rimini. Tragediya v pyati deistviyakh*, tr. V. Bryusov and V. Ivanov (St Petersburg, 1908)
Pervaya pifiiskaya oda Pindara, tr. Vyacheslav Ivanov (St Petersburg, 1899)
Petrarka, *Avtobiografiya. Ispoved'. Sonety*, tr. M. Gershenzon and Vyach. Ivanov (Moscow, 1915)

WORKS ON IVANOV

The following section contains details of selected articles and books on Ivanov, relevant to the theme of this study. Further references can be found in the bibliographies appended to the works by Tschöpl and West, listed below.

Adamovich, Georgy, '*Vyacheslav Ivanov i Lev Shestov*', in *Odinochestvo i svoboda* (New York, 1955)
Altman, M. S., '*Iz besed s poetom Vyacheslavom Ivanovichem Ivanovym (Baku, 1921 g.)*', in *Uchenye zapiski Tartuskogo gos. universiteta, Vypusk 209, Trudy po russkoi i slavyanskoi fililogii, XI, Literaturovedenie* (1968), 304–25
Anichkov, E., *Novaya russkaya poeziya* (Berlin, 1923)
Annensky, I, '*O sovremennom lirizme*', *Apollon*, 1 (1909), 12–42; 2 (1909), 3–29; 3 (1909), 5–29
Averintsev, S., '*Poeziya Vyacheslava Ivanova*', *Voprosy literatury*, 8 (1975), 145–92
Bakhtin, M. M., '*Prilozhenie. Iz lektsii po istorii russkoi literatury. Vyacheslav Ivanov*', in *Estetika slovesnogo tvorchestva*, ed. S. G. Bocharov and S. S. Averintsev (Moscow, 1979), 374–83 and 412–15

Belkind, E. L., 'Blok i Vyacheslav Ivanov', in Tartuskii Gosudarstvennyi
    Universitet, Blokovskii sbornik II (Tartu, 1972), 365–84
Bely, Andrei, 'Vyacheslav Ivanov. Siluet', in Arabeski. Kniga statei
    (Moscow, 1911; reprinted Munich, 1969), 468–74
Berdyaev, Nikolai, 'Ivanovskie sredy', in Russkaya literatura XX veka
    (1890–1910), ed. S. A. Vengerov, 3 vols. (Moscow, 1914–16), III,
    Book 8: 97–100
Blok, Aleksandr, 'Tvorchestvo Vyacheslava Ivanova', in Sobranie sochine-
    nii v vos'mi tomakh, ed. V. N. Orlov, 8 vols. (Moscow and Lenin-
    grad, 1960–3), v, 7–18
Briusov, Valery, 'Russia', The Athenaeum, 4 July 1903, 22–5
Bryusov, Valery, 'Novye sborniki stikhov' [Review of Cor Ardens 1],
    Russkaya mysl', 7 (1911), 20–4
    [Review of] 'Vyacheslav Ivanov. Kormchie zvezdy. Kniga liriki. Spb.
    1903 g.', Novyi put', 3 (1903), 212–14
    'Vyacheslav Ivanov. Andrei Bely', in Dalekie i blizkie. Stat'i i zametki o
    russkikh poetakh ot Tyutcheva do nashikh dnei (Moscow, 1912;
    reprinted Letchworth, 1973), 115–36
Bulgakov, Sergei, 'Sny Gei', in Tikhie dumy (Iz statei 1911–15 gg.)
    (Moscow, 1918; reprinted Paris, 1976), 135–45
Charny, M., 'Neozhidannaya vstrecha (Vyacheslav Ivanov v Rime)',
    Voprosy literatury, 3 (1966), 194–9
Convegno Il. Rivista di letteratura e di arte, 8–12 (1933–34). This issue was
    entirely devoted to Ivanov and contains articles on him by Curtius,
    Deschartes, Ganchikov, Marcel, Ottokar, Pellegrini, Steiner, Stepun
    and Zelinsky
Davidson, Pamela, 'Vyacheslav Ivanov and Dante: Reflections of a Medi-
    eval Tradition in the Poetic Imagination of a Russian Symbolist',
    unpublished D. Phil. thesis, University of Oxford, 1983
    'Vyacheslav Ivanov and Dante: The Image of the Guiding Stars', in
    Dante i slavenski svijet, ed. Frano Čale, Yugoslav Academy of
    Sciences and Arts, 2 vols. (Zagreb, 1984), 1, 85–106
    'Vyacheslav Ivanov's Cycle of Sonnets "De Profundis Amavi" ', in
    Cultura e Memoria, ed. F. Malcovati, 2 vols. (Florence, 1988), I, 111–31
    'Vyacheslav Ivanov's Translations of Dante', Oxford Slavonic Papers,
    New Series, 15 (1982), 103–31
Deschartes, O., 'Etre et Mémoire selon Vyatcheslav Ivanov', Oxford
    Slavonic Papers, 7 (1957), 83–98
    'Vyacheslav Ivanov', Oxford Slavonic Papers, 5 (1954), 41–58
Ellis, [Review of] 'Vyach. Ivanov. Po zvezdam, K-vo "Ory". Spb. 1909',
    Vesy, 8 (1909), 53–62
Gertsyk, Evgeniya, 'Vyacheslav Ivanov', in Vospominaniya (Paris, 1973),
    37–72
Golenishchev-Kutuzov, Ilya, 'Lirika Vyacheslava Ivanova', Sovremennye
    zapiski, 43 (1930), 463–71

Gumilyov, N., [Reviews of V. Ivanov's *Cor Ardens* I, II, and *Nezhnaya taina*], reprinted in *Sobranie sochinenii v chetyrekh tomakh*, ed. G. P. Struve and B. A. Filippov, 4 vols. (Washington, 1962–68), IV, 266–8, 296–8, 314–15

Holthusen, Johannes, *Studien zur Ästhetik und Poetik des russischen Symbolismus* (Göttingen, 1957)

Vjačeslav Ivanov als symbolistischer Dichter und als russischer Kulturphilosoph (Munich, 1982)

Ivanova, Lidiya, '*Vospominaniya o Vyacheslave Ivanove*', *Novyi zhurnal*, 147 (1982), 136–54; 148 (1982), 136–60; 149 (1982), 100–26; 150 (1983), 130–59

'*Vospominaniya. Neizdannye pis'ma Vyacheslava Ivanova*', ed. D. V. Ivanov, *Minuvshee. Istoricheskii al'manakh*, 3 (1987), 45–77

Jackson, Robert Louis and Lowry Nelson, Jr, eds., *Vyacheslav Ivanov: Poet, Critic and Philosopher* (New Haven, 1986). This volume contains papers on the poetry, criticism, philosophy, translations and life of Ivanov, given at the first international symposium on Ivanov held at Yale University in 1981. The contributors are Carol Anschuetz, Sergei Averintsev, Valery Blinov, Pamela Davidson, Victor Erlich, Cyril Fotiev, Johannes Holthusen, Dimitri Ivanov, Lydia Ivanova, Robert Louis Jackson, Alexis Klimoff, Fausto Malcovati, John Malmstad, Vladimir Markov, Lowry Nelson, Aleksis Rannit, Vasily Rudich, Ilya Serman, Heinrich Stammler, Edward Stankiewicz, Anna Tamarchenko, Victor Terras, Tomas Venclova, René Wellek, James West

Kotrelyov, N. V., '*Vyach. Ivanov – Professor Bakinskogo universiteta*', *Uchenye zapiski Tartuskogo gos. universiteta*, Vypusk 209, *Trudy po russkoi i slavyanskoi filologii*, XI, *Literaturovedenie* (1968), 326–39

Kuzmin, M., [Review of] '*Cor Ardens V. Ivanova*', *Trudy i dni*, 1 (1912), 49–51

Literaturnoe nasledstvo, vol. 85, *Valery Bryusov* (Moscow, 1976), See pp. 428–545 for Bryusov's correspondence with Ivanov, introduced and annotated by S. S. Grechishkin, N. V. Kotrelyov and A. V. Lavrov

Literaturnoe nasledstvo, vol. 92, *Aleksandr Blok: Novye materialy i issledovaniya*, Book 3 (Moscow, 1982). Several letters from Ivanov and Zinoveva-Annibal are published in the section '*Blok v neizdannoi perepiske i dnevnikakh sovremennikov* (1898–1921)', 153–539

Malcovati, Fausto, *Vjačeslav Ivanov: Estetica e Filosofia* (Florence, 1983) ed., *Cultura e Memoria*. Atti del Terzo Simposio dedicato a Vjačeslav Ivanov, 2 vols. (Florence, 1988)

Mandelshtam, Osip, '*Pis'ma k Vyach. I. Ivanovu*', in *Sobranie sochinenii v trekh tomakh*, ed. G. P. Struve and B. A. Filippov, 3 vols., second edition (Washington and New York, 1967–71), II, 485–91

Mints, Z. G., '*O "Besedakh s poetom V. I. Ivanovym" M. S. Altmana*', in *Uchenye zapiski Tartuskogo gos. universiteta*, Vypusk 209, *Trudy po russkoi i slavyanskoi filologii*, XI, *Literaturovedenie* (1968), 297–303

Poggioli, Renato, 'A Correspondence from Opposite Corners', in *The Phoenix and the Spider. A Book of Essays about some Russian Writers and their View of the Self* (Cambridge, Mass., 1957), 208–28

'Vjacheslav Ivanov', in *The Poets of Russia. 1890–1930* (Cambridge, Mass., 1960), 161–70

Pyast, V., '*Pervye sredy*', '*Eshche o sredakh*', in *Vstrechi* (Moscow, 1929), 44–62, 85–102

'*Vyacheslav Ivanov*', in *Kniga o russkikh poetakh poslednego desyatiletiya*, ed. M. Gofman (St Petersburg and Moscow, 1909), 265–75

Smirnov, I. P., ' "*Kormchie zvezdy*" *i esteticheskaya teoriya Vyach. Ivanova*', in *Khudozhestvennyi smysl i evolyutsiya poeticheskikh sistem* (Moscow, 1977), 59–72

Stepun, Fyodor, '*Vyacheslav Ivanov*', in *Vstrechi* (Munich, 1962), 141–159

'Wjatscheslaw Iwanow. Der Russische Europäer', in *Mystische Weltanschauung. Fünf Gestalten des russischen Symbolismus* (Munich, 1964), 201–78

Struve, Gleb, '*Vyacheslav Ivanov*', in *Russkaya literatura v izgnanii. Opyt istoricheskogo obzora zarubezhnoi literatury* (New York, 1956), 139–41

Tschöpl, Carin, *Vjačeslav Ivanov. Dichtung und Dichtungstheorie* (Munich, 1968)

Tyszkiewicz, S. I., 'L'ascension spirituelle de Wenceslas Ivanov', *Nouvelle Revue Théologique*, 72, no. 10 (1950), 1050–62

West, James, *Russian Symbolism. A Study of Vyacheslav Ivanov and the Russian Symbolist Aesthetic* (London, 1970)

Woloschin, M., *Die grüne Schlange* (Stuttgart, 1954)

GENERAL

This section includes works which are relevant to the general themes discussed in the book without being directly concerned with Ivanov.

Alekseev, M. P., '*Pervoe znakomstvo s Dante v Rossii*', in *Ot klassitsizma k romantizmu. Iz istorii mezhdunarodnykh svyazei russkoi literatury*, ed. M. P. Alekseev (Leningrad, 1970), 6–62

[Aquinas, Saint Thomas], *The 'Summa Contra Gentiles' of Saint Thomas Aquinas*, tr. the English Dominican Fathers, 5 vols. (London, 1924–9)

Auerbach, Erich, ' "Figura" ', in *Scenes from the Drama of European Literature*, tr. Ralph Mannheim (New York, 1959; reprinted Gloucester, Mass., 1973), 11–76

Balmont, K., *Izbrannoe. Stikhotvoreniya. Perevody. Stat'i* (Moscow, 1980)

Baudelaire, Charles, *Les Fleurs du Mal*, ed. Enid Starkie (Oxford, 1966)

Bely, A., *Nachalo veka* (Moscow and Leningrad, 1933)

Bely, Andrei, '*O teurgii*', *Novyi put'*, 9 (1903), 100–23

Pervoe svidanie (St Petersburg, 1921)

Vospominaniya ob Aleksandre Aleksandroviche Bloke (Letchworth, 1964)
Bely, A., [Review of] '*I. Skartatstsini, Dante, Peterburg 1905 goda*', *Vesy*, 11 (1905), 75
Belza, Svyatoslav, '*Bryusov i Dante*', in *Dante i slavyane*, ed. I. Belza (Moscow, 1965), 69–94
Blok, Aleksandr, *Sobranie sochinenii v vos'mi tomakh*, ed. V. N. Orlov, 8 vols. (Moscow and Leningrad, 1960–3)
  Zapisnye knizhki, ed. V. N. Orlov (Moscow, 1965)
Blok, L. D., '*I byl' i nebylitsy o Bloke i o sebe*', in *Aleksandr Blok v vospominaniyakh sovremennikov*, 2 vols. (Moscow, 1980), 1, 134–87
Boyde, Patrick, *Dante Philomythes and Philosopher. Man in the Cosmos* (Cambridge, 1981)
Bryusov, Valery, *Izbrannye sochineniya v dvukh tomakh*, 2 vols. (Moscow, 1955)
  Stikhotvoreniya i poemy, ed. D. E. Maksimov and M. I. Dikman (Leningrad, 1961)
Bulgakov, Sergius, *The Wisdom of God. A Brief Summary of Sophiology* tr. P. Thompson, O. Fielding Clarke and X. Braikevitch (New York and London, 1937)
Chukovsky, K., *Kniga ob Aleksandre Bloke* (St Petersburg, 1922)
Cioran, Samuel David, *Vladimir Solovyov and the Knighthood of the Divine Sophia* (Waterloo, 1977)
Comparetti, Domenico, *Vergil and the Middle Ages*, tr. E. F. M. Benecke (London, 1895)
Concordanza della Commedia di Dante Alighieri, 3 vols. (Turin, 1975)
Danchenko, V. T., *Dante Alig'eri. Bibliograficheskii ukazatel' russkikh perevodov i kriticheskoi literatury na russkom yazyke 1762–1972*, ed. M. P. Alekseev (Moscow, 1973)
Dante Alighieri, *Epistole*, ed. Ermenegildo Pistelli, in *Le Opere di Dante. Testo critico della Società Dantesca Italiana* (Florence, 1921), 413–46
  Il Convivio, ed. G. Busnelli and G. Vandelli, second edition, 2 vols. (Florence, 1953–4)
  La Divina Commedia, with Scartazzini's commentary revised by G. Vandelli, twenty-first edition (Milan, 1979)
  La Vita Nuova, ed. M. Barbi (Florence, 1932)
  La Vita Nuova, tr. with an introduction by B. Reynolds (Harmonds-worth, 1971)
  Monarchia, ed. P. G. Ricci (Milan, 1965)
  The Divine Comedy, tr. with a commentary by Charles S. Singleton, second printing with corrections, 3 vols. (Princeton, 1977)
Davies, Richard D., 'Nietzsche in Russia, 1892–1917: A Preliminary Bibliography, Part 1', *Germano-Slavica*, 2, no. 2 (1976), 107–46; 'Part 2', *Germano-Slavica*, 2, no. 3 (1977), 201–20
Donchin, Georgette, *The Influence of French Symbolism on Russian Poetry* ('S-Gravenhage, 1958)

Elina, N. G., 'Dante v russkoi literature, kritike i perevodakh', Vestnik istorii mirovoi kul'tury, 1/13 (1959), 105–21

Ellis, Immorteli. Vypusk I-i. Sh. Bodler (Moscow, 1904)
  'Immorteli'. Vypusk II-i. P. Verlen, Zh. Rodenbakh, M. Meterlink, S. Pryudomm, Dante Aligieri, L. Steketti, D. Leopardi, F. Nitsshe, i drugie inostrannye poety (Moscow, 1904)
  Stigmata. Kniga stikhov (Moscow, 1911)
  translator, 'Iz "Bozhestvennoi Komedii" Dante, Pesn' 28-ya "Chistilishcha" ', Russkaya mysl', 10, Part 1 (1904), 134–8
  'Uchitel' very', Trudy i dni, 7 (1914), 63–78
  'Venets Dante', in Svobodnaya sovest'. Literaturno-filosofskii sbornik. Kniga pervaya (Moscow, 1906), 110–38

Enciclopedia Dantesca. Istituto della Enciclopedia Italiana fondata da Giovanni Treccani, 6 vols. (Rome, 1970–8)

Ern, Vladimir, Bor'ba za Logos (Moscow, 1911)
  Filosofia Dzhoberti (Moscow, 1916)
  Rozmini i ego teoriya znaniya. Issledovanie po istorii ital'yanskoi filosofii XIX stoletiya (Moscow, 1914)

Florovsky, Georges, 'Vladimir Soloviev and Dante: the Problem of Christian Empire', in 'For Roman Jakobson'. Essays on the occasion of his sixtieth birthday (The Hague, 1956), 152–60

Foster, Kenelm, The Two Dantes and Other Studies (London, 1977)

Frank, S. L., ed., A Solovyov Anthology, tr. N. Duddington (London, 1950)

Garin, Eugenio, Medioevo e rinascimento: Studi e ricerche (Bari, 1954)

Gilson, Etienne, The Spirit of Medieval Philosophy, tr. A. H. C. Downes (London, 1936)

Golenishchev-Kutuzov, I. N., Tvorchestvo Dante i mirovaya kul'tura, ed. I. Golenishcheva-Kutuzova and V. M. Zhirmunsky (Moscow, 1971)

Gorodetsky, Sergei, Stikhotvoreniya i poemy, ed. S. I. Mashinsky and E. I. Prokhorov (Leningrad, 1974)
  'Vospominaniya ob Aleksandre Bloke', in Aleksandr Blok v vospominaniyakh sovremennikov, 2 vols. (Moscow, 1980), 1, 325–42

Gorodetsky, S. M., 'Moi put'', in Sovetskie pisateli. Avtobiografii v dvukh tomakh, ed. B. Ya. Brainina and E. F. Nikitina, 2 vols. (Moscow, 1959), 1, 320–31

Grayson, Cecil, ed., The World of Dante. Essays on Dante and his Times (Oxford, 1980)

Houser, Caroline, Dionysos and his Circle: Ancient through Modern (Cambridge, Mass., 1979)

Jeanmaire, H., Dionysos. Histoire du culte de Bacchus (Paris, 1951)

Joret, Charles, La rose dans l'antiquité et au moyen âge (Paris, 1892)

Khlodovsky, R. I., 'Blok i Dante (K probleme literaturnykh svyazei)', in Dante i vsemirnaya literatura, ed. N. I. Balashov, I. N. Golenishchev-Kutuzov and A. D. Mikhailov (Moscow, 1967), 176–248

Khodasevich, V. F., Nekropol'. Vospominaniya (Paris, 1976)

Knowles, David, *The Evolution of Medieval Thought* (London, 1962)
Kovalevsky, M., '*Russkie perevody "Bozhestvennoi Komedii"*', *Kazanskii bibliofil*, 2 (1921), 58–60
Kuzmin, M. A., *Sobranie stikhov*, ed. John E. Malmstad and Vladimir Markov, 3 vols. (Munich, 1977)
Lo Gatto, Ettore, 'Sulla fortuna di Dante in Russia', in *Saggi sulla cultura russa* (Naples, 1923), 165–74
Lossky, N. O., *History of Russian Philosophy* (New York, 1951)
[Lyubker, Fr.], *Real'nyi slovar' klassicheskoi drevnosti Fr. Lyubkera*, tr. V. I. Modestov, 1 (St Petersburg and Moscow, 1884)
Mandelshtam, Osip, *Razgovor o Dante* (Moscow, 1967)
Minsky, N., *Ot Dante k Bloku* (Berlin, 1922)
Mochulsky, K., *Vladimir Solovyov. Zhizn' i uchenie* (Paris, 1936)
Moore, Edward, *Studies in Dante. First Series: Scripture and Classical Authors in Dante* (Oxford, 1896); reprinted with new introductory matter, ed. C. Hardie (Oxford, 1969)
Muratov, P., *Obrazy Italii*, 2 vols. (Moscow, 1911–12), 1
Nietzsche, Friedrich, *The Birth of Tragedy and the Case of Wagner*, tr. Walter Kaufmann (New York, 1967)
O'Flaherty, J. C., T. F. Sellner and R. M. Helm, eds., *Studies in Nietzsche and the Classical Tradition* (Chapel Hill, 1976)
Ovid, *Metamorphoses*, tr. Mary M. Innes (Harmondsworth, 1981)
Oxford Dictionary of the Christian Church, The, ed. F. L. Cross, second edition, revised by E. A. Livingstone (Oxford, 1974; reprinted with corrections, 1978)
[Petrarca, F.], *Le Rime di Francesco Petrarca di su gli originali*, ed. G. Carducci and S. Ferrari (Florence, 1920)
Podkopaeva, Yu. N. and A. N. Sveshnikova, eds., *Konstantin Andreevich Somov* (Moscow, 1979)
Preobrazhensky, V. P., '*Fridrikh Nitsshe. Kritika morali al'truizma*', *Voprosy filosofii i psikhologii*, 15 (1892), 115–60
Pushkin, A. S., *Sobranie sochinenii v desyati tomakh*, 10 vols. (Moscow, 1974–8), II, VI
Pyman, Avril, *The Life of Aleksandr Blok*, 2 vols. (Oxford, 1979–80)
Renaudet, Augustin, *Dante humaniste* (Paris, 1952)
Renucci, Paul, *Dante: Disciple et juge du monde gréco-latin* (Paris, 1954)
Rohde, Erwin, *Psyche. The Cult of Souls and Belief in Immortality amongst the Greeks* (London, 1925)
Sbornik pervyi. O Vladimire Solovyove (Moscow, 1911)
Seznec, Jean, *La survivance des dieux antiques* (London, 1940)
Sokolov, N., '*V. Ya. Bryusov kak perevodchik (iz pisem poeta)*', in *Masterstvo perevoda: Sbornik statei* (Moscow, 1959), 368–88
Solovyov, Sergei, '*Ellinizm i tserkov*', *Bogoslovskii vestnik*, 9 (1913), 50–76
    '*Vospominaniya ob Aleksandre Bloke*', in *Pis'ma Aleksandra Bloka*, with introductory articles and notes by S. M. Solovyov, G. I.

Chulkov, A. D. Skaldin and V. N. Knyazhnin (Leningrad, 1925),
9–45
Zhizn' i tvorcheskaya evolyutsiya Vladimira Solovyova (Brussels, 1977)
Soloviev, Vladimir, *La Russie et l'Eglise Universelle*, second edition
(Paris, 1906)
Solovyov, Vladimir, *Rossiya i vselenskaya tserkov'*, tr. from the French by
G. A. Rachinsky (Moscow, 1911)
Stikhotvoreniya, ed. Sergei Solovyov, sixth edition (Moscow, 1915)
Stikhotvoreniya, ed. S. M. Solovyov, seventh edition (Moscow, 1921)
S[olovyov], Vl., '*Mistika, -tsizm*', in *Entsiklopedicheskii slovar'*, ed. F. A.
Brokgauz and I. A. Efron, xix (St Petersburg, 1896), 454–6
Solovyov, Vl., *Pis'ma*, ed. E. L. Radlov (St Petersburg, 1923)
[Solovyov, V. S], *Pis'ma Vladimira Sergeevicha Solovyova*, ed. E. L.
Radlov, 3 vols. (St Petersburg, 1908–11)
Solovyov, V. S., '*Smysl lyubvi*', *Voprosy filosofii i psikhologii*, 14 (1892),
97–107; 15 (1892), 161–72; 1/16 (1893), 115–28; 2/17 (1893), 130–47;
21 (1894), 81–96
[Solovyov, V. S.], *Sobranie sochinenii Vladimira Sergeevicha Solovyova*,
ed. M. S. Solovyov and G. A. Rachinsky, 9 vols. (St Petersburg,
1901–7)
Southern, R. W., *The Making of the Middle Ages* (London, 1967)
Tyutchev, F. I., *Polnoe sobranie stikhotvorenii*, ed. V. Gippius and
K. Pigarev (Leningrad, 1939)
Veselovsky, A. N., '*Iz poetiki rozy*', in *Privet. Khudozhestvenno-nauchno
literaturnyi sbornik* (St Petersburg, 1898), 1–15
Zhirmunsky, V., '*Poeziya Bloka*', in *Ob Aleksandre Bloke* (Petrograd,
1921), 65–165
Zinoveva-Annibal, L., *Kol'tsa* (Moscow, 1904)

Index

Titles of works are listed under the names of the authors

313